China under Threat

Melvin Gurtov is professor of political science at the University of California, Riverside. He has written and contributed to several books on China and Southeast Asian affairs, including *Southeast Asia Tomorrow: Problems and Prospects for U.S. Policy, China and Southeast Asia—The Politics of Survival,* and *The United States against the Third World: Antinationalism and Intervention.*

Byong-Moo Hwang was formerly on the faculty of the Korea National War College.

China under Threat
The Politics of Strategy and Diplomacy

Melvin Gurtov and Byong-Moo Hwang

The Johns Hopkins University Press
Baltimore and London

Chapter 3 was originally published in *Modern China* 2, no. 1 (January 1976): 49–103. The present version has been slightly revised for inclusion in this volume.

Chapter 5 was originally published by Harry Harding, Jr., and Melvin Gurtov as a RAND Corporation Report (R-548-PR) in February 1971. The present version has been shortened and slightly revised.

Library of Congress Cataloging in Publication Data

Gurtov, Melvin
  China under threat.

  Bibliography: pp. 314–26.
  Includes index.
  1. China—Foreign relations—1949–1976.   2. China—Politics and government—1949–1976.   I. Hwang, Byong-Moo, joint author.   II. Title.
DS777.8.G87   327.51   80–7990
ISBN 0–8018–2397–8

Melvin Gurtov dedicates this book
   to the people of China;
   to the radical humanist legacy of Mao Zedong; and
   to all persons working for a new world alliance
      built on peace, nonviolence, and equity.

Byong-Moo Hwang dedicates this book
   to the memory of his father, Suh-Koo Hwang.

Contents

Preface

In this book we challenge the traditional approach to foreign policy that treats it as a realm apart from domestic politics. Instead, in agreement with the Chinese and other radical approaches, we see foreign policy as the external face of politics. We believe we offer in these pages a unique approach to understanding how Chinese foreign-policy decisions originate and why they take the forms they do. In a much larger sense, we are also motivated by the belief that a Marxist-Maoist framework for analyzing foreign policy is a valuable and essential tool: It sensitizes the analyst to issues of political economy—in particular, the connectedness of domestic and foreign affairs—in ways that conventional frameworks do not (and by their nature, cannot). We therefore hope to fill a major gap by offering a careful study of the relationship between domestic economic and political developments and foreign-policy perceptions and behavior. In so doing, we also suggest that many misconceptions exist about Chinese behavior in crisis situations.

Both authors assume responsibility for the ideas and manner of presentation in the book as a whole. Each has reviewed the contributions of the other. Byong-Moo Hwang is the author of the case studies of Korea, the Sino-Indian border war, and the Sino-Soviet border clashes (Chapters 2, 4, and 6). Melvin Gurtov is the author of the introduction, the Taiwan Strait study, and the conclusion (Chapters 1, 3, and 7), and with Harry Harding, Jr., is coauthor of the Vietnam chapter (5).

The authors would like to express their appreciation to several people. Byong-Moo Hwang wishes to thank Ronald Chilcote and Victor Lippit for their helpful comments on the studies of the Sino-Indian border war and the Sino-Soviet border clashes. These two studies were originally undertaken as part of Hwang's doctoral dissertation under the supervision of Gurtov. Melvin Gurtov acknowledges with appreciation the many thoughtful suggestions of Alice Langley Hsieh, Allen S. Whiting, and William W. Whitson on the Vietnam study, and of Edward Friedman, Harry Harding, and Jack Service on the Taiwan Strait study. Anna Sun Ford and Robert Herrick were very helpful in bringing together materials on the latter study.

Some of the ideas presented in the first chapter originated in collaboration with David Mozingo, whose support and friendship Melvin Gurtov has always valued greatly. Needless to say, neither Professor Mozingo nor any of the other persons named bears responsibility for any errors, omissions, or interpretations in this book.

The authors also acknowledge with gratitude the permission of Professor Harding and the RAND Corporation to reprint the original Harding-Gurtov research memorandum of 1971. Modest financial assistance was received from the Center for Chinese Studies of the University of California, Berkeley, to complete the Taiwan Strait study, and from the University of California, Riverside, for two years of research assistance under intramural and patent fund grants. We thank these institutions for their support.

One final note concerning the romanization of Chinese personal and place names. We have chosen to employ the Pinyin system that the Chinese government adopted at the start of 1979. Where appropriate, we have indicated in parentheses the previous rendering of a name or place following its first mention.

List of Abbreviations

CB	*Current Background*
CCP	Chinese Communist Party
CDSP	*Current Digest of the Soviet Press*
CPS	*Chinese Press Survey*
CPSU	Communist Party of the Soviet Union
CPV	Chinese People's Volunteers
DNR	*Daily News Release* (NCNA)
D.R.V.	Democratic Republic of Vietnam
FBIS	*Foreign Broadcast Information Service*
GLF	Great Leap Forward
GMD (KMT)	Guomindang (Kuomintang)
GPD	General Political Department
IISS	International Institute of Strategic Studies (London)
JPRS	Joint Publications Research Service (U.S. Department of Commerce)
MAC	Military Affairs Committee
MFA	Ministry of Foreign Affairs
NCNA	New China News Agency
N.E.F.A.	North East Frontier Agency (India)
NLF	National Liberation Front (Vietnam)
NPC	National People's Congress
PC	*People's China*
PLA	People's Liberation Army
P.R.C.	People's Republic of China
RCP	*Review of Hong Kong Chinese Press*
SCMM	*Selections from China Mainland Magazines*
SCMP	*Survey of China Mainland Press*
SEM	Socialist Education Movement
URS	Union Research Service (Hong Kong)

China under Threat

1 An Interactive Model of Chinese Foreign Policy

The Need for a Fresh Approach

Changes in the nature of the cold war seem to bring with them changes in scholarship. We have come a long way from the totalitarian model of communist politics that prevailed in official and academic circles during the 1950s and most of the 1960s. That model assumed, and contended, that communist systems were closed to debate and rivalry and were dominated by a single leader. Power struggles and personalities, not issues and priorities, were considered to lie at the heart of communist politics. In foreign affairs, the model depicted a single-minded communist threat centered in Moscow, with Beijing (Peking) as its Asian headquarters. The foreign policy of both powers was assumed to be a direct extension of their rigid, ruthless politics: unswervingly expansionist and amenable to moderation only when confronted with superior force. In recent years, as the cold war has shifted to less direct (although not less deadly) forms of competition and to more substantive forms of cooperation, scholarship concerning the socialist world has followed suit. In both academic and official papers, the image of monolithic communism has given way to a more refined view that emphasizes, for example, the roles of interest groups and bureaucratic politics in decision making, interparty and intraparty differences, and as a consequence, national interests that derive from political, economic, and domestic considerations other than an overarching ideology. There is now widespread acknowledgment on the part of Western writers that the policy-making process in socialist states bears many of the same features— diverse and complex, if not pluralistic—previously considered characteristic only of the industrialized capitalist systems.[1]

Out of this evolution has come a new understanding of the relationship between domestic and foreign policy under socialism. Previously, the cold war had influenced Western specialists (Americans in particular) to perceive, or presume, a clear separation of the two. Communist leaderships were described as being so tightly regimented in thought and behavior that domestic concerns—the state of the economy, popular unity, political factionalism—could be easily divorced from the foreign-policy-making process. According to this approach, a communist leadership could, if it desired, insulate its society from international events. Now there is a general acceptance that under socialism, as under capitalism, domestic and foreign policy making and policy consequences often interact. They are more properly considered parts of a single sphere of politics rather than separate spheres, and for a full understanding of motives and objectives in one sphere, the analyst must consult developments in the other.[2]

To date, however, that is about as far as anyone has been able to generalize confidently. The relatively scanty literature thus far available on the political process of foreign policy making in the socialist countries falls well short of providing students with a consensus, or even with testable and interesting hypotheses. To be sure, this circumstance is in large measure a function of limited information: we do not have material on politics in, say, China to rival the data available in the United States on public opinion, intraservice rivalry, bureaucratic bargaining and positioning in the executive branch, the media, lobbies, and corporate interests. There is plenty of room for speculation, informed and otherwise.

This book, working from several case studies and the writings of others, attempts to fill an important gap in the literature on Chinese politics and foreign policy. Here the reader will still find speculation and tentative conclusions; but these will be clearly identified as such and, more importantly, will be drawn from research and placed into a broad framework that seeks to comprehend the foreign-policy significance of China's total revolutionary experience. The propositions offered in this chapter are, we hope, a step forward toward understanding the domestic sources and impact of Chinese foreign-policy perspectives and behavior.

A word seems to be in order about the primary sources used in this study. Like most other detailed investigations of Chinese affairs, this one relies on the usual array of press, radio, and documentary materials that officially and otherwise have become available here. The "objective world" we present is largely the one seen through official Chinese eyes, a circumstance that gives ground for caution. It is not merely a matter of having to rely on "propaganda"; *any* government's official viewpoint is propagandistic. We also have to be wary of deliberate overstatements, since we find Mao Zedong (Mao Tse-tung) himself once cautioning his comrades not to be "hoodwinked by our own propaganda."[3] We have not devised a fail-safe formula for determining the veracity of Chinese (or anyone else's) statements. But by checking their internal consistency, comparing public with private statements, using non-Chinese sources, and especially matching Chinese claims against actual events, we can take account of the kinds of verbal excesses that Mao acknowledged. And we must say that having done so, we find that public Chinese commentaries on world affairs, shorn of rhetorical flourishes, are generally quite accurate, sincere, and logical. There is certainly every reason to take these statements as seriously as one would any other government's.

Since each of the five case studies in this volume examines Chinese decision making in a crisis, the question might be raised whether or not this fact limits the usefulness of our findings. We do not think so. A crisis dramatizes the interplay of domestic and foreign politics. If treated as such, rather than narrowly as a matter of diplomatic strategy and military tactics, crises can be highly instructive. The important thing, we have found, is to take into account as much as possible of the total domestic and international environment in which a leadership makes policy choices. Most studies of Chinese foreign policy—in crisis situations and not—fail to do justice to the scope of the problem. They focus on Chinese decision makers within the confines of the immediate situation, as if domestic affairs and international developments elsewhere at the time were of minor concern in Beijing. They surely were not; and in these pages we accept their importance, even though there are limits to how precisely we can indicate it.

In stressing the international and especially the domestic political setting of foreign-policy decisions, we hope to make a conceptual and methodological contribution to China studies, beyond whatever new insights we may provide about each crisis. For once it is accepted that China's foreign-policy establishment, like that of other governments, gives first place to politics when it looks abroad, and is itself subject to political maneuvering, the whole framework for assessing Chinese foreign policy must be reconsidered. Existing approaches that do not take these domestic-international linkages fully into account must be revised or discarded. Doing the case studies has compelled us to reevaluate our notion about the motive forces behind Chinese foreign policy as a whole.

Our procedure will be to offer this alternative framework, which is grounded in a reappraisal of Chinese foreign-policy methodology, before going on to the case studies. We will then introduce the three major "impulses" (as they will now be called) that seem to underlie China's external interests, and the domestic sources of those impulses. The main implication of this approach—that foreign policy is the outward extension of domestic political priorities, institutions, and values—will be spelled out in the form of several propositions. These are suggested by the case studies and related materials that are mentioned. The concluding chapter will amplify the propositions and explore their significance in past and current Chinese foreign policy.

International Relations through Chinese Eyes

An overview of published studies on China's foreign policy reveals one persistent methodological weakness: the failure to consider China within the context of that country's total developmental experience, and in a way that takes seriously the Marxist-Maoist analytical approach. With some notable exceptions,[4] these studies fall into two basic categories. One is historical-descriptive works, which are valuable for their insights about the antecedents of a Chinese world view. But studies of this type overemphasize China's historical and cultural uniqueness. They do not take adequate account of China in the contexts of international and comparative politics— for instance, China as a developing socialist state or China as part of the Asian or global state system. The second category consists of studies of crisis behavior that focus on Chinese diplomacy (or "strategy") in particular situations. Very often these studies, whether friendly or hostile to China's actions in their conclusions, are simply forms of threat analysis: they evaluate the nature and limits (if any) of Mao's guerrilla warfare model as it is projected abroad. Such studies have a peculiarly cold war character, especially since many of them adopt, explicitly or implicitly, the vantage point of American foreign policy makers.

Both of these kinds of studies share other drawbacks. Most of them consider Chinese foreign policy to be a function of only two domestic factors: the leadership's communist ideology, which is considered rigidly prescriptive, and its guerrilla warfare experiences. Little effort is made to explore the *politics* involved in foreign policy making, the ideology of other leaderships that interact with China, and the constraints on or opportunities for decision making afforded by China's and other nations' domestic economic and social needs. Consequently, the results are conceptually and analytically narrow and culturally (i.e., politically) biased. We are usually given a China that is either victimized or propelled by its history to act in a particular way, either constantly reacting to or constantly initiating international events. Neither perspective has sufficient breadth or depth to be convincing.

One thing we would seem to need are studies of Chinese foreign policy that look at the world *as the Chinese leaders do*—with a sensitivity to their philosophy of history, their methodology, and their experiences as revolutionary nationalist fighters, liberators, and bureaucrats. We also need studies that interpret China's foreign policy *from the inside out*—that is, as the product of domestic political, social, and economic forces that affect Chinese perceptions of the world just as surely as they affect the leadership's internal behavior. With such studies, we could begin to understand how Chinese thinking on, and actions in, world affairs are influenced by the country's radical socialist development. We might have to take a second look at the function of the Chinese revolution in the country's foreign policy. We would avoid tendencies in the literature to emphasize Chinese (or Mao's) strategy and tactics, Chinese communism (or communism), and U.S. foreign-policy objectives. We would have the tools for appreciating how Chinese decision makers must deal with competing or contradictory demands posed by international events. We would be able to avoid the unresolvable distinctions between, and the unproductive debate over, national interest and ideology in Chinese foreign policy making, since we would be treating revolutionary China's motives and goals as products of several elements—historical, experiential, ideological, bureaucratic, developmental—that combine, oftentimes uneasily, to give the state its theory and practice of politics.

A beginning step in gaining this broader perspective might be to consider anew Mao's philosophical writings of the 1930s, chief among them being "Dialectical Materialism,"[5] "On Practice,"[6] and "On Contradiction."[7] Here Mao unveiled his conception of the sources of revolutionary change and described the proper mode of political analysis. Thus, in the first of them, Mao distinguished between idealism and materialism, saying that "materialism recognizes the independent existence of matter as detached from spirit and considers spirit as secondary and subordinate." *Dialectical* materialism, the foundation of Marx's philosophy, enlarges on the concept of materialism by applying it to a class analysis of society that points the way to a revolutionary transformation of people's lives. As the Chinese communists see it, Marx made it possible to view history not as the development of ideas (Hegel) or static spiritual forces (the notion of traditional Chinese philosophers) but as "matter endlessly in movement from a lower form to a higher form." "That is to say," wrote Mao, "it is possible to investigate the world as development and process." The notions of process, synthesis, contradiction, struggle, and transformation that emerge from the Marxist-Maoist dialectic have profoundly influenced the way contemporary Chinese evaluate international politics, as we shall illustrate later on.

The process of "investigating the world" employs the "dialectical materialist theory of knowledge," Mao wrote in "On Practice." True knowledge comes from direct experience—such as personal involvement in revolution— where theory gained from books is tested in practice. Three important implications for political analysis derive from the "theory of knowledge." The *starting point* of analysis is "objective facts, not . . . abstract definitions."[8] Marxist theory, Mao often said, cannot be dogmatically applied; it is useful only when it is based on practice and proves to have practical value. Theories are made to be disproven, since as one major Chinese analysis of world politics put it in 1977, "the thesis that the logic of facts is stronger than any other logic still holds true."[9] Maoism, as Franz Schurmann has written, is best understood as a practical ideology, a guide to action.[10] It indeed proposes certain immutable truths based on Marx's reading of history and on China's revolutionary experiences (e.g., those pertaining to the behavior patterns of imperialist states). But Maoism also comprises precepts for revising perceptions based on new experiences (such as, in the 1970s, redefining the "socialist camp" or the united front of different classes).

The *framework* for political analysis is the "law" of contradictions—that is, the unity and struggle of opposing forces such as nationalism and colonialism or U.S. imperialism and Soviet revisionism. Historical change occurs as contradictions unite temporarily and struggle absolutely—as in the case of the Sino-U.S. relationship since Nixon's visit in 1972. The astute analyst knows how to identify the principal and secondary aspects of contradictions, and how to distinguish "antagonistic" contradictions (those between "the enemy and us") from "nonantagonistic" ones (those among "the people").

Contradictions thus change in importance over time. For example, in 1965 the principal contradiction in world politics was declared to be that between the United States and the revolutionary forces of the Third World, with Vietnam as the focal point of contention.[11] In 1969, shortly after the cessation of Sino-Soviet border fighting, Lin Biao (Lin Piao) identified four major contradictions in world politics—(1) between socialist countries and U.S. and Soviet imperialism, (2) between U.S. and Soviet imperialism and the oppressed Third World peoples, (3) between the proletariat and the bourgeoisie in capitalist and revisionist countries, and (4) between and among imperialist countries—without specifying which was the primary contradiction.[12] By the early 1970s numerous Chinese analyses were suggesting that the primary contradiction was between U.S. imperialism and Soviet "social-imperialism," on the one hand, and the nonsocialist developing and developed countries of the first and second "intermediate zones," on the other.[13] In 1977, in accordance with Mao's "theory of the differentiation of the three worlds," the Chinese leadership argued that capitalism and socialism had ceased to be useful analytical categories. The main contradiction was then proclaimed to be that between the two imperialist superpowers of the "first world" and *all* the "second world" and "third world" countries. Since the U.S.S.R. was the greater threat, its contradiction with China was deemed more important than that which exists between China and the United States.[14]

In line with the hope of arriving at a better understanding of the domestic sources of Chinese foreign policy, our main interest is in the *method* of analysis, which is dialectics. Dialectics is the study of contradictions in things. Drawing upon Marxism, the Chinese apply dialectical reasoning to their history, revolution, and socialism. *Historical dialecticism* emphasizes the contradictions between large social forces and classes that provided the mainsprings of China's revolution. Western political scientists are mainly concerned with personalities, power, systems, structures, and functions when explaining politics. Chinese analysts pay attention to imperialism and social-imperialism, colonialism and neocolonialism, revolution and reaction; and they assess the role played by particular classes at particular times, such as the national bourgeoisie in the 1930s and 1940s when China was said by Mao to be a semicolony under the control of several imperialist powers.

Here is how one Chinese historian defined the approach:

> Modern and contemporary world history is a record of the criminal acts of capitalism, colonialism and imperialism in exploitation and aggression at home and abroad and also one of the heroic struggle of the world's revolutionary people and the oppressed colonial people against exploitation, aggression and oppression. In the long course of struggle, capitalism, colonialism and imperialism have changed from strong to weak in moving step by step towards their extinction, while the revolutionary people and the oppressed colonial people have grown from weak to strong in advancing to victory. This is what historical dialecticism means.[15]

Such an analysis explicitly builds on confidence in the future—confidence that the weak will eventually prevail over the strong, that the oppressed will overthrow their oppressors, that one can defeat many, that the masses count for more than technology. Given the history of the Chinese communist revolution, such long-term conviction is easy to understand.[16]

By interpreting the world of politics in line with the historical dialectic method, one always risks becoming the subject of controversy in Chinese politics. To take the current period as an example, the "three worlds" theory leaves ambiguously answered the question of whether the United States is to be regarded as an ally or an opponent in the primary struggle with the Soviet Union. Can the U.S. leadership, which is considered imperialistic, also be part of the broad international united front against Moscow that China wishes to see develop? How far should China go in support of revolutionary movements in the Third World (e.g., in central Africa) and of workers' movements in the capitalist world (e.g., in Italy or the United States) when these are directed against the same imperialistic U.S. leaders whose support China needs againt Soviet power? These are very real issues for which the Maoist methodology does not (contrary to the assumption of many China analysts over the years) provide ready-made answers. There is plenty of room for debate, as evidenced by the quite credible charges leveled in Beijing against the "Gang of Four" for allegedly opposing several policy lines undertaken in accordance with the "three worlds" theory.[17]

Another component of the Chinese political methodology is *revolutionary dialectics*. It is concerned with the concrete circumstances of oppressed and oppressor as the Chinese experienced them against Chiang Kai-shek's Guomindang (GMD) (Kuomintang [KMT]) and the Japanese in the 1930s. It is a set of conclusions, put forward by the Chinese as laws or truths, about the behavior of the two parties that stand in contradiction to each other in conflict situations. Authoritative Chinese statements on international affairs constantly and frequently refer to this kind of dialectical relationship.[18] It is one that emerges directly from the Chinese leaders' (above all, Mao's own) revolutionary experiences; as such, revolutionary dialectics are applied to political conflict in China's international *and* domestic affairs.

Revolutionary dialectics can be presented in several ways. Our approach is to group them in three categories: the nature of imperialism; strategy for dealing with the enemy; and the revolutionary process. Here, we will provide only a few illustrations of their relevance to Chinese foreign-policy thinking, since the case studies contain additional references.

On the Nature of Imperialism

"All reactionaries are paper tigers."[19]   While imperialistic and reactionary forces may be technologically powerful, they are in fact weak and vulnerable because they lack popular support. Applied initially to the United States, this concept was later (in the early 1960s) extended to include the Soviet Union.

"Lifting a rock only to drop it on one's own feet."[20]   The logic of imperialists is to take precisely those actions that will lead to their doom. The U.S. alliance with Chiang Kai-shek's Taiwan is an example: by converting Taiwan into a U.S. base, the U.S. leaders created the conditions for three crises in the Taiwan Strait. Taiwan became "a noose around the Americans' necks."

"Make trouble, fail, make trouble again."[21]   Imperialists never learn from their mistakes; instead, they invariably repeat them. Thus do they become "teachers by negative example." Such was the case when the Russians invaded Czechoslovakia a second time in 1968, and when the United States became still more deeply involved in Vietnam after the 1954 Geneva conference.

"Things in contradiction change into one another."[22]   Revolutionary struggle leads to the transformation of opposites: as resistance to U.S. and Soviet power widens, the world's revolutionary forces will grow from weak to strong, while the counterrevolutionary forces will decline, eventually becoming the weakest. "All of history proves that point," Mao said in 1956.

"Several thousand years of people's class society proves this point: the strong will yield to the weak."[23]

"All reactionary forces on the verge of extinction invariably conduct a last desperate struggle."[24] The enemy is most dangerous at the end of its tether, and revolutionaries should not be deluded by its last gasp of strength. Such was the situation, for example, when Nixon ordered the invasion of Cambodia in 1970 and the Christmas bombing of Hanoi in 1972.

On the Correct Strategy for Dealing with an Enemy

"Strategically despise the enemy, but tactically take the enemy seriously."[25] From the longterm perspective, the enemy is inherently weak; but in the short run, the enemy may be quite dangerous, and its power should be respected. The imperialists are indeed paper tigers, said Mao in December 1958, after the second Taiwan Strait crisis; but "they are also living tigers, iron tigers, real tigers which can devour people."[26]

"To be attacked by the enemy is a good thing."[27] To be attacked by the imperialists means the Chinese are being influential in world affairs and are doing an effective job of making clear what distinguishes the two sides from each other. This is what the P.R.C. leadership said, for instance, when various Johnson administration officials portrayed China as the "aggressor by proxy" in Vietnam. The Chinese replied that the more the United States attacked China, the more clearly did it reveal itself as the real aggressor in Asia, against revolutionary nationalism.

"First, we are against [war]; second, we are not afraid of it."[28] Mao initially made this statement during the period of Soviet missile advances in the late 1950s. In the 1970s, Chinese officials often quoted it to show concern that the superpowers would begin a new world war. The statement expresses the belief that war is best deterred by preparing for it. Thus the Chinese will also say, "We will not attack unless we are attacked; if we are attacked, we will certainly counterattack"[29] and urge waging "tit-for-tat" struggle against the enemy.[30] Imperialism is both reckless and capable of imposing war on China. China should respond, first, by not being afraid to fight if forced to do so, and second, by being prepared to fight, psychologically and materially. Without fearlessness and preparedness, Mao was saying, the enemy would be convinced of China's weakness and would surely attack. "Strategic surrender"—refusing to fight for fear everyone will be annihilated—was totally unacceptable to Mao.

Looking at the situation in an all-round way. In "On Practice," Mao warned party officials not to be "subjective, one-sided and superficial in their approach to problems," since every situation contains a history, an essence, and a relationship to another situation.[31] Such was also the leadership's advice in 1977 on the question of how to treat Third World leaders of widely different political persuasions. Looking at the "essence" of the matter, the Third World, in spite of its many contradictions, should still be regarded as "the main force in the struggle against imperialism and hegemonism."[32]

Understanding line and policy. "Policy is the starting-point of all the practical actions of a revolutionary party and manifests itself in the process and the end-result of that party's actions."[33] But policies carried out independently of awareness of the party's general line, which gives policies their ideological and programmatic direction, are bound to be unsuccessful.[34] When Sino-American diplomacy got under way in 1971, culminating in Nixon's China trip, the party leadership went to great pains to explain to lower-level officials that its policy was in keeping with Mao's "revolutionary diplomatic line." Policy shifts are appropriate, the leadership argued then, so long as they are based on correct principles—which is what the general line is all about.

Distinguishing enemies and friends: The united front. One of the first lessons Mao drew from his attempts to mobilize the peasantry was the necessity to "unite with real friends in order to attack real enemies."[35] Forming a united front (from "below") with different classes and (from "above") with noncommunist parties and governments in order to defeat a common enemy has always been a central feature of Chinese revolutionary strategy. The makeup of the united front will change as contradictions change. In 1977 Premier Hua Guofeng (Hua Kuo-feng) said China's goal would be to "form the broadest united front against the hegemonism of the two superpowers."[36] Should the governments of Chile, the Philippines, Iran (under the Shah), and Zaire, which are closely tied to the United States and face substantial popular unrest, be part of the front? The Chinese leadership answered "yes" on the basis that these governments' interest in asserting their independence and adopting anti-Soviet policies was more important than the contradictions between them and their people.

On Making a Revolution

"A single spark can start a prairie fire."[37]   When one sees the contradictions of a situation, rather than make a superficial examination, one can detect the limitless possibilities for radical changes. "Where there is oppression, there is resistance." Much depends on whether or not the

revolutionary has faith in the power of people who are united. "Who is more afraid of whom?" Mao asked at the height of the Taiwan Strait crisis in 1958. He answered that Dulles and the Western powers were more afraid of the socialist camp than it was of them. "It's a question of strength," he explained; "it's a question of popular support. Popular support means strength, and we have more people on our side than they do."[38]

"All wars that are progressive are just, and all wars that impede progress are unjust."[39] Just wars prove themselves by their breadth of popular support and the political character of the opposing forces. In May 1970, after U.S. and South Vietnamese forces invaded Cambodia, Mao issued a statement that Beijing has often repeated since: "Innumerable facts prove that a just cause enjoys abundant support while an unjust cause finds little support. A weak nation can defeat a strong, a small nation can defeat a big. The people of a small country can certainly defeat aggression by a big country, if only they dare to rise in struggle, dare to take up arms and grasp in their own hands the destiny of their country. This is a law of history."[40]

Self-reliance. The policy of "regeneration through one's own efforts" rather than reliance on foreign help has long characterized the Maoist approach to revolution.[41] As a Chinese commentator put it, only Third World nations and peoples that "adhere to the principle of maintaining independence and keeping the initiative in their own hands and relying on their own efforts" will be successful.[42] Self-reliance has been the guiding concept of China's foreign-aid program, its limited support of revolutionary movements, and its quest for an independent nuclear deterrent.

"While the prospects are bright, the road has twists and turns."[43] Optimistic Chinese statements about the ultimate success of just struggles are often tempered with admonitions about "twists and turns," "zigs and zags" along the way. "Revolution is not a dinner party," Mao said. Once revolutionaries understand this truth, they will be able to turn inevitable difficulties into useful experiences that will strengthen them.

"A bad thing can be turned to good account."[44] Part of making a complete analysis of a situation is to see the advantages of adversity. U.S. intervention in Vietnam gave rise to the antiwar movement in the United States and increased popular support in Vietnam against the Saigon regime. The Soviet leadership's turn away from genuine socialism, in the Chinese view, gave them valuable lessons on how to prevent the rise of capitalism in China. When a group of visiting Japanese apologized to Mao in 1958 for

their country's aggression against China in the 1930s, he replied that actually it was "a good deed" because it helped bring about the unity of the Chinese people and the visit of these Japanese to Beijing.[45]

A third form of dialectical reasoning is *socialist dialectics,* which concerns the handling of contradictory forces in Chinese society since 1949. Mao's speeches "On the Ten Major Relationships" (1956), "On the Correct Handling of Contradictions among the People" (1957), and to an enlarged central work conference (1962)[46] are among the principal sources for the application of dialectical thinking to China's political economy. Here and elsewhere Mao raised issues that were vital to China's development as an egalitarian, self-reliant society: the relationship between democracy and centralism, between agriculture and light and heavy industry, between the party and the masses, between internal and external resources, and between theoretical (intellectual) and practical (manual) work. In Mao's view, a proper balance between these conflicting relationships could not be achieved without contention, since under socialism and even under communism contradictions will always exist. The essence of socialist dialectics thus lies in the contradiction between modernization (improvements in material productivity) and development (improvements in people's spiritual, no less than material, well-being).

The Three Impulses

Historical, revolutionary, and socialist dialectics together provide the theoretical tools that China's political leaders seem to rely on as they analyze their society and the world. The domestic and external experiences that give content to the dialectics and frame the way they are employed are now introduced as *impulses.* We treat Chinese foreign policy as the product of Asian, revolutionary, and socialist impulses that have shaped the development of communism in China itself. Dialectics provides a methodology, and the impulses provide an internal and external direction for policy making.

As we have said, foreign affairs is not entirely separate from domestic affairs; the two realms are connected by the fact that in China, as in other societies, perceptions of and actions in foreign affairs are the consequence of a variety of experiences, the most critical of which originate internally. The fact that these experiences are by no means uniform is reflected in contradictions between the impulses that give foreign policy making in China its political (contentious and collaborative) quality. We maintain that Chinese behavior in international politics is at bottom the external form of domestic political values and objectives. Chinese officials share this view.[47]

Like the three dialectics, each impulse reflects a distinct aspect of Chinese experience that gives the impulse a particular political focal point. Thus, the *Asian* impulse stems from China's history; consciousness of imperialism, nationalist sensitivity, and concern about national security are the chief consequences. The *revolutionary* impulse draws upon Marxism, as adapted by Mao, and upon the experience of civil war. The focal point of this impulse is the revolutionary transformation of society—*fanshen.* The *socialist* impulse concerns politics in action, the development of the state along socialist lines. For every Chinese leadership, the central challenge of policy making is how to serve and harmonize these impulses, which often compete for priority. There is by no means always a direct line from impulse to policy choice; the road invariably contains "zigs and zags," as the Chinese like to say—contradictions that may occasion political struggle. The case studies bring out some of these disputes.

What, then, are the main domestic and international characteristics of these three impulses? The historically grounded Asian impulse comprises the need to demonstrate the Chinese revolution's continuity with nineteenth-century rebellions (the Taiping [T'ai-p'ing] rebellion in particular) and early twentieth century nationalist movements (May 4, 1919). It therefore also embraces China's strong cultural identity, sensitivity to foreign penetration and control (anticolonialism and anti-imperialism), and revolutionary pride—all of which are common themes in Mao's preliberation writings[48] and are epitomized by his September 1949 speech "The Chinese People Have Stood Up!"[49]

Chinese attitudes toward and perceptions of the outside world are, needless to say, strongly influenced by the Asian impulse. A clear example was provided when Foreign Minister Qiao Guanhua (Ch'iao Kuan-hua) addressed the UN General Assembly in 1971 as head of the first P.R.C. delegation:

> The Chinese people have experienced untold sufferings under imperialist oppression. For one century and more, imperialism repeatedly launched wars of aggression against China and forced her to sign many unequal treaties. They divided China into their sphere of influence, plundered China's resources and exploited the Chinese people.... Since the founding of the People's Republic of China, we, the Chinese people, defying the tight imperialist blockades and withstanding the terrific pressure from without, have build our country into a socialist state with initial prosperity by maintaining independence and keeping the initiative in our own hands and through self-reliance. It has been proved by facts that we the Chinese nation are fully capable of standing on our feet in the family of nations.[50]

In this and other parts of Qiao's statement may be found many of the issues the Asian impulse embraces: border questions; the security threat posed by historical enemies (such as the Russians and the Japanese) and contemporary imperialism; foreign bases in China (which the Russians proposed in

1958 and 1965) and surrounding China; principles of equality and mutuality in state relations that have been incorporated into the various peaceful coexistence treaties China has concluded since 1954; and China's concern to have a proper role in the affairs of Asia, with assurances that the two superpowers will not collude against China or seek regional hegemony.

The focal point of the Asian impulse is anti-imperialism. Over the years, as some recent studies have shown,[51] the Chinese leadership has made opposition to imperialism—traditionally, that of the United States; more recently, that of the U.S.S.R.—the key factor in determining the friendliness or hostility of other states. Anti-imperialism means independence, territorial and decision-making sovereignty, and security, all of which China did not begin to possess until the victory of the communist revolution. In deciding on the character of China's relationship with another state, therefore, the Chinese leadership has made a government's attitudes toward imperialism, and not its ideology or social structure, the determining factor. A good example is the official P.R.C. statement of October 10, 1970, concerning Cambodia, after General Lon Nol had overthrown Prince Sihanouk and acquiesced in a U.S.-South Vietnam invasion:

> Whether a state is progressive or reactionary depends not on whether it bears the name of a kingdom or a republic, but on whether or not the policy it follows represents the interests of the people and whether or not its policy is anti-imperialist. There are certain kingdoms which pursue a policy of peace and neutrality, oppose imperialist aggression and defend their national independence, thus winning the approval and support of the people and playing a progressive role in history.[52]

The fact that the P.R.C. will conduct state relations with reactionary and repressive regimes while being willing to disrupt relations with some socialist ones can be understood only with reference to the anti-imperialist issue.

The revolutionary impulse refers to China's commitment to seek a fundamental transformation of the structure of the international system. It is a commitment that flows from Mao's ideology and practices of political and economic development—his interest in "changing people's souls," cultivating self-reliance, decentralizing power, promoting egalitarianism and voluntarism, subverting bureaucratism, and preventing the growth of an intellectual, scientific elite. His philosophy that "to rebel is justified" is reflected both in his dialectic of domestic development and in his international outlook, for in both we see clearly his belief that great masses of people can ultimately prevail over the power of technology (including nuclear weapons), finance (including international-monopoly capital), and political alliances (including those directed against China). The revolutionary impulse may be thought of as the transference onto the international stage of Mao's conviction that one of the greatest assets of the Chinese people is that they are "poor and blank."[53]

The revolutionary impulse coincides with the emphasis in historical and revolutionary dialectics on converting weakness to strength, relying on the oppressed masses to make revolution, and avoiding situations of dependence on big powers such as that which China encountered with the U.S.S.R. right after the 1949 liberation. The impulse therefore has specific relevance to developmental choices faced by all other Third World leaderships, a relevance that Chinese officials emphasized throughout the 1970s by identifying China as a Third World country, not a superpower.[54] Yet it is more than a matter of identification, since for many years China's pattern of development has been held up as an alternative model for Third World leaderships to consider. Just as China has overcome feudalism, colonialism, and dependency, so too can other underdeveloped societies find an independent socialist road. What one writer has called China's "ethical diplomacy"[55] is an important component of the revolutionary impulse: it embraces issues of international political economy such as territorial waters, energy, multinational corporations, population planning, and ecology, on all of which the P.R.C. stands with the Third World. The impulse also concerns trade and foreign-aid programs, with China offering conditions that promote self-reliant, independent growth in recipient countries. In all these areas, the P.R.C.'s primary interest is to redefine the international system in ways that begin to equalize power (economic power particularly) and end exploitation of the weakest states, China included.

The other side of the revolutionary impulse is the issue of revolution itself. That China has not uniformly or consistently promoted revolution beyond its borders is by now amply documented.[56] The commitment, at least verbally, to "support" revolution is a fixture in the Chinese world view, but Under what circumstances? For how long? and With what means? are among the practical questions Chinese leaders have addressed since 1949. Conditions in the late 1970s, for instance, were clearly considered different from those in the mid-1960s, when the Vietnam War was China's paramount external concern. The revolutionary impulse by no means determines a favorable Chinese response to those in revolt. China is a model of successful revolution, but its revolution took place under specific historical, geographic, and political conditions that Chinese leaders have always been conscious of (and sometimes have had to remind revolutionaries abroad about), conditions that have made them careful not to promote their revolution as a blueprint for anyone else's.

The socialist impulse emanates from the commitment in China's development strategy to socialist methods and goals—for instance, to collective well-being and communal values, to egalitarian rather than hierarchical relationships, and to the centralization as well as the democratization of decision making. Looked at as a unique impulse, socialism gives Chinese leaders a special sensitivity to the corrosive political effects of "dogmatic" thinking and habits, on the left, and of "revisionist" thinking and habits, on the right. While Mao was alive, at least, revisionism was considered the greater danger to the Chinese way to socialism.

These domestic characteristics of Chinese socialism have important implications for China's place in world politics. As a member of the socialist community, the socialist impulse focuses attention on China's relations with the Soviet Union, Eastern Europe, and the socialist governments and parties of the Third World (in Asia particularly). Specific issues include Chinese concerns about the growth of revisionism in the U.S.S.R. and the resulting threat posed to China's political economy and stability; China's promotion of autonomy within the socialist bloc, and more recently, its leaders' assertions that a socialist bloc no longer exists; and the competition between Moscow and Beijing for political preeminence among the world's communist parties.

Outside the socialist community, this impulse is concerned principally with the effects of Sino-Soviet relations on China's outlook and policies toward the United States, Western Europe and Japan in the "second world," and toward Third World countries. In the bygone era of cordiality in Sino-Soviet relations, the socialist impulse was responsible for cooperative, or at least noncompetitive, policies toward these countries and areas. Russian technical and economic help was important enough to China's economy to warrant Beijing's muting of disagreements and suspicions. By the late 1950s, however, most writers would agree that Chinese attitudes had changed profoundly, and the long period of heated rivalry, which includes the present, had begun. Since the late fifties, as the Soviet threat has risen to dominate Chinese strategic thinking, China's socialist impulse has probably prompted questions like these: Should China attempt to build socialism in relative isolation from the international political economy (thus strictly defining self-reliance), or should it engage in "realist" diplomacy to take advantage of what the capitalist economies have to offer? In what ways should China respond to political developments in the Third World—such as internal upheavals, changes of leadership and ideology, and interest in nonalignment—so as to promote China's own security from imperialist threats? What commonalities in the politics of the "second" and "third" worlds would facilitate the formation of a united front against the U.S.S.R.?

Politics and Foreign Policy

Having defined the three impulses, we may now amplify an earlier remark about their importance to understanding the politics of Chinese foreign policy making. Most significantly, the impulses approach draws attention to *the priority of domestic objectives over international ones in official Chinese thinking.* Secondly, the approach sensitizes the analyst to the range of policy choices Chinese officials may have, and to the different positions that are likely to be taken on specific issues. Each of these points requires some elaboration.

We have attempted to show that the principal concerns of Chinese foreign policy makers—security, legitimacy, system transformation and redistribution, and the future of socialism—can be traced to domestic sources: China's history of confrontation with imperialism, the revolution of consciousness and economic and political structures that Mao spearheaded, and socialist development strategy. Looked at this way, Chinese foreign policy *serves* domestic political values, institutions, and programs. Hence our first proposition:

1. The chief purpose of foreign policy in China is to protect and promote the radical socialist revolution at home.

A former ambassador and leading figure in China's Ministry of Foreign Affairs phrased the issue this way:

> The foreign policy of a country is the extension of its domestic policy, and moreover follows and serves its domestic policy. . . . Lenin, speaking of the basic tasks of Soviet foreign policy, said: "We need peaceful construction. We must carry out peaceful construction with all our spirit and life." Because only with peaceful construction can production greatly develop, can the goals of socialist production be fully realized, and can the people's continually increasing material and cultural needs be satisfied. For these things, a peaceful international environment is demanded; war can only obstruct and destroy the carrying out of construction.[57]

This first proposition, and the three major impulses from which it flows, suggest the decidedly defensive orientation of Chinese foreign policy: *preventing* imperialism, revisionism, capitalism, and other counterrevolutionary forces from threatening the very fabric of Chinese political life; and *promoting* the self-strengthening and self-reliance of the social system and its people. This is quite different from the interpretation of many other writers, who suggest that among the leadership's highest priorities is the promotion of socialist revolution abroad. The case studies in this volume will do much, we think, to support the idea that "national security" for China has above all meant protecting the domestic socialist revolution from outside interference. Quite apart from historical factors, such as ethnocentrism and justifiable fear of encroachment by imperialist powers, China's defensiveness is the consequence of practical considerations. An activist foreign policy must be a luxury for a country with limited resources *and* a

leadership committed to revolutionizing the society. Foreign entangle-
ments must always be carefully weighed against pressing domestic obligations; the former cannot have the same priority as the latter without
incurring expensive new commitments abroad that may not merely detract
from domestic programs but may also bring about major redirections in the
domestic revolution as a whole. Even the world's wealthiest nation found
that it could not indefinitely afford guns and butter; all the more so for
China. Its leaders are as "realistic" as any other state's: they understand
that the costs of foreign policy must inevitably be calculated in domestic
political terms. In contrast with the superpowers, the security and stability
of China's domestic institutions and values have not required the sustained
and far-flung projection of state power. There is nothing in Chinese doctrine
or practice that compares with the Brezhnev doctrine in its application to
Eastern Europe, or with the Truman, Eisenhower, Johnson, and Nixon
doctrines in their applications to the Third World.

Rather than seek to achieve domestic goals *through* foreign-policy
actions—which is the course Chinese analysts always assert imperialist and
social-imperialist regimes follow, particularly when their economies are
faltering or their leaderships are in political trouble[58]—Chinese leaders
have sought to *insulate* domestic politics from foreign-policy repercussions.
As the quotation from the former foreign affairs official intimates, one way
to achieve that kind of separation is to work for a peaceful international
environment, since:

> 2. A quiescent (nonthreatening) international environment is the opti-
> mum condition for radical socialist development.

We can find Mao and other Chinese officials asserting before their
colleagues the desirability of international peace not only in the 1950s,
when the agricultural collectivization movement was under way,[59] but also
in recent years, when attention has turned to long-term modernization
programs.[60] To the oft-heard charge that the P.R.C. has supported
revolution at least as often as it has promoted peaceful coexistence, the
Chinese reply that such support has been given only to those popular
movements that contest U.S. intervention in their country's economy,
politics, and national defense system. Revolution, they say, is an internal
affair of the country concerned; but it becomes a Chinese concern when
foreign intervention transforms "revolutionary civil war" into "local war."
There is a necessary contradiction between a peaceful foreign policy in
support of the socialist impulse, and a revolutionary foreign policy in behalf
of the global transformation of power.

Given a long period of international peace, China's prospects increase
for the fulfillment of social and economic plans. As those plans are realized,

in turn, China's security—political and economic as much as military—and international legitimacy are enhanced. Specifically,

   3. *Economic performance is considered by Chinese leaders to be the key to national security and international legitimacy.*

Echoing the view of American Realists like George Kennan, Chinese leaders believe that "the first requirement of a successful foreign policy is that one places oneself in a favorable posture for its conduct."[61] Successful economic performance, they say, is the prerequisite to political unity. With these achievements, China will be listened to with respect by the international community; without them, as in the Cultural Revolution, China is bound to lose influence and friends.

There is abundant evidence to document this proposition. On a number of occasions before and during China's Great Leap Forward (GLF) (1958–62), Mao may be found telling his colleagues that once grain, steel, and machinery production targets are met, the capitalist countries will be compelled to recognize the P.R.C. and negotiate on equal terms with it.[62] Senior army cadres were confidentially told in 1961 that the tasks of strengthening domestic unity and continuing the anti-imperialist struggle are "like two needles pointing at each other. In order to succeed in all these, we must carry on well the internal construction of our country and realize the importance of construction of our country and realize the importance of our foundation. Only through successful internal construction can we expect great accomplishments in international affairs."[63] Whether China had a short or a long respite from the forces ranged against it, said Mao at that time, "depends how well we do our work." It might take forty years; but by then, levels of production, education, and political consciousness would be much higher, so that "in all likelihood the whole of society will have passed on to communism. To sum up, the answer to all our problems lies in us being good at unity and good at work."[64] Nearly twenty years have passed since those remarks were made, but today's Chinese leaders are still clearly motivated by the belief that in modernization—which they specify as industrial, agricultural, military, and scientific and technological—lies the foundation for domestic political unity and influence and respect abroad.

From these first three propositions we can see how closely intertwined are China's goals of continuous revolution (or, today, socialist modernization) at home and the minimization of threats from and dependence on external powers. Domestic policies cannot be successfully pursued when foreign governments are able to exert military or economic leverage on China. Nor can external leverage be readily neutralized when there is domestic political or economic instability. Hence the desirability of international peace—when there are no foreign threats to China or to its chief revolutionary allies—and a strong, independent economy. The absence of those conditions has always been considered very dangerous, not only by communist leaderships but also by Chinese governments and nationalist movements of the last hundred years. All of them have been preoccupied with the capacity of big powers to compromise China's sovereignty, particularly at times of domestic weakness.[65] Like the leaders of other developing states, China's leaders throughout the modern era have been acutely sensitive to the security problems posed by the country's economic needs, military weaknesses, and periodic political mobilizations. For instance, how to maintain China's independence and preserve its "essence" while obtaining foreign technology and expertise has been a central issue since the initial Chinese confrontation with the West in the 1840s. For all Chinese governments have found that undue reliance on foreigners runs the risk of dependency, and openness to foreign ideas may subvert the official ideology and transform people's attitudes and life styles.

Accordingly, our next set of propositions concerns how Chinese perceptions of international politics influence and are influenced by domestic circumstances.

4. Chinese sensitivity to external threat is highest at times of domestic political weakness or conflict.

4a. The most dangerous aspect of external threat is its subversive influence on revisionist elements within the country.

5. Foreign policy becomes a domestic political issue by addressing economic or political choices that are under debate.

6. Domestic stability promotes conditions that are favorable to foreign-policy initiatives.

6a. Domestic instability discourages foreign-policy initiatives.

During the initial period of encounter with the Western imperial powers, the phrase *nei luan wai huan* ("within, chaos; without, catastrophe") was often used to describe the perceived connection between domestic disorder and foreign exploitation. Modern-day Chinese· leaders agree: foreign powers will most likely attempt to take advantage of China at times of domestic political instability or economic weakness. Such was the dominant perception in Beijing in the months before liberation in 1949, when Mao warned—correctly, as it turned out—that "the imperialists," not resigned to defeat, "will smuggle their agents into China," attempt to "blockade China's ports," and even "send some of their troops to invade and harass China's frontiers."[66] During the Cultural Revolution, Beijing warned Washington not to attempt to exploit China's domestic unrest.[67] The case studies in this volume will provide still other instances in which Chinese leaders perceived their adversaries to be bent on exploiting domestic weaknesses in the P.R.C. by applying military and other kinds of pressures.

External threats at times of domestic weakness are troublesome to the Chinese leadership not only or even primarily because war might result. In case of attack, China's enormous size and population, guerrilla tradition, and modern weapons give its leaders some confidence that the aggressor will eventually be repelled. The greater dangers are considered to come from within the country. Factions within the P.R.C. elite may seek to capitalize on the leadership's problems by applying pressure to compel major policy changes. Foreign powers may use their financial and technical resources and ideological appeals ("sugar-coated bullets," the Maoists would say) to win over influential Chinese to their political viewpoint.

An example of the first type of subversion allegedly occurred during the Great Leap Forward period. According to Zhou Enlai (Chou En-lai):

> When China's economy experienced temporary difficulties and when the imperi-alists, the reactionaries and the modern revisionists launched repeated cam-paigns against China, the class enemies at home launched renewed attacks on socialism, and consequently once again fierce class struggle ensued. In the domestic field, quite a few people actively advocated the extension of plots for private use and of free markets, the increase of small enterprises with sole responsibility for their own profits or losses, the fixing of output quotas based on the household . . . ; in the international field they advocated the liquidation of struggle in our relations with imperialism, the reactionaries and modern revision-ism, and reduction of assistance and support to the revolutionary struggle of other peoples.[68]

Thus, certain officials in high places—led by Liu Shaoqi (Liu Shao-ch'i), it was later claimed—urged conserving resources, liberalizing economic programs, and moderating tensions with the superpowers in order to gain time for (and possibly assistance in) economic recovery. After the Cultural Revolution the charge was broadened:

> Historical experience proves that, invariably, the activities of domestic counter-revolutionaries and the opportunists in the Party are not only political struggles in character but are co-ordinated with those of foreign reactionaries. Liu Shao-chi and company regarded the rabid anti-China campaign launched by the U.S. imperialists, the Soviet revisionists and the Indian reactionaries between 1959 and 1962 as their golden opportunity to restore capitalism.[69]

China's central leadership often has relied on Lenin in asserting that "imperialism and social-imperialism will always try to find their agents within our Party," just as "revisionists and opportunists hidden in our Party . . . will always go to them for backing."[70] Looking abroad, Chinese analysts cited the intellectuals who led the Hungarian uprising in 1956, allegedly with foreign support;[71] and Yugoslavia in the late 1950s, when

Marshal Tito encouraged criticisms of the state's power and thereby facilitated antisocialist activities and "the restoration of capitalism," all because, according to the Chinese, he wanted U.S. economic aid.[72] The lesson of Yugoslavia drawn by the Chinese leadership is instructive, since it clearly reflects concern about "another Hungary" occurring in China:

> It shows us that the restoration of capitalism in a socialist country can be achieved *not necessarily through a counter-revolutionary coup d'état or armed imperialist invasion* and that it can also be achieved through the degradation of the leading group in that country. *The easiest way to capture a fortress is from within.* . . . It shows that revisionism is the product of imperialist policy. . . . Sparing no cost, imperialism has now extended the scope of its operations and is buying over leading groups in socialist countries and pursues through them its desired policy of "peaceful evolution." U.S. imperialism regards Yugoslavia as the "bellwether" because it has set an example in this respect.[73]

In the years immediately preceding the Cultural Revolution, as the "struggle between the two lines" of socialism escalated within the Chinese Communist party leadership, Mao's constant concern about the influence of Soviet revisionism also intensified. The party Central Committee's 1964 letter, "On Khrushchov's Phoney Communism and Its Historical Lessons for the World," bears the clear imprint of Mao's concern. "The bourgeoisie and international imperialism both understand," says the letter, "that in order to make a socialist country degenerate into a capitalist country, it is first necessary to make the Communist Party degenerate into a revisionist party." The lesson to be drawn was to strengthen the dictatorship of the proletariat and democracy among the masses and within the armed forces in China so as to prevent domestic revisionism from poisoning China's revolutionary foreign-policy line.[74]

One phase of Mao's campaign against revisionism was the movement to train "revolutionary successors." Fittingly, the campaign was said to have "great strategic significance," since it was designed to counteract revisionist thinking that Mao believed had become dominant in the school system. Spokespeople for Mao's position observed how U.S. officials, like their counterparts in the revisionist countries (i.e., the Soviet Union), sought to corrupt the minds of younger Chinese with soft talk of "peaceful evolution" and of prospects for better relations with a "new generation" of more pragmatic Chinese leaders.[75] Kennedy administration officials were indeed saying exactly that; and evidently their words were considered potentially attractive to some Chinese comrades:

> The imperialists abroad headed by the United States pin their hope on the "peaceful evolution" of China through the degeneration of our third and fourth generations. Who can dismiss this view as entirely groundless? So long as there are classes and class struggle and a conflict between the socialist and capitalist roads . . . there will not be one road and one prospect, but two roads and two prospects, for future social development.[76]

The Cultural Revolution was the culmination of Mao's several efforts to prevent China from "changing color" and following the Soviet road of "goulash communism." To the American leaders, who were said to be encouraged by the advent of revisionism in Russia, one Chinese writer said: "Your hope for the emergence of 'softening and moderation' in China will never come to pass" now that the Red Guards have been formed.[77] The concerns of a decade earlier remained, however. The lesson of Yugoslavia had not lost its vitality:

> The history of the international communist movement provides almost no instance of proletarian state power being toppled in a socialist country by the international bourgeoisie through armed attack from without. *But a fortress can most easily be taken from within.* Imperialism, which is at the end of its rope while using war threats as intimidation against the socialist countries from without, is now mainly using the Khrushchov clique to carry out subversion from within and has effected "peaceful evolution" in the Soviet Union without using a single soldier or a single round of ammunition. Is this not a major historical lesson?[78]

So saying, the Chinese revealed why the Soviet Union constitutes a much graver threat to China than the United States does. While the American threat is military, the Soviet threat is preeminently political. The United States can be deterred by strategy and diplomacy; but the Soviet Union, because (in Chinese eyes) it represents the worst kind of socialist deviation—the restoration of capitalist incentives, bureaucratic elitism, and technocratic leadership—is an ongoing challenge to the legitimacy and permanence of the Chinese revolution. Doubtless there are bourgeois liberals in China who find the American political scene appealing; but there are surely many more and higher-ranking Chinese revisionists, as the Cultural Revolution brought out, whose politics would take Chinese socialism "down the capitalist road." Mao's view was that deterrence of this kind of threat required not only guns but also constant purification and mobilization of the party and people—which is precisely what the various mass campaigns in China, from the Hundred Flowers to the Cultural Revolution, were about. His successors seem to agree with his perception of the Russians, but in the interest of rapid technological change and administrative efficiency, play down the seriousness of domestic revisionism and therefore of mass movements to combat them.

This discussion of external threats and pressures brings out some important ways that a foreign policy becomes a domestic political issue in China (proposition 5). First, when the character or future of Chinese socialism is the topic of official action and discussion in the United States or the Soviet Union, that cannot help but arouse attention in Beijing, where the "struggle between the two (socialist) lines" has been going on since before the founding of the P.R.C. "Foreign" affairs then becomes inseparable from domestic affairs; what happens abroad may be emulated at home. Second, when China is itself embroiled in an external crisis, the central leadership may have to bargain for the support of key officials and interest groups. To obtain a consensus on crisis diplomacy may require making concessions on domestic and foreign policies—or risking a confrontation over them. Either way—bargaining or not bargaining—has important repercussions on leadership unity.

The case studies in this volume deal with the second type of situation, in which external threats create or enlarge debate within the P.R.C. leadership over economic and political choices. Foreign policy enters the domestic arena, mainly by compelling the chairman (Mao) and his bureaucratic leaders to *re*decide planning priorities and resource allocations. In one sense, external threats produce unity; but in another sense—and one that is often slighted by analysts—they prompt differences about China's best response that may reflect different personal, political, and organizational priorities. More is said about this matter in Chapter 7.

Propositions 4, 4a, and 5 deal with the impact of foreign policy on domestic affairs. Propositions 6 and 6a present the reverse situation. When there is political order at home—when the leadership is unified and confident about political, social, and economic order in the country— the way is clear to press Chinese interests abroad. Such was the case at the end of 1968, for example, when Mao and Zhou Enlai made their first overtures to the new U.S. administration for an improvement in Sino-American relations; and again ten years later, when Chinese and U.S. leaders reached agreement on diplomatic relations. The winding down of the Cultural Revolution was an important precondition of the first initiative, as the defeat of the "Gang of Four" was of the second. During the Cultural Revolution, however, circumstances had been entirely different. Policy-making resources were directed inward, all but one of China's ambassadors had been recalled, and Chinese interests abroad were represented by ultraleftist, often inexperienced young diplomats who created havoc in P.R.C. relations with a number of Third World governments. Order was not restored to these embassies, and to bilateral relations with these governments, until it was restored to the Ministry of Foreign Affairs in Beijing.[79] In a word, when great debate sweeps the land in China, the leadership's priority is Chinese socialism and not foreign affairs.

A very important exception to that last generalization will be underscored by the case studies and is implied in proposition 4. Preoccupied as the P.R.C. leadership may be with domestic matters, it will not shy away from a foreign threat when the nation's most vital interests are in question. We will see several instances in which the state of domestic affairs did *not* affect the leadership's willingness to act abroad, although it *did* seem to affect *how* it acted.

2 *The Korean War, 1950*

Introduction

The Chinese intervention in the Korean War took place in October and November 1950. Prior to the war, Chinese leaders, having just emerged from a prolonged and costly civil war, had to cope with crucial domestic problems in order to consolidate their power. China's economy and financial structure were on the verge of total collapse, the People's Liberation Army (PLA) was needed to help with production, and the civil war remained to be completed with the liberation of Taiwan and Tibet and the pacification of remaining anitcommunist groups. Overwhelmingly, the new government's concerns were domestic and focused on national rehabilitation.

Despite these pressing domestic issues, the P.R.C. responded with force to U.S. action in Korea, which most Chinese leaders perceived as an imminent danger to China's national security. The Chinese seemed to fear that invading UN and U.S. forces would occupy North Korea and push their attack beyond the border of Korea into China.

China's Korean War decision was influenced by and in turn affected its domestic affairs. Precisely how domestic and external events interacted in Chinese foreign policy making is the central concern of this chapter. We begin with an exploration of China's economic and political picture, move on to view world and regional politics as seen from Beijing, and then piece these together to describe China's motives and objectives in entering the Korean conflict.

The Domestic Situation

The Economy

Once the Chinese Communist party had established a new regime in October 1949, its central concern was the rehabilitation of the economy.

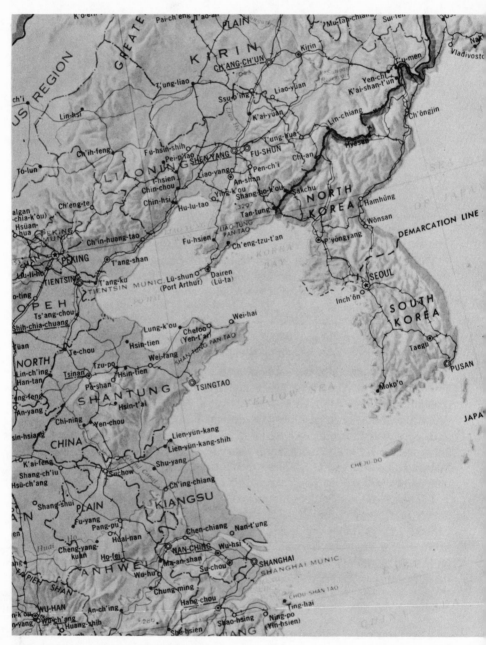

THE CHINA-KOREA BORDER

The Chinese economy and financial structure were in serious disrepair due to the twelve-year war, natural calamities, and a continuous increase of military and government expenditures. These economic difficulties were compounded by destruction of the transportation system in the war and a blockade of the Chinese coast by the GMD Nationalists. The Chinese communist leadership's first efforts were therefore directed at relieving famine, stabilizing commodity prices, checking inflation, balancing the budget, and restoring basic transportation and communication.

Long years of war had drastically lowered productivity in agriculture and industry and caused widespread unemployment. In 1949 the mainland was hit by natural calamities over wide areas. About 120 million *mou* of farmland and 40 million people were affected by floods or drought to a greater or lesser degree. Mainly due to the shortage of food and commodities, as well as to increases in military and government expenditures, the financial situation and commodity prices underwent periodic fluctuations. These extended into early 1950. In a report to the Central People's Government, Chen Yun, vice-premier of the Government Administration Council and concurrently chairman of the Committee of Financial and Economic Affairs, sensed acutely how a heavy burden of expenditures would adversely affect the financial situation and economy in the future: "During the interim period [of 1949] between the price fluctuation, there were times when currency and commodity prices were comparatively stable. But such stability was transitory. It was not the result of any reduction in the deficit. . . . On the contrary, owing to the monthly increase in military and government expenditures, the deficit also increased month by month, bringing about instability in currency and commodity prices."[1]

In the months prior to the Korean War, the Chinese leadership was seriously concerned about rehabilitating the war-torn economy in order to balance the budget, check inflation, and stabilize prices. From its point of view, economic hardships would have a deteriorating effect on people's welfare, which in turn might undermine efforts to consolidate power. An article in *People's China* on February 1, 1950, noted that complete military victory over the GMD would depend on the outcome of the communists' efforts to restore the war-torn economy: "The imperialists rejoice over our financial hardships. After the liberation of Shanghai last May, they remarked: 'The Chinese communists get a full mark in military achievements, 80 in political affairs and 10 in economic matters.' They believed that the Kuomintang blockade, undertaken at the instigation of the American imperialists, would surely result in the collapse of our financial structure and general economy."[2]

To rehabilitate the economy, the government decided on a partial demobilization of the PLA and on transferring soldiers to production and construction work. It also decided to restore "key points" of the economy—

heavy industry, agricultural irrigation, and railway communications—and to favor a production-first policy, with less emphasis on class struggle. In late June 1950 China's first five-year national economic plan was drafted.[3] All these policies seem relevant to China's decision on Korea, directly and indirectly.

On December 5, 1949, Mao Zedong released instructions on the PLA's participation in production and said: "State revenue is inadequate and expenditures are very great," and thus "the PLA must undertake specific production tasks . . . from a long-term construction point of view."[4] In June 1950, Mao again stressed the partial demobilization of the PLA: "While preserving its main forces, the People's Liberation Army should be partially demobilized in 1950, provided that the forces must be adequate to liberate Taiwan and Tibet, consolidate national defense and suppress counter-revolutionaries. This demobilization must be carried out carefully so as to enable the demobilized soldiers to return home and settle down to productive work."[5]

A low rate of investment in economic reconstruction (23.9 percent of the nation's total expenditures) and Beijing's emphasis on "key point" restoration appeared to benefit the northeast region of Manchuria (adjacent to North Korea), which has rich resources and is the center of heavy industry in China. Long before the complete liberation of Manchuria, the Chinese Communist party had given the northeast region a special economic status by permitting it to retain its own currency system, thus insulating the area from the economic effects of the war still in progress south of the Great Wall. The 1950 budget of the northeast region reflected continuation of that special status. Fifty-three percent of its total expenditures were appropriated for economic reconstruction, while military expenses were only 8.9 percent of the total.[6] Gao Gang (Kao Kang), secretary of the northeast bureau of the Chinese Communist party and concurrently vice-premier of the central government, stressed in a report in March 1950 Manchuria's important role in national economic recovery. He noted that in 1943 the northeast region had produced about 87 percent of the country's pig iron, 93 percent of its steel products, and 78 percent of its electric power, and that it contained 42 percent of the total railway mileage of the nation.[7]

Taking together Manchuria's special status economically and geographically, Gao's position in the central government, and Manchuria's need of technical aid for industrialization, it seems highly probable that Beijing's decision in 1949 to "lean to one side in foreign policy" (the side of the Soviet Union, as discussed in the next section) was strongly favored by regional leaders like Gao. This speculation is reinforced by the reluctance of regional leaders to support Beijing's plan, starting in March 1950, to control financial economic operations, including tax collection, on a national level in order to prevent local authorities from making use of the revenue collected in localities for local purposes.[8]

Beijing's emphasis on increased production, especially in agriculture, caused policy debate within the leadership. In 1948–49, three factions could be identified.[9] One faction was concerned about the need to arouse mass involvement in the ongoing liberation movement as well as in production. It advocated a high wage for workers and peasants. This faction seemed to expect to eliminate capitalism and realize socialism in a short period of time; it downgraded the role of the national bourgeoisie and rich peasants in the rehabilitation of the economy. A rightist faction thought that the most acute struggle against GMD elements was over by the end of 1948. It argued that economic recovery was the most difficult problem facing the party. Regarding production and growth as compelling goals, this faction emphasized the potential of the national bourgeoisie. In its view, rapid recovery of the war-torn economy required maximum utilization of the private sector and meant rescinding state control over private industry. As Fan Hong (Fan Hung), dean of economics of Beijing Academy, wrote in October 1949: "The national bourgeoisie still has a historical task . . . the development of capitalism through exploitation. Workers' welfare and their majority employment is inseparable from the right of exploitation. Enough restrictions are present: the private sector is utterly dependent on the state sector for raw materials; hence, the changeover from capitalism to socialism will be easy through state control."[10]

The Maoists seemed to take a middle road. As for the long-term purpose of socialist revolution, they stuck to a radical line: the state sector should lead the private sector and restrict private capitalism; and workers should increasingly assume their position as the leading class in Chinese society. However, in the short run, where the main objective was economic recovery, they seemed to side with the rightists' goals: increasing production by uniting with the national bourgeoisie and preventing a continuing "left" deviation in Chinese socialist construction.

The debate ended in victory for the rightists, probably by their having made a coalition with the Maoists. In June 1950, two weeks before the Korean War broke out, Mao continued to emphasize class struggle, but his main concern seemed to be the economy, especially the early rehabilitation of rural production. In a report on June 6, Mao pointed out that agrarian reform should proceed "step by step and in a systematic way" so as to maintain the rich peasant economy, which embraced considerable expertise, capital, and productive means. He warned against an ultraleft line in socialist construction: "The view held by certain people that it is possible to eliminate capitalism and realize socialism at an early date is wrong. It does not tally with our national conditions."[11]

However, the emphasis on national recovery soon led to the spread of rightist tendencies. Chinese capitalists and rich peasants reverted to the preliberation pattern of corruption, bribery, and nepotism. As will be discussed later, it was during the Korean War that the Chinese leadership took a militant line internally to check capitalist tendencies in Chinese society, radicalize the country's rather moderate land reform, and thereby heighten enthusiasm for production.

The Military

Military policy was determined by Beijing's domestic priorities soon after the founding of the P.R.C. The PLA had to carry out three major military tasks—the liberation of Taiwan and Tibet, and the pacification of GMD elements and other bandits. In terms of domestic economic policy, however, it was needed to participate in economic construction. To resolve the contradictions between these two objectives, part of the armed forces were demobilized and transferred into production work, as Mao's instruction in December 1949 and his report in June 1950 had indicated.

On June 24, 1950, the State Administrative Council and the People's Revolutionary Military Council reportedly held meetings to discuss the work of demobilizing the armed forces.[12] In the late spring and early summer of 1950, it is widely known that the Chinese began to redeploy 60,000 troops of the Fourth Field Army from south and central China to Shandong (Shantung) and Manchuria.[13] General Zhu De (Chu Teh) was said to have remarked that this redeployment was aimed at having the troops take up garrison duty in Manchuria and run a mechanized state farm.[14] In reporting these redeployments, General Douglas MacArthur later linked them to a Chinese contingency plan just prior to the attack on North Korea.[15] But John Gittings interpreted it as a preliminary step toward demobilization, reasoning that this move "would most naturally be effected in the troops' original recruitment area."[16] Allen Whiting did not rule out "additional functions" of troop redeployment "beyond peaceful purposes," but noted: "This redeployment implemented directives on assignment of units to construction projects. It was paralleled by troop movement elsewhere, returning units to points of origin from which they had begun pursuit of Nationalist forces, or to permanent bases in designated army command areas. No troops other than those from the Fourth Field Army entered Northeast China at this time."[17]

The central government also had the PLA launch production campaigns. The PLA's participation in production was not intended to be temporary; rather, it was to be long-term, a commitment to construction projects, including agriculture and water conservancy and other production tasks for industry and transportation. An article in *People's China* claimed that the PLA production campaign was unprecedented in scope and character: "No longer is the sole aim to reduce the people's tax burden and to raise army living standards. ... Today the main aim is to help put the nation back on its economic feet and to speed the process of industrialization."[18] PLA authorities set up the necessary organizations to lead the production drive, and with the help of the party branches, production committees were organized at each level from the company up. By March 20, the 1950 plan had been promulgated among all the field armies.[19]

In the meantime, Beijing continued to be concerned about the suppression of remnant Nationalist forces and hostile elements engaged in armed opposition to the occupation of Tibet and Taiwan. The tasks of pacifying anticommunist elements and occupying Tibet appeared not to impose an excessive burden on the PLA, although they caused alarm in several provinces and raised Beijing's sensitivity to the linkage between enemies at home and China's enemies abroad.

It is estimated that between April 1949, when the PLA crossed the Yangze (Yangtse) River, and the early months of 1950, 980,000 Nationalist guerrillas were wiped out, but that more than 400,000 bandits remained scattered in remote regions. The major affected provinces were Henan (Honan), Hubei (Hupeh), Hunan, Jiangxi (Kiangsi), Guangdong (Kwangtung), and Guangxi (Kwangsi) in the central-south region, and Xinjiang (Sinkiang), Yunnan, Guizhou (Kweichow), and Sichuan (Szechwan) in the southwest region.[20] As viewed from Beijing, these forces posed a serious threat to the newly established regime by operating through many secret agents and spies, sabotaging economic projects, assassinating officials, and resorting to guerrilla warfare. In east China, for instance, it was reported that in 1950 there were 770 cases of grain pilferage, disturbance, and mob uprisings; 206 cases of poisoning; and 315 cases of political sabotage. In addition, more than 20 privately and publicly owned vessels were plundered. In Fujian (Fukien) Province alone, the number of cadres and progressives ambushed and assassinated by special-service bandits reportedly reached 1,084.[21] Chinese leaders regarded these activities as being directed from behind the scenes by Americans and Nationalists. This apprehension about internal enemies colluding with external enemies probably was heightened by the fact of domestic economic difficulties. As General Ye Jianying (Yeh Chien-ying), in a report of April 9, 1950, pointed out:

> Remnant forces of the counter-revolutionary rulers . . . are still everywhere, and they are still very active. The activities of these criminals are international in character. Surrounding us are the "Sino-American co-operation organization," "Sino-American Information Bureau," "Southeast Asia Information Bureau" and other secret organizations supported by imperialists and Chiang Kai-shek's bandits. . . . These organizations operate from Hong Kong and Macao, and are financed by American imperialists. . . . These activities are possible because we still have many weaknesses, especially an economic problem.[22]

In the first half of 1950, the PLA had to engage in extensive campaigns to, with the help of local militia, mop up bandit remnants. In Hunan, for instance, almost 200,000 men participated in a "bandit suppression campaign" in the spring of 1950.[23] The invasion of Tibet was an exception. Preparation for it began in January 1950. In October, some 40,000 troops of the Second Field Army in the southwest military region crossed into Tibet and, meeting negligible military resistance, occupied Chamdo, a garrison town in eastern Tibet.[24]

Recovering Taiwan appeared to be the most important of the P.R.C.'s military objectives. For Chinese leaders, the battle for the liberation of Taiwan would be the final battle for the liberation of all the territories of China. For them, it was also to be the last military campaign before the nation embarked on peaceful reconstruction. In strategic terms, however, the liberation of Taiwan was, according to General Su Yu, vice-commander of the Third Field Army and coordinator of the Taiwan campaign, an "extremely big problem" and the "biggest campaign in the history of modern Chinese warfare." General Su seemed concerned about logistical difficulties, suggesting that "these islands can't be occupied without sufficient transports, suitable equipment and adequate supplies." As he noted, "Only when we have fully prepared the material and technical conditions for overcoming difficulties can we smoothly carry out this tremendous military assignment." General Su's emphasis on full preparedness for the invasion of Taiwan was based on his assessment of the risks involved:

> Furthermore, a considerable number of Chiang Kai-shek's land, sea and air forces are concentrated there, together with a batch of the most intransigent reactionaries who have fled from China's mainland. They have built strong defense works, depending on the surrounding sea for protection. At the instigation of the American imperialists, they have invited in a group of Japanese militarists.[25]

According to the Chinese press in Hong Kong at that time, it seems that most of Beijing's leaders shared General Su's view. They probably were persuaded that China could not deploy air and naval forces across the Taiwan Strait that would be sufficient to contest the well-entrenched and better-armed Nationalist forces.[26]

In April and May of 1950, the successful liberation of Hainan Island appeared to encourage Beijing in its plan to invade Taiwan. *People's Daily* celebrated two successful operations as preludes to victory against Taiwan.[27] In a May Day speech, Liu Shaoqi said that the liberation of Hainan was the "PLA's mastery of the art of sea-borne landings," and stressed that the campaign would be a harbinger of a successful invasion of Taiwan.[28] But it should be pointed out that despite the successful Hainan campaign, Chinese leaders seemed to adopt a defensive perspective and cautious planning regarding Taiwan. One article in *People's China* claimed that the Hainan landings destroyed "desperate KMT naval and aerial opposition" and the hope that "Chiang will counterattack on the main-land."[29] A *Dagong bao* (Hong Kong) editorial on April 17 expressed cautious optimism about the future battle for the liberation of Taiwan. The editorial noted that the battle would be "materially different from the military campaign on the mainland," and would be won only "after adequate preparations."[30]

On the eve of the Korean War, the PLA remained an infantry army with acute deficiencies in heavy artillery, armored vehicles, and ammunition. Military officers still lacked technological know-how as well as familiarity with operational tactics such as coordination of joint operations, armor-infantry-artillery team work, and close air support. There was, at that time, no sign of plans to modernize and regularize the PLA.[31] China maintained five major field armies, each of which controlled combat forces in a distinct geographical area. One might hypothesize that the distribution of military and political power among five major field-army elites would lead to a challenge of Mao's personal power and would delay the reunification of national economic and political systems.[32] But this did not pose a problem for the central government immediately after the P.R.C.'s founding. Beijing was able to institutionalize centralized control of the PLA through the People's Revolutionary Military Council, which was the highest authority in military affairs. In regional politics, northwest and southwest China and Inner Mongolia were garrisoned and controlled by the army mainly because of unfinished military business. In the north and northeast, a full-fledged people's government had functioned since mid-1948. In central-south and east China, military control was prevalent only in the major cities and the seaboard provinces.[33] This is not to say, however, that the decentralization of political and military power ruled out the involvement of military leaders in national policy issues that affected their interests. An external threat posed by a militarily superior enemy like the United States would have been one such issue, since it would have forced Beijing to reorder domestic economic priorities in planning for a major new military commitment.

Thus, just prior to the Korean War, except for the announced campaigns in Tibet and Taiwan, which Chinese leaders regarded as domestic issues, China was not in a position to undertake external involvements. At that time, its top priority was rehabilitation of the nation's economy. Accordingly, the leadership was preparing for a partial demobilization of the PLA, which would contribute labor to production and help to reduce the government's financial burden. This policy seemed to depend on a peaceful international environment undergirded by the strength of the Soviet Union. In the June 1950 report cited above, Mao Zedong said: "The present international situation is favorable to us. The world front of peace and democracy headed by the Soviet Union is stronger than it was last year. . . .

The new treaty [of February 1950] between China and the Soviet Union enables us to carry on our national construction more freely and more speedily."[34]

The International Situation

Beijing's Position in 1949

China's initial foreign-policy line was characterized by Mao Zedong in mid-1949 as one of "leaning to one side." It can be argued that leaning toward the Soviet Union was occasioned by a shared Marxist-Leninist ideology and China's naïveté in diplomacy because of its inexperience. The result, according to this view, was an immutable and exclusive Sino-Soviet alliance coupled with an intransigently hostile attitude toward the United States and other capitalist countries.[35] That there was an idological affinity and hostility toward the capitalist world is certainly true; but these factors provide a very incomplete explanation of China's choice. Beijing's search for partnership not only took account of China's need to promote socialist revolution at home and its determination to maintain independence and sovereignty. It also developed in reaction to the U.S. attitude toward the Chinese Communist party (CCP) and reflected bureaucratic political debate.

A year before the P.R.C. was established, the CCP's Central Committee issued a statement on the general principles of China's foreign relations. The statement, dated November 21, 1948, said: "The CCP are willing to enter into equal and friendly relations with any foreign nation, including the United States . . . provided China's territories are kept intact and immune from aggression."[36] This statement coincided with several events. Domestically as Mao indicated, the military situation in China had reached "a new turning point," to the extent that the PLA had become superior in numbers. The Chinese communists expected victory in the near future.[37] Internationally, President Truman, whom most Chinese communist leaders considered less hostile to the CCP than Republican Thomas Dewey, was elected in November 1948.[38] The Soviet Union, which maintained formal diplomatic relations with the GMD right up to the day of liberation in October 1949, did not endorse the CCP's policy to unify China by military means. In late 1948, Stalin apparently advised the CCP to accept a China divided into a communist-controlled north China and a GMD-controlled south China along the Yangze River in order to avoid direct American intervention.[39]

Some Chinese communist leaders who were generally identified by U.S. officials as "liberals" evidently thought that a flexible and independent diplomacy might contribute to achieving new China's objective of independence and sovereignty by using barbarians to control barbarians and by carrying out domestic reconstruction with aid from capitalist countries. For the liberals, diplomatic strategy, if it could be properly employed between the superpower camps, would be a useful counterweight against undue Soviet influence and possible pressure, and would also appease the hostile U.S. attitude toward the CCP. In any event, the liberals hoped for something short of full partnership with the Soviet Union and wished to have contact with the United States.[40]

In January 1949, when President Truman was inaugurated, articles appeared in *Shijie zhishi* [World Knowledge], a semiofficial publication of China's Ministry of Foreign Affairs, dealing with the prospect of Truman's policy toward China.[41] The articles asserted that the Truman administration, which appointed Dean Acheson as secretary of state, would not implement any basic change in foreign policy, but might undergo a "somewhat technical change." American policy toward China was characterized as a "watch-and-wait policy," according to the authors of these articles, mainly because China's new situation compelled American leaders to consider and devise new methods. What were the new methods? One article pointed out that Washington might borrow from George Marshall's European Recovery Program in order to influence the policies of the new Chinese government: "At present one of the methods being studied by the United States is perhaps to reconsider the problem, since it has not been successful in giving 'military' aid to the old government, turn its head toward the new government, stretch out its hand giving economic 'aid' and to try again the method which has already turned out to be a failure toward the European nations."[42]

Indeed, the CCP was considering "all means" of diplomatic relations with foreign countries to safeguard China's territorial integrity and sovereignty. An article in March 1949 in *Chunzhong* [Masses], a procommunist newspaper in Hong Kong, conveyed such an idea and aired the liberals' view of China's foreign policy: "Some are afraid that like the Kuomintang which is in the fold of the United States today, the Communists when in power may lead the country into the fold of the Soviet Union so that China will continue to lose her independence and sovereignty."[43]

In the first half of 1949, the liberals in the CCP attempted to make some diplomatic overtures to the United States in order to receive American aid and establish de facto working relations. According to secret documents of the U.S. State Department released in September 1978,[44] in late May 1949, Zhou Enlai, speaking for the liberal group,[45] informally delivered a message via a correspondent of United Press requesting economic assistance from the United States government. Zhou was said to desire working relations with the United States because, for the purpose of the nation's reconstruction, especially improvement of the "physical well-being of

Chinese people," China desperately needed foreign aid that the Soviet Union would not be able to provide. Zhou revealed concern about Moscow's foreign-policy line, noting that "the Soviet Union is risking war which it is unable to fight successfully." He even suggested that China's participation in international affairs would make Moscow discard policies leading to war; China would serve as a mediator between the U.S.S.R. and the Western powers. Zhou's desire for U.S. aid seemed to be reinforced by Shanghai Mayor Chen Yi's plea for help to John Cabot, U.S. consul general in Shanghai. According to a telegram sent to the State Department on June 6 from Cabot, Chen Yi was quoted as saying: "The Soviet Union and its satellites might not be able to offer assistance to China, and thus aid from U.S. and British would be accepted if presented on basis of equality with no strings detrimental to Chinese sovereignty attached."[46]

Another of the liberals' diplomatic probes was to seek U.S. recognition of the new government. On May 13, shortly after the PLA crossed the Yangze River and entered Nanjing (Nanking), the capital of the GMD, Huang Hua, a student of Yanjing (Yenching) University in Beijing when Leighton Stuart was its president in the 1930s, visited the now Ambassador Stuart. Huang reportedly raised the question of American recognition of the P.R.C. and of an ambassador's visit to Beijing in June. Huang was said to have added: "I am quite sure Mao Zedong and Zhou Enlai would be very glad to see you."[47] But the overture was brushed aside. Stuart replied: "When there emerged a new government which obviously had the support or at least the acceptance of the Chinese people, and *gave evidence of its willingness and ability to maintain relations with other nations according to international standards,* then the matter would naturally be discussed."[48]

By stressing preconditions for government recognition in accordance with international standards, the U.S. ambassador probably had in mind the arrest in April of American Consul General Angus Ward and four of his aides by local communist authorities in Mukden. But in addition, the United States seemed to want to utilize recognition as leverage to contain China's leaning to the Soviet Union. Huang was told by Stuart that a communist China could be recognized by the United States under the condition that Beijing would not ally with Moscow.[49] On May 21, Stuart's enquiry for permission to go to Beijing was rejected by the State Department, which replied that his contact with communist authorities would harm the North Atlantic alliance's endorsement of common action in dealing with the Soviet bloc.[50] Not until late June did Zhou Enlai receive any response from Washington to his plea for aid. It should be noted that during the summer of 1949, Truman's decisions on these issues were made in a changed domestic political environment, one that was influenced by an active pro-GMD lobby in the U.S. Congress.[51]

The diplomatic probes of the Chinese liberals appeared to meet considerable resistance from a more radical group within the CCP. This group perceived the basic development of the postwar world situation in terms of the acute antithesis between the two camps, and preferred to rely on the Soviet Union for economic rehabilitation, the maintenance of independence, and for deterring the imperialist threat to China and elsewhere. On June 6, 1949, *Liberation Daily* (Shanghai) republished Liu Shaoqi's essay "On Internationalism and Nationalism," written in November 1948.[52] The essay characterized world politics as being divided into two hostile camps, imperialist and socialist. Liu stressed that it was impossible for a country to adopt neutrality between the camps. In light of what the liberals were then saying, the essay seemed to be warning them not to adopt the anti-Soviet attitudes of the Titoists in Yugoslavia; to do so would expose them to American trickery and eventually deprive them of their independence. An article in *World Knowledge* on June 17 aired a related view, noting that "the peace front," united with the Soviet Union and the East European nations, was "strong enough to overpower the imperialist war-mongers."[53]

For the Soviet-oriented radicals, of particular importance were the domestic consequences of foreign aid. China's collaboration with imperialist countries in receiving "aid" would adversely affect the ongoing class struggle. Class enemies like GMD elements and the bourgeoisie would be encouraged in their hostility to the socialist revolution. "On Leaning to One Side," an article in *Liberation Daily* in September 1949, called attention to the effect of the Marshall Plan on Western Europe. Europeans, said the article, were increasingly under the thumb of American imperialism, and the only way to "break the economic yoke imposed by imperialism and guarantee the success of the new democratic reconstruction" was "to lean to the side of the peaceful and democratic front led by the Soviet Union."[54]

It appears that the foreign-policy debate ended in late June 1950. On June 24, one writer in *World Knowledge,* citing a dispatch of the Associated Press, announced that the U.S. State Department "was planning a policy of 'restricted trade' with China under Communist control," and for the first time noted a negative U.S. attitude toward recognition: "American imperialism plans to forge a united diplomatic front against New China in the matter of recognition . . . to prevent other countries from taking unilateral action and thus leave the United States in the lurch. American imperialism, ten days after the liberation of Nanking, sent notes to a number of governments suggesting joint action in dealing with the new government of China."[55] Apart from the negative U.S. attitude, for Mao and even for the liberals to have accepted the U.S.

preconditions for recognition would have required that Beijing assume any economic and political burdens incurred by the Nationalists. They would also have severely limited future Chinese foreign-policy options. Even if presented without strings, aid from the United States might undermine Chinese self-reliance in development, and therefore also China's prospects for consolidating socialist revolutionary power. As the article just quoted stressed: "It must be known that the liberation of China is principally being undertaken through the great efforts of the Chinese people themselves. While foreign assistance is of course welcome when given on the basis of equality and reciprocity, the Chinese people are not at all yearning for aid granted under any other circumstances."[56]

Mao's position in the debate was established on June 30, 1949, in his speech "On the People's Democratic Dictatorship," in which he declared, "We must lean to one side" in order to win and consolidate revolutionary victory. He criticized advocacy of British and U.S. government aid as being "a naive idea in these times."[57] But Mao never closed the door to future negotiations with capitalist countries. He clearly distinguished governments in Western countries from their peoples and the progressive forces in them. China's flexible position was reaffirmed: "There will be the possibility of establishing diplomatic relations with *all* foreign countries," Mao said, if they agree that relations should be on the basis of "equality, mutual benefits, and mutual respect for territorial sovereignty."[58] This formula was employed continuously after the P.R.C. was formally established.[59]

In early July, Gao Gang, who represented the People's Government of Northeast China, came to Moscow to negotiate the Sino-Soviet Barter Agreement, which was soon concluded. Coming soon after the debate in Beijing, the agreement had as much political import as it had economic significance. One report announced that the agreement covered "the barter of goods between the two areas for a period of one year," but was concluded "at a time when the imperialists are directing their running dogs, the remnant Kuomintang influences, to enforce an armed blockade of our coast in order to undermine the task of reconstruction in New China." The same report further noted: "The Soviet Union has demonstrated its great international friendship for this country, by concluding, on the basis of equality and reciprocity, a barter agreement with our Northeast, to help the people of China in breaking down the blockade via the overland route, and thus to tide over the economic crisis."[60]

As has been discussed, the CCP's decision to "lean to one side" was made largely in reaction to a negative U.S. attitude toward the new China. The reaction deepened on the eve of and soon after the outbreak of the Korean War because of developments in the U.S. containment policy in the Far East, which we will discuss next. Equally influential on P.R.C. policy making were Sino-Soviet relations and the question of how the liberals' independent line was handled within the CCP. It is crucial to consider these factors because the state of Sino-Soviet relations in 1949–50 would affect China's decision to enter the Korean War.

Containment in Asia

American policy toward communist China began with the conviction that the P.R.C., in alliance with Moscow, would pose a threat to the United States' strategic and economic position in Asia. Shortly after the publication of Mao's "lean-to-one-side" speech, Dean Acheson, in his August 1949 "Letter of Transmittal" to Truman introducing the China *White Paper,* publicly articulated the major premises of containment in Asia. He wrote that the United States and other members of the UN would be confronted with an alarming situation should the new communist regime be subservient to Soviet Russia (as he supposed it would be) and attempt to engage in aggression against China's neighbors.[61] Accordingly, between the last half of 1949 and the first half of 1950, the United States worked closely with friendly Asian governments to bolster both their anticommunist politics and their military potential. Containment in Asia did not begin with the U.S. intervention in South Korea. Hence, how the P.R.C. leadership perceived American activities in Asia and linked them to its national security is worth exploring.

In the first half of 1950, the Chinese government was suspicious and fearful of attempts by the United States to isolate the P.R.C. through nonrecognition and blocking P.R.C. representation in the UN. Beijing also became conviced that the United States would seek to prevent it from liberating Taiwan by providing economic and military aid to the Nationalists.

In January 1950, the P.R.C. was recognized by the Soviet Union, India, Yugoslavia, Great Britain, and Norway, all of which were members of the UN Security Council. France and Egypt were expected to extend recognition soon thereafter. P.R.C. leaders had every reason to think that conditions were highly favorable for its early admission. But on January 13, the Soviet draft resolution that demanded the expulsion of the GMD representative was rejected in the Security Council. On January 17, a *People's Daily* commentary noted the Soviet delegation's declaration— and stated that the Nationalist presence in the UN was being fostered by "American imperialism and its collaborators."[62] Two days later Beijing again tried to claim the Chinese seat in various organs of the UN. The request was made in a note to Carlos Romulo, president of the General Assembly, and Trygve Lie, secretary-general of the UN, from Foreign Minister Zhou Enlai.[63] Lie then asked Acheson whether Washington would consider recognizing the P.R.C. in the foreseeable future. But recalling

China's recent seizure of American properties, Acheson was said to have answered that "the United States would certainly not recognize Peking in such circumstances and was opposed to seating the Communist regime in the UN."[64]

Adding to China's frustration in gaining international standing was its fear of possible action by the United States to thwart reunification with Taiwan and even to support a counterattack from Taiwan against the mainland. One may argue that in view of statements made by high-level U.S. officials in January 1950, the United States was clearly opposed to defending Taiwan by military means or to assisting in a counterattack. In late December 1949, the State Department published a "policy information paper on Formosa" that minimized the island's importance.[65] In his famous speech of 1950, Acheson excluded Taiwan from the American "defense perimeter" in the Far East.[66] On January 5, President Truman, prior to consultation with Congress, defined the U.S. position on Taiwan as follows:

> The United States has no desire to obtain special rights or privileges or to establish military bases on Formosa. Nor does it have any intention of utilizing armed forces to interfere in the present situation. The United States will not pursue a course which will lead to involvement in the civil conflict in China. Similarly, the United States government will not provide military aid or advice to Chinese forces on Formosa.[67]

But such statements were interpreted differently in Beijing, where Chinese leaders remained apprehensive of U.S. intentions concerning Taiwan. They looked upon the December State Department paper as "a sly attempt to cover up aggressive designs on Taiwan." Despite the Truman declaration of "hands off Taiwan," Chinese analysts cited continuous American aid to Taiwan within appropriations already approved by the U.S. Congress.[68] The New China News Agency (NCNA) declared on January 3 that a secret agreement had been reached between Washington and Taibei in which the "American government decided to give further aid to the KMT remnants to resist the PLA and turn Taiwan into a strategic base for invading China's mainland and opposing the peoples of Asia."[69] On January 16, People's China editorially condemned Truman's statement as a "smokescreen" to hide imperialist intentions to annex Taiwan, and detailed how the United States was militantly reinforcing Taiwan at that time:

> A batch of 32 American military advisors has already arrived at Taipei. Military supplies, including 250 American tanks, had been shipped to the southern part of the island. A 27,000 ton aircraft carrier and two destroyers have been sent to reinforce the U.S. Navy's 7th Task Force. General MacArthur is reported to have recruited 4,000 Japanese aviation experts and naval specialists to help with the defense of Taiwan.[70]

Beijing's sensitivity to U.S. military support of Taiwan was heightened by reports of GMD air raids on cities in south China and a naval blockade along the southern coast. According to NCNA reports, in January and February 1950 alone, American-made GMD bombers raided Shanghai, Hangzhou (Hangchow), and Qingdao (Tsingtao), destroyed a power plant, and caused more than 1,000 casualties among the civilian population.[71] An NCNA correspondent commented that the series of air raids was "part of a coordinated bombing plan of the Americans and their lackeys," and expressed apprehension that if Washington sent additional airplanes to Taiwan, the GMD would extend the bombing to major cities in north China, including Beijing and Tianjin (Tientsin).[72] This fear was more clearly stated in an address by Zhu De, commander in chief of the army, on February 28:

> The remnant Kuomintang gang is now using Taiwan as its base to carry on all kinds of intrigues and plots against the Chinese people. American imperialism continues to help the KMT brigands with arms. The KMT gangsters are using war vessels supplied by America to blockade the China coast; using U.S. aeroplanes to bomb Chinese cities and using American and Japanese military personnel sent by the American occupationists to take part in bombing and other military actions. They aim to undermine the peaceful life of the Chinese people and the construction of New China. . . . Therefore, the liberation of Taiwan has become the most pressing task of the people of the entire country.[73]

In 1949–50, Chinese leaders were also deeply concerned about the so-called reverse course in U.S. postwar policy toward Japan, and regarded it as a threat to revolution in Asia as well as to China's security. As George Kennan suggested in 1947, American plans to rehabilitate Japanese industry, curb the left-wing influence in Japan, rearm Japan, and turn it into an anticommunist arsenal and base started with the conviction that the victory of communism in China would be bound to enhance communist pressures on Japan and other countries in Asia.[74] Shortly after the U.S. National Security Council, in November 1948, made "a strong and friendly Japan" a U.S. objective, the Supreme Commander for the Allied Powers (SCAP), General Douglas MacArthur, promulgated a nine-point program for the stabilization of Japan's economy and the revival of its industrial (including military) potential. In May 1949, Washington unilaterally announced the cancellation of Japanese reparation payments. The Japanese Diet was directed to pass an act enlarging the police force to a 150,000-man national force and labor laws to undermine the left-wing influence in labor unions.[75]

Simultaneously, the United States took steps to conclude a separate peace treaty with Japan (excluding the Soviet Union) as part of a plan to maintain an indefinite military presence in Japan. An authoritative NCNA commentary described these activities as constituting a direct violation of the Potsdam declaration and as directly undermining Japan's independence and the development of a democratic and peaceful economy.[76] More pertinent for China's interests was the fact that a reverse course in Japan under U.S. direction would harm the left-wing movement in Japan, which Beijing expected could prevent a revival of Japanese militarism, and convert Japan into a major jumping-off point for American interventions in the Far East.[77]

Beijing's fear of a militarily resurgent Japan had substantial basis in fact, as developments from late 1949 onward indicated. In October 1949, Washington started to construct expanded air-base facilities on Okinawa while accelerating the improvement of existing airfields in Japan. During the first half of 1950, MacArthur's headquarters carried out a large-scale reconstruction of naval bases in Japan and the Ryukyu Islands. This military plan was reinforced by the "Operation Roll-up Program," which was designed to equip the U.S. Eighth Army's infantry divisions with reclaimed equipment from stockpiles scattered throughout the Pacific during World War II. After a meeting between MacArthur and Phillip Jessup, ambassador-at-large, in January 1950, reports of the scheme for a unilateral peace with Japan were constant. In March, all Japanese war criminals were released, and in April, the Japanese Communist party was outlawed.[78]

The Chinese press was again apprehensive about these developments. One article in *World Knowledge* in February 1950 linked a separate U.S. peace treaty with Japan to the conclusion of a U.S.-Japanese military alliance, and expressed concern that "this alliance may possibly be developed into a Pacific pact" against the P.R.C.[79] *People's Daily* and other Chinese publications pointed out that U.S. bases in Japan were part of a vast network in the Pacific from Siberia to south China. U.S. policy in Taiwan was therefore "inseparable in Chinese minds from MacArthur's frenzied war preparations in Japan."[80]

Fear of U.S. containment schemes in the Pacific probably also accounted for concern about the nature of the U.S. commitment to South Korea. In the speech of January 12, 1950, cited above, Acheson excluded South Korea from the U.S. defensive perimeter, saying that "the perimeter runs from the Aleutians through Japan and the Ryukyus to the Philippine islands." But the Chinese were well aware that the South Korean government was receiving U.S. economic aid and military assistance to suppress the communist-supported guerrilla movement. Thus, a *People's China* editorial on February 1 referred to Acheson's address but still included South Korea in the defensive perimeter.[81] The authoritative "Observer" charged on April 11 that "South Korea is an anti-Communist base of the Americans in the North Pacific" and claimed: "The United States continues to exploit the United Nations as an instrument for interference in the internal affairs of Korea. The United States had dispatched a military advisory group in South Korea for the training of its puppet army. On January 27, 1950, an agreement was concluded whereby South Korea was given military aid to the tune of U.S. $10,000,000."[82]

Chinese concern extended to U.S. commitments in Southeast Asia too. Since the communist victory in China, the Americans, in collaboration with the French and British governments, had provided economic aid to several countries in Southeast Asia under Truman's Point Four program, and simultaneously had given a considerable amount of military assistance to Vietnam, Thailand, Burma, Indonesia, and the Philippines. The French-dominated Bao Dai government in Vietnam was one such recipient of both kinds of assistance. Another was the Philippines, with which Washington signed a military pact in early 1950 to help combat a communist insurgency. The Chinese regarded these aid programs as ways for the United States to tighten political and economic control over Southeast Asia and interfere in the liberation movements of the Asian peoples.[83]

A secret conference of U.S. Asian diplomatic personnel in Bangkok in February 1950 led Beijing to suspect a plot to encircle China. The conference reportedly was attended by seventeen embassy and consular personnel under the sponsorship of Ambassador-at-large Jessup and Assistant Secretary of State Butterworth. Noting a United Press comment that the conference was called for the purpose of discussing ways to "remedy" the deteriorating position of the various Western powers in Southeast Asia, a Chinese press article speculated that the main purpose of the conference was to discuss preliminaries to an "Asian military alliance": "It is as clear as day that the United States is greatly concerned with forming a military bloc of reactionary forces in Asia and this is directed chiefly against the New China just as the Atlantic pact is directed against the Soviet Union."[84]

As viewed from Beijing, U.S. steps in Southeast Asia not only presented a threat to China's security but also adversely affected China's plans for dealing with Tibet. In 1949 and early 1950, the Chinese authorities constantly expressed concern that the British, American, and Indian governments would encourage Tibetan leaders to launch an independence movement against the P.R.C. In late 1949, Washington allegedly was prepared to give about $75 million to the Dalai Lama regime for the defense of Tibet.[85] In January 1950, it became widely known that the Tibetan authorities in Lhasa were ready to send "goodwill missions" to the United States, Britain, India, and Nepal to discuss Tibet's independence.[86] The Chinese regarded American and British moves in Tibet as an attempt to "buy over the reactionary upper strata of Tibet against Peking," and linked those moves to U.S. moves in Southeast Asia: "The malicious schemes planned by the imperialists for Tibet cannot be divided from their plots carried out in the whole of Southeast Asia. . . . The imperialists are madly intensifying their efforts to suppress and plunder the peoples of Southeast Asia in an attempt to save their crumbling rule, and thence to turn around to resume their attacks on the Chinese people."[87]

Sino-Soviet Relations before June 1950

Whatever the origin of the Korean War—and recent scholarship has effectively challenged the conventional wisdom that North Korea committed unprovoked aggression and was supported in that decision by Moscow and Beijing[88]—it is important to clarify the relationship between the Soviet Union and the P.R.C. at the time the war began. We have already provided evidence of considerable suspicion within the CCP that a tight partnership with the Soviet Union would undermine China's independence and sovereignty. The conclusion by the two governments of the Treaty of Friendship, Alliance, and Mutual Assistance in February 1950 further strained rather than consolidated the relationship.

Soviet policy toward China in the mid-1940s, as numerous writers have suggested, appeared to be based on the so-called weak-neighbor policy, according to which a divided and weak China run by Nationalists and communists would most benefit Soviet interests.[89] There is ample evidence to support this argument. Shortly after the Soviet declaration of war against Japan in August 1945, the Red Army occupied Manchuria and seized whole factories and vast amounts of equipment. Contrary to the argument that the Russians facilitated the PLA's "phenomenal expansion" by providing it with captured Japanese equipment, they actually destroyed the major part of the great arsenals they could have given the Chinese communists. Later, General Lin Biao was quoted as saying: "Whatever came with the Red Army into Manchuria went back when the Red Army went."[90]

Similar behavior was evident in Soviet dealings with the CCP on civil-war strategy and on territorial issues. In late 1948, when the CCP was convinced it was on the verge of final victory over the Nationalists, it was advised by Stalin to continue guerrilla warfare and refrain from pushing for a decisive victory. In April 1949, when the communists occupied the Nationalist capital of Nanjing, only the Soviet ambassador among foreign diplomats followed the Nationalists to Guangzhou (Canton or Kwangchow). One Chinese reporter, after interviewing Soviet Ambassador Roschin on May 12, revealed that Roschin had gone to Guangzhou without prior consultation with the CCP.[91] In May the Soviet Union extended the agreement with the Nationalist government on joint rights in Xinjiang Province for five more years. The Chinese communists probably regarded these Soviet policies as designed not only to block the CCP's path to power but also to increase Soviet influence in China and exploit its natural resources. Later Mao recalled to André Malraux that Roschin's "good wishes were reserved for the Nationalists."[92] In 1962 Mao added: "The Russians did not permit China to make revolution."[93]

It seems likely that Stalin sought to acquire organizational footholds in China, as he did in Eastern Europe. Perhaps he intended to do so by influencing pro-Soviet leaders in the CCP like Gao Gang, head of the People's Government of Northeast China. The years 1948 and 1949 found Stalin extremely concerned about and suspicious of communists in Eastern Europe as well as of Mao, worrying that his breach with Tito and the defection of Yugoslavia from the Soviet camp might happen elsewhere. Before the P.R.C. was formally established, Gao Gang negotiated a treaty with Stalin in Moscow and was granted substantial assistance for the reconstruction of Manchuria. According to the official charges later leveled against Gao, who committed suicide not long after Stalin's death, Gao maintained "illicit relations with foreign countries" and set up in Manchuria a "separate kingdom of his own."[94] (Subsequently, Khrushchev hinted that there had indeed been collaboration between Gao and Stalin: "Gao's only crime had been to oppose his party's incorrect policy vis-a-vis the Soviet Union.")[95] Mao probably regarded Gao as a dangerous, Soviet-backed rival. In an important speech at the Tenth Plenum of the Eighth Central Committee in October 1962, Mao revealed Stalin's attempt to use the Sino-Soviet treaty to make Mao Moscow's pawn: "After the victory of the revolution, Stalin suspected China of being a Yugoslavia, and that I would become a second Tito. Later, when I went to Moscow to sign the Sino-Soviet Treaty, he was not willing to sign a treaty. After two months of negotiation, he at last signed. It was at the time of the Resist America, Aid Korea campaign that Stalin finally came to trust us."[96] The speech suggests that considerable tension existed between Stalin and Mao during the treaty negotiations. On January 2, 1950, several weeks after he arrived in Moscow, Mao hinted to a TASS correspondent that bargaining with Stalin was difficult. As Mao put it, "The length of my sojourn in the USSR depends on the period in which it will be possible to settle questions of interest to the PRC."[97]

The treaty and the supplementary documents signed on February 14 basically followed the pattern of the treaty of 1945 with the GMD, except for the surrender of Soviet rights in Manchuria and elsewhere within a time limit.[98] The Soviets' loan ($300 million at one percent interest, to be spread over five years) was not satisfactory to Mao. It was about a tenth of the amount Mao was rumored to have asked for, and its terms were poorer than those some East European countries had obtained.[99] The major Russian concession was to return the Changchun Railway to the P.R.C. by the end of 1952. A minor concession to China was joint use of Port Arthur (Luda).

But no change was agreed upon concerning the status of the port of Dalian (Dairen), which the Russians had established as a naval base. Stalin recognized Beijing's de facto sovereignty over Xinjiang, but secured the establishment of joint stock companies for the exploitation of Xinjiang's oil and mineral resources.[100]

Probably for these reasons, the Chinese press needed to address people's complaints about Soviet behavior toward China. People were raising questions such as "Why has the Soviet Union taken away our machinery?" and "Shall leaning to one side cease to bother us?"[101] An article in *Zhanwang* [Outlook] attempted to persuade the so-called ultranationalists not to raise objections over the delay of Russian withdrawal from the Changchun Railway, Port Arthur, and Dalian. The article reasoned:

> It must be pointed out that though victory has been scored in the liberation war, reconstruction of China is only just commenced, and national defense measures have not yet been consolidated. The evacuation of Soviet troops just now from Port Arthur will give the American and Japanese reactionaries an opportunity for encroachment, and therefore it must await the peace treaty with Japan. But in case, through American interference, the treaty cannot be concluded within three years, then by that time, China will be able to undertake the defense of her Northeast, and the Soviet troops would thus be able to evacuate.[102]

Indeed, for Chinese leaders the real value of China's alliance with the Soviet Union was a strategic and political one. It was 1950, and the new regime was vulnerable to subversion at home and to external threats. It needed to devote time and energy to national reconstruction and the consolidation of internal security. Noting that article 1 of the treaty was directed specifically against attack by Japan and "states allied with it," meaning the United States, China's leaders repeatedly emphasized that the treaty assured China of Soviet military backing and would enable the Chinese people to shift from military concerns to economic and political ones.[103] Previously we noted that Mao was inclined to link his plan for the PLA's demobilization to a peaceful international environment supposedly backed by the Soviet Union. Liu Shaoqi's May Day speech in 1950 also hinted that the international conditions established mainly by China's alliance with the Soviet Union were favorable for carrying out domestic construction in a peaceful environment.[104] How much confidence Mao and his colleagues actually had in Soviet protection is not known. The treaty had come at a high price; but it did have the potential to deter threats from the "imperialists." Only after U.S. and UN forces crossed the 38th parallel in Korea did it become plain to the Chinese that they and not the Russians would have to confront the imperialists directly.

The strained relations between Moscow and Beijing lead us to believe that Mao was not privy to any discussions that may have been held in North

Korea or in Moscow about an attack on South Korean forces.[105] Clearly Beijing was concerned about the viability of North Korea, which borders on the P.R.C. But its support of revolutionary war in Asia is an entirely different matter. In 1949–50, while Chinese officials and the press expressed strong sympathy for armed struggles of national liberation in several Asian countries, including South Korea, only in Vietnam did the P.R.C. provide active (and even then, limited) support. Beijing's support of such struggles appeared to be based on one principle: the liberation movement should develop like China's indigenous movement, on the basis of self-reliance and under the guidance of the local Communist party.[106]

There was a doctrinal preference for making revolution Mao's way, but the P.R.C. as a new regime was too weak to give significant material support to revolutionaries abroad, especially since difficult economic problems, the liberation of Taiwan and Tibet, and the wiping out of counterrevolutionary elements at home had top priority. Probably for all these reasons, Beijing was inclined to regard guerrilla fighting in South Korea as an internal Korean problem and to expect that direct American intervention against the revolutionary movement in South Korea was unlikely. Khrushchev held precisely that view, believing that "the USA would not intervene since the war would be an internal matter which the Korean people would decide for themselves.[107] A Chinese news analysis reflected such thinking in September 1949: "Though there were and are many revolts exploding in South Korea, only the Yosu revolt which occurred last autumn became known to the outside world. The Americans never used their own troops in quelling the past revolts except in Taiku where the rebelling Korean troops were intercepted and disarmed by U.S. troops as the former were passing the U.S. garrison."[108]

The Decision to Enter the Korean War

It was on October 8, 1950, that Chairman Mao ordered the Chinese People's Liberation Army to enter the war in Korea. By then, three months after the outbreak of the war, U.S./UN forces had made an amphibious landing at Inchon, the port nearest Seoul, and had speedily crossed the 38th parallel. Mao's order was not implemented until late October, when the PLA launched limited preemptive attacks on the UN forces as they approached China's border. These attacks suddenly stopped for a little less than three weeks until late November, when the PLA intervened in the war on a massive scale.

China's Korean War decision was not made suddenly, nor was it a unanimous party decision. The three months preceding the final decision to resort to force saw the Chinese using verbal warnings and diplomatic and military overtures in order to prevent the spread of war beyond the 38th parallel. In this section, we shall discuss these problems, focusing on how the Chinese leadership weighed alternatives and finally decided on military intervention.

China's Intervention

When North Korea launched a large-scale attack on South Korea across the 38th parallel at dawn on June 25, 1950, the United States reacted promptly. On the same date, the U.S. representative to the UN brought the case before the Security Council, which adopted a resolution calling for an immediate cease-fire and withdrawal of North Korean forces back across the 38th parallel and requesting UN members not to provide support to North Korea. On June 27, President Truman ordered the dispatch of the Seventh Fleet to neutralize Formosa. He stated that the determination of the future status of Formosa should await the return of security in the Pacific, a peace settlement with Japan, or action by the UN.[109] On June 30, Truman instructed U.S. ground forces to join sea and air units in support of South Korea. Despite U.S. intervention, the North Korean army achieved overwhelming victory on the battlefield. By the end of July, U.S. and South Korean troops were forced to withdraw to the Pusan perimeter around the southeastern extremity of the peninsula.[110]

In these early days of the war, the P.R.C. was primarily concerned about American action in the Formosa Strait and was less interested in the fighting on the Korean peninsula. As one study has pointed out, the Chinese media referred to the Korean war as a "civil war" or "war of national liberation," indicating that the fate of the war remained in the hands of the Korean people. In view of the likelihood of increased U.S.-UN military resistance, the media predicted that a communist victory, although certain, would not come quickly, suggesting that there would be a "period of hard struggle ahead for the North Korean Army." But nowhere did the Chinese press hint at the necessity of P.R.C. assistance to North Korea beyond rendering sympathy and moral support to its people.[111]

However, the Chinese reacted sharply to the changed U.S. position on Taiwan. In a statement of June 28, Zhou Enlai condemned Truman's new policy of June 27 as constituting "armed aggression against the territory of China in total violation of the United Nations Charter." He described the dispatch of the Seventh Fleet to the Taiwan Strait as a predatory action designed to prevent the communist liberation of Taiwan. Zhou called the U.S. action in Korea a "premeditated move designed to create a pretext for the United States to invade Taiwan, Vietnam, and the Philippines" (the latter two countries having been designated by Truman to receive increased

U.S. military aid). Zhou declared that "no matter what obstructive action the U.S. imperialists may take, the fact that Taiwan is part of China will remain unchanged forever."[12] This pledge was echoed by Mao Zedong and supported by various national organizations and representatives of national minority groups in China.[113]

It should be noted, however, that despite Beijing's lack of interest in making any direct commitment to the Korean War, the Chinese obviously began to worry that the Korean problem would decisively alter the future of Taiwan and other Asian countries. This concern was reflected in official Chinese protests, diplomatic moves, domestic anti-American campaigns, and redeployment of the PLA. As indicated in Zhou's statement quoted above, the Chinese viewed the American action in Korea in the broad context of Asian affairs. In a cable of July 6 to Secretary-General Trygve Lie, moreover, the P.R.C. labeled the June 27 resolution of the Security Council calling upon members of the UN to assist the South Korean authorities, and Truman's order of the same day, as acts of open aggression against and intervention in the internal affairs of Korea and the P.R.C.[114] In the middle of July, the P.R.C. welcomed the Indian government's proposal that the P.R.C. be admitted to the UN as part of a move toward a Korean settlement.[115] In the meantime, domestically, the All-China Federation of Labor had organized a national campaign against "U.S. aggression" in Taiwan and Korea. *People's China* indicated that the campaign was aimed at bringing home to the Chinese people by every possible means a clearer realization of the character and methods of American imperialist aggression in the Far East.[116] *People's Daily* carried a cable sent by a labor hero, noting that the American challenge had led China's workers to express the workers' support for the peoples fighting for liberation in Korea and other Far Eastern countries.[117]

Of particular importance is the fact that from early July to early August, Beijing ordered troop redeployments from south China to the north. Numerous reports in the Chinese press of Hong Kong revealed that no less than 50,000 men of various units of the Fourth Field Army which had been assigned to assist the Third Field Army to invade Taiwan, were being moved to the north.[118] This military reinforcement of China's northeastern border with Korea seemed to provide a clue to Beijing's reappraisal of strategy affecting both Taiwan and Korea. One implication was that the liberation of Taiwan would be delayed until the United States was defeated in Korea, which might cause a U.S. withdrawal from the Taiwan Strait. The other interpretation, of course, was that the Chinese were making contingency plans should the Korean War take a turn for the worse.[119] In any event, the troop redeployments resulted in a reduction in the PLA's strength opposite Taiwan and undercut the Third Field Army's preparations for the invasion of Taiwan. Citing competent sources, a Chinese newspaper in Hong Kong pointed out that Beijing had decided to transfer part of the Third Field Army to Guangdong to reinforce the local garrison, which had been considerably weakened as a result of the wholesale withdrawal of the Fourth Field Army units, and that the vanguard of the Third Field Army had already entered Guangdong from Fujian.[120] It seems reasonable to assume that some military leaders in the Third Field Army reacted against the central government's decision to postpone plans for the invasion of Taiwan, especially in view of North Korean successes on the Korean battlefield.

Two events in mid-August probably led the P.R.C. to be directly concerned about developments in Korea. Beginning in early August, the balance of power at the battlefront in Korea shifted steadily in favor of UN forces. On August 10 and 17, U.S. delegate Warren Austin was said to state before the Security Council that the American government had decided to reunify Korea under UN auspices, and thus presented a threatening signal to the P.R.C. that the Americans would bring their troops to the doorstep of Manchuria.[121] It is by no means coincidental that in the midst of these events General Ni Jieliang (Ni Chieh-liang), China's first ambassador to Korea, arrived in Pyongyang and presented his credentials. The report hinted that the P.R.C. would be prepared to consult formally with Pyongyang on any common problem regarding the Korean War.[122] In a cable of August 20 to the UN Security Council, the P.R.C. for the first time expressed China's interest in Korea as its most pressing external concern: "Since Korea is China's neighbor, the Chinese people cannot but be especially concerned about the solution of the Korean question, which must and can be settled peacefully."[123] Beijing was probably attempting to send Washington a signal that the Americans should not pursue the war to total victory, but should consider a negotiated settlement. The cable demanded that the P.R.C. delegate be allowed to take part in the discussion of the Korean problem in the Security Council, that the UN military operation in Korea be stopped, and that all foreign troops be withdrawn from Korea. Beijing's demand was echoed by Soviet delegate Malik, who warned that "any continuation of the Korean war will lead inevitably to a widening of conflict." But the demand was not considered by the Security Council.[124]

China's growing concern about the war was heightened by U.S. border violations in late August. On August 27 and 29, U.S. B-29 bombers allegedly entered Chinese air space in the northeast and strafed railway installations and the population. For the first time the P.R.C. lodged strong protests with Secretary of State Acheson and with the Security Council.[125] These protests were followed by nationwide demonstrations against U.S. provocations. Editorially, the *Guangming Daily* claimed that the Americans, having already invaded Taiwan and Korea, were now intruding into northeast China.[126] *People's China* expressed apprehension that the United

States might spread the war to China, noting that the fate of North Korea was linked with China's security interests:

> We must regard the Korean people's defensive war as our war, for the American invasion of Korea is as much a threat to us as it is to the existence of a free and independent Korean nation. That is why the attack on Korea has such sinister undertones for China, why the struggle of the Korean people is bound up with our struggle, and inevitably with the struggle of all Asian peoples against imperialism.[127]

China's fear that the war might spread to northeast China was reinforced by events in the last two weeks of September. The U.S. "X" Corps, after an amphibious landing at Inchon on September 15, rapidly eroded the resistance of the North Korean Army. The "X" Corps recaptured Seoul on September 28, while the U.S. Eighth Army drove north from the Pusan perimeter. On September 19, South Korean President Rhee announced that with or without U.S. assistance, the South Korean Army would continue its attack against the remnants of the North Korean forces.[128] For the P.R.C., these events meant that its efforts to deter UN forces from crossing the 38th parallel by primarily diplomatic means were not working. Chinese protests were being ignored, and efforts to participate in UN discussions were being rejected.[129] The stage was set for a shift to military countermeasures.

On September 25, three days before the UN forces recaptured Seoul, General Nie Yanrong (Nieh Yen-jung), governor of Beijing, attempted to send a warning signal to the United States via Indian Ambassador Panikkar, his message being that China would intervene in the war if UN forces crossed the 38th parallel. In his memoir, Panikkar wrote: "General Nieh told me that the Chinese did not intend to sit back with folded hands and let the Americans come up to their border." This was "the indication," the ambassador added, that "the Chinese proposed to intervene in the war." General Nie even spoke of Beijing's calculation of the costs and risks of stopping the Americans:

> We know what we are in for, but at all costs American aggression has to be stopped. The Americans can bomb us, they can destroy our industries, but they cannot defeat us on land. . . . They may even drop atom bombs on us. What then? They may kill a few million people. . . . China lives on the farms. What can atom bombs do there? Yes, our economic development will be put back. We may have to wait for it.[130]

China's leaders seemed prepared to risk war with the United States and sacrifice economic rehabilitation if the United States expanded the war to North Korea. In a formal speech on September 30, Zhou pointed out that the Chinese people wanted a peaceful environment for national reconstruction, one free from external threats. But he warned that "if the American aggressors take this as a sign of the weakness of the Chinese people, they will commit the same fatal blunder as the KMT [Guomindang] reactionaries." He declared that "the Chinese people absolutely will not tolerate foreign aggression, nor will they supinely tolerate seeing their neighbours being savagely invaded by imperialists."[131]

These warnings coincided with Chinese troop reinforcements in Manchuria. But on October 1, the South Korean Third Division pushed over the 38th parallel and sped up the east coast of North Korea. That night, Zhou summoned Panikkar to a meeting and stressed that if American forces invaded North Korea, China would intervene in the war.[132] It is apparent that at this time the P.R.C. was apprehensive about the crossing of the parallel by the United States Army, not by the South Korean Army. China's warnings were meant to deter U.S. troops from advancing beyond the 38th parallel, but on October 7, UN forces crossed it. The next day, General MacArthur issued an ultimatum calling upon Pyongyang to surrender unconditionally.[133] In this critical situation, P.R.C. leaders finally reached the decision to respond with force to the UN advance. On October 8, the central government sent the following order under the name of Mao Zedong, chairman of the Chinese People's Revolutionary Military Commission, to the Chinese People's Volunteers (CPV):

> In order to support the Korean people's war of liberation and to resist the attacks of U.S. imperialism and its running dogs thereby safeguarding the interests of the people of Korea, China and all the other countries in the East, I herewith order the Chinese People's Volunteers to march speedily to Korea and join the Korean comrades in fighting the aggressors and winning a glorious victory.[134]

The order was not implemented until October 14 and 16, when about 50,000 CPV moved secretly into Korea. On October 19, UN forces captured Pyongyang and speedily crossed the Chong Chon River, forty miles below the Yalu. The first clashes between the PLA and UN forces took place in late October and early November, when the PLA launched surprise attacks on a South Korean battalion that had reached the Yalu River and on several UN regiments. But the Chinese suddenly stopped their attacks and faded away for less than three weeks.[135] The limited attack and subsequent disengagement indicated that in this initial stage of its military intervention, the P.R.C. was being cautious, and that its objective was apparently not a decisive effort to destroy the UN forces in Korea. Mao and his colleagues may have intended to test the Americans' response to Chinese intervention, giving due consideration to the risks involved and determining to minimize them.[136] Encouraging the enemy's arrogance by withdrawing in early November and luring the UN forces deeper into North Korea, where their tenuous supply lines could be interdicted, the Chinese might have planned to annihilate the enemy by separating its units from one another.[137]

It is far more likely, however, that China's leaders were firing a warning shot: They wanted to check the advance of the enemy toward the Yalu River—the objective they had failed to obtain by verbal warnings and diplomatic maneuvers—and to force the Americans to reconsider their goal of total victory in Korea. The Chinese media recalled later that "had we been late by just one minute, these thugs might have advanced to the banks of the Yalu river."[138] Indeed, China's primary concern about national reconstruction, a debate within the CCP over the decision to enter the war, and the Soviet Union's reluctant endorsement of China's decision, as we shall see, all contributed to the initial hesitation on the part of China to undertake a massive counteroffensive and become enmeshed in a prolonged war with the Unites States. Shortly after China's limited display of force, the Chinese press, implying genuine doubts within the leadership about the outcome in the event of a large-scale intervention, began to prepare the population for the possibility of a prolonged war in Korea. For instance, *Dagong bao,* in an editor-in chief's talk with a reader, aired those doubts: "We are going to take action in order to put a stop to war. There can be only two kinds of consequences: Either the war will be stopped; or else, the war danger will be further aggravated when the Americans refuse to give up. . . . In this case, the war might go on for a long time."[139]

In the last half of November, the Chinese saw that mixing warnings with limited military involvement had failed to modify the U.S. policy of total victory. Shortly after the PLA's disengagement, the UN Security Council decided to invite the P.R.C. to discuss MacArthur's special report of November 5 regarding the PLA's entry into the war. On November 10, a British proposal was put before the UN for the creation of a buffer zone that would presumably protect China's frontier. The Chinese, however, seemed to be uninterested in discussing these two matters, since the special report included a proposal that the P.R.C. withdraw all its forces from Korea, and the British idea of a neutral zone was unreliable in view of MacArthur's ambitious plan for total victory in Korea.[140] But Beijing evidently thought that its participation in UN discussions might afford a chance to appeal its position, and if possible, to discuss the question of U.S. armed intervention in Korea. On November 24, China's representative, Wu Xiuquan (Wu Hsiu-ch'uan), arrived in New York. On the same date, however, General MacArthur announced the start of an offensive to end the war. Two days later, the Chinese counterattacked along the entire Korean front, thereby beginning a massive engagement that lasted for more than two and a half years.

The decision to intervene was not made unanimously within the CCP, nor was it made with the warm support of the Soviet Union. There is evidence that before reaching the final decision, Zhou Enlai went to Moscow to discuss China's action in Korea with Stalin, who for the first time disagreed with Zhou's proposal for intervention.[141] Huang Hua later recalled that when China announced the decision, Stalin disapproved because he worried that "our action would anger the United States, thus triggering World War III." "Having seen through the essence of the U.S. paper tiger," Huang added, "Chairman Mao insisted on entering into action; afterwards, practice educated Stalin and he eventually supported our joining the war."[142] Stalin evidently hoped to limit the Soviet role to diplomatic maneuvers in the Security Council for a negotiated settlement and limited air support for North Korea. Inevitably, the overt intervention by Chinese ground forces would increase the risk of escalation, and in this respect, Stalin was unlikely to exert any pressure in favor of intervention; rather, he agreed to it reluctantly.[143] This hypothesis is strengthened by the record of Soviet action in the early stage of China's intervention. Ratification of the Sino-Soviet treaty took place in late September 1950, but implementation of the credit agreement did not come until February 1951.[144] The offer of Soviet weapons was made long after China had intervened. In the first half-year of China's involvement, Chinese soldiers used Japanese and Ameircan arms captured during the civil war rather than Soviet military supplies.[145]

It is also likely that Beijing had developed a contingency plan for the war—one that was based on self-reliance rather than on reliance on Soviet military might. In the three months after the outbreak of the Korean War, the Chinese were not unaware of Moscow's unwillingness to risk war with the United States.[146] Given the strained alliance that existed between Beijing and Moscow, then, the Chinese had reason to doubt they could expect active and effective Soviet aid beyond limited military supplies; indeed, there were some indications at the time that support this speculation. The Chinese media expressed the hope that the Russians would deter American use of atomic bombs in China, saying that "the atomic bomb is no longer the sole possession of the American imperialists." But the media continued to refer to atomic bombs as "paper tigers" and expressed the belief that they could not be employed on the battlefield to destroy directly the fighting power of the opposing army.[147]

The P.R.C. therefore evaluated Soviet military protection as being of secondary value. In the first line of defense of the socialist camp, the Chinese were obviously determined to shoulder a heavy burden with the North Korean people. On November 27, one day after the Chinese launched their all-out counteroffensive, *Dagong bao* clearly aired this view: "The heroic resistance of the Korean people coupled with the active asistance of the Chinese people offered on a voluntary basis is sufficient to ensure the inevitable annihilation of the enemy in battle and the realization of ultimate victory. . . . In the case that developments in the Far Eastern situation reach the stage as to call for the application of the part of the

Treaty on mutual assistance, there can not be the least doubt that the Soviet Union shall discharge its obligations."[148]

The P.R.C.'s decision was apparently an arduous one. It has been reported that Mao Zedong paced the floor for three days and nights before reaching it.[149] Mao encountered opposition from various sectors of the party, government, and army. Certain leaders, especially those in charge of economic affairs, opposed the decision. For instance, according to a Red Guard document on the Cultural Revolution, Minister of Finance Chen Yun argued that "to fight the war of resistance against the Americans and to continue with economic construction was absolutely incompatible."[150] However, Mao ruled out such an absolutist position. He seemed to reason that the imminent threat posed by the United States put a peaceful environment for reconstruction out of China's reach, and that China would have to struggle to bring about such an environment. An editorial in *People's Daily* on November 6, 1950, developed Mao's position:

> Would it not be better that we should strive our utmost not to afford any pretext under which the enemy might undertake an attack on us and utilize the intervening period for the peaceful reconstruction of the nation? . . . Such reasoning is erroneous, because it presumes that the enemy who has started his attack will permit us an intervening period and environment for peaceful reconstruction which is contrary to the facts. . . . We can not forever afford to wait for the enemy to grant us the time and environment for peaceful reconstruction.[151]

Opposition also came from PLA leaders. The generals who were against intervention argued that involvement in Korea would get the PLA bogged down in a protracted war.[152] Other generals perceived the U.S. threat as being less dangerous than Mao asserted. Their view was that a military counterattack by China, even after a large-scale U.S. invasion of Chinese territory, would not be too late to defend China. They reasoned that even though the enemy was marching toward the Yalu River, had bombed and strafed China's border areas, and had occupied Taiwan, it had not undertaken any large-scale invasion of China's territory. (Although the Japanese began their aggression against Korea in 1894, it was not until 1931 that they occupied northeast China.) But Mao regarded the intention and capability of the Americans as a more immediate threat to China's security than those of the Japanese had been in the past. He preferred to intervene early. He obviously worried that to do nothing against an enemy that was advancing toward China's border would only whet its appetite for further aggressiveness.[153]

Some leaders were mainly concerned about the liberation of Taiwan. They opposed the decision to aid Korea because it would inevitably lead the central government to divert resources originally committed to the Taiwan front. But the Maoists considered the American attack on Korea to be part of a plan for aggressive moves in Taiwan and elsewhere in Asia. This perceived linkage led the Maoists to relate the fate of the Korean War to the planned liberation of Taiwan. A *World Knowledge* writer vividly expressed this view:

> Some people have said that to resist the U.S. and defend our country, it is only necessary for us to cross the ocean and liberate Taiwan and that it is not necessary to aid Korea. Of course we must liberate Taiwan, but we can not withhold aid from the Korean people in their war of resistance because of our preparations for the liberation of Taiwan. The liberation of Taiwan is closely tied up with aid to Korea, and aid to Korea will be instrumental to military actions for the liberation of Taiwan. To let the enemy accomplish the first step of his strategy—overcoming of Korea, our difficulties in liberating Taiwan across the ocean will be increased. It is therefore our urgent task to aid Korea.[154]

China's Motives and Objectives

In this section we shall discuss the motives behind China's commitment to the Korean War, focusing on how domestic and international events interacted to affect the decision to intervene.

In differentiating the two domains that might have influenced China's decision to intervene in Korea, our analysis of the domestic and external circumstances of China leads us to assume that external events, not internal ones, were primary in precipitating the decision. Chinese intervention was undertaken in reaction to external threats to China's security that P.R.C. leaders perceived as being imminent. China's central concern was to stop invading UN forces at the doorstep of the northeast region, to prevent the spread of the war into Chinese territory—that is, to localize the war in Korea. The Chinese also wanted to prevent the extinction of communist North Korea bordering the P.R.C. and to force the aggressors to accept a solution of the Korean question that took Chinese interests into account. After the failure of verbal warnings, diplomatic probes, and preemptive limited attacks to deter UN forces from advancing beyond the 38th parallel, and after the Soviets' limited reaction to American military activities in Korea, P.R.C. leaders had to weigh further, and massive, military intervention against pressing domestic needs and other military problems like the liberation of Taiwan and Tibet and the pacification of anticommunist elements still on the mainland.

The outbreak of the Korean War and U.S. intervention in it fed apprehensions about the regional scope of the U.S. threat in Asia. This fear was further heightened by apparent U.S. violations of China's territorial air space, by the United States' recommitment to protect the GMD in Taiwan, and by U.S. military aid to other anticommunist governments in Asia.

When UN forces crossed the 38th parallel, Chinese concern was for the security of the P.R.C. itself as UN forces, especially U.S. troops, seemed prepared to march to the Yalu and Tumen rivers, and possibly even push their attacks beyond Korea's northern border. These fears and suspicions were probably reinforced by the fact that the United States ignored several serious Chinese warnings not to cross the parallel, and did not show a deference to the PLA's limited but strong attacks on the UN forces that initially approached the Yalu River in last October and early November. As a *People's Daily* editorial in early November 1950 noted, assurances from U.S. government officials that China's security was not in jeopardy were therefore unpersuasive:

> When American invaders were pressing toward the 38th parallel the U.S. government started a rumor that the U.S. troops would stop at the parallel. Later it was said that the U.S. forces would stop at the point some distance from the borders of the Soviet Union and China. . . . Up to this moment, the U.S. invasion troops are pressing toward the Yalu river, the mouth-pieces of the American imperialists are still spreading the smokescreen of guaranteeing that Mac-Arthur's troops, who are advancing toward North Korea, will not push beyond the border of Korea. However, in the light of the experience afforded by history, such statement is in fact a prediction that U.S. aggressors will push beyond the border of Korea.[155]

Under such circumstances, P.R.C. leaders felt compelled to "resist America and aid Korea" by committing massive forces to the Korean front. Such an intervention would serve China's security objective to forestall an American attack across the Yalu River and limit the war to Korea. This objective was repeatedly emphasized in the Chinese media before and after the China's intervention. For example, on October 6, General Ye Jianying addressed himself to the "international situation" the P.R.C. had to cope with: "In our support of Korea and opposition to American imperialism, we are checking American imperialist aggression being brought to our doors, preventing the spreading of the war, and fulfilling the sacred duty of protecting our homes."[156] Soon after the limited PLA attacks in late October, *World Knowledge* expressed the hope (and objective) that "American imperialists will not dare to carry on all-out war against China, but rather will limit the war to Korea itself, only fighting those Chinese who take part in the Korean war as volunteers."[157]

It is also reasonable to assume that China's intervention was aimed at preventing UN forces from totally defeating the North Korean Army and unifying all Korea under UN supervision, which General MacArthur had announced as his objectives. China's repeated warnings that it would not tolerate its neighbor being invaded by imperialists, and the date of its decision to enter the war, suggest that its objective was closely related to the survival of the North Korean regime. It should be noted, however, that in the initial stage of China's intervention, the Chinese were motivated much more by concern for the P.R.C.'s security than by concern about North Korean interests. For instance, Foreign Minister Zhou's talk to Indian Ambassador Panikkar on October 2 hinted that the civil war in Korea was an internal Korean affair and that the P.R.C. might tolerate a partial occupation of North Korea by South Korean forces, but not by U.S. forces. Although it had secretly moved into North Korea in the middle of October, the PLA did not attempt to defend Pyongyang, the capital of North Korea, which was captured by UN troops. As late as early November, the P.R.C. seemed to be interested in a British proposal for a buffer zone in the vicinity of the neck of the Korean peninsula.

There is no convincing evidence that China's intervention was prompted either by Soviet pressure or by a legal (treaty) obligation to defend North Korea. Instead, in view of the strained alliance between Moscow and Beijing, and considering Moscow's unwillingness to risk war with the United States in order to deter a U.S. invasion of North Korea, China's leaders realistically concluded that Soviet military protection would be of secondary importance. They made the decision to enter the war with the awareness that they could expect only a very limited amount of help from the Russians.[158]

Mao's strategy evidently was to undermine U.S. plots to encircle China and to stymie U.S. adventurism in Asia by determined struggle against the United States in Korea. Before the Korean War broke out, the leadership had assumed the United States was responsible for Taiwan's bombing and blockading of the south coast of China. Shortly after the war began, Beijing feared that U.S. interjection of the Seventh Fleet into the Taiwan Strait and its plan to use Taiwan as a military base were steps aimed at preventing the liberation of Taiwan by the P.R.C. and at making use of Taiwan as a springboard for an invasion of the mainland and Vietnam.[159] Added to these developments was the U.S. plan to rearm and rebuild Japan, which to the Chinese augmented the American threat to the region substantially. The Chinese media repeatedly (and quite accurately) pointed out that the Americans were enlarging the Japanese armed forces; using Japan's military bases for the transport of supplies, munitions, and personnel to Korea, as well as for air operations; and was seeking permanent basing rights in Japan through a separate treaty that would exclude the Soviet Union and the P.R.C.[160]

As viewed from Beijing, the P.R.C.'s passivity to American intervention in Korea would probably encourage U.S. ambitions against China and throughout Asia. Chinese action in Korea thus took on a punitive as well as a defensive character. For instance, *Dagong bao* in November 1950 listed the four objectives behind Chinese entry into the Korean War. Two of them were concerned with U.S. action in Taiwan and Japan:

The American Seventh Fleet together with all other forms of military establishments must be withdrawn from Taiwan and its accompanying waters, and all aid to Chiang bandits must be stopped.

The American imperialists must stop rearming of Japan and a full-fledged peace treaty with Japan must be signed with the participation of China and the Soviet Union. Thus shall China be freed from threat and peace be maintained in the Far East.[161]

It has been argued that to some extent China became involved in the Korean War because of its domestic need to mobilize the people for production, a wholesale transformation of the social and economic order, and the pacification of anti-Communist groups.[162] But there is no convincing evidence that China's intervention was prompted by those needs. To be sure, the war presented advantages to the leadership. Soon after it began, the Chinese press continuously propagandized the anti-American campaign throughout the country, using that theme to promote increased production. The land program was pressed more vigorously; a widespread purge began against counterrevolutionaries; and the *Sanfan* ("three anti-") and *Wufan* ("five anti-") movements for cleaning up society took place. Indeed, for the leadership, a drastic external threat seemed to be of considerable benefit in intensifying those movements, as a *People's Daily* editorial in December 1950 intimated when it criticized some cadres for losing their vigilance over counterrevolutionaries in the belief the revolutionary order would be easily consolidated. The editorial stated that at a time when "the Chinese people are waging a sharp struggle against American imperialism," the people should intensify class struggle at home, thereby depriving counterrevolutionary elements of their political freedom.[163]

It should be pointed out, however, that for all these advantages, the P.R.C. leaders would not possibly have risked war with the United States to obtain them. Not only was the outcome uncertain; the war's costs imposed heavy burdens on China's economy and finances at a most inopportune time. The "Resist America, Aid Korea" campaign contributed to meeting the demands of war far more than it did to helping China to reconstruct. For instance, in a speech in October 1951, General Chen Yi described the campaign as a great contribution to reducing the central government's financial burden. He noted that "by October 10 (1951), the people of East China have pledged to donate 897 planes, 33 artillery, 17 anti-aircraft, and 2 tanks, constituting one-third of the donation of all the country."[164]

In the case of land reform, the sudden radicalization of policy seems to have come about because of the party's sensitivity—heightened by the Korean War—to internal insecurity. As Ezra Vogel has suggested after taking a close look at land reform in Guangdong, the war aroused Beijing's fear that landlords and other politically unreliable persons in south China might resist the government's directives, taking advantage of the transfer of troops from Guangdong to Korea.[165] Hence, the party center needed firmer policies to stir up peasant enthusiasm for struggle against landlords. These considerations suggest that the Korean War did affect the onset of more radical domestic politics, *not* by providing a pretext for them, but by further stimulating the leadership's insecurity and its need of increased production.

One may hypothesize that China's intervention in Korea was undertaken by the Maoists for reasons of military politics. They could not have been unmindful of the potential dangers inherent in the distribution of military and political power among five major field army elites. By sending many units from distant military regions to Korea and reallocating political-military power among the field armies, the Maoists might have stood to enhance their central power at the expense of regional party leaders and commanders.[166] But this hypothesis cannot be sustained if we take a look at internal circumstances before and after the Korean War. There was no hint that the party center had lost its grip over the military regions when the war began, as has been discussed, or that Chairman Mao was challenged from within the CCP and by regional leaders. Mao then had the power to rule out opposition raised by various sectors in the government against his decision to intervene in the war. Mao was said to have had full control over the movement of the armed forces and operational planes during the war period.[167] The hypothesis is further weakened when we consider Beijing's initial plan to cope with the UN forces. The P.R.C. initially deployed the best units of the Fourth Field Army to the front in Korea, presumably hoping they would be sufficient to hold off the enemy. The decimation of these units and the prospect of a prolonged war forced Beijing to send replacements from the First, Second, and Third field armies.[168]

So far as the connection between domestic and international events is concerned, domestic insecurity and external threat were linked in the perspective of the Chinese leadership on the eve of the Korean War. Internally, China's economy was stagnant after a prolonged civil war. Armed resistance by anticommunist groups of remnant GMD forces, landlords, and non-Chinese people made the newly established leadership vulnerable to internal subversion. One Chinese document asserted that these anticommunist groups were being assisted by American or GMD forces, saying that "apart from open aggression, the U.S. also tries to work against us from the inside," and that "60 percent of the principal bandit groups in the Southeast had their training under the U.S. and Chiang."[169] *Guangming Daily* in November 1950 pointed out that while sending a large number of special-service agents to engage in sabotage in Tibet, "the imperialist nations of the west have been using all manner of political intrigues to sow dissension between our Tibetan brothers and people of other nationalities of China in order to separate Tibet from China."[170] Despite the Truman administration's public commitment to cease interfering in China's civil war, the Chinese were acutely sensitive to the possibility that China's internal vulnerabilities would be exploited by the United States, either in hopes of bailing out Chiang Kai-shek once again, or in response to domestic political pressures to reverse the "loss of China." A NCNA (Xinhua she [Hsinhua she]) report expressed this sensitivity, which increased further once the United States intervened in Korea: "As soon as American imperialism started their war of aggression against Korea and right after American planes bombed and strafed our territory, these bandits, thinking that 'the time is ripe,' started operating in earnest by gathering together their bandit agents, expanding their organizations, establishing a comprehensive network of secret bases, and collecting intelligence reports, as well as in spreading rumors, staging robberies and disturbing social peace and order."[171]

In view of the linkage perceived in Beijing between external threat and internal vulnerabilities, the Chinese thought that resolute action in response to the growing U.S. threat would correct Washington's misperception of China's weakness and fear of U.S. power. [172] They probably also thought a strong response would erode a popular psychology of deference to American military might and encourage "wavering elements" not to collaborate with anticommunist groups. A powerful parallel seemed to exist between China's intervention in Korea and the PLA's occupation of Tibet. The PLA's preemptive action against U.S.-UN forces coincided with its march into Tibet in late October. The coincidence in timing may have reflected China's apprehension that while engaged in the Korean War, the PLA might have to cope with a threat on another front, a threat posed by internal enemies acting in collaboration with external ones. The local Chinese authorities declared that the PLA's entry into Tibet was aimed at "consolidating the national defense of the western borders of China and ridding Tibet of imperialist influence." They appealed to anticommunist groups not to stand against the central government. An authoritative proclamation on Tibet read: "Pro-imperialist and KMT officials concerning whom there is definite evidence that they had severed relations with the imperialists and KMT and who will not carry out any sabotage or put up resistance may remain at their posts, irrespective of their past history."[173]

A combination of domestic vulnerabilities and foreign threats tended to magnify the P.R.C. leadership's insecurity. In the summer and fall of 1950, the combination of U.S. forces advancing toward the Yalu and internal subversion may have considerably increased Beijing's perception of a direct threat to China's border security. It probably led Chinese leaders, especially the Maoists, to regard the U.S. threat to China's security as more imminent than was actually the case.

We have seen how domestic economic and military needs and political instability were constraining factors in Chinese foreign-policy decision making during a time of crisis. But these weaknesses did not prevent the leadership from initiating countermeasures against an imminent threat. China, as indicated in Zhou's speech in late September 1950, needed peace at that time more than ever; but Mao decided that peace was more likely to come about by entering the war than by sitting back and observing the next round of U.S. moves. Economic difficulties, internal vulnerabilities, the liberation of Taiwan all took a back seat to an immediate danger. Yet these pressing domestic concerns clearly influenced the way the Chinese intervened in the war. The slow implementation of Mao's order on October 8, China's initial limited attacks on UN forces, and its subsequent disengagement for three weeks all reflected domestic circumstances such as the status of the economy, military preparedness, and bureaucratic politics. By intervening, Mao evidently hoped to bring the Americans to their senses, negotiate a reasonable settlement, and withdraw.

The Chinese Korean War decision supports our hypothesis that when internal insecurity combines with external threat, foreign policy becomes a domestic issue and reorders China's policy priorities. As soon as the P.R.C. decided to enter the war, the Central Committee set forth a "three-sided financial policy"—that is, to fight the war of resistance, to achieve stability, and to get on with national construction.[174] This policy obviously was a modification of the construction-first policy that the P.R.C. had instituted in 1949. It meant that China would delay economic construction programs based on the First Five-Year Plan and would undertake an all-out mobilization of the society, thereby stopping a planned demobilization of the PLA. In addition, Beijing would stop pursuing its plan to liberate Taiwan and divert resources previously assigned for that task to the Korean front. In July 1950, the Planning Division of the Ministry of Heavy Industry was reported to have drawn up the initial steps in a production plan for China's heavy industry.[175] But such economic planning was not to be implemented until 1953 when the Korean War came to an end. During the war, the Chinese press did not publicize any further plan for the PLA's demobilization, except for a speech of General Liu Bocheng (Liu Po-chéng), chairman of the Southwest Military and Administrative Committee.[176] A clear indication of changing priorities from economic construction to defense expenditures may be seen in the report of the vice-minister of finance that appeared in *People's Daily* in March 1951. Reminding his audience that financial work in 1950 had been conducted on the basis of the overall policy of striving for a balanced government budget and stabilized finances and commodity prices, he hinted that the P.R.C. would again face increasing defense expenditures in 1951. "With regard to key points of expenditure," he noted, "we must draw special attention to those expenditures with which we are not much acquainted and which are flexible such as national defense construction and military expenses in the war expenditures."[177]

3 The Taiwan Strait Crisis, 1958

Introduction

In the literature on Chinese foreign policy, the dominant interpretation of the 1958 Taiwan Strait crisis is that the P.R.C. leadership initiated it, bears responsibility for the ensuing U.S.-China confrontation, and suffered a major setback as a result. Differences in interpretation are largely confined to the question of Chinese—which is to say Mao's—motives. Some writers speculate that Mao manufactured a crisis over the strait mainly for domestic reasons: in order to minimize dissent over his economic policies, or to stimulate the Great Leap Forward, or to help rationalize the "Everyone a Soldier" militia movement. Other writers concentrate on the strategic factors: Mao sought to vindicate his "paper tiger" thesis in the face of Soviet irresolution; or he wanted to test or demonstrate the vulnerability of the United States in the strait area; or he took a preliminary step in a "limited war" strategy to liberate Taiwan. What these explanations have in common is their assumption that Mao, whether for primarily domestic or foreign-policy reasons, "needed" an external adventure to make a point.

This case study will attempt to develop a plausible alternative explanation of Chinese motives. While it relies on sources that are already well known, it proposes a new way of ordering and interpreting the evidence. Like some other studies of the crisis, this one assumes an interaction between Chinese politics and foreign policy. But it rejects the conclusion that a foreign-policy crisis was manufactured for or stimulated by domestic concerns. Briefly stated, the thesis here is that had it not been for American actions—in Taiwan, elsewhere in Asia, and in the Middle East—Mao would have had no reason to order the bombardment of the offshore islands on August 23, 1958. At that time, domestic problems seemed to complicate rather than facilitate Chinese foreign policy making. Mao did not want a crisis over the strait before or after August 23; what he most needed was international quiescence.

THE TAIWAN STRAIT

If new light is to be shed on Chinese motives, we need to reexamine the decision-making environment before and during 1958. In particular, we want to understand how domestic circumstances (the economy and the state of politics and preparedness in the armed forces) affected and were affected by international developments. Domestic needs, especially if they are pressing and cannot be satisfied with scarce resources, can become the basis of leadership debate and bureaucratic competition. They may also, as in 1958, have foreign-policy implications, since China then was economically and militarily in need of Soviet assistance. An external crisis adds to the problem of resource allocation; but how deeply it will affect domestic political conflict and decision making depends on how seriously it is perceived as a threat to national security compared with its influence on personal and bureaucratic interests. The following descriptive overview of China's internal and external worlds prior to August 1958 attempts to assess the extent to which domestic politics and foreign affairs, independently and by their interaction, influenced Mao's policy choices.

The Domestic Situation

The Economy

As 1958 began, the central concern of Chinese policy makers was the performance of the economy. During the six previous years, agricultural collectivization had begun and expanded in the countryside; and in 1955 Mao had urged greater speed in a "socialist upsurge." Early in 1956 Mao proposed a "leap forward" in production and introduced a twelve-year program for agricultural growth.[1] Opposition to this program was apparently intense; but at the Eighth Party Congress in September 1956 it was resolved to conclude the First Five-Year Plan (1953–57) with a 51.1 percent increase in the total value of industrial and agricultural output (compared with that of 1952) in preparation for the Second Five-Year Plan, which would begin in 1958.[2] One year later, when the party Central Committee met again to discuss the pace of collectivization, "conservatives" in the leadership who had balked at Mao's program and succeeded at slowing it down were evidently defeated.[3]

In January 1958, Mao established the momentum toward establishment of the people's communes—the decision on which would not be made until late August—when he coined the key slogan of the Great Leap Forward (GLF): "We will catch up with Britain in about fifteen years." He stressed the importance of the new year: "In these fifteen years, we must emphasize the first five years; in these five years, we must emphasize the first three years; in these three years, we must emphasize the first year; in the first year, we must emphasize the first month."⁴ In February, Mao drafted and submitted to other party leaders for comment and approval "Sixty Points on Working Methods."⁵ The document reflected Mao's optimism that the masses were ready to respond to party appeals for a leap forward in production. He classified the GLF as the last of the "three great socialist reforms": the revolution in ownership of the means of production, completed in 1956; the ideological revolution, to be largely completed in 1958; and the "technological revolution," which he expected would get under way in July. Also in February, at the fifth session of the First National People's Congress, Vice-Premier Bo Yibo (Po I-po), chairman of the National Economic Commission, reported that conditions were satisfactory and new targets had been set for a "new leap forward" in the economy.⁶

By March 1958, when a secret party conference was held at Chengdu (Ch'eng-tu), concrete plans had been laid to further decentralize collectives and industry and to increase production by as much as 20 percent in 1958.⁷ Mao urged his colleagues to be bold and daring, to adopt an attitude of "craving greatness and success, being impatient for immediate benefits, scorning the past, and idolizing the future."⁸ An important organizational prerequisite was apparently initiated at this time: the decentralization of economic decision making through a large-scale *xiafang* campaign that moved millions of government and party workers into rural jobs.

It is well established that the drive toward full-scale collectivization in the 1950s was opposed nearly every step of the way by "some comrades" in the leadership who evidently balked at the pace, scope, and dynamics of Mao's development strategy.⁹ Their recalcitrance helps explain the need for Mao's pep talk on boldness. Politically, however, it is also clear that by 1958, Mao's line had won out. That development, coupled with the culmination of the antirightist campaign in the fall of 1957, gave Mao an indispensable condition for the Great Leap Forward: the approval or acquiescence of his chief associates in his program of depending on the enthusiasm of the masses rather than on the expertise of intellectuals. As members of the leadership stated frequently during early 1958, the ideological revolution—the struggle to consolidate the proletarian dictatorship and eliminate rightist thinking—had basically been won. Thus, in February, Mao felt able to submit his resignation as chairman of the P.R.C., saying, "Now [that] the country is at peace, it is better for me to be relieved of the Chairmanship." Apparently wanting to devote full time to the GLF, Mao requested acceptance of his resignation "before September" 1958 "in order to meet the demands [of the work] of the party."¹⁰ He was resigning, it would appear, from a position of strength rather than, as some writers have suggested, out of weakness.

Mao's enthusiasm to get the communes organized translated into a Central Committee resolution on August 29, 1958, directing that they be established nationwide. "It appears now that the realization of Communism in our country is no longer a thing of the distant future," the resolution stated.[11] Mao would later express surprise and regret at the speed with which the commune decision was reached.[12] But there were, in addition, important domestic and international political consequences. Internally, the commune program meant that economic decision making would be concentrated in the central and local party organizations, a move that would curtail the authority of the government bureaucracy over economic affairs.[13] As will be discussed shortly, this centralization of party authority occurred simultaneously with a reemphasis on party control over the armed forces at a time when budgetary and other resources were being diverted to economic construction and away from national defense. Externally, the GLF, and especially the communes, made their mark on Sino-Soviet relations, at first ideologically and economically, and later militarily. They were not simply the last stage of collectivization, but were an integral part of Mao's strategy to break China's relationship of dependency on the U.S.S.R.

The Military

Politics in the PLA has always been a reflection in microcosm of political change in China as a whole. The period from 1956 to 1958 illustrates this phenomenon very well. As the party center sought to isolate and erode rightist, bourgeois thinking; as it campaigned for a more self-reliant economy; as it centralized authority in party committees; and as it began to emphasize moral incentives over material ones, it took steps to ensure that these priorities would be adhered to in the armed forces. The results would have a bearing on the Taiwan Strait crisis in two respects: in the preparedness of the PLA to deal with an external threat, and in the degree to which China would have to rely on Soviet support in foreign-policy matters.

The mid-1950s, as various writers have concluded,[14] was a time of considerable stress in the PLA. Different and in some cases diametrically opposed views had developed between the military professionals and the party center over the following issues: the scope of authority of party committees in the armed forces; the relative priority of military training and technology as against political training and morale (hence, the question also of modernizing by relying on foreign military aid or by becoming increasingly self-reliant); the relative merits of doctrinairism (the Soviet model) and eclecticism (Maoist adaptation and the guerrilla model); the probability of a major war; and the usefulness of a people's militia.

The political direction in which Mao wanted the PLA to move was established in January 1956 with a party directive for increased political training for officers. Following his speech on contradictions in February

1957, this directive was extended. It was complemented by the start of an officers-to-the-ranks movement that reached a peak in September 1958, a month *after* the Taiwan Strait crisis began, when 10,000 officers were reported to be serving one-month stints as privates.[15] In early 1958 the study of Chairman Mao's military writings was made the cornerstone of basic training in the armed forces, and a major study campaign was carried out after the Military Affairs Committee of the party Central Committee met in the spring. As in the case of the economy, the party insisted on enforcement of the committee leadership system in the PLA. It noted that "purely military views, warlordism, and doctrinairism have revived among a part of the [PLA's] personnel," causing "certain ideological confusion and weakening the fine tradition of our army in practical work."[16]

The party center needed to strengthen its authority over the PLA at this time for the same reason it needed to reinforce its grip on the economy. The Great Leap Forward would be taking an increasing share of the nation's resources, and parochial bureaucratic interests could not be permitted to interfere. Politics would have to take command in the PLA in order to prevent misguided professionals from continuing to emphasize military training, modernization of equipment, and "regularization" of the command structure, objectives that were out of phase with Mao's decisions to give economic production first place and leave professional military interests for later attention. By 1958, as John Gittings has written, there was a "crisis of confidence in the PLA at the height of the Great Leap Forward [which] was in large measure caused by this ever-widening circle of party control and interference, as well as by the somewhat mechanical and clumsy methods which were adopted in order to resurrect the 'revolutionary' ideals of former years."[17]

The term "crisis of confidence" does not seem overly dramatic when one considers the specific ways in which the GLF affected the PLA's strength and mission. For one thing, beginning in 1956 there were important cutbacks in the military budget and manpower. While expenditures for economic construction increased about 23 percent from 1955 to 1956, defense expenditures declined by nearly 6 percent, or from 22 percent to about 20 percent of the national budget. In the 1957 budget, total economic expenditures declined somewhat (although those for agriculture continued to increase), but they still accounted for about 47 percent of the budget, whereas the PLA's share dropped to 18.9 percent. In 1958, party inroads into the PLA budget were even greater, and left the PLA with only an estimated 15.1 percent of the national budget.[18] Significant demobilizations in each of those years led to some cost reductions. The army's strength dropped from 3 million in 1955 to 2.5 million in 1958.[19] As General Su Yu, the PLA chief of staff, had warned in mid-1957, the armed forces were being challenged to raise their quality while having to economize, and were being reduced in strength.[20] What he did not say was that with the emphasis in training on politics rather than fighting, the army would be hard put to maintain, much less raise, its defense preparedness.

General Su, who would be replaced in October 1958, may have been among those professionals who came under attack in midyear for arguing on behalf of the military's interests and neglecting politics, the party's wishes, and the national interest.[21] These officers evidently questioned the party center's judgment that in the development of a modern state, industry and agriculture should take precedence over military work, and therefore that military personnel should actively contribute to local production activities.[22] Such a program had actually been started in 1956, when four million man-days of work were contributed by PLA personnel. But the figure climbed to twenty million in 1957 and to fifty-nine million in 1958.[23] In addition, as General Su explained in 1957, servicemen would be "demobilized for participation in industrial and agricultural production, to conserve the reserve forces for combat."[24] In May 1958 the New China News Agency reported that 6.8 million servicemen demobilized since 1950 "are now taking part in national construction."[25]

The militia movement also came into being at this time, for reasons that in some degree were military but that for the most part were economic. Faced with the problem of providing the army with replacements for regular and demobilized soldiers earmarked for construction work, the party center hit upon the idea of a popular militia. Here was the ideal solution, because the militia would bolster the PLA's reserve force while saving money and keeping able-bodied citizens at work on their collectives. In 1957 a new system was inaugurated that merged the reserve and the militia. Non-conscripts would be brought into the militia and discharged into it. By the end of 1957 there were reportedly about thirty million militia members. Soon after the "Everyone a Soldier" movement was announced in September 1958, there were said to be some 220 million peasant-soldiers.[26]

The chronology of the militia movement's development indicates that its main purpose was to assist in the organization and consolidation of the unfolding commune system—as revealed, for instance, in the slogan "getting organized along military lines." Only secondarily was the militia intended to be a backup force for the PLA. In all key respects—in its emphasis on mass participation, voluntarism, indigenous methods, decentralized authority, self-reliance, and the Chinese revolutionary model— the militia movement was consistent with the spirit and essence of the GLF as a whole.[27]

Here again, the PLA was being shortchanged. Undoubtedly there were many in its leadership who accepted the party's contention that the militia would be a valuable auxiliary force in wartime, and in peacetime would broaden the economic base of national defense. As the saying went, "a rifle in one hand, a hoe in the other." But for the military professionals, having a militia was probably considered a poorer alternative than not having one. Far from enhancing the army's strength, the militia detracted from it: the PLA would have to detach instructors to give peasants basic training; it would have to supply weapons; and since local party committees would be in charge of militia units, the army would be weakened bureaucratically.[28] The diversion of precious resources to the militia must have been especially onerous to the professionals inasmuch as the PLA had also to provide vehicles for the communes, manufacture and repair articles for local need, and assign thousands of officers to assist in commune organization.[29]

The overall spirit of the GLF was self-reliance, and a concerted effort was made by the party leadership to imbue the PLA with it. "Starting in 1958," Mao would later say, "we adopted the guiding principle of self-reliance to be supplemented by seeking foreign aid."[30] In June 1958, midway through a lengthy enlarged conference of the Military Affairs Committee that thoroughly reviewed the party's role in the PLA, Mao criticized the dogmatism of Chinese military officers in learning from Soviet military experiences, ordinances, and plans. On the question of military aid, he said: "It is necessary to strive for Soviet aid, but what is of primary importance is self-help." Lin Biao echoed the chairman's thought, telling the same conference that the U.S.S.R. should be studied only "halfway," meaning that "we study the use of naval and air forces and the cooperation of the various services. The half that we need not study includes such things as tactical ideas, because we have Chairman Mao's."[31]

Professional military people were being told quite plainly, as in an editorial in the *Liberation Army Daily*[32] after the conference, that they would have to make do with "inferior equipment" and adopt "a spirit of independent activity" during the ensuing period of full-scale collectivization. They were informed anew that "erroneous tendencies" such as "one-sidedly stress[ing] the part of atomic weapons and modern military technique" and mechanically copying Soviet experiences would not be tolerated.[33] The service chiefs faithfully reported on Army Day (August 1) that the military was responding to the party's wishes while also making a great leap forward in training to maintain quality.[34] But their declarations had a hollow ring.

In fact, as several writers have commented,[35] military modernization and the acquisition of atomic weapons in particular had for some time been a matter of intense debate within the PLA hierarchy as well as between members of the PLA leadership and the party center. Mao's insistence on self-reliance was emerging as a divisive issue as early as the mid-1950s. The military professionals who wanted to minimize it—according to Alice Hsieh, they were largely confined to the PLA General Staff (which included Su Yu)—perceived (or rationalized their position on the basis of) an immediate U.S. threat to China, including a possible nuclear first strike, and argued for rapid modernization of Chinese forces and weapons. A second group, apparently headed by Minister of Defense Peng Dehuai (P'eng Teh-huai), gave far less credence to the view that nuclear war was imminent, but argued that it was necessary for China to rely on the Soviets to deter that eventuality. The two factions thus differed over how much the PLA could safely sacrifice to Mao's economic policies, with Peng's faction evidently being more willing to divert military expenditures to socialist construction.

In terms of Sino-Soviet relations during the period of the Taiwan Strait crisis, the point to highlight is that *neither* PLA faction seemed to be promoting a viewpoint that was consistent with Mao's. The General Staff's implicit unwillingness to rely for long on a Soviet defense of China *was* in line with Mao's thinking. The chairman also wanted the P.R.C. to have its own nuclear weapons. Three senior officials—Chen Yi, Guo Moruo (Kuo Mo-jo), and Air Force Chief of Staff Liu Yalou—predicted in May 1958 that China would have them in the near future;[36] and in June, Mao issued a directive: "Let us work on atom bombs and nuclear bombs. Ten years, I think, should be quite enough."[37] But the chairman's timetable for getting them was much longer; his chief concern was the economy, and only an imminent national security threat seemed likely to force him to alter his priorities. The General Staff labored under the "purely military viewpoint" of wanting immediately to devote a major share of the budget to creating a modern, independent Chinese military machine that would have nuclear weapons and much more besides.

As for Peng, his position accorded with Mao's insofar as it put long-term economic objectives ahead of immediate military requirements. But according to accusations leveled against Peng after his purge in 1959, he opposed the communes, wanted to abolish the militia, worked against party supremacy in the armed forces, was inattentive to military research, and perhaps most crucially, promoted policies that would have maintained the armed forces' dependence on the U.S.S.R.[38] Indeed, Peng may have tried to use Mao's priorities against him. By endorsing the notion of the economy first and military affairs second, Peng had a powerful argument for continued Chinese reliance on all kinds of Soviet aid. Mao, as we shall see in the next section, accepted the necessity of Soviet help and protection in the transition to military self-sufficiency. One area in which he and Peng may have had a parting of the ways was over Soviet proposals for defense cooperation in 1958 and over strategy in the Taiwan Strait, both of which issues sharply focused the question of what price China would have to pay to have Soviet aid and the strategic deterrent. Among the top military leaders, then, it seems that only Lin Biao spoke for those who subordinated their professional interests entirely to Mao's programs for self-reliance.[39]

Summary

During the first half of 1958, Mao Zedong seemed to be firmly in command of Chinese domestic affairs. He had set, and had had accepted, the primacy of rapid economic growth under the "three red flags": the general line of socialist construction, people's communes, and the Great Leap Forward. He had placed economic advancement ahead of military modernization and had reasserted the party's authority in both spheres. In the face of opposition, he had set self-reliance as an overall objective, and with apparent success, had brought the military leadership to cooperate in promoting it within its own ranks and in the countryside. China was about to enter a period of rapid change marked by political stability (but potential instability) in the party center, enthusiasm and uncertainty about the economy, and a PLA weakened by economic constraints and the factionalism the army itself and strategic issues had combined to produce. Mao's expressed concern for international stability in March 1957 was even more applicable a year later: "The new social system has only just been established and requires time for its consolidation. . . . To achieve its ultimate consolidation, it is necessary not only to bring about the socialist industrialization of the country and persevere in the socialist revolution on the economic front, but to carry on constant and arduous socialist revolutionary struggles and socialist education on the political and ideological fronts. *Moreover, various contributory international factors are required.*"[40]

The International Situation

Sino-Soviet Relations

Was the Chinese action in the Taiwan Strait on August 23, 1958, undertaken with Soviet approval, acquiescence, or opposition? The place of the strait crisis in Sino-Soviet relations is an important piece in the puzzle of Chinese motives because it can help establish the external environment in which decisions were made and the nature of Chinese objectives. To develop an answer requires putting Sino-Soviet diplomacy in mid-1958, at the time of Chairman Khrushchev's surprise visit to Beijing, in the context of the two countries' relations during 1956 and 1957.

As is well known, in the early 1960s the Chinese leadership saw fit to declare that the "origin of the differences" between it and Moscow was a series of events in 1956. Khrushchev's denunciation of Stalin, the Soviet response to uprisings in Poland and Hungary, the Soviet reconciliation with Yugoslavia, and the mild Soviet reaction to the Suez crisis were sharply criticized by Beijing. Moscow's openness to a relaxation of tension with the United States in 1957, including talks on a nuclear test ban, also displeased the Chinese leadership. At one level these policy differences reflected different national-interest calculations. But at another and deeper level they reflected different domestic political and economic circumstances and, as Khrushchev's memoirs more recently attest,[41] clashes of personality and style between himself and Mao.

Yet during these two years, and for that matter into 1958, P.R.C. leaders, while expressing doubts about the wisdom of Soviet policy, continued to endorse Soviet leadership of the socialist world. If anything, the basis of Chinese disappointment with the Soviets lay in their failure to be more assertive, either in Europe or in confrontations arising out of U.S. interventions. Mao's policy of self-reliance was greatly accelerated by this disappointment. China, like the Soviet Union, would have to act in its own best interest; China would need material assistance from the U.S.S.R. for some time to come, but would have to find independent means of promoting the revolution at home and pursuing its interests abroad. In the late 1950s, China lacked the capabilities to assert its complete political and economic independence of the Soviet Union. Soviet help was very much needed— where else could it come from?—and besides, a split was then not inevitable. As Mao described the relationship at a meeting of party secretaries in January 1957: "Sino-Soviet relations have their differences at present, but they are not major differences. As a matter of fact, the two countries are drawing closer together. The Soviets do things differently than we. We have to wait and do some work."[42]

Continued cordiality in Sino-Soviet relations was not only needed by China in order to obtain Russian technology and other practical aid for the Second Five-Year Plan. It was also useful for China's protection against the United States. Domestic uncertainties of the kind described previously made China vulnerable to external pressures and interference, and Mao had decided to forgo rapid military modernization in order to concentrate on the economy. The Soviet deterrent probably loomed large in Mao's thinking at this time, and he did all he could to upgrade it. This may explain why Mao was so full of praise for the U.S.S.R. at the November 1957 Moscow conference of Communist parties, why he suggested then that "the East Wind is prevailing over the West Wind," and why he declared that in the event of a third world war, the result would be "the end of the world capitalist system." His message should be read as a verbal tactic, not a strategy for foreign-policy adventurism. Primarily, Mao wanted to use the Soviet missile and space achievements of August (the ICBM test) and October (Sputnik) 1957 to protect the Chinese socialist revolution. One way of doing so was to talk tough and try to rally the socialist camp around Moscow.

Of course, Mao's public confidence in the U.S.S.R. had an immediate practical goal: the expansion of Soviet military technological aid to China, which would accelerate China's attainment of self-reliance in defense. On

October 15, 1957, the Chinese reported years later,[43] an agreement was signed in Moscow "on new technology for national defense." The Russians thus committed themselves to go beyond the initial nuclear aid arrangements of 1955 in helping the Chinese to develop their own weapons and the missiles to deliver them.[44] In January 1958, a protocol was signed for joint research on 122 scientific and technological projects over the next five years. This agreement, too, probably included projects relevant to China's defense.

So far as the Russians were concerned, however, Sino-Soviet military cooperation had limits, and these were to be the source of increased friction in 1958. By providing China with technical nuclear help, but not with finished weapons or the facilities for producing them, Khrushchev could not only maintain a measure of Chinese dependence but could also ensure Chinese political support (as at the November 1957 Moscow conference) and hope to make the joint military arrangments he would propose in 1958, which would likewise have a restraining effect on China, all the more attractive to some Chinese leaders. Khrushchev probably accepted the inevitability of an independent Chinese nuclear capability. In the agreements of October 1957 and January 1958, like the proposals to follow, the Russians sought maximum leverage for as long as possible over China's nuclear and missile research, production, and use in foreign policy.[45]

In early 1958, before U.S. intervention in the Middle East and the "revisionist" program of the Yugoslav Communist party would add to the list of Sino-Soviet differences, the nature of their military relations became a critical and divisive issue. "In 1958," the Chinese would later charge,[46] "the leadership of the C.P.S.U. put forward unreasonable demands designed to bring China under Soviet military control. These unreasonable demands were rightly and firmly rejected by the Chinese Government." The reference is to a series of proposals by the Soviet leadership for joint military cooperation, some of which were made before May 1958, when high-ranking Chinese officials for the first time referred publicly to China's production of its own nuclear weapons.

The first set of Soviet proposals included construction of a radio station in China to facilitate communication with the Soviet Pacific fleet. According to Khrushchev's account,[47] the Chinese replied by requesting—but never using—assistance to build the station themselves. Khrushchev's memoirs do not, however, mention a more far-reaching proposal about which there is evidence:[48] that the Soviet Union station nuclear weapons on Chinese soil, undoubtedly under Russian lock and key. Beijing's rejection of this proposal may also have settled the debate between the party and the military professionals over the price to be paid for the acquisition of finished Soviet nuclear weapons.[49] For Mao, evidently, any "quick fix" to improve deterrence, such as the proposal represented, was far outweighed by the threat to Chinese sovereignty that a Soviet base or permanent presence in

China would entail. The May announcement of China's future acquisition of its own weapons signaled Mao's final answer: the P.R.C. would take the long road to military self-sufficiency.

These proposals were followed by others during Khrushchev's secret visit to Beijing (to be discussed later), including refueling and basing privileges for Soviet submarines. In and of themselves, they might not have upset the Sino-Soviet relationship as seriously as they seem to have. But in the climate of Chinese domestic affairs in which they were put forward—at a time when the PLA was being called on to sacrifice and when Mao was pressing for communalization and a breakthrough in agriculture—the Soviet proposals may well have been viewed by Mao and his colleagues as dangerous interference. Khrushchev may have been seen as not simply attempting to keep China dependent on Moscow but also trying to strengthen the professionals' position in their debate with the party center, to stir up renewed conflict within the party leadership itself, and in those ways to upset Mao's development strategy. The Chinese were surely aware of Khrushchev's hostility to the GLF—that he considered it not merely wasteful and impractical but, more fundamentally, a challenge to Soviet doctrinal primacy (with Chinese talk of being first to make the transition to communism), to the Soviet development model, and to political stability in Eastern Europe and even the Soviet frontier regions.[50] Mao would give Khrushchev no opportunity to widen the latitude the Russians already had, by virtue of their aid program, to influence the style and pace of China's economic development.

In the months preceding the Taiwan Strait crisis, then, the limits of Sino-Soviet cooperation became fairly well set. Mao accepted Soviet paramountcy in the bloc, but was assiduously working to carve out an autonomous Chinese role. Seeing the limits of Soviet defense aid, sensing the divergent needs created by two different economies, and beginning to doubt Soviet reliability in promoting China's international interest, Mao opted for a long-term program of national defense based on a leap forward in production between 1958 and 1962. In the interim years, he apparently hoped for continued Soviet technical help and a sharing of scientific, including nuclear, know-how. But by the time Khrushchev arrived in China, Mao already knew that any more substantial or direct kind of Soviet support carried an unacceptably high price tag. He let Khrushchev and his own military chiefs know this by rejecting proposals for military collaboration and opting for the development of China's own nuclear arsenal.

Sino-American Relations and the Taiwan Question

The interrelationship of Chinese military politics, the Chinese economy, and Sino-Soviet relations forms one analytical set relevant to the Taiwan Strait crisis. Another set of relations involves the P.R.C., the United States and Taiwan. Khrushchev's visit would almost certainly not have occurred had the second set not intersected the first in mid-1958. The catalyst was a new threat to China's security posed, as its leadership interpreted events, by actions of the United States and the GMD authorities in the Taiwan Strait area.

In the wake of the 1954–55 strait crisis, President Eisenhower had reversed his previous policy of "unleashing" Chiang Kai-shek's forces as a means of putting pressure on the mainland. Instead, under the December 1954 Treaty of Mutual Defense between Washington and Taibei (Taipei), Eisenhower committed the United States to the defense of Taiwan and the Pescadores. The Formosa Resolution, pushed through Congress by the administration in January 1955, had the effect of reinforcing and even enlarging that commitment. In return, Chiang agreed to withdraw forces from the Dachen (Tachen) Islands, to have a "joint understanding" with the United States before launching any "offensive military operations" from Taiwan, and not to increase forces on the offshore islands (Quemoy and Matsu) except by mutual agreement.[51] Hardly was the ink dry on these agreements than Chiang began a substantial military build-up on the offshore islands—from 30,000 men on Quemoy in September 1954 to 90,000 by August 1958. With 10,000 men on Matsu by 1958, Chiang had 100,000 troops, or one-third of his total ground forces, on the islands at the time the crisis broke out.[52]

U.S. officials apparently attempted to head off this build-up in its early stages; but their efforts, confined to trying to persuade Chiang rather than coerce him, failed. Not until the 1958 crisis had started did U.S. officials, including President Eisenhower and Secretary of State Dulles, publicly criticize the build-up as *militarily* foolish. As Dulles added, however, Washington had done nothing to prevent it; the administration had not *approved* the build-up, he said, but had "acquiesced" in it.[53] One possible reason, apart from traditional American reluctance to put pressure on a long-time anticommunist ally, was bureaucratic politics: the build-up may have been "the price which the Navy was exacting from the White House for rejection [in 1955] of its proposal to use tactical nuclear weapons in defense of the offshore islands."[54]

One can imagine that the distinction between U.S. "acquiescence" and approval of the build-up was lost on the Beijing leadership. From its vantage point, Chiang's action belied reports that he had been "released." To the contrary, it encouraged the perception that Chiang's forces would be deployed on the mainland if, as American officials were openly hoping, domestic turmoil developed in the P.R.C.[55] Secretary Dulles consistently fed that perception. In a speech in San Francisco on June 28, 1957, for instance, Dulles rejected arguments for any kind of relationship with the P.R.C. and said the United States looked to the eventual dissolution of the

Chinese and all other dictatorships. The United States, he continued, would contribute to that process: "We can confidently assume that international communism's rule of strict conformity is, in China as elsewhere, a passing and not a perpetual phase. We owe it to ourselves, our allies, and the Chinese people to do all that we can to contribute to that passing."[56]

This remark is particularly noteworthy because it came only about six weeks after the State Department had announced that Matador surface-to-surface tactical nuclear missiles would be set up on Taiwan by a U.S. Air Force unit.[57] Defense Department officials said that the Matador, with a range of 600–650 miles, would add to the U.S. "atomic punch" in the Far East. They did not say whether atomic warheads would accompany the missiles.[58] Coming on top of plans announced in Washington in January 1957 to build a new $25 million air base in central Taiwan for use by the Nationalist and American air forces,[59] the Matador action, missiles first being test-fired on May 2, 1958,[60] aroused considerable interest in Beijing, and may have caused a basic change in China's way of dealing with the Taiwan problem.

For two years prior to the U.S. decision to deploy Matador, the P.R.C. leadership had relied on the Geneva ambassadorial talks to bring about American concessions on Taiwan and stimulate direct negotiations with GMD leaders. Beijing evidently hoped that the GMD elite, fearful of a behind-the-back deal between Beijing and Washington, would accept various feelers for direct talks and would be enticed by Zhou Enlai's references, in 1956, to "peaceful means" of liberating Taiwan. Like the GMD, the P.R.C. had augmented its forces facing the Taiwan Strait after the 1954 crisis; unlike the GMD, Mao and Zhou seemed to have a serious interest in reducing tension there and in peaceably working toward a reconciliation between Taiwan and the mainland.[61]

The Americans, in more ways than one, turned off these Chinese initiatives. At the Geneva talks,[62] the Chinese delegation sought acceptance of the principle of noninterference—the United States had no right to "occupy" Chinese territory, patrol the strait, or have any security relations with Taiwan. But the U.S. delegation countered by insisting that China renounce the use of force in determining Taiwan's future and accept Taiwan's right of self-defense, meaning defense partnership with Washington and separate status for Taiwan. In Chinese eyes, it may reasonably be speculated, the Americans were looking for ways to legitimize their intervention in Taiwan while denying the possibility of a reconciliation with Beijing. The 1954 Mutual Defense Treaty, the subsequent expansion of U.S. military aid to Taiwan, the build-up of Chiang's forces on the offshore islands, official American rhetoric on China, and the Matador deployment all solidified the GMD-U.S. relationship and gave Beijing a clear picture of the remoteness of a diplomatic settlement.

American hostility toward China was further implanted by Washington's reaction to P.R.C. proposals in 1956 and 1957 to improve bilateral relations.[63] On August 6, 1956, Beijing lifted its ban on visits to China by American newspeople. But the State Department, citing six Americans still being detained in Chinese prisons, refused to validate passports. The U.S. reaction was the same when, also in August, Ambassador Wang Bingnan (Wang Ping-nan) proposed at the Geneva talks that discussion turn to U.S.-Chinese trade and cultural contacts. In response to the protests of U.S. correspondents, the State Department subsequently relaxed its stance to permit a trial run of visits by U.S. newspeople to China, but it remained adamantly opposed to visits to the U.S. by Chinese newspeople. Beijing rejected the conditional U.S. position, and when, in September, Wang proposed agreement on "an equal and reciprocal" exchange of journalists, his American counterpart, U. Alexis Johnson, turned him down immediately. With Johnson's transfer to Bangkok in December 1957, the State Department closed the door to further debate on Sino-American contacts—much to Beijing's consternation.

Beijing, in short, was receiving no signals from Washington that could give it confidence in either a diminution of the threat of attack from Taiwan in the short run or a peaceful resolution of the Taiwan issue in the long run. The signals all ran in a contrary direction, and of them, the Matador decision may have been most influential in Beijing. As Zhou Enlai said when word leaked of the decision, the United States was seeking to turn Taiwan into another Hawaii, and far from negotiating seriously on a reduction of tension in the Taiwan area, was strengthening military bases there.[64] Although it would be early summer 1958 before the P.R.C., in a more unstable international environment, made its own military adjustments to the threat posed by Taiwan, developments in 1956 and 1957 seem to have been the immediate background to them.

One can only infer from Mao's decisions on the economy, on the Soviet proposals for military cooperation, and on independent long-term nuclear development that through May 1958 he did not consider the U.S. threat from Taiwan to be serious enough to warrant renewed attention to Chinese national security. The picture to be presented in the remainder of this section and in the next is that a whole range of developments—in Taiwan, in Asia, and internationally—convinced Mao, perhaps at the end of May, that he must take direct action in the Taiwan Strait, although in a way that would not mean abandoning course domestically.

With respect first to Taiwan, in the eight months preceding the first artillery bombardments, not only did the build-up to 100,000 men continue on Quemoy and Matsu, but provocative GMD actions in and over P.R.C. territory also intensified; several visits were made by high-ranking U.S. and GMD officials to Taiwan and the offshore islands; important changes were made in the GMD armed forces; numerous "offensive" training exercises were held by those forces in the strait area; and direct U.S.-Chinese diplomacy came to a halt.

With the completion of the offshore islands build-up, Chiang Kai-shek had cleverly achieved his purpose: "to create an artificially manufactured tie between the defense of the offshore islands and the protection of Taiwan."[65] If the P.R.C. responded by attacking the islands, the Eisenhower administration would either have to defend them, and probably carry the conflict into China (which is precisely what Chiang wanted, as he made clear when the crisis was under way),[66] or let the islands fall and risk exposing Taiwan. Eisenhower and Dulles were now suffering for their policy of "acquiescence"; as the president stated in his memoirs, "To restrain Chiang from his cherished ambition of aggressive action against the mainland was not always easy."[67] Throughout the first half of 1958 the administration apparently debated ways to reassure Chiang of the U.S. commitment to Taiwan without specifically including defense of Quemoy and Matsu. But on the very day the bombardments began, August 23, the commitment to the offshore islands was stated with little ambiguity, along with a warning to Beijing that "attacking and seeking to conquer these islands . . . could not be considered or held to a 'limited operation.' "[68]

Washington had become further enmeshed in Taibei's web. Instead of attempting to reverse the build-up, it had again condoned it. More than that, the administration had failed to discourage—in fact, in public statements seemed to encourage—the kinds of provocative actions by Chiang's forces that might well lead to the confrontation with Beijing it supposedly did not want. These actions, most of which were reported as anticommunist retaliations in the Taibei *Central Daily News* (the official GMD organ), included military exercises on the offshore islands and in Taiwan by the three services, high-level inspection tours and visits, propaganda leaflet drops over the P.R.C. coastal provinces, sabotage missions along the coast by GMD agents, reconnaissance overflights of P.R.C. territory, and air and naval clashes. The sources and dates of this information, as well as brief descriptions, are provided in Table 1.

Whatever American officials may have tried to do privately to discourage these activities, publicly they gave the strong impression of approving their purpose. For example, the commander of the U.S.-Taiwan Defense Command, General Doyle, told an audience of Taiwan naval officers in early July 1958: "The task you bear of counterattacking the mainland is absolutely certain to succeed—there is no need to have the slightest doubt—because your training has reached the highest standards. Add to that your admirable spirit and awesome determination—these are the conditions for the success of China's [that is, Taiwan's] new navy."[69] Probably more ominous from Beijing's viewpoint was the State Department's memorandum

Table 1. Summary of Reported Guomindang Military Activity in the Taiwan
Strait Area, January–July 1958

Source/Date	Activity
CDN, Jan. 10	Military exercise in the Pescadores
CDN, Feb. 8	"Full-scale" military exercise for one week in Matsu chain
Fujian ribao, Mar. 6 (*SCMP* 1788)	Capture of four Chiang agents who are named and who had mission of collecting military information; newspaper says such sabotage has been going on "constantly" in past year and represents "only a portion of similar cases we have smashed."
NYT, Mar. 15	Visit by Dulles to confer with Chiang
CDN, Apr. 9	GMD defense minister and U.S. advisers inspect Matsu
CDN, Apr. 11	Military exercise by Pescadores Garrison Command
CDN, Apr. 17	Joint military exercise by army, navy, air force on Matsu for first time, attended by deputy cmdr. of U.S. Military Assistance Command
CDN, Apr. 28	GMD deputy cmdr. of navy leads inspection tour of Quemoy
CDN, May 1	GMD defense minister inspects Matsu islands
CDN, June 1	Military exercise by naval headquarters at a southern base for atomic defense
CDN, June 2	Armed clashes in Matsu Strait reported
CDN, June 4	GMD defense minister inspects Matsu defenses
CDN, June 8	Military exercise in Taiwan for defense against special weapons
CDN, June 12	Naval battle in Matsu Strait reported
NCNA, Fuzhou (Foochow), June 18 (*SCMP* 1798)	One of two GMD RF-84 aircraft shot down over Fujian (Fukien)
CDN, June 19	GMD forces on Matsu reportedly repulse P.R.C. gunboats

of August 11, 1958, on the reasons for U.S. nonrecognition of the P.R.C.[70] That policy, according to the memorandum, "keeps alive the hopes of those Chinese who are determined eventually to free their country of Communist rule." Although "there is no reason to believe that the Chinese Communist regime is on the verge of collapse," neither is there "reason to accept its present rule in mainland China as permanent." There are signs of "dissatisfaction and unrest" that support the U.S. view "that communism's rule in China is not permanent and that it one day will pass. By withholding diplomatic recognition from Peiping it seeks to hasten that passing."

As part of their strategy of manufacturing a crisis, GMD officials, from January 1958 on, frequently cited war preparations in the mainland's coastal provinces to justify their own harassment, sabotage, and military build-ups. Yet as a few writers have noted,[71] not until July was there an increase in the level of military activity in Fujian (Fukien), which in our view was clearly a response to the GMD actions. That is why, in early

Source/Date	Activity
CDN, June 22	GMD forces on Matsu reportedly again clash with P.R.C. gunboats
CDN, June 23	Third report of naval battle off Matsu
CDN, June 24	Armed clash off Fujian coast reported
CDN, June 25	GMD defense minister inspects Matsu; naval units have entered state of war preparedness
CDN, July 4	Propaganda leaflets dropped over Guangdong (Kwang-tung) and Fujian under heavy artillery fire
CDN, July 5	Propaganda leaflets dropped over Guangdong and Guangxi (Kwangsi)
NCNA, Guangzhou (Canton), July 6 *(SCMP* 1811)	Seven GMD agents sentenced to death for subversion in Guangdong
Dagong bao, July 7 *(SCMP* 1811)	Four more GMD agents arrested in Guangdong
CDN, July 7	U.S. assistant secretary of army visits Taiwan
CDN, July 8	Mobilization exercises completed in southern Taiwan following those in north
CDN, July 14	Visit to Taiwan of U.S. cmdr., Seventh Fleet
CDN, July 18	All military leaves in Taiwan canceled
CDN, July 20	A number of GMD jets flown to Quemoy to carry out patrols
NYT, July 26	GMD six-day air defense exercise
NCNA, Guangzhou (Canton), July 29 *(SCMP* 1825)	P.R.C. air force reports shooting down two of four RF-84's, as well as recent sighting of other RF-84's over Fujian
NCNA, Beijing (Peking) broadcasts, July 31	Three GMD agents captured after being airdropped into China

Abbreviations: *CDN (Central Daily News,* Taibei); *NYT (New York Times);* NCNA (New China News Agency, Beijing); *SCMP (Survey of China Mainland Press,* Hong Kong).

March, General Doyle told reporters in Taiwan that there were no significant changes in Chinese Communist military activities across the strait. He denied a U.S. newspaper report that the P.R.C. was preparing to launch a full-scale invasion of Taiwan in June.[72] And that is also why Eisenhower, in his memoirs, wrote: "The first definite word that the Chinese Communists might again try to seize the offshore islands came to me through intelligence sources on *the 6th of August.* "[73] The belligerency of GMD rhetoric about returning to the mainland, which accompanied the accelerating provocations, likewise preceded emphasis in Beijing's propaganda on "liberating Taiwan." The *Central Daily News* carried officials' statements about "counterattacking" from January 1958 onward; the "liberate Taiwan" campaign of rallies and speeches lasted for two weeks in the latter half of July—again, apparently, in response to Chiang's militant actions and, by that time, U.S. intervention in Lebanon and the break-off of the Geneva ambassadorial talks between the P.R.C. and the United States.

Another kind of threatening signal from Taiwan involved military organizational changes. In 1958 and before the crisis, a program called "Forward Look" was instituted "to increase the firepower, the mobility, and the logistic support of the [GMD] ground forces" and "to make the army an effective fighting force in a nuclear war." The entire army was reorganized into smaller, more independent units.[74] In the same period, the American military command on Taiwan also was streamlined. The Taiwan Defense Command and the Military Assistance Command were reorganized into the U.S.-Taiwan Defense Assistance Command.[75] Both changes were duly noted in the Beijing press.

As mentioned previously, the Matador missiles on Taiwan were test-fired on May 2, 1958. General Doyle reportedly told a Taibei press conference in January that the missiles would be used in retaliation for a Chinese communist attack in the strait area. The same report stated that although Doyle had declined to say whether or not the missiles already had nuclear warheads, "observers" believed the warheads were either on Taiwan or on nearby Okinawa.[76] During the crisis, as the Eisenhower administration made certain to publicize, eight-inch atomic howitzers were moved to Quemoy, and U.S. aircraft carriers with atomic warheads aboard were deployed in the Taiwan Strait. Beijing's strategists, one may surmise, had to calculate before the crisis that the weapons were already there.

Beijing portrayed all these military developments in alarming terms, especially when the Middle East crisis over Iraq and Lebanon began in July. Prior to that period, the Chinese press and various officials had condemned the deployment of the Matador missiles, which was said to denote the presence of nuclear weapons on Taiwan.[77] It was linked in a number of articles[78] to other U.S. military moves in the region, such as training exercises for South Korean forces using nuclear artillery; U.S. missile-basing arrangements with Japan, Korea, and other countries; and a naval exercise by SEATO forces in the South China Sea. When the reorganization of the U.S. command on Taiwan was announced, the Chinese media interpreted it as bringing Chiang's forces more firmly under U.S. control—which was considered to be more rather than less threatening in light of the expansion of U.S. missile, air, and naval facilities there and the reorganization of the Nationalist army into five "atomic divisions."[79]

By July the coloration of these perceptions distinctly darkened. One reason almost certainly was the breakdown of the ambassadorial talks. When Ambassador Johnson was transferred to Bangkok, he was not replaced by anyone of ambassadorial rank. Edwin Martin became acting head of the delegation. The Chinese claimed this was a violation of the agreement that had established the talks.[80] On June 30 the P.R.C., in a lengthy statement, linked the U.S. action to its Taiwan policy and its negative attitude toward Chinese proposals for improving bilateral relations. For three years, the statement charged, the United States had used the talks to cover up its intervention in Taiwan and its "two-China" policy. Like other Chinese commentaries on military developments, this one did not threaten direct action to liberate Taiwan. It demanded, rather, that Washington send a delegate of ambassadorial rank to Geneva within fifteen days. "Otherwise, the Chinese Government cannot but recognize that the United States has already determined to break up the Sino-U.S. ambassadorial talks."[81]

Dulles replied at a press conference on July 1 that the United States would be proposing resumption of the talks at a new site, Warsaw, with Ambassador Jacob Beam as chief delegate. No attempt was made to inform Wang Bingnan of the proposal until July 28, however, well after the fifteen-day deadline had passed. Wang apparently never did accept a copy of the proposal; nor did he respond to Beam's attempt, on August 4, to arrange a meeting with him in Warsaw.[82] A spokesman for the Chinese Ministry of Foreign Affairs had rejected the proposal on July 2, asserting that Dulles could not with one hand violate the ground rules for the talks and with the other hand insist on a change of venue.[83] But by later in the month, Beijing may have interpreted the American delay as signifying lack of interest in responding substantively to Chinese concerns about U.S. policy in the Taiwan Strait area. Indeed, it is possible that Dulles deliberately ordered an attempt to deliver his proposal held up for two weeks beyond the Chinese deadline to enhance the chance that Beijing would *not* accept it. And if this is the case, Dulles was right, for by then Mao's thoughts had turned to direct action and the Khrushchev visit. The U.S.-Chinese talks did not resume until September 15.

The Impact of Events in Asia and the Middle East

The second major reason for the heightened Chinese sense of threat was the U.S. intervention in Lebanon, which occurred amid a number of other developments in Asia that were unfavorable to Beijing's interests. The leadership's perception, to judge from statements in the media, was that these events formed a pattern of revived American aggressiveness.

Among the most important of these was the American support given to the anti-Sukarno rebellion of dissident military officers in Sumatra. The strong Chinese reaction was surely due as much to the fact that Taiwan-based CIA aircraft were used in the operation as to the American involvement in an attempted overthrow of a government.[84] The coordination of U.S.-GMD activities was also under way in Tibet. Zhou and the Chinese government charged during early 1958—and there is evidence to confirm the charge[85]—that U.S. and GMD agents, working with Tibetan émigrés who were given aid and comfort in India, sought to stimulate armed revolt in Tibet. Rebellions had been occurring in eastern Tibet since early 1956, and Chinese officials, deeply concerned about foreign involvement, had frequently complained to the Indian government about them. By August 1958, Chinese sensitivities on the Tibetan matter were no doubt especially acute because an appeal to the United Nations to bring about the removal of Chinese troops from Tibet had been issued from Kalimpong, the main resistance base in India, by rebel delegates and "every Tibetan official of note in India."[86]

Probably also relevant to Chinese perceptions in this period were the start of construction of U.S. missile bases in Korea and the introduction of nuclear weapons there; signs of potential American intervention in Laos (which came to pass) to upset the Vientiane agreements for the political and military integration of the Pathet Lao; and difficulties with the Kishi government in Japan because of the Nagasaki flag incident, which led to suspension of Japanese-Chinese trade relations and to close political and military collaboration between Tokyo and Washington. Citing some of these developments, a resolution at the close of the Eighth National Party Congress, second session, on May 23, 1958, declared:

> We should be alert. U.S. imperialism and the imperialist cliques headed by the U.S. still are actively making war threats, preparing for a new war, intensifying their political, economic, and cultural aggression against many Asian, African, and Latin American countries, destroying the domestic unity of these countries, to the point of directly using military force to suppress the national liberation movements. Our task is to unite all peaceloving forces in the world to protect peace and smash the war plans of the imperialist aggressor clique headed by the United States.[87]

The U.S. intervention in Lebanon may have convinced Mao and his colleagues that the GMD's activities in the Taiwan Strait and elsewhere in Asia, far from being isolated events, were part of a pattern of anticommunist pressure engineered from Washington. For at least a month before the U.S. Marines landed in Beirut, the Chinese press had correctly warned of the drift toward direct intervention. When it came, Beijing reacted strongly. It called the action "an outrageous provocation," a "naked act of aggression," and a threat to world peace.[88] Demonstrations were reported throughout China. In a lengthy editorial on July 17, *People's Daily* urged that "all governments in favor of peace act in unison" to compel U.S. withdrawal from Lebanon; otherwise, "a new world war would be unavoidable." In recalling how the Anglo-French–Israeli invasion of Suez had been halted, Beijing seemed to be demanding that Moscow take the lead—which it did not, and which may have been one of the reasons for Khrushchev's visit.[89]

Both before and, with greater precision, after the Taiwan Strait crisis had begun, numerous Chinese statements linked the U.S. intervention in Lebanon to an increased threat from Taiwan. For example, at the same time that the U.S. was preparing to intervene in the Middle East, said a commentator in early August,[90] "the United States again directed the Chiang Kai-shek clique to intensify the tense situation in the Taiwan area and harass and provoke the China mainland. . . . Peace is indivisible. U.S. armed aggression against Middle East nations, like the armed occupation of China's territory of Taiwan, is part of its overall plan of imperialist aggression." Zhou Enlai, speaking about the strait crisis on September 6, said:

> Supported by the United States, the Chiang Kai-shek clique has for long been using coastal islands such as Quemoy . . . and Matsu . . . as advance bases for conducting all sorts of harassing and disruptive activities against the Chinese mainland. Recently, since the United States launched armed intervention against the Arab states, the harassing and disruptive activities of the Chiang Kai-shek clique against the Chinese mainland have become more unbridled. The Chinese government has every right to deal resolute blows and take necessary military action against Chiang Kai-shek's troops entrenched on the coastal islands. . . . The Chinese people's determination to liberate their own territory of Taiwan and the Penghu Islands is unshakable. In particular the Chinese people cannot tolerate the presence in their inland waters along the mainland of an immediate threat posed by such coastal islands as Quemoy and Matsu.[91]

A *People's Daily* editorial on September 7 similarly recited the recent series of GMD harassments and attacks and added:

> Since the U.S. launched a war of aggression in the Middle East, the Chiang Kai-shek clique, with U.S. support, has intensified its harassing activities from Quemoy, Matsu, and other coastal islands, and moreover has repeatedly shouted about "opportunely speeding up preparations for counterattacking the mainland." As early as over a month before the PLA sternly warned the traitor Chiang army on Quemoy, the Chiang Kai-shek clique cancelled leaves for officers and men and actively prepared for war. The Chiang Kai-shek clique intensified its surprise air attacks on the mainland and the activities of its ships against coastal areas. Precisely for these reasons, the Chinese PLA dealt Chiang's forces occupying the coastal islands serious blows. This was entirely within the province of the Chinese government's internal affairs.

Statements such as these can be matched with more frequent reports in the Chinese press from late July to mid-August citing particular cases of air and ground infiltrations by GMD forces. The acute sensitivity of the leadership to GMD harassments at this time is revealed in a *People's Daily* article in August that warned of the need for added vigilance. Increasing tensions in the Middle East were related to excited talk from Taiwan of "counterattacking," the article said. And, it continued, "experience tells us that whenever there is any unrest in the international situation the remnant counter-revolutionaries at home are likely to cause disturbances and intensify sabotage and some of them may even want to support from within

the Chiang Kai-s[h]ek group in their so-called 'offensive against the mainland.'"[92]

Another point that is consistent with the Lebanon connection, with Zhou
Enlai's above-quoted statement, with the September 7 editorial, and with
other Chinese analyses explaining P.R.C. policy is that *the bombardment
of the offshore islands was almost always described as punitive and
retaliatory*, not as the first step in Taiwan's liberation.[93] Accordingly, the
first shots fired in the crisis were reported by *People's Daily* on August 24,
in two lines, as having been directed at a GMD troop ship bound for
Quemoy. Supply vessels and GMD troops were the only targets of PLA
artillery for the first three weeks of the crisis.[94] The U.S. State Department
made much of a mainland broadcast to the Quemoy garrison on August 28
which said that the PLA "has determined to liberate Taiwan ... as well as
the offshore islands, and the landing on Quemoy is imminent," and which
urged the soldiers there to surrender or revolt.[95] Over the next several days,
however, this and similar ultimata were not broadcast by Radio Beijing or
the New China News Agency, but were beamed only to the offshore islands
or to Taiwan. Even Pentagon sources were reported to believe that, on
military grounds, the bombardments could not be considered the prelude to
an attack on the offshore islands.[96] The logistical nature of the P.R.C.'s
operation in the Taiwan Strait—including its failure to amass sufficient
troops to attempt to seize the islands, its lack of enough landing craft to cross
the strait, its choice of a season when bad weather and rough seas were
about to start, and its refrainment from aerial bombardment—was such as
to make its purpose indisputably defensive.[97]

The State of the World, from Beijing, in Mid-1958

Premier Khrushchev would arrive in Beijing on July 31 to find the
Chinese Politburo in basic accord about a mounting American threat to the
P.R.C. from Taiwan. The incidence of GMD harassments and probes had
increased, but the danger was greater because such actions now seemed tied
in with a growing American aggressiveness world-wide. Events in Lebanon
were particularly salient to the Chinese world view, since they involved
direct U.S. intervention and did not lead to any meaningful Soviet
counteraction. And here is where the Chinese and Soviet positions on the
meaning of Sputnik diverged: Beijing thought Sputnik would enhance the
ability of the socialist world to defend its interests against imperialist
encroachments, such as in the Middle East, whereas Moscow decided it
could be best exploited in negotiating conditions for détente. In light of the
emerging threat in the Taiwan Strait, Chinese leaders surely were ponder-
ing the reliability of Soviet protection of China's domestic revolution: How
much was Sputnik worth now?

Mao's thinking was defensive; he wanted to protect a socialist revolution that was about to enter a new stage, and not to create new international situations of stress. Before Lebanon, the dominant theme of his and other high-level Chinese analyses of world politics in 1958 was that the socialist camp was getting stronger and the Western camp weaker, and that thus there was reason for optimism that the revolution could proceed with minimal disturbance from outside. One sees this line of thought, for instance, in Zhou's foreign-policy report to the National People's Congress in February,[98] in Liu Shaoqi's work report to the Eighth Party Congress, second session, in May,[99] and in Mao's speech to the same congress.[100] "Imperialism is squabbling within itself," said Chairman Mao; "it is suppressing Indonesia, Lebanon, and Latin America and fighting over Algeria." He urged his colleagues not to become downcast over this "temporary darkness," because "between war and peace, the possibility of peace is greater." The socialist camp and its allies were increasing in strength while there was instability in the West; "the working class, a part of the bourgeoisie, and the American people do not want war." Like Liu, however, Mao said there was need for alertness because "there is also the possibility of war. There are maniacs, and imperialism wants to extricate itself from economic crises."[101] The way to get Dulles's respect, Mao remarked in another speech to the May congress, was through economic growth; he said nothing that would suggest an adventuristic foreign policy to test American strength.[102]

This same essential optimism evidently carried over into Chinese strategic estimates.[103] Again, there seemed to be a basic disagreement between the General Staff, headed by Su Yu, and the Defense Ministry, under Peng Dehuai. The General Staff pointed to the "frenzied [U.S.] preparations for war," and to the possibility of a nuclear first strike, in making its case for rapid modernization. The Defense Ministry's view prevailed in the aftermath of the Russian ICBM and Sputnik achievements. America's ability to launch an all-out war was now virtually eliminated, this view held, and U.S. involvement in a local war would be, if not less likely than before, less effective and more difficult to carry out. The Soviet deterrent had not neutralized American power, but it had placed new limitations on it.

One may readily imagine, from the foregoing analysis, that the U.S. intervention in Indonesia and then in Lebanon, and the absence of a Soviet reply to both, significantly deflated China's—including the Defense Ministry's—confidence about the future. A major foreign-policy analysis that appeared in the August 16 issue of *Red Flag,* the party journal, under the authoritative pseudonym of Yu Zhaoli (Yü Chao-li), supports this speculation. The tone of the analysis is thoroughly defensive, in marked contrast to the optimism that had prevailed earlier in the year. While the article extols Soviet strength, its primary theme is how weakness ("the forces of the new") can overcome strength ("the forces of decay")—a variant of Mao's concept, which Yu discusses, that "all reactionaries are paper tigers." The United States is portrayed as being "isolated as never before," "over-extended," and "vulnerable at many points." But it is still said to be carrying out aggression everywhere and building military bases around the world. Confidence is expressed in the capacity of the socialist states to prevent war; "but we must keep a watchful eye on the atomic war maniacs." In two places there are references that could be taken, out of context, to signify foreign-policy toughness—in the quotation "War is like fire; if you do not quench it, you will get burned yourself," and in the statement "There is only one way to deal with madmen—to expose and fight them." But read as a whole, Yu Zhaoli's article is an argument for watchfulness, not for adventurism. It bespeaks insecurity, which we suggest was the predominant feeling of the Chinese Politburo as Khrushchev arrived.

The Taiwan Strait Decision

Khrushchev in Beijing

Khrushchev apparently understood the threat to China's security from Taiwan.[104] But of greater importance to the Soviet leader were international interests in the Middle East and in Berlin; moreover, Khrushchev realized that the United States, if it were squarely behind the GMD's operations, would be very difficult to deter because of the superior military power it could introduce in the Taiwan Strait area.[105] Whether because he had some inkling of a forthcoming Chinese military initiative in the strait or because of a more general determination to restrain Mao from acting irresponsibly and embroiling the U.S.S.R. in a confrontation with the United States elsewhere in the world, Khrushchev came to Beijing with new proposals for military cooperation.

Khrushchev's memoirs[106] and statements by Mao[107] concur on two points about the nature of the meeting between the two leaders: (1) Khrushchev was alarmed by China's strong reaction to his previous proposals and wanted to present his latest ideas personally; and (2) the Taiwan Strait situation per se was not discussed. The Soviet chairman put forward what the Chinese later termed "unreasonable demands designed to bring China under Soviet military control."[108] These involved a request that Soviet submarines be permitted to refuel in Chinese ports, that Soviet sailors be granted shore leave in China, and that submarines of both countries—presumably when the Chinese possessed them—be allowed reciprocal use of each other's ports.[109] (Either then or during the crisis, the

U.S.S.R. also offered to station interceptor squadrons in China to assist in China's defense against possible attack from Taiwan.)[110] It is difficult to conceive of Khrushchev making these new requests, which were more far-reaching than those Mao had previously rejected, unless he had an additional bargaining card. And that card must have been the Soviet Politburo's evaluation that the Chinese urgently desired a show of Russian support of the P.R.C.'s security.

The Russians were correct if that was their evaluation; but they were incorrect to assume that Mao would pay a high price for the Soviet deterrent. Mao interpreted Khrushchev's latest offers in the same way he had the others; they meant control over Chinese policy, not support of it, because they entailed an attempt "to block the China seacoast, to launch a joint fleet in China to dominate the coastal area, and to blockade us."[111] Perhaps Mao considered that Khrushchev was trying to play a role similar to Eisenhower's with Chiang: Khrushchev would have the leverage to decide whether or not Mao should be "leashed" or "unleashed."

We suggest, therefore, that the August 3 communiqué issued at the end of Khrushchev's visit, which made no mention of Taiwan, as well as subsequent public Soviet statements on the strait crisis during its initial and most critical stage (from August 23 to September 6), *gave Mao the extremely limited support he knew was all he could expect in the absence of concessions to the Soviet interest in a military presence in China.* Even though Taiwan was not on their agenda, there could have been no misunderstanding that China was on its own in the event of trouble with the United States. The August 3 communiqué contained only a vague warning that "if the war maniacs of imperialism dare to impose war on the world's people all the nations and peoples that love peace and love freedom will closely unite." It described Sino-Soviet relations as harmonious and closely cooperative, and as proceeding with "complete equality and comradely mutual help."[112] Once the artillery bombardments began, the Soviet leadership, while expressing support for China's claims to Taiwan and the offshore islands, minimized the seriousness of the crisis ("there is no cloud from which thunder could roll," said Khrushchev on August 24) and avoided making firm commitments to China in the event it came under attack.[113]

As has been widely noted, it was only after Zhou Enlai, on September 6, had picked up the American offer of July 28 to resume the ambassadorial talks at Warsaw that Chairman Khrushchev's rhetoric in defense of China became bold. Before September 6 the Soviet leadership would say only that "whoever attempts to use an offensive to threaten the PRC should not forget that he is also threatening the Soviet Union."[114] But on September 7 Khrushchev warned Eisenhower: "An attack on the Chinese People's Republic, which is a great ally, friend, and neighbor of our country, is an attack on the Soviet Union."[115] During and immediately after the crisis, various Chinese officials expressed warm thanks for Soviet help. But when the rift became public during the polemical exchanges of 1963, the P.R.C. leadership condemned Soviet behavior in the crisis, claiming that the U.S.S.R. had come to China's defense only when it was clear that "there was no possibility that a nuclear war would break out and no need for the Soviet Union to support China with its nuclear weapons."[116] Aside from the probability that there was no danger of a nuclear war before September 6, the analysis here suggests that Mao knew well in advance of the crisis what he could and could not expect from the U.S.S.R., and clearly the Soviet nuclear umbrella was one kind of support Mao decided he would rather do without.

There is now evidence, however, that Mao's way of dealing with Khrushchev during his visit was not unanimously endorsed within the Politburo. At least one of Mao's colleagues, Peng Dehuai, reportedly disagreed. According to a Red Guard document:

> In 195[8], traitor Peng Teh-huai worked in collusion with a foreign country. In that year, bald-headed Khrushchev suddenly came to China without being invited in the vain hope to control us. He put forward what he called "united action," and traitor Peng Teh-huai had played a lot of monkey tricks in this connection. Their conspiracy was at once pierced by Chairman Mao and rejected. After bald-headed Khrushchev left, Chairman Mao ordered the shelling of Quemoy. This was a forceful reply to Soviet revisionism, and traitor Peng Teh-huai was very dissatisfied over this. Chairman Mao personally directed this important military action, but traitor Peng Teh-huai stealthily slipped away on the ground of making an inspection tour.[117]

What was the basis of Peng's disagreement? Considering his stated and alleged perspective—his confidence in the Soviet deterrent, his willingness to put off rapid military modernization, and his conservative, Soviet-style approach to military organization—Peng was unlikely to favor responding to an external threat unless he had solid assurances of Soviet backing. Khrushchev's "united action" proposals probably appealed to Peng—first, because they afforded China deterrent coverage; second, because they would restore needed harmony in Sino-Soviet relations, which would have long-term benefit for China's economy and national defense; third, because the military would have continued access to the kind of technology that he realized Mao's economic program would not allow the PLA to have for years to come.

Peng's argument may therefore have been that China could not have guns and butter. If the economy had top priority, he was saying to Mao, China could not risk a direct confrontation with the United States. The Politburo should either accept Khrushchev's proposals or not challenge

Taiwan militarily. Rejecting them and bombarding the GMD's military supply lines and fortifications would play into Chiang's hands and court conflict with the "war maniacs" in Washington at a time of dissension and unpreparedness in the PLA, overriding economic concerns, and increasing distance from Moscow. Conceivably, Peng's evaluation of the external threat was appreciably lower than Chairman Mao's.[118]

Mao's rejoinder, we may suppose, was that the time had arrived for taking direct action to counter the imperialist threat; otherwise, it would grow beyond control.[119] An appropriately cautious use of force in the Taiwain Strait would not require significant Soviet support, would signal that China's interest was in deflecting a threat and not in generating an international crisis, and could be pursued without taking resources away from economic mobilization. Sino-Soviet relations were already strained because of Chinese rejections of earlier Soviet proposals, differences in foreign policy, and the Great Leap strategy, Mao may have said. To ease those relations at the cost of increasing dependency on the Soviet Union was, to him, unacceptable militarily, politically, and economically.

China's Motives and Objectives

Mao's strategy in the Taiwan Strait was not a test, a demonstration, or an external adventure for internal manipulation. Consequences must always be distinguished from intentions. Mao's strategy clearly had repercussions in Sino-Soviet and Sino-American relations and in the Chinese economy and politics. But a comprehensive look at the international and domestic settings of the August 23 action suggests that Mao's first concern was to deflect a dangerous and growing threat to China's security at a time of rapid domestic change and military weakness. He tried to do this with a limited, low-risk preemptive move against the offshore islands in order to bring the Americans to their senses about their ally on Taiwan.

Mao had no need to "test" the Soviet leadership's reliability; nor could he expect to demonstrate to that leadership that the United States was indeed a paper tiger. Soviet *un*reliability and U.S. strength and aggressiveness were already well entrenched in Mao's and the Politburo's thinking by August 1958. As has been proposed, Mao knew the limits of Soviet support and developed his strategy within them. He was also acutely aware of American capabilities and, particularly after Lebanon, of the potential for direct American intervention abroad. Both before the strait crisis and after,[120] he and other high-level commentators stressed the standard dictum that the United States was a paper tiger to be strategically despised *but tactically respected*—in the long run, not to challenge imperialistic behavior would be viewed as passiveness, but in particular cases, not to take the enemy's strength seriously would be labeled adventurism. China's involvement in the strait crisis was undertaken with these revolutionary dialectics in mind; it had the twin effects of *clarifying* the nature of both the main enemy and the number one friend.

Mao was not betrayed by the U.S.S.R. He and Khrushchev, to judge from the Soviet leader's memoirs, do not seem to have disagreed over strategy. Each knew what to expect from the other, so that the Chinese charge in 1963 of belated Soviet deterrent help does not ring true. But the other Chinese charges of Soviet efforts in 1958 to hamstring Chinese foreign policy and "blockade" China are credible. And for that reason, the Taiwan Strait crisis *was* a watershed in Sino-Soviet relations. For Mao, it had the desirable outcome of showing that the Chinese leadership could conduct crisis diplomacy independently of the U.S.S.R. But he learned anew that the Soviet Union was a rival and a hard bargainer, not an ally, and that China would have to be as self-reliant internationally as it was seeking to become economically and militarily on the home front. The crucial outcome of the Taiwan Strait crisis may therefore be that it helped shorten the timetable of Sino-Soviet cooperation, eventuating in Soviet abrogation of the October 1957 agreement in June 1959 and the withdrawal of all technical Soviet assistance in 1960.

As for the Americans, Mao's strategy indicates that he took their strength and willfulness into account and sought to demonstrate Chinese concern while minimizing the risk of a direct confrontation. Mao had to avoid a military initiative that would give the Americans a *casus belli* or that would enable Chiang to manipulate them into a broader commitment to his "counterattack" ambitions. Yet how could a preemptive move in the Taiwan Strait not further complicate Mao's problem? One possible source of his apparent confidence was the knowledge, gained from numerous Western accounts, that there had been disagreement within the Eisenhower administration in 1954 and 1955 over defense of the offshore islands. Secondly, Mao could feel perfectly justified in responding with measured force to Taiwan and U.S. provocations—a typical "tit-for-tat" action, as John Service has reminded us. That may explain Mao's confession of surprise, shortly after the crisis began, that "firing a few shots at Quemoy and Matsu" would stir up such a world-wide storm. And since public outrage was directed mainly at the United States, the Taiwan Strait action only proved again that "tense situations" can be beneficial to China.[121]

Rather than demonstrate American vulnerability in the Taiwan Strait area, China's actions seemed to acknowledge the overpowering U.S. position there[122] and to signal, among other things, that Mao wanted a reduction of tensions. China's cessation of the shelling of Quemoy on September 5 and Zhou Enlai's announcement on September 6 that the P.R.C. wished to resume the ambassadorial talks are usually interpreted as an admission that the Chinese blockade had failed and as a surrender of the game in the face of superior power. But a better explanation, in line with the thesis put forward here that Mao's strategy was punitive and preemptive in nature, may be that resumption of the talks was one of Mao's objectives. His strategy, which was calculated to alert, not threaten, the Americans, left room for a renewal of bargaining. It was Dulles's action, after all, that had led to suspension of the talks and added to the precrisis climate of diplomatic deadlock and U.S. hostility. Now, if the United States could be persuaded of the necessity of discussing Taiwan and of reconsidering its support of the GMD, the Chinese leadership would register an important achievement.

A key Chinese objective, then, was to channel perceived U.S. aggressiveness back into the diplomatic arena. Achieving that objective would not only deflect an immediate security threat but would also erode the U.S.-GMD relationship—first, because it would mean the failure of Chiang's efforts to bring about a U.S.-P.R.C. confrontation; second, because it would again arouse Chiang's concern about a behind-the-back deal at Taiwan's expense. But Chinese efforts were not limited to exerting pressure on the Taiwan leadership indirectly.

Another important P.R.C. objective seems to have been, in Tang Tsou's words, "to pry the Nationalists from the United States."[123] This objective can be surmised from P.R.C. messages to Taiwan and from the PLA orders broadcast by Peng Dehuai in October 1958.[124] Clearly distinguishing the Chinese civil war from the question of American involvement in Chinese affairs, Peng expressed hope for a peaceful settlement among the Chinese in order to create one China. He recalled Zhou's proposals of a few years earlier. The artillery bombardments, Peng said in his first message on October 6, were "of a punitive nature . . . just to call your attention" to the provocative actions taken against the mainland. The stopping and starting of the bombardments in October—they were suspended for one week on October 6, for two weeks on October 13, and on alternate days beginning October 25—were explained as lenient treatment in the hope of encouraging direct talks. Comrades on Taiwan were warned of the day "when the Americans will leave you in the lurch." Dulles first wanted to "isolate" Taiwan and then "place Taiwan under trusteeship." The Americans had begun to treat the P.R.C. as a reality, giving Taiwan "the title of a small China" and thus moving closer to realization of a two-China policy.

Mao needed to work at both ends of the U.S.-Taiwan alliance. Long before the crisis, there had been American proposals for a cease-fire in the strait. Beijing had always rejected them because they implied acceptance of a separate Taiwan tied to the United States. "Two-Chinas" preoccupied Beijing by 1958, abetted by increasing U.S. contributions to Taiwan's "security"—for example, the Matador. Not surprisingly, the Politburo flatly and instantly rejected Dulles's statement at a September 30 news conference[125] that "if there were a cease-fire in the [strait] area which seemed to be reasonably dependable, I think it would be foolish to keep [Nationalist] forces on these [offshore] islands." Mao had not been and would not be interested in such a deal; China's security from American threat would not be solved by negotiating for Taiwan's continuation under American tutelage. The appeals to "Taiwan's compatriots" in the wake of the punitive bombardments were Mao's alternative method of weakening Taiwan's ties to the American military system.

In like manner, Mao also seemed concerned not to disturb Quemoy's status as a part of Taiwan. Just as a cease-fire in the strait would have promoted American plans for a separate Taiwan (an alternative China), so Chinese seizure of the offshore islands would have strengthened that prospect. As Robert W. Barnett has written, "Before, during and after the Quemoy crisis, Mao and Chiang looked upon that island alike: the linchpin that made Quemoy and Taiwan parts of One China."[126] Strategically, Mao and Chiang in 1958 had much in common: both avoided breaking the link between the offshore islands and Taiwan; both ultimately had political objectives in the crisis; and both believed in the value of a GMD *presence* on the islands in order to perpetuate Taiwan's link to them and hence the reality of one China. The kind of trade Dulles implied on September 30 was doubly unacceptable because it held out the prospect of a Nationalist withdrawal from the islands which, when coupled with a cease-fire in the strait, would have strengthened the two-China policy.

There are several indications that Chinese policy was designed to reduce the threat posed by the increased GMD strength on the offshore islands without seeing them abandoned. As has already been mentioned, the Chinese neglected various military moves that would have signaled an intention to seize the islands. The artillery fire was directed at the sources of a potential threat to the mainland, and its punitive purpose was explicitly stated. These actions contradicted the initial broadcast to Quemoy announcing an imminent landing and urging the garrison to surrender. But it remained for Peng Dehuai, in his October messages, to make this Chinese motive crystal clear. On October 13 he said that the shelling of Quemoy had been halted in order "to enable our compatriots on Quemoy, both military and civilian, to get sufficient supplies, including food and military equipment, *to strengthen their entrenchment.*" And on October 25, Peng announced there would be no shelling on even-numbered days so that all the islands may "get sufficient supplies, including food, vegetables, edible oils, fuels and military equipment, to *facilitate your entrenchment for a long time to come.* If you are short of anything, just say so and we will give it to you" (italics added).[127]

Sometime after the crisis had passed, Khrushchev recalled having asked Mao why the Chinese stopped short of taking over the offshore islands and in that way removing the threat. Mao's reported answer perplexed

Khrushchev, but it seems to fit well with the purposes we have described: "All we wanted to do was show our potential. We don't want Chiang to be too far away from us. We want to keep him within our reach. Having him [on Quemoy and Matsu] means we can get at him with our shore batteries as well as our air force. If we'd occupied the islands, we would have lost the ability to cause him discomfort any time we want."[128] What Mao seemed to be saying was that by "allowing" Chiang to maintain forces on the offshore islands, the P.R.C. would retain both the link to Taiwan and the ability to frustrate any new GMD attempt to retake the mainland. More than that, Mao probably recognized that seizing the islands could only have increased the Americans' commitment to defend Taiwan and prolonged their disengagement from the strait area. In short, there were powerful political reasons for the limited counteraction against the islands that the PLA took; and there were few if any purposes to be served by trying to liberate them. Using Mao's colorful dialectical metaphor, U.S. military bases around the world were nooses around the Americans' neck, and in Taiwan the Chinese people were holding the rope.[129]

With the foreign-policy rationale for Chinese actions in the Taiwan Strait set out, it remains to ask whether or not these were prompted by domestic considerations. The evidence appears to argue persuasively that they were not. Mao's strategy was, if anything, constrained by domestic conditions. He would do nothing to endanger his self-reliance and Great Leap programs and compel a redistribution of domestic resources.

Actually, the Chinese leadership seemed deliberately to keep the Taiwan Strait crisis *out* of national politics. One would expect that if the party center loyal to Mao wanted to use the crisis for domestic advantage— to stimulate enthusiasm for the GLF, for example, or to consolidate political leadership at the top—it would have propagandized the American-GMD threat regularly in the months preceding and during the crisis. In fact, a review of *People's Daily* and local and national broadcasts indicates that Taiwan was a peripheral news subject through September 6, when Zhou Enlai urged a resumption of the ambassadorial talks. Aside from the brief "liberate Taiwan" campaign in late July, which occurred amid mounting reports of captured Chiang agents and other harassments, newspapers and broadcasts were remarkably quiet about Taiwan. The overwhelming emphasis of media and official commentaries was on the economy and the communes. With only occasional exceptions, these domestic matters were reported without connection to external developments. Mao dramatized his priority by continuing to tour the provinces in September, as did Liu Shaoqi. Even after Zhou Enlai made the front page with his announcement, intensive newspaper and radio coverage of the crisis occurred only in spurts, and gave considerable attention to foreign reactions. Mass demonstrations, which were called for by a meeting of the Supreme State Conference on September 15, occurred mainly in the latter half of the month. For China's domestic audience, the strait "crisis" lasted only about six weeks in the early fall.

The argument that Mao used the crisis to silence resistance to his economic programs is further weakened by the fact that at the Chengdu party meeting in March 1958, Mao had won out over his critics. The party center had already consolidated its ranks, even if not with enthusiasm; Maoist authority over the economy and the PLA was secure. Not until the Sixth Plenum in Wuchang in December 1958 was the commune system reevaluated and the decision made to slow down the communization process.[130] Mao admitted his overoptimism at that meeting and his failure "to combine revolutionary fervor and the practical spirit."[131] Even if, as we do not believe was the case, Mao's resignation as chairman of the P.R.C. was accepted at this party conference because of deficiencies in the commune program, during the Taiwan Strait crisis he was solidly in command. There is little logic or factual basis for concluding that he would involve China in a crisis over Quemoy and expect to save himself from domestic opposition.

It has been suggested that the crisis was at least in part a mobilizing device for the leadership's militia campaign. As has already been noted, however, the "Everyone a Soldier" movement fit so well with the character and aims of the GLF, and grew so directly (and early) out of Mao's notion of self-reliance, that the militia must be explained above all in economic terms. Not only would it facilitate communal organization under the party leadership; it would also provide some backup for a depleted army. That the crisis was *useful* to the party leadership in stimulating the militia program is beyond much doubt. This was signaled by Mao in September when, after touring several provinces, he said: "The imperialists have been insulting us so much that it is necessary to deal with this seriously. We not only want to have a strong army; we also want to organize militia in a big way."[132] On November 30, 1958, he also reportedly said: "It was good for Taiwan to fire artillery shots, for otherwise the militia could not have been organized so quickly."[133] "The process of the [militia] movement has been accelerated since the struggle against the U.S. invasion of Taiwan was broadened," one typical broadcast in the fall of 1958 stated.[134] But to say that the crisis gave the militia movement a boost is far from saying that the crisis was a pretext for it.

Mao's above-quoted statement implies that the decision to broaden the militia came directly in response to developments in the Taiwan Strait. One reason may have been purely tactical: In view of the United States' large-scale response to the Chinese shelling, Mao may have decided on the need for a modest step-up in preparedness. But he chose to strengthen the militia as an alternative to a general mobilization of the regular army because he considered a U.S. invasion unlikely and a redirection of resources into the PLA—in which the officers-to-the-ranks movement was just beginning—

undesirable except *in extremis.* Another reason for the militia campaign may have been bureaucratic. Perhaps under pressure from the military professionals once the crisis began, Mao called for organizing the militia "in a big way" to answer those who were still pushing the line of "moderization and regularization." Yet another possible explanation is that the militia, representing the postliberation equivalent of the guerrilla forces, was Mao's answer to Khrushchev's proposal, evidently supported by Peng Dehuai, of a joint fleet for shoreline defense. If Mao had to appear to be doing something to enhance China's security from the U.S. threat, a strengthened militia was a time-honored and far less costly choice than was the joint-fleet scheme.

Further Implications

Aside from raising questions about existing interpretations of Chinese motives in the 1958 Taiwan Strait crisis, the preceding analysis also permits discussion of broader foreign-policy issues. One of these concerns the linkage between domestic politics and foreign policy. Some analyses of Chinese behavior in 1958 propose that external adventurism was the product of domestic instability. Common to them is a narrow focus. They either neglect to make a circumspect examination of the domestic Chinese scene during the period in question or they slight the relevance of other governments' actions to Chinese foreign-policy choices. Almost all studies of the 1958 crisis, for instance, fail to say virtually anything about U.S. foreign policy in the Taiwan Strait area or elsewhere during that year.

Applied to China, linkage analysis of this kind draws attention away from the crucial relationship that this study has tried to show existed in 1958 between Chinese insecurity and a foreign-policy initiative. Even though the country was in the midst of a major economic and social transformation, the Beijing leadership replied with force to an external threat to China because the threat was judged sufficiently dangerous. "We will not attack unless we are attacked; if we are attacked, we will certainly counterattack" has long been part of China's revolutionary dialectics; and Mao always interpreted "attack" to include imminent threat. China's leaders did not make an initiative abroad entirely dependent on domestic circumstances.

This study also has implications for interpretations of the 1957–58 period in Chinese foreign policy. The post-Sputnik phase is commonly treated in the literature as one of Chinese bellicosity and foreign-policy adventurism. Yet in the Taiwan Strait crisis we find Mao taking heart from Sputnik, though not in order to advance Chinese interests abroad. Rather, he appears to have wanted the *Soviet* leadership to confront imperialist aggression more assertively, and to have used Soviet technological achievements to increase China's margin of external security for accelerating its domestic revolution. Far from being in an adventuristic mood in 1958, Mao seems to have been confident that with Sputnik, China's security would be much less vulnerable to the adventurism of the Eisenhower-Dulles administration—which proved to be a miscalculation.

There was another element of miscalculation on the Chinese side. The Chinese leaders (except possibly Peng Dehuai) attached more urgency to the American threat from Taiwan than actual circumstances warranted. The Eisenhower-Dulles policy was to use the GMD armed forces as a means of keeping military pressure on China, not for "rolling back" communism in China. In neither word nor action, however, did the Eisenhower administration show sensitivity to China's concern about American intentions in the wake of the offshore islands build-up, the Matador decision, and other developments. The Americans fed Chinese images of imminent U.S. aggressiveness in the Taiwan Strait; the forceful Chinese response only confirmed the State Department in its prevailing assessment of a P.R.C. threat to Taiwan; and the ensuing American show of power went considerably beyond Mao's expectations. As happened early in the Korean War, the security concerns that were expressed in the Chinese media (and perhaps in other forms not yet made public) were ignored, starting a cycle of mutual misperceptions that ended in a confrontation.

Was the Taiwan Strait crisis a defeat for Mao? It can be so interpreted only if it is assumed that his objectives were far greater than they are portrayed to have been in this study. Once it is accepted that Mao acted defensively and without desiring or anticipating a crisis, the events of late 1958 take on a different color. The Chinese leaders deflected what to them was an immediate threat to the mainland's security. Faced with a dramatic escalation of the conflict, they helped move it from the military to the diplomatic arena. Furthermore, Mao conducted foreign policy without deference to the Soviet leadership or to his own opponents in the military; he artfully controlled the risks in the strait and hence maintained his domestic priorities.

With respect to Taiwan, Mao's policy kept the island linked to Quemoy and Matsu and thus answered American proposals for a cease-fire in the strait that would have had the effect of implementing the two-Chinas concept. Mao's policy also compelled the American leadership to reassess the military value of the large GMD force deployed on the offshore islands and to attempt to reduce it. Washington also sought to commit Chiang to a formal abandonment of his ambition to recover the mainland by force.[135] Both of these efforts failed, as became apparent in the 1962 Taiwan Strait crisis, so that Mao's 1958 policy was successful only for the short run. Not until the Sino-American diplomacy of the Nixon administration would the threat to the P.R.C. posed by U.S. and GMD military activities in the Taiwan Strait area be addressed directly and largely neutralized.

4 The Sino-Indian Border War, 1962

Introduction

The Sino-Indian border war took place in October and November 1962 in the midst of major Chinese domestic and foreign difficulties. The Chinese economy had suffered severe setbacks due to three years of natural calamities and the rift with Moscow. Food shortages had brought malnutrition and political dissension to a sizable part of the population and had resulted in unplanned population movements across the Chinese border and rebellions accompanied by food riots. Facing serious internal insecurity, the Chinese leadership was primarily concerned with the rehabilitation of the country's economy. Priority in allocating resources was placed on reinforcing the agricultural front and improving the welfare and livelihood of the people, thereby cutting new industrial investment and reducing arms production. The Maoist leadership was subject to challenge from various fronts within and without the party. But Mao Zedong remained *influential* in Chinese policy making and took firm command over those policies that were vital to his socialist line. The party center controlled military affairs and subordinated the modernization of the army to long-term economic construction. The standard of war preparedness of the armed forces was low. The strategic outlook of military leaders was cautious and essentially defensive.

Internationally, the P.R.C. confronted not only Tibetan insurgency supported by the United States, Taiwan, and India, but also Indian military activities pressing forward on Chinese territory along the borderlines in Xinjiang and Tibet. These activities included the establishment of more than forty new military posts in Chinese-claimed territory and intensified border patrols in response to provocative intrusions by Indian ground troops, motorboats, and aircraft. China had to cope simultaneously with external threats from two more fronts. Tension in the Taiwan Strait, which

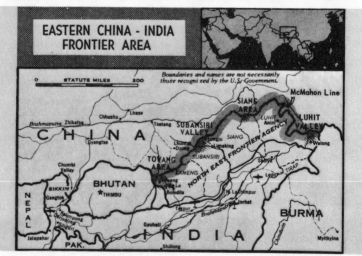

THE WESTERN AND EASTERN SINO-INDIAN BORDER
AREAS

reached its peak in mid-1962 when Nationalist officials in Taibei called, in collaboration with the United States, for invasion preparations, posed a grave threat to China's security. The Soviets' support of Moslem insurgents in Xinjiang provided another kind of threat to China along the Sino-Soviet border. The events in the Taiwan Strait and on the Sino-Soviet border, as well as Washington's and Moscow's support of the Indian stance toward the Sino-Indian border dispute, added a new context to the Chinese leadership's perspective on the Himalayan frontiers.

These domestic and external events, and the interaction of both, provided background for Chinese decision making during the border crisis. In this chapter we will discuss the major domestic and international events and finally bring them together in a summary of the border decision itself.

The Domestic Situation

The Economy

Between 1959 and 1961, the middle years of the Great Leap Forward, the Chinese economy suffered sharp setbacks. Poor weather, unprecedented in a hundred years, combined with errors in planning and economic management to produce a succession of three very bad harvests. The decline in agricultural production resulted in an acute shortage of food and eventually precipitated a full-fledged agricultural crisis. This crisis then spilled over into the rest of the economy and was reflected in declines in industrial production, consumption, and trade.

During the same three years, China was hit by severe droughts, typhoons, and floods. In 1959, the area stricken was more than 650 million *mu,* over one-third of the total cultivated area. In both 1960 and 1961, more than 900 million *mu,* or half of the cultivated area, were affected. In 1962, natural calamities were less serious than in previous years, but still affected north China, which experienced a drought, and the coastal areas, which were hit by floods.[1] No official figures on grain production have been published since 1959, but Mao Zedong hinted at a bad harvest in his interview with Field Marshal Montgomery in September 1961. Mao told Montgomery that China's normal grain harvest was 180 million tons, but that in 1960 it had been 150 million tons. He also said that he expected the harvest to increase by 10 million tons in 1961.[2] The output of grain in 1962 was officially recorded as slightly higher than that in 1961.[3] Perhaps the 1962 harvest was in the range of 160–170 million tons. It has been estimated that grain production declined by about 24 percent between 1958, the year of peak Great Leap output (200 million tons), and 1961, the year of post-Leap collapse (160 million tons). Nevertheless, the food shortage in 1961 amounted to about 60 million tons, or nearly 30 percent of the supply level, because about 20 percent of the expected supply had to be converted to nonfood uses.[4]

The impact of crop failures and the withdrawal of Soviet aid from China's industrial sector contributed to a stagnation of industrial production. Particularly, the withdrawal of Soviet aid appears to have had a severe impact. In July 1960, the Soviet Union decided on a complete withdrawal of the 1,390 experts who were helping in China's industries, tore up 343 contracts for experts, abolished 257 programs involving scientific and technical cooperation, and drastically reduced the supply of complete sets of equipment.[5] Later the Chinese leadership blamed the Soviets for having "inflicted incalculable difficulties and losses on China's economy, national defense, and scientific research," aggravating greatly China's difficulties during this time of severe economic crisis.[6] It has been estimated that China's industrial production in 1961 remained at a level slightly above that of 1957 and that production in 1962 was slightly better than it had been in 1961.[7]

In 1960–62, the decline in production in both agriculture and the manufacture of consumer goods in turn affected the volume of exports, of which more than 70 percent were farm produce or processed farm products.[8] In sum, the vicious cycle of 1960–62 was reflected in China's Gross National Product. The GNP declined by almost 30 percent compared to the highest point in 1959, and per capita income dropped by about 32 percent.[9]

Much more serious to the Chinese leadership was the fact that economic collapse brought with it numerous unexpected social problems such as an increase in the occurrence of debilitating diseases, unplanned population movements, and discontent among large sectors of the population, including rebellions and food riots. According to one visitor to China in 1961, food rationing had become much more severe since 1959. In big cities like Beijing, Tianjin, Nanjing, and Hangzhou, monthly grain rations had declined from 17 kilograms for a person in 1955 to 13–15 kilograms in 1961. Eggs were very scarce. Milk, fats, and sugar had hardly any place in the diet of the masses. No meat had been distributed for two months.[10]

The food shortage was also felt in the armed forces. The *Bulletin of Activities* of the PLA indicates that in 1960 the supply of food to army units remained short: "After August of last year [1960], the food ration standard of the company decreased. Formerly, each soldier had one and a half catties to eat. The General Rear Services Department prescribed that each person should save a half ounce each day. However, owing to the further reduction of food at each level, a soldier actually can only get less than one catty and two ounces each day. Many considered that they did not have enough to eat."[11]

This situation improved a little by the latter part of 1961, but the armed forces were still suffering from the food shortage. In August 1961 the *Bulletin* pointed out the seriousness of the food shortage in the PLA by noting that "about 5 to 10 percent of the persons in a company do not have sufficient food to eat" and that "they have to transfer part of their food to solve the problem of food needed by their families."[12]

The food shortage also caused widespread malnutrition and contributed to the spread of infectious diseases in the armed forces. It was reported that typhus, typhoid, malaria, and other diseases had become a serious problem in the armed forces in 1960–61.[13] Luo Ruiqing (Lo Jui-ch'ing), chief of staff of the PLA, also reported widespread disease among soldiers' families at that time: "The 60 soldiers of the company are all natives of Szechwan. Twenty-four of them were from places which suffered serious disasters last year (1960). This accounts for 40 percent. From last May to the end of last year, 16 persons in 10 soldiers' families died, and 9 of them died of dropsy resulting from the famine."[14]

Owing to some difficulties in earning their livelihood, a sizable part of the populace, including members of the armed forces, may have nurtured feelings of disaffection toward the party and local authorities. Investigating the letters received in one company from soldiers' families in the disaster areas and reduced-production districts, the *Bulletin* also pointed out that many soldiers' families (about 30 percent) complained about the natural disasters, illness, and hardship. Some soldiers whose family members had died of dropsy explicitly revealed their complaints to the party by asking "Where did the food go?" and "Why are people dying?"[15] The complaints of the people most likely increased because of the illegal and disorderly conduct of some local officials. During the economic difficulties, some local party members became selfish and engaged in excessive consumption and corruption.[16]

The Chinese leadership appeared to face the worst situation in north-western and southwestern China, where food riots and armed rebellions had occurred. These regions included Gansu (Kansu), Qinghai (Chinghai) Sichwan, Tibet, and Yunnan. It was reported that there were still 3,000 armed bandits left at the end of 1960.[17] Furthermore, as will be discussed later, economic difficulties and political discontent among the population, particularly in minority areas like Xinjiang and Tibet, contributed to the rapid increase of a Chinese exodus to Hong Kong and the Soviet Union during 1960–62. Such events made the Chinese leadership acutely sensitive to the security of China's borders by late June 1962.

Facing serious economic difficulties combined with political disaffection, the Chinese leadership was primarily concerned to rehabilitate the economy. In September 1960, Liao Luyan (Liao Lu-yen), minister of agriculture, called on the whole party and all the people to give full support to agriculture, stressing that "all possible material, technical and financial aid" would be funneled into agriculture in a crash program to boost farm production.[18]

In January 1961, the Ninth Plenum of the Eighth Central Committee of the Chinese Communist party officially approved a basic change in economic priorities. Agriculture was given top priority as the foundation of the economy, while industry was assigned the role of "leading factor." The plenum also proclaimed policy guidelines known as "readjustment, consolidation, filling out and raising standards" in order to overcome the imbalance that had emerged in the national economy.[19] According to such policy guidelines, the first priority of resource allocation should be placed on reinforcing the agricultural front so as to rehabilitate and increase farm production as quickly as possible. Industrial production targets and the number of capital construction projects were readjusted downward. New industrial investment was cut back. The production of articles for daily use and for agriculture was stressed.[20] These guidelines were further consolidated through the "ten tasks in adjusting [the] national economy" put forth by Premier Zhou Enlai at the Second National People's Congress held between March and April 1962.[21]

In this period of consolidation, the Chinese leadership continued to pursue a policy of self-reliance, which had been the standard of economic development since 1958. China did not borrow a penny from foreign countries, and even paid off on time the debts and interest owed to the Soviet Union.[22] Food imports were only rarely undertaken. China imported from five to six million tons of grain from Australia, Canada, and other capitalist nations in 1961 and 1962 at an annual cost of from $300 million to $400 million. Actually the value for grain imports jumped almost two-fold between 1960 and 1961.[23] Because foods replaced capital goods as the leading import category, imports of capital goods and defense items declined by about one-third of the peak year of the GLF, according to Alexander Eckstein.[24]

Additionally, China's revenue structure further contributed to constraining heavy arms production on a self-reliance basis. According to one official Chinese source, agriculture was one of the main sources of accumulation of funds by the state, and about half of the nation's revenues were related, directly or indirectly, to farm production in 1960.[25] Given substantial drops in the production of farm and light industrial products, as well as the withdrawal of Soviet technical aid, China was probably in a poor position to finance heavy industries related to arms production. The PLA *Bulletin* indicates that resource allocation for arms production was much below planned targets. In the first half of 1961, PLA units could get only one-third to one-half of the materials (e.g., steel, lumber, and cement) they ordered. Army capital construction projects were drastically reduced by 50–70 percent from the original plan.[26] Futhermore, state factories could complete only 15.9 percent of the planned target in the manufacturing of weapons and equipment.[27]

Apart from resource allocation, the response of the Beijing leadership to such serious domestic difficulties was moderate, defensive, its focus being on temperance and practicality for the purpose of increasing production. Production seemed to be not only the key word but also a real criterion of success in any work. The leadership stressed the decisive importance of increasing agricultural production in order to improve the welfare and livelihood of the people.[28] Material incentives were stressed.[29] The people's communes were radically modified to place power in the hands of production teams, which replaced brigades as the basic accounting and planning units. The production teams were gradually authorized to program their own utilization of manpower, land, and draft animals, and were permitted to determine expenditures and income distribution.[30] The private plots that had been confiscated during the GLF were restored. Peasants had more freedom to manufacture their own handicrafts and to sell their products at free markets.[31]

Throughout 1960–62, a campaign for increased production, particularly agricultural production, had been sweeping the nation. But the Beijing leadership abandoned the ambitious schemes it had attempted to implement early in the GLF for the large-scale mobilization of labor in industrial and rural areas. During September and October 1958, a mass movement launched under the slogan "All Out Big Leap Forward" mobilized sixty million people to participate in steel making and ten million people to be trained as technicians and workers in iron smelting and steel making.[32] In contrast, the leadership did not adopt a policy of social mobilization on the land, but opted for a campaign of selective capital and technical investment in agriculture. The "return to the village" (*huixiang*) campaign was launched, but the mass movement, like the *xiafang* movement of earlier years, under which the wholesale organization of teams was transferred to the countryside, was abandoned.[33]

The Party

After weathering the challenge from Peng Dehuai, minister of national defense and concurrently a Politburo member, and his colleagues at the Eighth Plenum of the Central Committee in August 1959, the Maoists appeared to maintain a shaky coalition of power. But by mid-1960, this coalition had begun to disintegrate, mainly due to leadership tensions derived from domestic difficulties and external threats. By 1962, policies of socialist construction were again under attack by dissenters in the party and had to be revised in the wake of readjustments in the national economy.

Considerable opposition to Mao's established policies came from two quarters: the government and party leadership group of Liu Shaoqi and Deng Xiaoping (Teng Hsiao-p'ing); and the intellectual group comprised of people such as Wu Han and Deng Tuo (Teng T'o). In mid-1960, Liu, as chairman of state, and Deng, as general secretary of the party, were preoccupied with the improvement of agricultural production and promulgated "urgent directives concerning rural work" which undermined Mao's policy concerning the people's communes established during the Great Leap Forward.[34]

At the March 1961 Guangzhou work conference, Liu's group drafted the "Sixty-article Regulations for the Rural People's Communes." In May, Liu chaired meetings of the central work conference and approved Deng Zehui's (Teng Tzu-hui's) proposal to dissolve 200,000 agricultural producers' cooperatives and economic liberalization measures in the face of the Great Leap crisis.[35] At the September conference of party secretariats held at Lushan, Liu's group was told to draft the "Seventy-article Regulations on Industry," and in their application to enforce the bonus system in an effort to accelerate the overall fulfillment of the various tasks of commercial enterprises.[36] Because they encouraged material incentives and the technical and practical training of workers, the regulations were later criticized as deviating seriously from the Anshan Constitution[37] of 1960, which was based on Mao's principle "politics takes command" in production and the management of factories.[38]

It is highly probable that during this period the line *sanze yibao* ("three privates and one guarantee") was suggested as an alternative to Mao's domestic policies. During the Cultural Revolution, Liu Shaoqi confessed that Deng Zehui, director of the party's Rural Work Department, had formulated the *sanze yibao* line, but added that he had not rejected Deng's proposals.[39] By promoting liberal policies in agriculture and industry, with emphasis on the extension of peasants' private plots and free markets, an increase in private business, and the fixing of output quotas based on individual households, the line encouraged the restoration of private family economy, thereby undermining the collective economy.[40]

At the January 1962 party work conference, the first public clash between Liu's group and the Maoists occurred. Liu was said to have attacked Mao's policies of the previous few years, particularly noting that the difficulties of the recent past had been brought about "30% by natural calamities and 70% by man-made disaster." Liu claimed that, contrary to Mao's view that "the situation is very favorable," eight or ten years would be required to make the necessary readjustments. Deng Xiaoping and Chen Yun joined Liu in critiquing Mao's domestic policies and aired the view that opposition to Chairman Mao was only opposition to an individual.[41] It was Lin Biao and Zhou Enlai who defended Mao's leadership at the conference.

Lin Biao in his speech urged the party to act "according to Chairman Mao's instructions," stressing that "Mao's thought is the soul and the root of life." Zhou supported Mao by noting that the general line had been correct in the past few years and there had been more gains than losses.[42]

More critical to the Maoists at and after the January work conference was the call for a reversal of the verdicts on party officials, including Peng Dehuai, who had officially been denounced as antiparty right-wing opportunists at the Lushan plenum. A reversal of verdicts was suggested in intellectual circles in early 1961, and was later promoted by certain party leaders. In February 1961, the Maoist leadership had been subject to criticism from within intellectual circles in the form of a Beijing opera entitled *The Dismissal of Hai Rui from Office*. In this opera, Wu Han complained about Peng Dehuai's dismissal in these words: "It's unjust to relieve me of my post."[43] Deng Tuo, the former editor of *People's Daily*, also denounced the Great Leap Forward and ridiculed Mao's decision on Peng Dehuai.[44] At the enlarged work conference in January 1962, Liu Shaoqi was said to claim that "much" of Peng's antiparty program was "in conformity with the facts" and "shouldn't be regarded as a mistake."[45] In June 1962, Peng himself was encouraged by certain Beijing leaders including Liu Shaoqi and Deng Xiaoping, to bring out an 80,000-word document that was aimed at reversing the verdict passed against him.[46]

Some party leaders were apprehensive of domestic weakness as a constraint on foreign policy and advocated lessening tensions with the "imperialists, the reactionaries, and the revisionists," as well as reducing the assistance and support given to the revolutionary struggles of other peoples. Liu Shaoqi recalled in his confession that an "unnamed comrade" proposed a policy of *sanhe yishao* ("three reconciliations and one reduction").[47] Liu was later accused of having a capitulationist attitude toward Khrushchev, as well as of advocating less support for the revolutionary struggle of peoples abroad, and therefore of undermining the proletarian revolutionary line and the antirevisionist struggle promoted by Mao.[48] In several essays, Deng Tuo mocked a basic assumption of Mao's world outlook that "the East Wind prevails over the West Wind," noting that "these words are just hackneyed phrases without much meaning." Deng suggested that China ally with more advanced countries. He even called for a rapprochement with the United States, claiming that the Chinese had been closely associated with Americans as early as the fifth century (!), and consequently, the "long tradition of Sino-American friendship is an important historical fact." Deng also criticized Mao's alienation of the Soviet Union and further advocated emulating Soviet economic models in modernizing China.[49] The existence of the *sanhe yishao* line hinted, as will be discussed later, that during the interplay of domestic weakness and external threats there was a different foreign-policy perspective at work among the Beijing leadership, a perspective which would provide policy implications for the Chinese border war with India. But the point here is that the *sanze yibao* and *sanhe yishao* lines became additional factors in the Liuists' challenge to the Maoist leadership.

Throughout 1962, particularly in the months prior to the Tenth Plenum, there is no doubt that the Maoist leadership was subjected to challenges from various fronts within and without the party. However, it is not true that Mao was out of power in the Chinese decision-making process or unable to take command over the essentials of his policies, as some writers argue.[50] Mao was not omnipotent as party chairman and responded to certain issues defensively. Nonetheless, he remained the prime ideological spokesman and placated and reasoned with those party members who deviated from his line in order to obtain their compliance. Furthermore, he took firm command over those policies that were vital to his socialist line, rejecting compromise at least until the Tenth Plenum in September 1962, one month before the outbreak of the Sino-Indian border war. However, several remarks must be made in clarification of this argument.

There is no entirely convincing evidence, even in the documents of the Cultural Revolution, that Mao was forced to retire into the background during this period, or that Liu and others took command or conspired to overthrow him. As will be discussed elsewhere, Mao remained in control of the ultimate source of power, the PLA. Mao even perceived in January 1962 that China's class struggle was "less ferocious compared to the year of 1957," when the so-called right-wing bourgeois faction attacked the Maoist leadership.[51] Mao's position was probably more stable at the Tenth Plenum than it had been at the Eighth Plenum in August 1959, when the Maoists were subjected to serious challenge from the military leadership. In his final struggle with Peng and his followers at the Eighth Plenum, Mao personally appealed to and claimed the loyalty of the PLA to him: "If we deserve to perish, then I will go to the countryside to lead the peasants, to overthrow the government. If those of you in the Liberation Army won't follow me, I will go find a Red Army. . . . I think the Liberation Army would follow me."[52] In contrast, Mao's January 1962 speech was generally moderate with regard to China's class struggle, and even stressed Liu's basic agreement with his policies. Mao commented on Liu's report as follows: "Comrade Liu Shao-ch'i said in his report that in the past four years our line was correct, and that our achievements were the main feature; we made some mistakes in our practical work and suffered some hardships, but we gained experience; therefore we are stronger than before, not weaker."[53]

Several important concrete policies on rural areas, industry, and education might have been made by the Tenth Plenum with Mao's participation, but he felt reservations and a lack of commitment toward those policies. There is considerable plausible evidence of this. In overcoming economic difficulties and adjusting the priorities of the national economy, Mao seemed to believe that a tactical retreat from his economic policies was inevitable as well as that some concrete policies were needed to adjust the domestic situation. But he lacked knowledge of concrete policies that would overcome the difficulties that followed in the wake of the three successive years of calamities. In a discussion with Edgar Snow in 1960, Mao revealed that "as far socialist construction [is concerned], China still has no experience"; eleven years of experience is not enough.[54] Mao's speech in January 1962 further indicated his lack of knowledge about economic construction as follows:

> For us the socialist economy is still in many respects a realm of necessity not yet understood . . . there are many problems in the work of economic construction which still I don't understand. I haven't got much understanding of industry and commerce, I understand a bit about agriculture, but this is only relatively speaking—I still don't understand much. . . . I myself also would like to study more. Up to now, however, my knowledge of these matters has been very scanty. I have paid rather more attention to problems relating to the productive relationships. As for the productive forces, I know very little.[55]

In such a context, it is highly probable that Mao was unable to make up his mind on certain policies and agreed to some policy proposals despite reservations. In the summer of 1962 he was said to have been undecided on the question of loaning land to individual houses, a proposal previously drafted by Deng Zehui. But Liu Shaoqi had interpreted this noncommitment as permissive approval by Mao.[56] With reservations, Mao seemed to have already agreed to several concrete policies like the sixty regulations on work in the countryside, the seventy regulations on industrial enterprises, the sixty regulations on higher education, and the forty regulations on scientific research. In his January speech, he noted that such draft regulations were merely summaries of the experiences of two years (1960–61) and that "some may have to be greatly revised" in the future after experimentation and determination of their suitability to Chinese conditions.[57]

Mao never failed to refute and correct important policies that appeared to threaten the essence of his rural policies. At the central work conference in August 1962, Mao called a halt to further retreat, and took the initiative in dismissing Deng Zehui as director of the party's Rural Work Department. He also terminated Deng Tuo's criticism against him. Top-level party and government leaders in charge of rural, industrial, and financial affairs, particularly Chen Yun, Li Fuchun, Li Xiannian (Li Hsien-nien), and Bo Yibo came under self-criticism during the conference.[58]

Most important is the fact that the Maoist leadership was strong enough to mobilize political support in the framework of formal decision-making procedures in dealing with the matter of reversing the verdicts against Peng Dehuai. Just before the Tenth Plenum, the Standing Committee of the Politburo met and decided that Peng and his associates who had already been labeled as a right-opportunist antiparty clique at the Eighth Plenum, were not qualified to attend the Tenth Plenum.[59] In his speech at the Tenth Plenum, Mao renamed "right-wing opportunism" as "Chinese revisionism" and further stood firmly against the reversal of the verdicts.[60] He warned that "the recent trend towards the reversal of verdicts is incorrect. Only those verdicts which were truly incorrect can be reversed. Those verdicts which were correct can't be reversed. . . . We can't reverse all of them indiscriminately."[61]

About the time of the Tenth Plenum the domestic and international situations were more favorable for the stability of the Maoist leadership than they had been in the spring of 1962. The actual harvest of summer crops showed a slight gain over that of 1961, and the yields of autumn crops were also expected to register an increase.[62] Beijing's leaders thus faced an improved economic outlook. As will be discussed elsewhere, the exodus of Chinese to Hong Kong and to the Soviet Union declined. The 1962 Taiwan Strait crisis began to recede in July with credible assurances from the United States that it had no intention of backing Chiang Kai-shek's invasion.

The Tenth Plenum communiqué revealed optimism for the future by noting that "though certain difficulties still exist, it is entirely possible to overcome them"; thus, "our future is bright."[63] The Maoists were now in a relatively better position to deal with the dissension in the party and populace as well as with external threats. In Mao's speech at the Tenth Plenum, there was already the hint of a growing call for ideological and political purity in the party and society, and equal emphasis on the need for vigilance against Soviet revisionism.[64]

The Military

As we discussed in the previous chapter, from the mid-1950s to 1959, there was considerable disagreement between the military professionals and the party center over the problem of how to modernize the PLA. During the GLF, Mao gave priority to socialist economic construction and tried to allocate the maximum of domestic resources to achieve this objective on the basis of self-reliance. This economy-first policy caused a delay in the modernization of the PLA.

The Lushan plenum in 1959 marked the end of the controversy between the Maoists and the professionals. The Maoists were victorious, which meant, generally speaking, the victory of the proletarian military line over the professional military line and indicated "a return to the revolutionary model" in China's army building.[65] The order of priorities was set in early 1960: the party commands the gun, and politics commands technology, with emphasis on man's superiority over weapons; the modernization of the PLA must be subordinated to long-term economic construction and must be pursued on the basis of self-reliance—that is, without relying on aid from the Soviet Union; China's defense doctrine must be based on the people's war tradition of the PLA rather than on foreign, especially Soviet, military experience.[66] These priorities would have considerable implications for the capability and strategic outlook of the PLA, particularly with regard to the external threats that developed in 1962.

Lin Biao, who had strongly supported Mao's army-building policies in the late 1950s, took command of the PLA as vice chairman of the Military Affairs Committee (MAC) and defense minister in September 1959.[67] Lin was primarily concerned about party control over the armed forces and ideological and organizational purity at the company level, the army's basic unit. Political work in the PLA began to be stressed in late 1960 when an enlarged meeting of the MAC called attention to the political and ideological work of army building. At this meeting, Lin Biao clearly defined the direction the political work of the PLA would take using his formula of the "four firsts." According to this formula, man is primary over weapons; political work is primary over other work; ideological work is primary over routine work; and practical thought must be placed before book learning.[68] A "four-good" company movement was launched in the spring of 1961.[69] To strengthen the basic units of the armed forces, many cadres were required to go to the companies for training. Some regiments are reported to have regularly assigned 70–80 percent of their cadres to work in the companies.[70]

The high command in the PLA simultaneously pushed up the work to strengthen the party's control over the army under the principle of collective leadership by party committees. A rectification campaign of party organization in the armed forces and a drive to strengthen the party's presence in the PLA were launched. By early 1961, over 80 percent of the party structure at the basic level had been reorganized through a rectification campaign, and 229,000 new party members had been recruited into the armed forces on the basis of their class background and political quality. As a result, all PLA companies had established party committees by March 1961.[71] "The Four Sets of Regulations on Political Work" that were promulgated in the fall of 1961 provided a further step to crack down on professionalism among the military commanders by strengthening the leverage of the political commissar against the leadership of individual commanders.[72]

The military high command also appears to have strengthened military training within the PLA. It attempted to combine politics with military affairs and "redness" with expertness under the principle "politics takes command."[73] An outline of the 1961 defense plan clearly indicated the importance of military training and allotted more time for it than for political education, noting that skills and equipment technology were much more complicated and difficult to learn than they had been in past years. For the ground forces, the ratio of military training to political education was 60 percent to 40 percent, and in the special forces it was 70 percent to 30 percent.[74]

The party center's interest in directing the PLA to participate in production rapidly declined after early 1960. Uncompensated participation of the armed forces in production was 59 million work days during the peak of the GLF. But by 1960, the figure was 46 million work days, and by 1961, 22 million.[75] In 1962, only 4 million days were recorded.[76] The reasons for this decline might be interpreted in terms of both the abandonment of many projects initiated during the Great Leap and the need of the armed forces for partial economic self-sufficiency at a time of food shortages in the PLA itself.[77] Additionally, an aggravated international situation, especially in the Taiwan Strait, along the Sino-Soviet border (Xinjiang), and on the Sino-Indian border in 1962 may have contributed to the reduction in the PLA's role in production and to the increase in its strategic role against external threats. In particular, the Taiwan Strait crisis was so serious that a captured document described the first half of 1962 as a "war-preparation period."[78] An Army Day editorial in *People's Daily* on August 1, 1962, described the PLA's vigilance against a Nationalist adventuristic plan backed by the United States during the period by noting that since the beginning of 1962 the PLA had not slackened its vigilance "even for a single day." It called for the PLA's continued vigilance as well as for stepped-up training to make itself better prepared.[79]

Despite its increasing attention to the strategic role of the PLA by mid-1962, China was not in a position to reallocate resources for the PLA. In the late 1950s, just prior to the Taiwan Strait crisis of 1958, the mission and strength of the PLA had been affected by the party center's primary concern with the GLF. The PLA's budget and manpower had been cut down.[80] But in 1960–62, the economic difficulties of three successive years would further contribute to constrained defense expenditures. The total defense budget for 1959 (5,800 million *yuan*), was slightly higher than that of 1958 (5,000 million *yuan*), and the defense budget of 1960 (5,826 million *yuan*) was almost equivalent to that of 1959. But the ratio of defense budget to national budget continued to decline from 15.2 percent in 1958 to 11.2 percent in 1959 and 8.3 percent in 1960.[81] Figures for the defense budgets of 1961 and 1962 are not available. But considering that the leadership again "adjusted and reduced" the defense budget for 1961,[82] one may assume that the defense budget for 1961 was equivalent to that of

1960 at best, or below the level of 1960 at worst. The PLA *Bulletin* indicates as much by stressing that the 1961 defense plan had to be based on the policy of "making little, buying little, using the present equipment until it was worn out and finished."[83]

Under the above conditions, high-level military leaders probably had to adjust the limited defense budget to the urgent need for combat readiness in the PLA. The MAC urged in January 1961 that all army units build up "fighting forces with diligence, thrift and economy," economizing on administrative expenses and reducing the use of various kinds of materials.[84] But so serious was the shortage of military equipment and materials that it caused trouble in the training program in 1961. In a report to the MAC on June 22, 1961, Marshal Ye Jianying said that numerous units in the armed forces were not obtaining adequate training with modern weapons, mainly due to the low standards of the national defense industry. According to his assessment, this was especially true

> in the technical branches of service of the Ground Force, Navy, and Air Force. There is X% of the vessels and ships of the Navy to be repaired. . . . XX ships are operational and can't be submerged. The air planes of the Air Force which were grounded were as high as XX%; the flight training time of pilots was reduced to half in comparison with previous years. . . . The Ground Force is also facing the difficulties of obtaining fuel, ammunition, and batteries for the use of their vehicles and in training.[85]

It seems doubtful that the preparedness of the PLA for dealing with external threats was rapidly improved during the war-preparation period, the first half of 1962. It is reported that the enlarged meeting of the Politburo's Standing Committee in February 1962 found the national budget to be several hundred million dollars in the red, and likened the financial and economic situation to "a time of emergency."[86] The New China News Agency revealed on July 27, 1962, that the PLA had continued to develop the honorable tradition of fighting with industry and thrift amid hardships and had saved a great amount of money for the state.[87] The PLA was reported to have reduced but intensified military training in 1962, its emphasis being on "compactness and [the] quality principle."[88] There was no hint of expanded military production. Steps to increase military production were not taken until 1963, when China had improved economic conditions and established three more machine-building ministries.[89]

The Chinese leadership did not expect any Soviet assistance in modernizing China's armed forces, and appears to have maintained continuously a "go-it-alone" policy that was the outcome of a decision made by Mao in 1958.[90] In April 1961, the General Political Department of the PLA reaffirmed Mao's policy by saying that "principally," China would depend on itself for development and "secondarily" it would strive for foreign assistance.[91] Despite serious natural disasters, the military leaders asserted their confidence in the self-reliance policy. The General Political Department claimed: "We are facing temporary and partial difficulties," but "we should under no circumstances lose our confidence."[92] This policy of self-reliance was reflected in China's military doctrine and strategic outlook. The military writings of Mao Zedong and learning from China's own experiences were emphasized by the compilers of China's combat laws and ordinances.[93]

The party center may have been worried about the likelihood of an unexpected or accidental war, particularly one triggered by an unauthorized decision of military personnel, at a time when China faced domestic difficulties and tensions. In a notice in January 1961, the MAC called for all units in the PLA to respect strictly "the ruling not to exceed the limit of entry into the neighboring countries beyond 20 kilometers" when they responded to domestic rebellions in places close to the borders of neighboring countries—for example, the Sino-Indian border, the Sino-Nepalese border, and the Sino-Sikkim border.[94] The MAC was determined to have firm control over any military decision concerning China's borders. In the directive just cited the MAC also stated: "In the neighboring countries (including fraternal nations and nationalistic countries) if and when in these border regions there occurs any international incident, it is required to report quickly to superiors and await decisions and orders, if any. *Under no circumstances should an officer upon his own personal responsibility take steps to carry out an unauthorized decision.*"[95]

The strategic outlook of China's military leaders was cautious and essentially defensive. They stressed the doctrine of people's war and the superiority of "man over weapons."[96] Military training stressed preparations to meet the contingency of an enemy invasion, concentrating on close combat and night fighting rather than on large-unit maneuvers.[97] The military leaders rejected the policy of dividing the world into spheres of influence according to the interests of a few great powers. The PLA *Bulletin* noted that aside from China's 9,597,000 square kilometers (the total area of China's national territory), the Chinese did not want one inch of land from others.[98] Chief of Staff Luo Ruiqing reaffirmed this principle in a speech in August 1962 on the occasion of the thirty-fifth anniversary of the PLA's founding: "The Chinese people will never encroach upon a single inch of others' territory, nor will they ever allow anyone to encroach upon a single inch of China's territory."[99]

So long as the central concern of the Chinese leadership was the country's domestic problems, particularly the recovery of the economy, we may speculate that it did not want to increase the strategic role of the PLA unless external tensions were high and the nation's security was directly endangered. The leadership had made it clear that its priority in the allocation of limited resources was economic recovery, not military modernization. But external threats complicated China's efforts to recover from the economic difficulties caused by three years of natural calamities, poor planning, and the rift with Moscow. The leadership had to cope with threats posed by India, the United States, Taiwan, and the Soviet Union, and to deal with internal insecurity caused by economic difficulties.

The Sino-Indian Boundary Dispute

In the mid-1950s, Chinese and Indian leaders began to realize that they were far apart in their understanding of the border between the two countries in the area of Xinjiang and Tibet, but they did not then deal with the issue in a contentious manner. India's awareness of Chinese efforts to liberate Tibet near India's North East Frontier Agency (N.E.F.A.) was heightened after the Chinese People's Liberation Army entered the eastern sector of Tibet. In November 1950, using the device of a parliamentary question, India's Prime Minister Nehru affirmed that the frontier from Bhutan eastward had been clearly defined by the McMahon line, which had been fixed by the Simla Convention of 1914.[100] After this affirmation, India continued to regard the McMahon line as the well-established border in the eastern sector of Tibet and as not being subject to discussion with China for a delimitation of the Sino-Indian boundary there. Beginning in September 1951, however, when Premier Zhou Enlai raised the question of stabilization of the Tibetan frontier in talks with the Indian ambassador in Beijing, China kept sending India the signal that the boundary in Tibet had *not* been formally demarcated and that China had not accepted the McMahon alignment as India's northeast boundary.[101] In 1956, Zhou met Nehru in New Delhi and suggested that China did not recognize the McMahon line, but was willing to maintain the status quo in the eastern sector of Tibet, thereby revealing China's intention not to cross the line.[102]

Both governments realized that there was a boundary question in the middle sector of Tibet, but they made every attempt to minimize and conceal it. For instance, in April 1954, when the two governments signed an agreement regulating trade and travel between India and the Tibetan region of China, they merely named six passes near the middle sector of the frontier (west of Nepal and east of Ladakh) as routes for trade and pilgrimages without delimiting or specifying the boundary.[103] Boundary differences were first raised in relation to Wure (Wu-je) (Indian: Barohati) in the middle sector in the summer of 1954, but were treated in a relatively noncontentious manner.[104]

In the western sector, the Chinese regarded the Aksai Chin plateau, the area from Karakoram Pass in Xinjiang to Kongka Pass in western Tibet (Indian: Ladakh) as a traditional Chinese artery linking Xinjiang and western Tibet. According to Chinese claims, a major part of the Aksai Chin was under the jurisdiction of Hetian (Hotien) County of the Xinjiang Uygur Autonomous Region of China, while the minor part was under that of Rudok Dzong County of the Tibetan Autonomous Region of China.[105] This official Chinese position was revealed for the first time in January 1959. Neither government had raised the Aksai Chin boundary issue in a meeting to negotiate a 1954 trade agreement involving Tibet or in Zhou's talks with Nehru in 1956. In October 1958, when a map controversy developed over an entire border,[106] India officially claimed legal ownership of some 12,000 square miles of the Aksai Chin in a note to the Chinese ambassador in New Delhi. It was the first time in recorded history that India had claimed ownership of the Aksai Chin.[107]

In a letter to Zhou in December 1958,[108] Nehru again made a formal claim to the Aksai Chin and denied the existence of a major boundary dispute between China and India, noting that there could be "no question of these large parts of India being anything but India." Nehru appeared to emphasize especially the de facto and de jure existence of the McMahon alignment, asserting that the boundaries delimited in the N.E.F.A. were the well-known and fixed ones. In his reply to Nehru in January 1959, Zhou challenged Nehru's impressions and put forth the basic positions thereafter adopted by China. In that letter,[109] Zhou claimed that the Sino-Indian boundary had not yet been formally delimited and that some differences existed. He officially reminded Nehru that "no central Chinese Government had ever recognized the McMahon Line" and that it was "a product of the British policy of aggression." Premier Zhou was very sensitive to India's claim to the Aksai Chin, and noted that part of Xinjiang had "always been Chinese jurisdiction," that it was regularly patrolled by Chinese border guards, and that through this area China had built the Xinjiang-Tibet highway from Yecheng in southwestern Xinjiang to Gaer (Gartok) in southeastern Tibet. He even explained why this matter had not been raised in the 1954 Sino-Indian negotiations—"because conditions were not ripe for its settlement and the Chinese side, on its part, had no time to study the question." China's proposal, according to Zhou's letter, was that pending a satisfactory negotiation of all outstanding boundary differences, both sides should maintain their existing positions. This proposal, as well as the basic Chinese attitude toward all boundary issues, implied that China intended to retain the territory in its de facto possession in the western sector of Tibet; would not cross the McMahon line in the eastern sector, despite rejecting the line as the legal basis for its boundary with India there; and considered a formal demarcation of all boundaries an issue that remained to be solved through negotiation.

Meanwhile, the situation in Tibet aggravated the Sino-Indian border dispute. Beginning in the mid-1950s, the Khamba tribesmen in eastern

Tibet, opposed to Beijing's policy of preparing Tibet for autonomy and democratic reform, organized a military revolt and jeopardized Communist Chinese communications with Tibet from the east.[110] Probably for this reason, the PLA, together with more than 3,000 civilians, undertook the construction of the 1,200-kilometer Xinjiang-Tibet highway across the Aksai Chin under extremely difficult natural conditions from March 1956 to October 1957.[111] By the middle of 1958, when the Khamba revolt and China's military counteraction had assumed major proportions, Chinese sensitivities regarding the disputed and largely uncontrolled Sino-Indian frontier were no doubt especially acute. In a note to India on July 10, 1958, the Chinese leadership revealed that "subversive and disruptive activities against China's Tibetan region were carried out in Kalimpong in India, near Darjeeling," and implied all sorts of possibilities for collusion between the Tibetan insurgents and Indian agents, and perhaps American and Chiang Kai-shek special agents as well.[112]

The revolt in Lhasa and the flight of the Dalai Lama to India in March 1959 triggered a new outburst of public polemics between New Delhi and Beijing, intensified the border dispute, and aggravated the Sino-Indian cordiality that had been carefully maintained since 1954. The Indian government granted asylum to the Dalai Lama with courtesy and sympathy and permitted the release of his famous Tezpur statement in April 1959.[113] Indian public opinion became even more pro-Tibetan. Many thousands of Tibetans escaped into Nepal and India, and many mysteriously got arms and recrossed the border.[114]

From the Chinese point of view, the Tibetan revolt was aided and supported by outsiders, including Indians and American and Chinese Nationalist agents operating from bases in India.[115] India's sympathy and support for the Tibetan movement was aimed at separating Tibet from China and pursuing Tibetan independence.[116] In these circumstances, the Chinese leadership obviously felt it was necessary to seal off the Indian frontiers along the McMahon line for the purpose of preventing armed Tibetan rebels from crossing the border and acquiring external aid and support.[117] India, in turn, was sensitive to Chinese military activities along its borders and moved its border patrols forward into the frontier of Tibet. The result was brief but bloody clashes between Indian and Chinese patrols at Kongka Pass in western Tibet as well as Longju in eastern Tibet in the fall of 1959.[118]

Despite its criticism of India's pro-Tibetan attitude,[119] the Beijing leadership did not want to send a threatening signal to India. Rather, the leadership appears to have worried that the unprecedented clashes between the two countries would cause a further deterioration of Sino-Indian relations at a time when China considered the United States its primary enemy abroad and urgently needed to devote its efforts to long-term economic construction at home. In a formal statement to Indian Foreign Secretary S. Dutt on May 16, 1959, China's ambassador claimed that China didn't want war with India at a time when its main attention and policy of struggle internationally were being directed against U.S. imperialism. He further noted that "the enemy of the Chinese people lies in the east—the U.S. imperialists have many military bases in Taiwan, in South Korea, Japan and in the Philippines which are all directed against China.... China will not be so foolish as to antagonize India in the West ... we can't have two centers of attention, nor can we take friend for foe. This is our state policy."[120] In a note to the Indian embassy in Beijing on December 26, 1959, the Chinese Ministry of Foreign Affairs implied that "China is still very backward economically and culturally, needs decades or even over a hundred years of arduous efforts to overcome such backwardness," and stated that "in order to attain the great goals in peaceful construction the Chinese people are in urgent need of a long-term peaceful international environment."[121] In a letter to Prime Minister Nehru on December 17, 1959, Premier Zhou also suggested that China urgently needed a period of long-term peaceful construction and that the Chinese didn't want to create tension, mainly because it would "dissipate and divert the Chinese people's attention from domestic matters."[122] The Chinese leadership perceived that domestic and international constraints would add to Chinese motives and behavior in the conduct of general foreign relations, particularly in dealings regarding border disputes with neighboring countries, which through friendly consultations would take into account both the historical background and the present situation.

By April 1960, China had been successful in resolving boundary disputes with two of its neighbors, Burma and Nepal. In an agreement with Burma, China accepted the McMahon alignment in the far north in return for Burma's concession of some areas contiguous with China.[123] Both the Burmese precedent—a way to put pressure on Nehru—and China's presence in Aksai Chin since 1950 (an area in which China had a strong strategic interest), would lead China to negotiate on the basis of de facto possession of the disputed territories. In a meeting in April 1960, Premier Zhou offered Prime Minister Nehru a diplomatic package, particularly suggesting that China would accept Indian control of the N.E.F.A. in return for India's acceptance of China's possession of Aksai Chin (eastern Ladakh).[124] The package also included China's past proposals that pending an overall settlement, the two sides should maintain the existing border, and that the armed personnel on the two sides of the border should withdraw twenty kilometers in order to maintain the tranquility of the border region.[125] Prior to this meeting, China announced that since the Kongka Pass incident the Chinese government had stopped sending out patrols along the entire frontier.[126]

Zhou's diplomatic package did not affect India's policy on the boundary question. India took a position during the meeting that neither the McMahon line nor India's claim to Aksai Chin was subject to negotiation and that China's withdrawal from the disputed area in western Tibet was a prerequisite for talks between India and China.[127] From the Indian point of view, the proposal to trade the N.E.F.A. for eastern Ladakh was seen as "a derogation of the juridical validity of the northern border," and the proposal to suspend patrolling along the border was considered "a derogation from India's right to send patrols into her claimed territory in the west," as Maxwell puts it.[128]

More important is the fact that after the summit meeting, eastern Ladakh emerged as the major area in contention, the uncompromising attitude of both sides toward the border disputes remained unchanged up to October 1962, and India began to implement the policy of advancing patrols into western Tibet. Beginning in the late 1950s, the Indian defense community began to consider that the presence of Indian troops in the disputed Aksai Chin region would restrict a further Chinese advance into the region, strengthen India's diplomatic leverage in dealing with China, and force the ultimate withdrawal of Chinese patrols from the disputed territories, thereby cutting China's lines of communication.[129] Nehru was reported to frame this policy politically, "for the benefit of the Parliament and the public which has criticized the way he was handling the border situation."[130]

But the actual implementation of India's Tibetan policy was delayed until mid-1961 because of the need to build roads and create communication infrastructures, as well as because of the regional commander's resistance.[131] In 1958–59, a Border Roads Development Board was created with India's prime minister as chairman and the defense minister as vice-chairman. By 1961, India had acquired AN-12 aircraft, MI-4 helicopters, and engineering and other equipment from the United States and the Soviet Union.[132] By the end of 1961, India had established more than fifty posts in Ladakh and the N.E.F.A. and occupation rights in some 200 square miles of Indian-claimed territory.[133] The number of new Indian military posts increased by more than forty in western Tibet between the spring and fall of 1962.[134] The new posts were established with the military effectiveness of year-round barracks and overlooked Chinese posts so as to interpose Indian posts and patrol activities between them, cutting supply lines where possible.[135]

On August 14, 1962, Nehru reported to the Parliament that India had three times as many outposts in the disputed western sector of Tibet as China had and that India had regained control over nearly 2,500 miles of the 12,000 square miles previously lost to China.[136] In addition to establishing new military posts, India strengthened its border patrol. Numerous official army directives in December 1961 formalized the forward patrols, saying that "in Ladakh we are to patrol as far forward as possible from our present positions towards the international border as recognized by us."[137]

As viewed from Beijing, such forward patrols constituted Indian troop intrusions into Chinese-claimed territory, especially in western Tibet, to which China attached the greatest importance. According to Chinese protest notes to the Indian Embassy in Beijing, the intrusions by Indian ground troops and motorboats numbered as many as 121 from June 1961 to October 1962.[138] More than 100 cases occurred from April 1962 to October 1962, while only 12 cases occurred from mid-1961 to early 1962. Nearly all the intrusions were made in western Tibet, with the remainder in the N.E.F.A.[139] India's forward patrol and other ground activities appear to have been closely supported by the Indian Air Force. Numerous Chinese notes protested Indian intrusions into Chinese air space, citing 513 sorties for the period from mid-1961 to September 1962.[140] Of these, 431 sorties occurred from April to September 1962.[141] According to Chinese notes, the intruding aircraft not only circled for reconnaissance purposes but also often airdropped military supplies and personnel on Chinese-claimed territory, sometimes even airdropping military supplies on Chinese posts.[142]

India's forward patrols into Tibet were accompanied by an unprecedented display of Indian militaristic nationalism elsewhere as well as by an optimistic view based on Indian politicians' perception of China's difficult domestic and international situation—all of which obviously heightened China's concern. In December 1961, India occupied the Portugese colony of Goa and hinted that it would link the military victory in Goa to the future border dispute with China.[143] In February 1962, Indian Home Minister L. B. Shastri was said to declare that "if the Chinese will not vacate the areas occupied by her, India will have to repeat what she did in Goa." In an article on June 8, 1962, the *Hindustan Times* encouraged India's continued firm stand with armed force against China. It noted that in view of the heightened Taiwan Strait crisis in the first half of 1962, China was not in a position to face the prospect of war on a second front simultaneously.[144] In early 1962, even Nehru himself had the conviction—based on reports by some of his ambassadors and on the advice of some of his political and other confidants—that the forward policy would not result in any serious Chinese resistance. General Kaul, who was close to Nehru, later recalled Nehru's conviction:

> Nehru believed . . . that the Chinese were really not so strong as they were made out to be, and had many of their own troubles; they had internal disorders due to food shortages, floods, and an unpopular dictatorial regime; that there were revolts in Tibet, and on the whole, the morale of the Chinese people and their armed forces was cracking up; and that *if we dealt with them strongly we should have the better of them.* . . . Nehru felt that due to this background, the Chinese were in no position to divert their attention to anything except putting their internal matters right.[145]

In the autumn of 1961, when the Chinese recognized India's increased military activity in the western sector of Tibet, they perceived it as a "purposeful and coordinated attempt to realize India's territorial claims unilaterally and by force."[146] In the middle of 1962, when the Beijing leadership realized that Indian forces were pressing forward on Chinese territory along a wide front, it directed its main attention to the recovery of its economy and to the Taiwan Strait crisis but took note of India's policy as "an audacious Napoleonic planning" to nibble away Chinese territory bit by bit and to change the status quo of the boundary.[147] China's leadership was obviously apprehensive of the possibility that its attitude of restraint and tolerance would be taken by India as an expression of weakness and would further India's territorial claims by armed force. A *People's Daily* editorial on July 9, 1962, was addressed to Indian authorities: "It seems that the Indian government takes China's restraint as an indication of weakness. But the Indian authorities would be making a big mistake if they thought that the Chinese frontier guards would submit to the armed Indian advance, that they would renounce their sacred duty of defending the frontiers of the motherland, and give up the right of self-defence when subjected to unwarranted attacks."[148]

That China would certainly respond to unwarranted attacks, despite its domestic and international constraints, was signaled when on July 10, 1962, Chinese military pressure was brought to bear on new Indian posts in the Galwan Valley of western Tibet for the first time since the border clashes of late 1959. Facing a Gurkha platoon that had been sent forward to cut off Chinese outposts in the Galwan Valley, a battalion of the PLA surrounded an Indian company in assault formation, thereby cutting off the Indian post from its ground supplies but avoiding an open clash.[149] This attempt was a major PLA countermove to halt the Indian forward movement and to apply pressure that would bring Nehru to the conference table, as several scholars put it.[150] But the PLA countermove failed to attain these two aims. The Galwan post was supplied by air during the incident and until October 1962.[151] Additionally, a wave of triumph appeared to sweep the press and politicians in India. For instance, *Hindu* published an article in which it noted that the Chinese had withdrawn "in the face of the determined stand of the small Indian garrison," and that if the Indian troops were resolute, the Chinese would not carry out their physical threats to attack the post.[152]

Nehru's persistent intransigence toward repeated Chinese proposals for negotiation may have led the Chinese leadership to perceive that the Indian authorities did not want a peaceful settlement of the border dispute and forced China to accept the military situation that India had created along the borders in both the western and middle sectors of Tibet. The two months prior to the October military confrontation were a period of "diplomatic interlude," Allen S. Whiting argues.[153] India had continued to take the position since the April meeting of 1960 that any border discussions should be preceded by China's withdrawal from Indian-claimed territory, particularly in Tibet's western sector.[154]

But in July 1962 there were some hints that India was changing its attitude. On July 13, after the Galwan Valley incident, Nehru suggested preparing for discussions with Chinese Ambassador Pan.[155] On July 25, Chinese Foreign Minister Chen Yi, who was attending the Geneva Conference on Laos, proposed negotiations to Krishna Menon, India's defense minister.[156] On July 21, the first skirmish since the Kongka Pass incident in October 1959 occurred in the Chip Chap Valley of western Tibet. On July 26, in reply to China's strong protest, the Indian government sent a note saying that India would be prepared to resume discussions "as soon as the current tensions have been eased and the appropriate climate is created."[157] But Nehru's attitude suddenly changed, probably because of pressure from public opinion and Parliament. Reading a prepared statement in Parliament on August 13, he stated that "any discussion . . . can't start unless present tensions are removed and the status quo of the boundary which existed before and which has since been already altered by force is restored."[158] In a note of August 22, the Indian Ministry of External Affairs maintained a position identical to that employed by Nehru in Parliament, but communicated its readiness to discuss "preliminary measures" essential to the holding of further discussions.[159]

From the Chinese perspective, if China were to accept India's precondition for discussions, China would remain defenseless in western Tibet, including the Ladakh corridor between Tibet and Xinjiang, which the Chinese government regarded as an important strategic road.[160] The Chinese leadership interpreted "essential preliminary measures" as another kind of precondition for negotiation and attacked India's dual policy of "phoney negotiations and real incursions."[161]

Not until October did China decide that the boundary question could not be settled through negotiations. On September 13, the Chinese government again proposed formally that the two governments hold discussions without setting any preconditions and suggested October 15 as the date to start these discussions, first in Beijing and then in New Delhi.[162] India replied on September 19 that it would accept the Chinese proposal only if China accepted India's preconditions for the agenda.[163] After the Chedong (Dohla post, N.E.F.A.) clash of September 10, the first in eastern Tibet since the Longze (Longju) incident in August 1959, India made an additional demand. In its reply of October 6 to China's note of October 3, in which China expressed opposition to setting any preconditions for the agenda, but willingness to receive Indian representatives in Beijing on October 15,[164] India insisted that Chinese troops withdraw from a locality in the Chedong area before discussions could be held.[165] One more serious skirmish took place northwest of

Chedong on October 10. Twenty-two Chinese were reportedly killed or wounded.[166] On the same day, just before his departure for Madras and Ceylon, Nehru clearly revealed India's position, saying that he had instructed Indian troops "to clear Chinese forces from the Northeast Frontier Agency." He called the Chedong skirmish a "major incident" in which the Chinese had suffered about 100 casualties, and emphasized that there was no chance for talks "so long as this aggression is continuing."[167]

The continuation of India's forward policy in spite of Chinese military pressure, India's rejections of China's repeated proposals for negotiations, and Nehru's declaratory policy followed by the Chedong incidents all signaled an imminent threat to China. The Chinese leadership perceived that the Indian government had already decided to launch a massive attack against Chinese troops. A *People's Daily* editorial on October 10 no longer proposed talks with the Indian authorities. Instead, it stated that India had decided to go to war with China. The editorial noted that the Indian paper *Tribune* had reported on October 5 that after the Cabinet meeting on October 4, the Indian government had decided to use armed force to deal with China, and that "according to a DPA report of October 8, Nehru has authorized India's new commander-in-chief of the eastern border area to fight a limited offensive operation."[168] On October 14, another *People's Daily* editorial stated that Nehru had made up his mind to attack the Chinese frontier guards on "an even bigger scale," and that the Indian army had completed preparations and was waiting to be unleashed. The editorial reminded readers that all foreign aggressors—the Japanese Imperial Army and the U.S. Army—had been cleared out of Chinese territory in the past. It then turned its attention to the PLA: "All comrade commanders and fighters of the People's Liberation Army guarding the Sino-Indian border, redouble your vigilance! Indian troops may at any time attempt to carry out Nehru's instruction to get rid of you. Be well prepared! Your sacred task now is to defend our territory and be ever ready to deal resolute counter-blows at any invader!"[169]

Internal/External Problems and U.S.-Indian Relations

For the Beijing leadership, the spring of 1962 was a time of external problems as well as domestic difficulties. In addition to the food shortages and social unrest that prevailed among the Chinese people at large, there were problems such as insurgents in Tibet and the exodus to Hong Kong and the Soviet Union. There was tension in Southeast Asia, the Taiwan Strait, and on the Sino-Indian and Sino-Soviet borders.

Since the Tibetan revolt in 1959, the insurgents in Tibet had not been fully suppressed, and in fact were becoming more rather than less of a problem. In the spring of 1962, famine struck Tibet, and the food situation in this area became desperate. At the end of 1960 and in early 1961, more than 10,000 rebels were reported to be at large in the mountains of eastern Tibet. They increased their raids on China's convoys, garrisons, and food supplies, and with the collusion of numerous indigenous feudal cliques were able to cross the Sino-Nepalese and Sino-Indian frontiers without hindrance.[170] Much more dangerous for China was the fact that the insurgents in Tibet were encouraged and supported by the American Central Intelligence Agency, Nationalist China, and India.

The success of the Dalai Lama's escape to India in March 1959 was reportedly due to an American CIA operation.[171] After that the CIA continued to support the clandestine activities of the Tibetan rebels in training and reequipping anticommunist insurgents in Tibet. By 1961 the CIA was reported to have trained groups of 200 and 300 Tibetans at Camp Hale, Colorado, and to have supplied more than 40,000 Tibetans with arms through airdrops. These activities were said to be directed by "private planes of Civil Air Transport (CAT) Complex on Taiwan which was a CIA proprietary." CAT reportedly carried out more than 200 overflights of mainland China and Tibet in 1960 and airdropped military supplies at CIA operational bases in Tibet and northeast India. Bases in Taiwan, Thailand, and Nepal also were used as jumping-off points for the CIA's clandestine operation in Tibet.[172] One secret CIA document described vividly the aims of the Tibetan operation:

> From the beginning of the Tibetan operation . . . spot raids against Chinese facilities in the backward mountain country [were] an annoyance to Peking and a reminder of its vulnerability. . . . The raids accomplished little beyond giving the Tibetan troops some temporary satisfaction and fanning their hopes that someday they would lead a true invasion of their homeland. Communication lines were cut, some sabotage was carried out, and from time to time an ambush of a small Chinese communist force was undertaken.[173]

Nationalist Chinese support for the insurgents in Tibet complemented CIA activities there. To judge from a Communist Chinese statement, Nationalist secret agents infiltrated groups of Tibetan refugees in India, organized a "Tibetan Welfare Association" among the refugees at Kalimpong and Darjeeling in India, and recruited underground leaders from among them. The Nationalist Chinese government reportedly trained about 2,000 Tibetan youths in Taiwan as "future leaders" of Tibet.[174] In addition, Indian public opinion and India's political leaders were pro-Tibetan and demonstrated anti-Chinese sentiments. According to the Chinese press, the Indian paper *Statesman* on January 26, 1962, proposed that "the support for the Dalai Lama and for the Tibetan refugees be made part of Indian policy towards China." In a BBC television interview on March 12, 1962, Nehru called the Dalai Lama a significant factor in the Sino-Indian border dispute and criticized China for its occupation of Tibet, claiming that "it has done a lot of harm to Tibet and its people.[175]

The U.S. and Nationalist Chinese support of the insurgents in Tibet, as well as India's pro-Tibetan attitude, caused China concern. The Beijing leadership worried that India would collaborate with the United States and Nationalist China on Tibet and decide to help the Tibetan rebels by supplying arms through exiled Tibetan leaders in India in the wake of increasing border tensions.[176] This scenario logically heightened the Beijing leadership's concern that the situation in Tibet might invite foreign intervention, probably coordinated by the United States, at the very time when China was grappling with severe economic difficulties. Another domestic dimension of the problem, from Beijing's point of view, was that the intervention of capitalist countries in Tibet would result in a collusion of feudal cliques with imperialists and foreign reactionaries and encourage the class enemies at home to plot to split Tibet away from the mainland.[177] In this respect, the Tibetan problem constituted a new threat to China's security.

The activities of the United States in Southeast Asia and the manifest Nationalist Chinese willingness to prepare for a counterattack against the mainland, followed by the exodus to Hong Kong and the Soviet Union, all constituted another kind of threat to China's security. Even though they occurred independently of one another, these events added a new context to the Chinese perspective on the Himalayan frontiers.

Early in 1962 the Chinese leadership began to receive a threatening signal as a result of U.S. military activities in Southeast Asia. In Beijing's view, the Kennedy administration, since its inauguration, had consistently plotted a "new strategy" for aggression against Laos and South Vietnam under the slogan "making Asians fight Asians," had collaborated with the SEATO countries to prepare "special warfare," and had stepped up armed intervention in the two countries. U.S. bases in Okinawa, the Philippines, Taiwan, and Thailand were being used as forward logistical bases for the U.S.-inspired limited warfare in Laos and South Vietnam.[178] Beijing perceived "U.S. aggressive moves" in Southeast Asia as "a serious threat to the security of China"[179] and equated the fresh U.S. plot of "making Asians fight Asians" with a plot by non-Communist countries, including India, to encircle the mainland. A *People's Daily* editorial on April 27, 1962, commented:

What is the "new strategy" of the Kennedy Administration? The Paris newspaper *L'express* has noted: "The American strategists dream of an Asian anticommunist crescent—from India to Japan." ... the United States would like to see a group of noncommunist countries in Asia "adding their weight" against China. The sinister U.S. plot of "making Asians fight Asians" is being carried out under an anti-China and anti-communist banner. Of course, on the one hand, the United States is attempting to invade China, and on the other hand, it is reaching out its aggressive claws to what it calls noncommunist countries.[180]

Beijing's apprehension about a U.S. plot of encirclement was doubled by Taiwan's direct threat to invade the coastal areas of the mainland at the time when China confronted domestic problems like the exoduses to Hong Kong and the Soviet Union. In the spring of 1962 there was an unprecedented exodus to Hong Kong mainly from Guangdong Province and to the Soviet Union from Xinjiang. Several thousand Chinese were reportedly seeking refuge in Hong Kong in the wake of three years of extreme economic difficulties at home. The number entering Hong Kong illegally increased gradually in the early months of 1962, but swelled suddenly into a mass flight of refugees in mid-1962. At the end of July, Hong Kong officials estimated that in the first half of 1962 the Colonial Department in Hong Kong had registered 1,200 illegal refugees a day, and predicted that by the end of 1962 the department would register 150,000—more than three times the 1961 total.[181] Hong Kong newspapers covered the exodus almost daily, commenting that the mass flight of refugees was mainly due to food shortages and the heightened discontent of the population. Pro-Nationalist Hong Kong newspapers carried accounts of riots and demonstrations on the mainland and commented that the Beijing leadership appeared to be losing control over the mainland.[182]

The exodus to Hong Kong in the spring of 1962 was paralleled by a similar flight of refugees from Xinjiang into the Soviet Union. In May 1962, more than 60,000 inhabitants of Xinjiang—primarily Uygurs, Kazakhs, and natives of Russia—reportedly crossed the Sino-Soviet border.[183] Unlike the exodus from Guangdong, the exodus from Xinjiang was stimulated by outsiders, reportedly local Soviet authorities who distributed thousands of Russian passports to Xinjiang Moslem refugees.[184] In late May, when the Chinese authorities tried administrative ways to stop the flow and sealed the border, thousands of Xinjiang Moslems formed mobs, attacked the government headquarters in Yining (Kuldja), a town fifty miles from the Soviet border, and fled across the border.[185]

Pro-Soviet Moslem insurgents had been fleeing across the border from Xinjiang since 1958. They were armed with Soviet weapons, accorded sanctuary in Soviet territory, and continued to threaten Chinese supply lines along the Xinjiang-Tibet highway until mid-1962.[186] The Soviets were pro-Moslem during and after the exodus from Xinjiang, claiming that "over 60,000 inhabitants of Sinkiang, unable to stand harsh living conditions, hunger, national discrimination made a spontaneous dash for the Soviet Union."[187] Much more important was the Soviets' allegation that Uygur broadcasts from Soviet stations repeatedly declared after the exodus that

"Sinkiang is our land and sooner or later we will return to occupy it."[188] Later, on September 6, 1963, in an official charge to the CPSU, the Chinese leadership replied: "In April and May 1962 the leaders of the CPSU used their organs and personnel in Sinkiang, China to carry out large scale subversive activities in the Ili region and enticed and coerced several tens of thousands of Chinese citizens into going to the Soviet Union."[189]

In Beijing's view, the exodus from Xinjiang could result in an incident on the Sino-Soviet border just when China was having to deal with Indian military pressure on the Himalayan frontier. In an interview with Japanese journalists on May 29, 1962, Chinese Foreign Minister Chen Yi revealed this concern by indicating that "we must provide against incidents that may occur on other borders."[190] Beijing's leaders obviously worried that the Soviet leadership would exploit China's difficult situation and intervene in Xinjiang.

Simultaneously with the exodus of refugees from Guangdong and Xinjiang, tension in the Taiwan Strait rapidly increased. In the early months of 1962, a series of bellicose statements by high-level Nationalist officials called for invasion preparations more directly than ever before and predicted an imminent return to the mainland. It is reported that in March 1962, Chiang Kai-shek said that "either subjectively or objectively we can no longer vacillate or hesitate to perform our duty to reunify our country."[191] By objective conditions, Nationalist leaders obviously meant taking advantage of the domestic vulnerability of mainland China. A Taibei official reportedly claimed that in the wake of serious economic difficulties and the discontent prevalent among the population, "the mainland is a powder keg on the verge of explosion."[192] As early as March, the Nationalist government issued a conscription mobilization decree in an attempt to draft additional manpower. In April the Taibei authorities adopted a special defense budget for wartime economic mobilization, and in early May imposed a special new "preparation-for-invasion" tax.[193] In the spring of 1962, high-level U.S. military and government officials visited Taiwan one after another. They included W. Averell Harriman, assistant secretary of state; Lyman L. Lemnitzer, chairman of the Joint Chiefs of Staff; and Allen W. Dulles, former director of the CIA and at that time head of the agency's "special warfare" unit. In early May, Washington appointed an ambassador to the Republic of China, Admiral Alan G. Kirk, who had had extensive experience with amphibious warfare during World War II.[194]

The tension in the Taiwan Strait reached its peak in late June 1962. The Chinese government reportedly redeployed seven or eight divisions of the PLA along the Taiwan Strait.[195] On June 26, the Guangzhou Municipal People's Council issued civil defense regulations to govern air-raid warning signals and traffic control.[196] On June 23, the New China News Agency released its correspondent's report on the preparations of the Nationalists, backed by the United States, to invade the coastal areas of the mainland. Describing Chiang's preparations for war against the mainland, the report stressed that the Nationalists dreamed of taking advantage of certain temporary difficulties on the mainland, but that without U.S. support they would be unable to carry out a military adventure.[197] On the same date, John M. Cabot, U.S. ambassador to the Geneva Conference on Laos, reportedly informed Chinese Ambassador Wang that the United States would not support any attempt by the Chinese Nationalists to invade the mainland. President Kennedy confirmed that position at his news conference of June 27, but declared that the United States would continue to defend Taiwan and the offshore islands if necessary. Beginning in July, the heightened Taiwan Strait crisis appeared to blow over.[198]

During and after the Taiwan Strait crisis, the Beijing leadership perceived a linkage between the Indian and Nationalist Chinese threats. It worried that the United States would use India to put pressure on the Himalayan frontiers and on Tibet while the Nationalists prepared to attack the mainland. In his May interview, Chen Yi expressed this concern, noting that "the Pentagon generals might support Chiang in starting a counter-offensive on the mainland along the coastal area, or they might be planning to raise trouble on the western border area of China by utilizing the China-Indian border dispute," and that the future of the dispute might depend upon India's willingness to be utilized by the Americans.[199]

Chen Yi's perception was the prevalent one in Beijing. A *People's Daily* editorial on July 9, 1962, noted that in the Indian Parliament on June 20, 21, and 23, Nehru had boasted that the position in Ladakh was "more advantageous to India than it was previously," and that "India had opened some new patrol posts to overlook the Chinese posts."[200] In Beijing's view, Nehru's boastful statements, followed by the increasing provocations of Indian troops, were by no means accidental, since June 1962 was a time of heightened Chinese concern about the Taiwan Strait. An "Observer" article in *People's Daily* on July 21 revealed the linkage between the intensified Indian intrusions into China and Chiang's preparations to invade the mainland with support from the United States. The article particularly noted the *Hindustan Times* comment on June 8 that China "might have to face prospects of war on two fronts simultaneously."[201]

The Beijing leadership also received signals of U.S.-Indian collaboration against China from Washington. During and after the Taiwan Strait crisis, high-level American officials emphasized U.S. aid to India. In testimony before the Senate Foreign Relations Committee on June 6, 1962, U.S. Ambassador to India John Kenneth Galbraith spoke of the importance of the U.S. aid program in India.[202] In a television interview in Washington on June 9, 1962, Acting Chairman of the Senate Foreign Relations Committee

John Sparkman affirmed continued U.S. aid to India, noting that "India is pressing very hard against communist China upon her northern boundary and northeastern frontier."[203] President Kennedy was reported to have said on August 22: "It is our interest to support India."[204] In Beijing's view, U.S. aid to India was a barometer of India's anti-China campaigns. An article by the Editorial Department of *People's Daily* on October 27, 1962, equated the intensification of India's anti-China campaign with the increase in U.S. aid to India.[205]

In the months prior to the Sino-Indian border war, U.S. sympathy with India on the Sino-Indian border issue may have been perceived by the Chinese leadership as an element intended to block peaceful negotiations between India and China. When the Chinese proposed speedy negotiations on the Sino-Indian boundary question in early 1962, Galbraith was said to have encouraged India to reject the Chinese proposals. Arguing that "India should be firm, and if necessary, enter into hostilities," he expressed the belief that "China's power of resistance today is at its lowest."[206] In this respect, the Chinese leadership may have thought that India's persistent refusal of China's proposals for negotiation was partly inspired by U.S. sympathy or support on the Sino-Indian border question and by U.S. aid to India.

The Moscow–Beijing–New Delhi Triangle

The linkage perceived by the Chinese leadership between threats from the U.S. and Taiwan and from India forms the basis for analysis of the Sino-Indian border war from one perspective. Chinese perceptions regarding Indo-Soviet and Sino-Soviet relations form another. During and following the Sino-Indian border clashes in 1959, Sino-Soviet relations worsened while Indo-Soviet relations led the Soviets to take a neutral position in the Sino-Indian border dispute in 1959.

In 1958–59, there was conflict between the Soviet Union and China over a number of issues, including the Soviets' criticism of China's communes and the GLF, the precise terms of planning for and commanding a joint fleet for shoreline defense, and the issue of nuclear sharing.[207] At both the Third Conference of the Rumanian Communist Party at Bucharest and the Moscow Conference of Eighty-one Communist Parties in 1960, the earlier rift between the two countries was further exposed in disagreements over the political character of the current epoch, tactics concerning war and peace, the unity of international communism, and support for national liberation movements.[208] In particular, after the Bucharest conference in June 1960, the Soviet government decided to withdraw more than 1,300 Soviet advisers, abolish about 300 contracts for experts, and cancel 250 projects for scientific and technical cooperation.[209] The Russian decision came just when the Chinese were devoting major efforts to economic recovery.

In the context of worsening relations between Moscow and Beijing, the Soviet leaders adopted a neutral attitude toward the Sino-Indian border clashes. After the Longze incident in August 1959, the Chinese government reportedly told the Soviet chargé d'affaires the facts behind the clash and advised him that the Soviet government should not make a public statement on the Sino-Indian boundary dispute.[210] Despite this advice, the Soviet government, in a TASS statement on September 9, expressed general regret over the incident and exposed Sino-Soviet differences on the boundary dispute.[211] In October 1959, in a speech to the Supreme Soviet, Khrushchev called the incident "sad" and "stupid," saying that the disputed areas were sparsely populated and of no great value to human life. He emphasized that the Soviet Union was bound by "unbreakable bonds of friendship" to India as well as to the P.R.C., thereby equating the worth of a communist country with that of a noncommunist country.[212]

The Soviet attitude on the Sino-Indian border clashes was received very differently in India and China. In New Delhi, Nehru and other high-level officials paid full attention to comments made by TASS and Khrushchev and interpreted them as being indirectly helpful to India. Nehru was reported to have said at a press conference on September 11 that the TASS statement was a fair and unusual one.[213] Defense Minister Krishna Menon emphasized that the Soviet Union had spoken for the first time about a peaceful settlement between a communist and a noncommunist country.[214] The Soviets' neutrality in the Sino-Indian border dispute, together with Sino-Soviet disagreement on a number of other issues, may have encouraged India's leaders to think the balance had tipped in India's favor in dealings over the border clashes. India's decision to pursue a forward policy in late 1959 may have been reached in part because of the Soviets' attitude. Immediately after the Soviet Union revealed that it would not support the Chinese, Nehru probably gained confidence that he could count on Soviet support for India's position. In late October 1959, Nehru reportedly sent a secret memorandum to Indian diplomats abroad, suggesting that they should prepare for the eventuality of India's using armed force in order to push Chinese troops from the disputed area in Ladakh.[215]

In contrast, the Beijing leadership regarded the Soviet stand on the border dispute not only as censureship of China but also as a violation of the spirit of proletarian internationalism.[216] In December 1959, Chinese leaders allegedly met with the Soviet ambassador on six occasions to protest the strictly neutral position of Moscow.[217] At both the Bucharest and Moscow conferences in 1960, China's leadership again tried and failed to persuade the Soviet leaders to modify their position. Instead, Chinese activities along the border were rebutted by the Soviet leaders as expressions of purely nationalist sentiment that departed from the principles of Marxism-Leninism.[218]

Beginning in late 1959, the Chinese began to pay attention to the emerging economic ties and military transactions between the Soviet Union and India. The Soviet Union showed a willingness to aid India's economic development and in September 1959 decided to authorize credits worth more than $500 million in support of India's Third Five-Year Plan.[219] This decision reportedly prompted the Chinese leaders to charge, at the Bucharest conference, that Soviet aid was being used to bolster the Nehru government.[220] What must have especially rankled Beijing was the fact that Soviet aid to India had begun at the same time that China's economic difficulties were aggravated by the withdrawal of Soviet advisers.

Soviet military aid to India undoubtedly added to China's concern. In April 1961, India purchased eight Antonov transports from the Soviet Union for use in the Ladakh area. Forty Russian pilots, navigators, and mechanics came to India to instruct Indians in the operation and maintenance of the aircraft. The Soviet Union also supplied India with two dozen Ilyushin-14 transports and Mil'-4 helicopters. The latter were known to be used for lifting men and supplies to altitudes of 17,000 feet.[221] In the spring of 1962, American congressmen reported that India would purchase two squadrons of the latest type of MIG jet fighters. India may have wanted these two squadrons to offset the two squadrons of F-104s that the United States had promised to provide Pakistan in 1961,[222] but Beijing was hardly likely to make that interpretation.

In mid-August 1962, Menon announced that the Indian government had signed an agreement with the Soviet Union on the manufacture of MIG-21s.[223] This was the first agreement for military hardware between the two countries. The Soviet Union could now license India to manufacture very sophisticated equipment that it had not given to the P.R.C. On September 13, the *Times* of India also reported that the Indian government had decided to buy two squadrons of Soviet MIG jet fighters.[224] It should be noted that the MIG deals between the Soviet Union and India appeared to have been pushed at the very time when skirmishes were occurring frequently on the Sino-Indian frontier.

In Beijing's view, the Soviets' economic and military support to India in 1961 and 1962 meant that the Soviet attitude was no longer neutral. The Chinese probably believed that the Russians had decided to align with India against China and to provide India with military supplies for its forward policy in the border areas. On October 8, 1962, the Chinese leadership reportedly protested to the Soviet ambassador that "Soviet-made helicopters and transport planes were being used by India for airdroppings and transporting military supplies in the Sino-Indian border," and that such supplies made a "bad impression" on Chinese frontier guards.[225]

In the months prior to the border war, Beijing's concern about the pro-Indian attitude of the Soviet Union was surely heightened by the exodus from Xinjiang and by Yugoslavia's stand on the border dispute. After the exodus of refugees from Xinjiang to the Soviet Union, the Chinese clearly remained suspicious of Soviet intervention in Xinjiang as well as of Soviet subversive activities elsewhere. Beijing reportedly closed the Soviet consulates in Wulumuzhi (Urumchi) and Yining in Xinjiang in the summer of 1962.[226] Beijing was said to have asked Moscow to close its consulates in Shainghai, Dalian, and Huibin (Harbin) in late September 1962, when the Tenth Plenum of the CCP was being held.[227] In the meantime, the new Soviet-Yugoslav rapprochment was accelerated in mid-1962 and climaxed in late September 1962 when Leonid Brezhnev, leader of the CPSU, visited Belgrade. The two governments repeatedly confirmed the fundamental identity of their views on foreign affairs.[228] In an interview with an American correspondent on August 7, 1962, Tito reportedly agreed with Soviet policies for East-West détente and supported the avowedly neutral Soviet position on the Sino-Indian border issue, urging the Soviet government to play "a pacifying role" in the dispute.[229]

In Beijing's view, Tito's support for the Soviet stand on the border dispute was not only part of a coordinated anti-China campaign by two revisionist countries but was also backing for India's anti-China policies. At the Tenth Plenum, Beijing's hostility toward Khrushchev- and Tito-led revisionist activities appeared to reach its height. In a speech at the plenum on September 24, Chairman Mao attacked Soviet-Yugoslav revisionism and particularly reminded the audience of the Soviets' pro-Indian attitude on the border incidents of 1959. As he stated, "During the Sino-Indian border dispute, Khrushchev supported Nehru in attacking us and TASS issued a communique."[230] On October 27, a lengthy article by the Editorial Department of *People's Daily* attacked the pro-Indian attitude of the Soviet Union and Yugoslavia, noting that "on the Sino-Indian boundary question, Tito and his ilk have always hurled shameless slanders against China and become an echo of the Indian reactionaries."[231]

As has been suggested, the Chinese leadership worried that China's domestic difficulties would lead India to misperceive China's military strength. Added to this apprehension of an Indian miscalculation was the fear that worsening relations between Moscow and Beijing, Moscow's pro-Indian attitude and policies, and U.S. support of India would lead India's leaders to think that China was isolated internationally and was therefore in no position to challenge India's border position. Both of these concerns were made public after the border war. In a television interview with Karlsson, a correspondent of the Swedish Broadcasting Corporation, on February 17, 1963, Foreign Minister Chen Yi recalled India's miscalculation of the domestic and international situation China faced in 1962.[232] An article by the Editorial Department of *People's Daily* on November 8, 1963, also emphasized that point: "The Indians mistook China's long forbearance as a sign that China was weak and could be bullied. They thought that with the backing of the imperialists and the support of the Soviet leaders they had nothing to fear, and that as soon as they took action China would be forced to retreat and their territorial claims would be realized."[233]

There was a time correlation between the Chinese attack on India on October 20, 1962, and the confrontation between the Soviet Union and the United States over Cuba (October 22–28). Heightened Chinese concern about Washington's and Moscow's support of India and the possibility of a joint intervention in Tibet by Washington, Taiwan, and New Delhi may have led Beijing to time its attack to coincide with the Cuban missile crisis. Moscow and Washington were immobilized as a result of their confrontation over Cuba and could not intervene on behalf of New Delhi. It has been further speculated that the duration of the Chinese attack on India was closely related to the duration of the Washington-Moscow confrontation over Cuba. In other words, Beijing appears to have pressed its attack when the two superpowers were locked in confrontation over Cuba, but withdrew as the Cuban crisis ended.[234] This argument seems logical and sound, but remains an untested assumption.

In late September and early October, rumors about the presence of Soviet missiles in Cuba were being leaked by U.S. intelligence sources. In a speech on October 10, Senator Kenneth Keating disclosed that the construction of six IRBM bases was under way in Cuba. On ABC's "Issues and Answers" program on October 14, Presidential Assistant McGeorge Bundy, sensitive to the rumors, denied that Soviet offensive weapons had been moved to Cuba.[235] These developments suggest that Beijing would have been aware of the U.S. leaders' sensitivity to the presence of Soviet missiles in Cuba before October 20. But it is questionable, as Whiting notes, that the Beijing leadership could have predicted the timing of the American reaction, or the nature and duration of the confrontation. It was not until October 22, after highly secret deliberations with his Executive Committee, that President Kennedy announced a naval quarantine of Cuba.[236]

The heightened military tension on the Himalayan frontiers from September 20 onward, together with the frequent border skirmishes and China's apprehension of a massive attack by India, suggests that China had already made, at a minimum, a contingency plan for the border war. In a television interview with Karlsson, Chen Yi hinted that China had been prepared for war from July onward, a time when the Indian government continued to reject China's proposals for negotiations, persisted in applying armed pressure on the frontiers, and issued instructions relevant to the preparation for a large-scale offensive.[237] In this respect, it is highly improbable that China's October offensive was primarily motivated by the Cuban missile crisis.

Neither is it a convincing argument that the duration of the Cuban missile crisis affected the nature and duration of the Chinese border offensives in the one-month interval from October 20 to November 21, given the original Chinese plan and the Indian government's attitude and military moves during and after the PLA offensives, which we will discuss later. But this is not to say that the Chinese would not have considered the way the Soviets dealt with the Cuban missile crisis and Washington's support of India during and after the crisis.

The Border-War Decision

Diplomatic Line versus Militant Line

In previous sections, we have discussed the status of the Chinese economy, the extent of leadership stability, policy differences among Beijing's leaders, and the strategic outlook of the PLA. We have identified the policy priorities of the party center. We have also discussed the main threats from various sources perceived by the leadership and have linked them to the Chinese perspective on the Sino-Indian border dispute. It has been noted that the interplay of domestic difficulties and international threats provided different perspectives within the Beijing leadership on domestic and international events and that the Maoists and the Liuists were divided over how to deal with these problems. Both groups appeared to have different perceptions and different policy priorities, and the split between them seems to have been relevant to China's decision on the Sino-Indian border war. In this section, we will discuss why and how Beijing's leaders weighed policy priorities in terms of the interaction between domestic weaknessess and external threats, coordinated militant action with diplomatic methods, and responded with force to the threats posed by India. We will conclude with an overview of the main Chinese motives behind the October and November PLA offensives and a look at the general nature of linkages and their significance in the Chinese border-war decision.

In early 1962, the evaluation of the domestic and international situation by the Liuists, including Deng Xiaoping and Luo Ruiqing, was highly pessimistic. In their view, China was facing the most difficult domestic economic situtation encountered since its founding, and it would take more than ten years for the country to overcome the setbacks caused by the failure of the GLF. As for the international situation, the Liuists were suspicious of a basic assumption of Chinese foreign policy from 1957 onward—that "the East Wind prevails over the West Wind" (an allusion to potential communist superiority)—and believed that the anti-China campaigns being waged by the Soviet Union, the United States, and other capitalist countries would become even more frenzied. As a result, China would be isolated internationally. In these perspectives the Liuists appeared to be preoccupied with the recovery of the economy and to advocate a line of *sanze yibao*. Their promotion of more liberal policies in agriculture and industry was described as undermining the collective economy. Their voicing of a *sanhe yishao* line internationally was intended to lessen tensions with foreign opponents and to soften China's support for revolutionary struggle abroad.[238]

In the Liuists' view, the linkage between the *sanze yibao* and *sanhe yishao* lines had major policy implications. The party center (Liu and Mao) gave top priority to the recovery of the economy and was apprehensive of domestic weakness as a constraint on foreign policy. The Liuist group may have considered that to mute confrontations with the Soviet Union, the United States, and other capitalist countries at a time of domestic difficulties would help to decrease external threats to China's national security. There is considerable evidence that the Liuists did not want a heightening of tensions with the two superpowers and other capitalist countries and tried to relax them. According to a later account, Luo Ruiqing, chief of staff of the PLA, was criticized for underestimating Soviet subversive activities in Xinjiang and for carrying out unwillingly the directive of the Central Committee of the CCP and Mao that the army units in Xinjiang should strictly block the Chinese exodus to the Soviet Union.[239] As indicated in Deng Tuo's essays, by favoring a rapprochement with the United States, the Liuists appeared to want to lessen tension in the Taiwan Strait. Liu was said to have openly called on the Communist party of Burma to lay down its arms and cooperate with Ne Win, whom the Maoists regarded as the Chiang Kai-shek of Burma.[240]

In addition to the foreign-policy rationale behind the line, the Liuists' advocacy of *sanhe yishao* seemed to be prompted by their careful consideration of pursuing a welfare doctrine and importing foreign techniques. During the Cultural Revolution, the Liuists were charged with advocating a one-sided welfare doctrine and the adoption of foreign techniques against the Maoists' strategic policy of making simultaneous preparations against war and famine on the basis of self-reliance when China confronted temporary economic difficulties.[241] It is highly probable that for the Liuists, generally lessening tensions with foreign enemies would allow China to maintain its policy priority of economic recovery without reallocating scarce resources to national defense. It was expected that improvement of China's relations with the Soviet Union would revive the Soviet assistance required to overcome China's economic difficulties.

China's relaxation of tensions with capitalist countries, including the United States, would gradually open doors through which necessary techniques could be imported.

It is very hard to identify the Liuists' attitude toward the Sino-Indian border dispute. There is no specific information that ties the Liuists to a particular point of view on relations with India. We can only deduce their position from the *sanhe yishao* line they were later accused of having advocated. In that light, we can hypothesize that the Liuists preferred a peaceful solution of the Sino-Indian border dispute through diplomatic means to a solution of the dispute through military pressure on the Himalayan frontier.

The Maoists' perception of the domestic and international situation was significantly different from that of the Liuists. On the domestic side, the Maoists believed that while China in 1962 still confronted economic problems in the wake of the failure of the Great Leap, the most difficult period had passed and the situation had gradually begun to improve.[242] As for the international situation, Mao observed in January 1962 that China was being provoked by "ceaseless" anti-China campaigns by "imperialists, reactionary nationalists, and revisionists," but called these "transient phenomena."[243] In the Maoists' view, China was not isolated in world politics, and the general international situation was still favorable to China. For instance, Premier Zhou's report to the Second National People's Congress in April 1962 reasserted "the East Wind prevails over the West Wind" thesis and stressed that the socialist camp and the national liberation movement in the Third World were growing, while the world capitalist system was going through a process of further decline and disintegration.[244] As a New Year's Day editorial phrased it, the Maoists' strategic thinking was based neither on adventurism nor on capitulationism, but on watchfulness against the possibility of war. According to the editorial, "Dark clouds may appear in the skies and storm may break all of a sudden on the sea," and "the Chinese people should maintain the keenest vigilance against them."[245]

At the time when the party center's primary concern was the economy, the Maoists obviously thought that any adventuristic attempt to deal with external enemies would require them to consider a reallocation of scarce resources for a rapid build-up of the PLA's fighting capability, which in turn would further aggravate the country's economic difficulties. In this regard, their viewpoint coincided with that of the Liuists. But a relaxation of struggle with foreign opponents, which the Maoists condemned as rightwing opportunism or capitulationism, might lead China to submit to unwarranted anti-China campaigns that would be exploited by domestic political opponents. This line of thought was revealed in a later Maoist account: "Historical experience proves that, invariably, the activities of domestic counter-revolutionaries and the opportunists in the Party are not only political struggles in character but are coordinated with those of foreign reactionaries. Liu Shao-ch'i and company regarded the rabid anti-China campaign launched by the U.S. imperialists, the Soviet revisionists and the Indian reactionaries . . . as their golden opportunity to restore capitalism."[246]

Given this strategic outlook, the Maoists appeared determined to cope with domestic difficulties and external threats simultaneously without sacrificing their primary objective, the recovery of the economy.[247] In other words, while consistently giving priority in resource allocation to economic recovery, the Maoists intended to maintain the PLA in minimal combat readiness for the worst possible military situation. We have noted that rather than reallocate resources to the PLA and rely on Soviet aid, the P.R.C. leadership dealt with the preparedness of the PLA in the early 1960s by adjusting the limited defense budget to the urgent needs of combat readiness and focusing on a build-up of fighting forces with diligence, thrift, and economy.

It is not possible to specify the extent to which the *sanhe yishao* line may have affected the Beijing leadership's deliberations on the Sino-Indian border dispute. But judging from Chinese diplomatic notes, the press, and the PLA's activities on the Himalayan frontier, it is safe to say that beginning in the spring of 1962, a coordination of diplomatic and military means was pursued by the leadership in coping with the dispute. From March 27 to April 16, the Second National People's Congress (NPC) of the P.R.C. held its Third Session in Beijing. At its opening meeting, Zhou Enlai referred to ten tasks that were needed to adjust the national economy and also pointed out the necessity of strengthening the national defense and the PLA.[248] During and after the Third Session, the Beijing leadership kept to its belief that the border dispute would be moderated by diplomatic reconciliation, but that China also had to deter India's forward movement by both limited military means and political pressure.

On April 13, the Chinese Ministry of Foreign Affairs made public twenty-two notes exchanged by the Chinese and Indian governments between December 1961 and March 1962 and a report on the boundary question that Chinese and Indian officials had submitted in December 1960. At about the same time, Chen Yi distributed these notes to the deputies of the Third Session of the NPC, and a spokesman for the Chinese Foreign Ministry issued a statement that revealed China's hope for a peaceful settlement of the boundary issues: "The Chinese government will continue to make unremitting efforts for the peaceful settlement of the boundary question and improvement in Sino-Indian relations and hopes that its view will be given positive consideration by the Indian government."[249]

Just after the Third Session, however, the Chinese government protested to the Indian government, in a note on April 30, the increasing forward movement of Indian forces on the frontiers of Xinjiang (eighteen successive intrusions were alleged to have occurred from April 11 to April 27). Beijing therefore announced a limited resumption of its border patrols in a sector from Karakoram Pass to Kongka Pass in Xinjiang for the first time since 1959, when the Chinese had unilaterally stopped the patrols. It also noted that "if India continues to invade and occupy China's territory and expand the area of its intrusion and harassment on China's border, the Chinese government will be compelled to consider the further step of resuming border patrols along the entire Sino-Indian boundary."[250]

Beijing's leaders may have expected that sending both deterrent and diplomatic signals would alter India's forward policy and reverse Indian intransigence toward China's proposals for negotiations. But the months of May and June brought developments that contradicted the expectations of those Chinese leaders who advocated a deterrent line and those who favored a diplomatic line. The Indian Army pressed forward on Chinese-claimed territory along a wide front, and the Indian Air Force increased its incursions into Chinese air space. Nehru's boastful posture in Parliament and his underestimation of China's strength belied a willingness to discuss the border question. Furthermore, tension on the Himalayan frontier accompanied the expiration of the Sino-Indian Treaty of Trade and Intercourse on June 3, despite China's efforts to renew it.[251]

In those two months, China's reaction to India's aggression was muted in terms of both military posture and diplomatic effort. The Beijing leadership revealed its sensitivity to the border dispute only through serious warnings that the "Chinese government will not stand idly by seeing its territory once again unlawfully invaded and occupied."[252] But there was no hint of a strengthening of the PLA's posture on the Himalayan frontier or of new diplomatic efforts to reopen a dialogue between Beijing and New Delhi. We must consider Beijing's position in the larger context of unprecedented domestic problems in Guangdong and Xinjiang and external threats perceived elsewhere, especially in the Taiwan Strait area. In May and June, Beijing's leaders probably diverted time and energy from the Sino-Indian boundary question to more urgent domestic and international problems.

Beginning in July, however, as those more urgent problems receded, Beijing's efforts to halt India's forward movement and to bring the Indian government to the conference table appeared to be energetically resumed both militarily and diplomatically. The pressure brought to bear on Indian posts in the Galwan Valley on July 10 was the first tactical maneuvering of a PLA battalion against the small Indian garrison. But this offensive was a total failure and led the PLA to strengthen its communication, logistical, and combat capabilities on the Xinjiang-Tibetan fronts. One Indian note on August 22 claimed that in July in western Tibet the PLA blasted the mountainsides with heavy explosives, constructed military bases, and expanded the military bases it had already set up along the border.[253]

In July and August, Beijing's leaders simultaneously tried to apply diplomatic pressure to bring the Indian government to the conference table. According to a later account by Zhou Enlai, Chinese diplomacy was successful to the extent that in late July, Chen Yi and Menon almost issued a joint communiqué from Geneva stating that the two sides would hold negotiations on the prevention of future border conflicts.[254] Nehru's suggestion to the Chinese ambassador that discussions be held and the July 26 note of the Indian government hinted that the Beijing leadership seriously intended to solve the border dispute through diplomatic negotiations.

After the collapse of diplomacy on August 22, however, the options available to China's leaders were limited. Diplomatic probes accompanied by minimal military pressure had almost been exhausted. It is likely that a more militant line gained ascendency over the line of diplomatic reconciliation. Considering China's behavior in September, it can be suggested that Beijing's leaders were prepared to translate their threat into action if deterrence and diplomacy proved ineffective in halting India's forward moves and in bringing the Indian government to the conference table. On September 13, when the Chinese government again proposed talks with India, it specified a date for the first time (October 15) and warned that "he who plays with fire will eventually be consumed by fire."[255] In the meantime, the PLA further improved its combat capabilities on the fronts in Xinjiang, Tibet, and the N.E.F.A. There was no sign of a massive transfer of manpower to Tibet by fall,[256] but the anticipation of combat required that the PLA stockpile ammunition, weapons, gasoline, and spare parts. One Indian officer described how, beginning in late August, the PLA increased construction of ammunition dumps all along the line across which Indian and Chinese troops faced one another.[257]

One may argue that the September 13 proposal for negotiations was made for a number of tactical reasons: Beijing's leaders intended to exhaust the potential of diplomatic probes in order to test India's intentions before finally resorting to military means; the PLA lacked the capability of launching a major offensive in Tibet and the NEFA and needed reinforcement; the PLA had to launch and complete a military offensive before winter.[258] Putting aside these tactical considerations, Beijing's leaders, particularly the Maoists, may have wanted time to consider military alternatives to either capitulationism or adventurism in order to stabilize the border dispute. In his speech at the Tenth Plenum, Mao reminded the party leadership that China's military line had always been cautious, but that China had never failed to respond to a serious threat to its security. He then alluded to the behavior of the two most famous military strategists in ancient China: "Chu-ko Liang was cautious all his life, while Lü Tuan was clear-headed in big matters."²⁵⁹

Mao's confirmation of the Chinese military line during a meeting of a high-level decision-making organ seems particularly relevant to China's decision on the border dispute in view of the events of late September. On September 19, the Chinese proposal that indicated a deadline of October 15 for a discussion of the border question was rejected by the Indian government. On September 20, the Chedong clash in the N.E.F.A. resulted in the loss of five Chinese frontier guards, including one officer. In notes on September 20 and 21, China's leaders no longer used diplomatic language with a hope of softening the border dispute. Instead, they strongly suggested a more militant line by declaring that as a defense measure against the intensified aggressive activities of India, Chinese frontier guards had been ordered to resume border patrolling in the western, middle, and eastern sectors of Tibet and to set up additional posts in the western sector.²⁶⁰ One note further claimed: "The Chinese government reserves the right to ask for an apology and compensation from the Indian government. If the Indian government does not immediately accept the Chinese government's demand . . . the Chinese side will be compelled to take the necessary defensive measures."²⁶¹ The logic of the situation and circumstantial evidence suggest that during the Tenth Plenum, Beijing's leaders, or a dominant faction among them, agreed to adopt "Lü Tuan's" position and use force before again resorting to diplomacy. This speculation is reinforced by the Chinese press, which quotes the Tenth Plenum communiqué as declaring: "The PLA is the strong and reliable armed forces of the people" and "stands ready to smash the aggressive and sabotage activities of any enemy."²⁶² Premier Zhou also emphasized, in a speech at the reception celebrating the thirteenth anniversary of the founding of the P.R.C., that "the Chinese people would never submit to any pressure much less bargain away principles."²⁶³ On September 28, one day after the close of the Tenth Plenum, a ceremonious funeral for the five frontier guards was held in Lhasa and simultaneously a mass rally was launched. The mass rally adopted a resolution declaring that "we will never tolerate the occupation of our territory by the Indian troops, nor shall we sit by with folded arms and let them kill our frontier fighters."²⁶⁴ In this respect, the fact that Chinese notes in early October still proposed negotiations might be interpreted as a mere formality, or as an effort to assuage the Liuist faction, which possibly still hoped for a diplomatic solution.

Considering military action, Beijing's leaders may have decided on a preemptive but limited attack on the Indian armies that would allow the PLA to clear them out of Chinese-claimed territory before they had a chance to reinforce their military strength on the frontier. There is evidence to support this assessment. In the October attacks of the PLA on Indian posts in Xinjiang-Tibet and in the N.E.F.A., the sudden-attack tactics of a conventional military operation were employed.[265] After the offensive, the PLA quickly overran the Indian armies all along the frontier. According to an Indian account, for instance, within forty-eight hours after the PLA attacks, the Indian armies had given up the whole of northern Ladakh.[266] On the western front the Indian withdrawal even outpaced the Chinese attack, but the PLA did not chase the Indian armies beyond the Chinese-claimed line.[267] This suggests that the October offensive was politically controlled and carefully preplanned. For the Beijing leaders, a quick war using a small-sized force had a number of advantages: it would attain China's limited territorial goals without eliminating prospects for a peaceful settlement later; it would minimize the possibility of military escalation; and it would maintain the party center's policy priority on domestic economic problems.

The October offensive appeared to be accompanied by a diplomatic line. During the fighting, there was no publicity in the Chinese press commending Chinese victories and no mass rally in support of the PLA. Rather, the press emphasized the Cuban missile crisis, and throughout the country, mass rallies were launched in support of the Cuban people's struggle against the United States.[268] The initial PLA offensive on the Sino-Indian border lasted less than one week, and from October 25 until a mid-November offensive, the PLA held its position on all fronts. In the meantime, using polite diplomatic language, Zhou put forward to Nehru a three-point proposal indicating that to end the border conflict, the two sides should respect the line of actual control along the entire Sino-Indian border, withdraw twenty kilometers from this line, and reopen negotiations for the peaceful settlement of the boundary question.[269] This suggests that even during the fighting, the Chinese leadership was waiting, hoping to co-ordinate a limited military offensive with a resumption of diplomatic talks.

It should be noted, however, that despite their achievement of a military victory on all fronts, the Chinese failed to bring the Indian government to the conference table. Nehru officially responded to Zhou's proposal on October 27 by refusing to talk with the Chinese government "under threat of military might" and without Chinese withdrawal from territory "all along the boundary prior to 8th September 1962."[270] Furthermore, the Indian government carried out anti-China campaigns throughout the nation in preparation for a long winter campaign. On October 22, in a broadcast to the nation, Nehru declared: "We shall carry on the struggle as long as we do not win." On October 26, India's president proclaimed a "state of emergency" throughout the country. All retired army officers and generals were ordered to active duty, and students were asked to join the "National

Cadet Corps." India's arms industry was given orders to start maximum production, and national defense bonds were issued in order to raise a national defense fund.[271] On the Himalayan fronts, India's armies were reinforced. Two divisions deployed along the front in Pakistan were transferred to the N.E.F.A.[272] In Xinjiang and Tibet, the western command reorganized split troops, brought them into Ladakh, and pooled all available transport.[273] On the eve of Nehru's birthday, November 14, the Indian armies appeared to be prepared to launch a major counteroffensive.[274]

It is likely that the second PLA offensive was launched as a result of India's intransigence and military moves. It is also apparent that when the Beijing leadership saw that preparations for a prolonged conflict were being made by the Indian government, it considered a second offensive necessary not so much to solve the border conflict through military means as to reinforce China's interest in diplomacy. Evidence of this is the fact that even though the second offensive inflicted heavy casualties on Indian forces and for the first time since the October offensive set off a panic in New Delhi that threatened to disintegrate public morale in India,[275] the Chinese halted the offensive, proclaimed a unilateral cease-fire on all fronts, and withdrew twenty kilometers behind the 1959 line of actual control in the eastern, middle, and western sectors of Tibet.[276]

The decision of Beijing's leaders to declare a unilateral cease-fire and withdrawal of forces was probably prompted by both tactical and political considerations. Tactically, as Chen Yi asserted, the Himalayas presented logistical difficulties for the waging of a long-term war.[277] The coming winter weather would surely have added to such difficulties. Politically, as noted earlier, the Chinese leadership was never willing to wage a prolonged war with India, primarily because of its central concern with the national economy. Beijing attained its essential security goal in the two military offensives and showed its superior strength. Any sign that the PLA planned to remain permanently in the newly occupied territories of western Tibet and the N.E.F.A., however, would be exploited by New Delhi as expansionism and would convey a bad image of Beijing to the Third World. China's sensitivity to a negative response by Afro-Asian countries to the PLA's offensives appeared in a lengthy letter that Zhou wrote on November 15, 1962, to Third World leaders. In the letter, Zhou adroitly capitalized on Nehru's leaning toward Washington, attempted to counterbalance U.S. support for India with pro-China support from Afro-Asian countries, and appealed to the Third World to mobilize pressure on India for direct negotiations between China and India.[278] Finally, China's unilateral cease-fire and withdrawal were meant to demonstrate Beijing's sincerity in attempting to end the border conflict and settle the boundary question peacefully, by means of negotiation.[279]

China's Motives and Objectives

China's decision to launch a limited border war with India in 1962 had clear repercussions in terms of domestic and international events. But the main motives behind the decision did not lie in the need to create an external crisis for domestic political or economic reasons. A comprehensive analysis of the external and domestic settings of the Chinese offensives of October and November suggests that China's decision to attack India was made primarily in terms of its assessment and confrontation of perceived threats from the outside world.

The Chinese leadership's first concern was to secure its territory against India and stabilize the border when it felt provoked by India's forward policy, which, supported by the United States and the Soviet Union, was being pursued at a time of domestic difficulties in China. China's limited preemptive military action against India was intended to halt India's forward movement on the frontiers and bring New Delhi to the conference table. The leadership's secondary objective was to punish India's further encroachment on Chinese territory, particularly in the western sector, in the area of the Aksai Chin plateau. Thirdly, the Chinese action against India was aimed at discrediting Washington's and Moscow's collusion with India against China. When that failed, Nehru's nonalignment policy was maligned by China's leadership, the hope apparently being to persuade Nehru not to lean toward Washington. Soviet conduct during the Cuban missile crisis added a final motive: to show Moscow how a communist country should conduct a crisis involving capitalist countries.

It was not China's intention to conquer India by military invasion; nor, contrary to some analyses, was China out to discredit the Indian development model. China's use of small-sized forces without tactical and strategic air support, the confinement of the PLA's advance to Chinese-claimed territory, and China's unilateral announcement of a cease-fire and troop withdrawal all suggest that the Chinese did not attempt to exploit their power for maximum advantage militarily or politically. In fact, during the October fighting, the Chinese leadership signaled to India its clear intention not to gloat over India's difficulties caused by the PLA's successes or to intervene in the domestic affairs of India.[280] These considerations lead us to argue that China was not willing, much less able, to compel India to divert its resources from economic development to defense so as to weaken the Indian political and economic system.

One of China's primary objectives was to achieve essential territorial security by halting India's forward policy at a minimum and by securing Chinese-claimed territory at a maximum. Achieving that security would serve China's interests in stabilizing the territory in contention from 1959 onward and in excluding or minimizing foreign influence and intervention in the region. The collusion of the U.S., Taiwan, and India was of particular concern to Beijing in view of Tibet's instability. Securing the Aksai Chin area was essential if China was to tighten its grip on the Ladakh corridor between Tibet and Xinjiang, which, since the founding of the P.R.C., had assumed a key strategic role as the supply and communication route linking the two provinces. This territorial objective had been clearly and repeatedly signaled to the Indian government in Chinese notes and diplomatic proposals before and during the fighting of October and November. For instance, in a reply to Nehru's letter of October 27 urging China to withdraw its troops to the position in the western sector it had occupied prior to September 8, 1963, Zhou Enlai reminded Nehru that the Aksai Chin area had always been under China's jurisdiction. Through this area the PLA had entered the Ari district of Tibet from Xinjiang in 1950, and it was there that the Xinjiang-Tibet highway, a gigantic engineering project, had been built. Zhou further asserted China's unwillingness to revert to the military position its forces had held prior to September 8, mainly because this would have permitted India to control forty-three military strong points in the western sector and thus would leave China defenseless.[281] On November 21, even as the Chinese government announced a unilateral troop withdrawal to a position twenty kilometers behind the 1959 line of actual control, it ruled out India's recovery and reoccupation of "the Kechilang River area north of the McMahon Line," "Wuje in the middle sector," and India's "43 strongpoints" in the western sector, solemnly declaring that "should the above eventualities occur, China reserves the right to strike back in self-defense."[282]

An equally important objective was to force the Indian government to accept China's desire for a peaceful settlement. As has been discussed, the Chinese repeatedly expressed hope for a peaceful settlement of the border dispute on the basis of de facto possession of the contested territories and exerted diplomatic efforts privately and publicly to bring the Indian government to the conference table. Having reached an agreement with India, China would have expected to formalize and demarcate the disputed boundary in accordance with the line of actual control and thus to stabilize the border on the basis of a permanent solution. But the collapse of diplomacy in late August, followed by Nehru's persistent rejections of Chinese proposals and an increase in military tension along the entire front, led the Chinese leadership to apply limited military pressure on India in order to reinforce China's interest in diplomacy. Shortly after the October offensive came Premier Zhou's three-point proposal, the halt of the PLA within Chinese-claimed territory, and China's unilateral cease-fire and troop withdrawal to the 1959 line of actual control, all of which suggest that indeed the Chinese were attempting to utilize military action to create a new diplomatic environment for a direct dialogue between the two states rather than to resolve the border conflict only through military means.

Another important objective, partly related to the above two objectives, was "punitive": to correct India's miscalculation of China's military strength and to get India to refrain from further encroachment on Chinese territory. Before the war, a predominant thought in the Beijing leadership was that despite the temporary difficulties that China confronted at home and abroad and the support and encouragement by Washington and Moscow of India's anti-China campaigns, China should never allow itself to appear to be too weak to respond to Indian military moves. The Chinese repeatedly warned the Indian government that it should not take China's restraint as a sign of weakness.

There are several indications that the PLA's crossing of the McMahon line was designed to correct such an Indian misperception, to punish India's further encroachment in all sectors, particularly the western sector, and to compel India to reassess its policies. From 1959 onward, China's position on the McMahon line had been that it was illegal, but would not be crossed by China. Despite this position, during the border war, the PLA crossed the McMahon line for the first time in Chinese history, advanced to several regions far south of Chedong, and on November 18 occupied Walong at the eastern end of the N.E.F.A., which India considered a vital stronghold barring an easy path to the valley on the Brahmaputra.[283] The fall of Walong forced Nehru to confront a difficult situation in Parliament[284] and set off panic in New Delhi and the disintegration of public morale throughout India. Nevertheless, the Chinese government declared a unilateral cease-fire and troop withdrawal from the newly occupied area south of the McMahon line without showing any intention that the P.R.C. would utilize the occupied area as a bargaining chip in future negotiations.[285] Furthermore, China's statement did not rule out India's restoration of the status quo ante in the N.E.F.A. in accordance with the 1959 line of actual control, which would permit India to reoccupy Walong and two other towns.

The PLA's crossing of the McMahon line was an ambivalent move in view of the army's immediate withdrawal from its position south of the line without trying to achieve diplomatic compensation. A statement by the Chinese Ministry of National Defense on October 22 clearly indicated that China had crossed the line in a punitive expedition aimed at restraining Indian armies from making further forward movements into the eastern sector. Citation of that statement seems worthwhile.

In its efforts to seek a friendly settlement of the Sino-Indian boundary question through peaceful negotiation, the Chinese government has repeatedly declared that "we absolutely do not recognize the illegal McMahon Line in the eastern sector, but we will not cross this line." However, taking the great restraint of the Chinese Government as a sign of weakness, the Indian Government pushed farther and farther ahead and its troops crossed the so-called McMahon Line, invaded and occupied larger tracts of Chinese territory and launched large-scale attacks on China's frontier guards. . . . The Chinese Government now formally declares that *in order to prevent the Indian troops from staging a comeback and launching fresh attacks, the Chinese frontier guards, fighting in self-defense, need no longer restrict themselves to the limits of the illegal McMahon Line.*[286]

The date of this statement suggests that the plan to cross the McMahon line was made in advance.[287] But the statement attributes the PLA's attack across the line to India's military movement north of the line. Actually, another Chinese objective in crossing the line was to punish India for its forward policy elsewhere, especially in western Tibet, by striking a stunning blow in the N.E.F.A., to which India attached the greatest importance. Considering China's sensitivity over control of Aksai Chin,[288] there is reason to suppose that the Chinese also needed to check Indian troop advances in Xinjiang and western Tibet. One yardstick of actual fighting suggests that the PLA was more seriously engaged in and concerned about the battle in the N.E.F.A. than about the fighting in Ladakh. According to Indian figures for October and November, five times more men were killed in the N.E.F.A. than in Ladakh, ten times more were wounded, and twenty-six times more were reported as missing.[289]

Another objective behind China's selection of the N.E.F.A. as the area in which to inflict a heavy blow against India may have been to prove to India that the McMahon line was not the de facto or the de jure boundary in the eastern sector and would remain negotiable, particularly if India continued to challenge China's de facto possession of Aksai Chin.[290] A later Chinese account of the crossing of the McMahon line reinforced the view that the attack in the N.E.F.A. was meant to affect India's attitude toward "the entire border dispute." According to that account, "After the PLA advanced to the area south of the McMahon Line the Indians had begun to have a little more sense and the Sino-India border tension basically eased."[291]

China's action was also designed to discredit Washington's collaboration with India and to put the two nations—particularly the United States—on notice that China would not be encircled. After the PLA's October offensive, this objective was stressed in the Chinese press and in speeches by high-ranking Chinese officials. Chen Yi warned on November 7 that the stepping up of U.S. military assistance to India would not be effective in "attaining its vicious aim of dominating India and using Asians to fight Asians."[292] An "Observer" article in *People's Daily* on November 11 recalled the three years of "self-restraint and forbearance" exercised by the Chinese government. Yet the United States had made every effort to back up and embolden the Nehru government in its maneuvers against China during this period. The "Observer" asserted that the P.R.C. could make

Washington and New Delhi "a bit more sober-minded only by waging necessary struggles against these rabid adventurists."[293]

The Chinese were determined to expose and challenge this coalition of enemies without deference to Washington's support of New Delhi. Mao's standard dictum was followed: "Strategically despise the enemy, tactically take it into account." Evidently, the Maoist leadership believed that avoiding confrontation would encourage China's enemies to carry out more vigorously their policies of intervention in China or elsewhere. The PLA's November offensive was prepared and launched during the very time when China knew that the United States was supplying India with small arms and ammunition. It was reported that President Kennedy sent a letter to Nehru on October 29 indicating that Washington was ready to help India as much as possible short of direct military intervention.[294] As a *Red Flag* editorial dated November 16 (but probably prepared during the November offensive) asserted: "If communists fail to recognize the outwardly strong but brittle nature of imperialism and the reactionaries of the various countries, are awed by the temporary power of the enemy and overestimate his strength, they will vacillate in the struggle and dare not win victory that can be won. . . . This only adds to the arrogance of imperialism and the reactionaries in the various countries."[295]

Once involved in the fighting, China may have attempted to influence the Soviet Union to adopt a different line concerning the struggle between a communist and a noncommunist country and to reassess its pro-Indian attitude. China's military offensive appears to have been aimed at stirring up reaction from Communist parties around the world to the Soviets' stand on the border dispute. In an article entitled "World Opinion Round Up," published after China proposed a peaceful settlement, the Chinese cited comments made by numerous Communist parties on the border dispute, stressing that they had begun to draw a clear distinction between "right and wrong" concerning the border conflict between a communist and a noncommunist country. The article also asserted that China's military action and its unilateral cease-fire had demonstrated "vivid proof of correct policy" in the sense that "the imperialists and modern revisionists standing on the Indian side would come to grief" as they began to recognize that their "anti-Chinese slanders were having less and less effect on China."[296]

The Chinese may have briefly considered their October military action successful in affecting the Soviets' attitude when a *Pravda* editorial was published supporting Beijing's three-point proposal. But quickly thereafter the Chinese charged that such support was tactically motivated by the Cuban missile crisis and really amounted to another Russian betrayal of friendship.[297]

China's November offensive, followed by the quick announcement of a cease-fire and troop withdrawal, appears to have been prompted by another objective: to teach Moscow how to cope correctly with crises involving capitalist countries. The Maoists' policy seemed to be directed toward dispensing with the twin errors of adventurism and capitulationism that Moscow had committed in dealing with the Cuban missile crisis. Numerous articles in *People's Daily* and *Red Flag* in November had as their main theme "the way to deal with imperialists and reactionaries."[298] For instance, a *People's Daily* editorial on November 15 described "imperialists and reactionaries" as "having always bullied the faint-hearted but feared the firm." Criticizing Moscow's deference to Washington's firm stand, it cited Castro's remark: "The road to peace is not the road of sacrificing the rights of the peoples and infringing on their rights because this is precisely the road leading to war." The editorial went on to suggest that the correct strategy for Marxist-Leninists was to wage a blow-for-blow struggle against imperialists and reactionaries in order to defuse their aggression, but never to refuse to negotiate with enemies and make compromises that did not involve bartering away principles.[299]

The Chinese may have decided that by discrediting Washington's and Moscow's collaboration with India they would simultaneously weaken India's intransigence. It is highly probable that this was their expectation, for the Chinese believed throughout the conflict that one source of India's intransigence toward China's proposals for a peaceful settlement was the backing of American and Soviet leaders. But Nehru firmly rejected China's proposals, prepared for a long winter campaign against China, and leaned still more toward Washington, proving that the Chinese had miscalculated his intentions. Probably for this reason, a Chinese political offensive to "expose" Nehru's nonalignment policy was launched in an attempt to reduce Nehru's further leaning toward Washington. Beginning on October 27, when Nehru officially rejected Beijing's three-point proposal, a number of articles in the Chinese press attacked India's nonalignment policy. Indian leaders were asked to reconsider their appeal for U.S. aid, the argument being that a prolonged war between China and India would only serve the needs of the United States.[300] This suggests that in attacking Nehru's nonalignment, Beijing was primarily interested in weakening the threat posed by closer collaboration between Washington and New Delhi during the fighting, rather than, as several writers have suggested, in eroding Nehru's image among leaders of the Third World and in increasing Beijing's prestige in the Afro-Asian countries.

In addition to the foreign-policy rationale behind China's actions in the Sino-Indian border war, were there domestic reasons such as the need for mass mobilization, the diversion of the people's attention from serious internal problems, and the consolidation of authority? There is no evidence that there were. Instead, China's foreign policy was *restrained* by economic weakness and the leadership's internal priorities. China's leaders would not do anything either to endanger economic recovery based on self-reliance or to impel a redistribution of scarce resources to modernize the PLA.

Supposing that the Chinese had wanted to exploit the border crisis for the purpose of boosting mass enthusiasm for production and diverting the people's attention from their economic difficulties, they would have propagandized and dramatized the Indian threat regularly in the public press. A review of the articles and party leaders' speeches that appeared mainly in *People's Daily* suggests that the border problem was peripheral news from the spring of 1962 onward. The number and nature of serious warnings in *People's Daily* articles and speeches changed significantly after July, however, when China became involved in a series of skirmishes on the frontier, and almost coincided in number and nature with the protests appearing in Chinese notes to the Indian government. Still, there was no hint of a mass meeting to mobilize the anti-Indian zeal of the people nationwide, with the possible exception of the local one held at Lhasa on the occasion of the funeral of the five frontier guards killed in late September. Even during the war in October, the Chinese press did not dramatize the fighting and victories of the PLA. Mass rallies were launched only in support of the *Cuban* people's struggle against the United States. As has been discussed, the Beijing leadership carried out a campaign for increased agricultural production throughout 1960–62, but abandoned the policy of social mobilization on the land, thereby shifting its efforts to a campaign of selective capital and technical investment in agriculture. These campaigns suggest that the Chinese leadership did not want to divert the time and energy of the nation to external problems, and deliberately kept the Sino-Indian border question out of national politics.

It has been hypothesized that the Chinese military move on India was made to silence resistance to the Maoists' economic policies at a time when the Maoists were being challenged by high-level party and government leaders mainly because of unusual domestic difficulties. Thus the Sino-Indian border war was said by some to be a by-product of the intraparty tussle in Beijing.[301] But this hypothesis is weakened by the fact that in the months prior to the border war, and especially at the Tenth Plenum, Mao was influential enough to counterattack critics of his policies within the party and to mobilize political support for the so-called antirightist action in formal decision-making organizations. As has been noted, at the central work conference in August 1962, Mao was in a position to compel the top party leaders in charge of rural, industrial, and financial affairs to undergo self-criticism for their sabotage of his policies. Mao also terminated a move to reverse the purge of former Minister of Defense Peng prompted by the Liuist group at a meeting of the Standing Committee of the Politburo just before the Tenth Plenum. At the Tenth Plenum, Mao's greater emphasis on economic recovery than on class struggle showed that the chairman appeared to feel confident in commanding the party. According to Mao's thinking, "Work and class struggle should proceed simultaneously, but we must not let the class struggle interfere with our work."[302]

Nothing in the documents of the Cultural Revolution period reveals that the Liuists challenged or deviated from the Maoists' policy on the Sino-Indian border problem. In this regard, it is highly probable that the diplomatic line that appeared in numerous Chinese notes and was reflected in the actual behavior of high-level officials in charge of diplomatic affairs was not a policy in opposition to the Maoist line, but was part of a policy coordinated within the party center. This suggests that so far as the Chinese decision on the border war was concerned, policy alternatives were considered by a cohesive Chinese leadership; the border question would not have seriously affected the disunity of the leadership before the decision. The Maoists seem to have had little reason to utilize the border issue for such political advantage as consolidation of the leadership.

From the perspective of bureaucratic politics, one might argue that local commanders in the PLA, individually or in association with higher-level military leaders, manipulated the border war as a means to increase professional military interests such as a higher defense budget and a loosening of the party center's grip over military commanders. Conceivably, these commanders were overzealous in carrying out their mission to the extent that they crossed the McMahon line.[303] A circumspect examination of politics in the PLA does not, however, bear out these arguments. The Maoists' firm grip on the PLA was maintained through Lin Biao's loyalty to Mao and the emphasis on a drive to strengthen the party's presence at the basic level of the PLA. Strict control by the party center over an unexpected or accidental war was reinforced in the MAC's directive of January 1961 to all units in the PLA that any international incident in border regions should be reported quickly to superior officers, who in turn would make decisions and give orders. In addition, the fact that the PLA's offensives did not advance beyond Chinese-claimed territory means that they were politically controlled actions, and therefore provides no evidence that the Chinese military was allowed to use adventurism on the border to further parochial bureaucratic interests.

There is no plausible evidence to support the argument that China's decision on the border war was motivated primarily by domestic instability or bureaucratic politics. A Chinese foreign-policy initiative was made independently of domestic circumstances. In particular, the Chinese leadership showed that it would respond with force to an external threat the leadership perceived was serious enough to threaten the national security, despite economic difficulties and political realignments. As was clearly declared in the speeches of Chinese political leaders[304] during the border dispute, a principle of Chinese strategy applied to the border decision was that "we will never encroach upon a single inch of other's territory, nor will we ever allow anyone to encroach upon a single inch of our territory." Perceiving encroachment in the Sino-Indian border area, the Chinese leadership no longer regarded domestic weakness as a constraint on its foreign policy and decided to meet an imminent threat with force.

This conclusion is not to say that domestic problems did not affect the *kind* of response China made to the external threat. The preemptive, limited military offensive chosen by Beijing appeared to be directly related to the state of domestic affairs. At a time when its top priority was economic recovery, the Beijing leadership was not in a position to wage a prolonged war against India.

The link that the Chinese leadership perceived between domestic weakness and external threats was that domestic vulnerabilities or difficulties might invite foreign intervention and increased foreign influence, which in turn would encourage Chinese enemies at home to plot with enemies abroad. Facing the insurgency in Tibet at a time of economic difficulties, the Chinese were more sensitive than usual to the joint intervention of the United States, Taiwan, and India in Tibet, as well as to the harmful effects of the intervention on China's socialist system. After the exodus from Xinjiang, the Beijing leadership was extremely suspicious of Soviet intervention and of the so-called revisionist influence on the Chinese people. China's action in India thus appears to have been prompted by a consideration of this domestic political implication. According to a later Chinese accounting, "When the imperialists, the reactionaries and the modern revisionists launched repeated campaigns against China, the class enemies at home launched renewed attacks on socialism, but both external and domestic enemies miscalculated [the] strength of the Chinese people."[305]

The interplay between domestic weakness and external threats from several fronts triggered a Chinese attitude of self-weakness, which in turn caused China's overestimation of the nature of India's threat. As has been discussed, China's hope for a peaceful settlement of the border dispute seems to have been negatively affected by the crises in May and June, which led to a serious reassessment of external threats and internal weaknesses. During the summer of 1962, China perceived that Indian forces were becoming well established on the Himalayan front by taking advantage of China's domestic troubles and by colluding with Washington and Moscow, and that, therefore, diplomatic negotiations would not lessen the threat to China's security. This attitude seems to have been reinforced by two events: the failure of the PLA's encirclement of an Indian post in Galwan Valley in western Tibet in July, and the collapse of Sino-Indian diplomacy in August. Frequent skirmishes on the frontier in September added to Beijing's magnification of the real Indian threat. It has been observed, however, that Nehru was not able to permanently reject the idea of Chinese control of

Aksai Chin, mainly because of India's confrontation with Pakistan.[306] General Kaul also pointed out that the strength of India's armies on the frontier both in western Tibet and in the N.E.F.A. was remarkably inferior to that of China and that the military advantage of the forward Indian posts in western Tibet was not as great as Nehru's frequent statements to Parliament indicated.[307]

The Chinese leaders' overestimation of India's strength also stemmed from their belief that Washington and New Delhi were actively colluding against China militarily. But apart from their clandestine cooperation with Tibetan insurgents, neither Washington nor New Delhi had much reason to be allied militarily—primarily because of Washington's commitment to Pakistan and India's commitment to nonalignment.[308] It was not until the October PLA offensive that India appealed to Washington for direct military aid, and only after the November offensive was India's request to Washington for air intervention made.

In summary, it is highly probable that the interplay between domestic weakness and external threats misled the Chinese leadership to perceive the threat from India to be much greater than was actually the case, and then to take drastic action against India in order to enhance its own sense of security and correct India's misperceptions of China.

5 Vietnam, 1965

Introduction

Long after the event, the purge of Luo Ruiqing, chief of the General Staff of the PLA, still invites inquiry. U.S. escalation of the air war over North Vietnam in 1965 coincided with major domestic political events in China to produce, it seems clear, a wide-ranging debate among Chinese leaders over foreign-policy, strategy, and political and economic alternatives. Although this case, unlike the others we are exploring, does not involve a military confrontation between China and another power, it warrants inclusion because of what it illustrates about the politics of a foreign-policy crisis. By trying to fit the purge of Luo into the total context of China's political climate, we may be able to shed light on the interaction of domestic politics, strategy, and foreign policy, and on the implications of that interaction for Chinese decision making. Furthermore, we will attempt to identify different views within the party and the army over the proper place of political training, and to discern differences in the perception of external threats and of the deterrence postures and force dispositions needed to counter them.

Reconsideration of the Luo Ruiqing affair also has contemporary value. As a political instrument and a major source of political authority, the PLA requires continuing attention to its leadership, doctrine, and behavior as a bureaucracy. Many of the issues that were apparently raised and debated in 1965 were not resolved by Luo's dismissal. Consequently, questions must still be asked about how party and army leaders can be expected to react to foreign crises: what will their priorities be, how will these affect their arguments and preferences, and how might external threats influence the formation and durability of domestic and international political alliances?

The Political and Strategic Context of the Vietnam "Debate"

The Political Context

Chinese domestic politics in 1964 were marked by an increasing concern over the political and ideological directions of Chinese society. Though

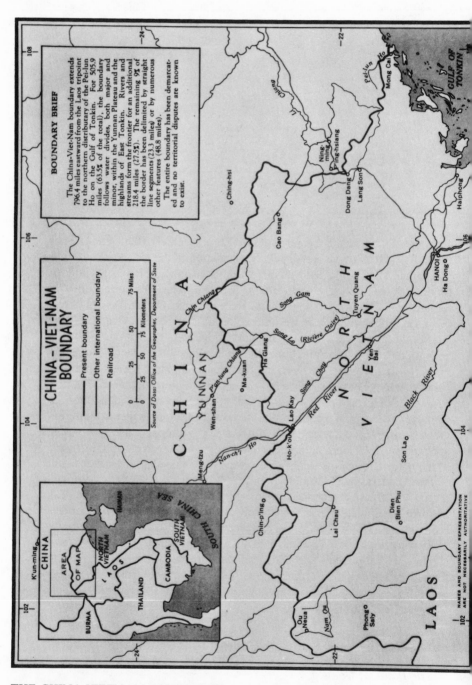

THE CHINA-VIETNAM BOUNDARY

China's economy appeared to have recovered from the "three hard years" following the Great Leap Forward, Chinese leaders were alarmed about developments in three other critical areas of Chinese society: dissatisfaction and individualism among the youth, serious deviations from major ideological principles among intellectuals, and organizational ossification and decay in both party and state. Were corrective measures not taken, some leaders feared, the nation would be susceptible to either a restoration of capitalism or the entrenchment of revisionism. To meet these threats, the party center devised remedial policies that relied to a great extent upon the PLA as a model and vanguard of reform.

The center's first cause for concern was the increasing alienation of China's educated youth. The surface manifestations of their discontent included interest in Western music, "decadent" entertainment, "bourgeois" fashions, and material comfort. But their disenchantment stemmed primarily from the government's inability to provide them with challenging and rewarding employment. The youth openly resented being asked to accept menial labor in the countryside, where they could make little use of the specialized technical skills they had acquired in high school and college. In short, China was unable to absorb the burgeoning intellectual class that its educational system was creating. Instead, it was producing an intelligentsia that was profoundly dissatisfied and impatient with the career choices available to it.[1]

Perhaps the most important campaign aimed at China's youth in 1964 was a drive to create "revolutionary successors."[2] Young people were urged to follow the same political education methods employed by the PLA in its efforts to create "four-good" companies and "five-good" soldiers: to study and apply the thought of Mao Zedong in all their activities; to emulate selected models (many of them army men) who had demonstrated through heroic action their proletarian standpoint; to learn about the hardships of the old society by exchanging experiences with older workers and peasants; and to engage in physical labor. The aim of this campaign—as in the PLA— was to rectify the "bourgeois" tendencies in the students' thinking so that they could meet the five criteria for "revolutionary successors" set down by Mao in "On Krushchov's Phoney Communism."[3] Only then would they be qualified to assume leadership positions in Chinese society.

China's intellectuals troubled the nation's leaders in another way. In the spring and summer of 1964, newspapers and magazines began to carry a series of attacks against Yang Xianzhen (Yang Hsien-chen), head of the CCP Higher Party School. Yang was accused of emphasizing the "unity of opposites" rather than the "struggle between the aspects of a contradiction" when lecturing on Mao's theory of contradictions. Yang's discussions of the resolution of social conflict, in other words, were said to have underestimated the role of struggle and exaggerated the possibility of compromise. But even more important than his distortion of Mao's theory of dialectics were the purported implications of Yang's theories for both domestic and foreign policy. Yang's notion that "two combine into one" (*he er er yi*) provided, it was said, the philosophical justification for a relaxation of the class struggle at home and an improvement of China's relations with the Soviet Union and the United States.[4]

In order to combat these ideological deviations, the central leadership launched a series of campaigns against Yang and other scholars associated with him. The campaigns, which obtained extensive media coverage, involved nationwide discussions of the basic pertinent political issues (issues that were considered so crucial that the discussions were held at levels as low as the factory), and congresses of intellectuals that were convened to expurgate Yang's writings. A major component of this early "cultural revolution"[5] was the growing participation of PLA cultural teams under the General Political Department (GPD) in the movement for the reform of the Beijing Opera that would later come to be associated with Mao's wife, Jiang Qing (Chiang Ch'ing). Army opera troupes were credited with major contributions in the effort to "revolutionize" this traditional art form.

Finally, the party leaders were also concerned about organizational problems, particularly those in basic-level rural units and in offices dealing with economic affairs. The documents captured in the Lianjiang (Lien-chiang) raids,[6] for example, indicate that the basic levels were plagued by corruption, speculation, extortion, waste, and capitalist tendencies. To cope with these problems, the party undertook increasingly stringent rectification measures during 1964. In September, the work teams that as a part of the Socialist Education Movement (SEM) had been sent into the countryside to "enlighten" the basic-level cadres were ordered to intensify their investigations of rural conditions and to permit the masses to struggle against errant officials.[7]

In the same month, An Ziwen (An Tzu-wen), director of the Organization Department of the party's Central Committee, published a major article that underlined the party center's concern about the political reliability of party and state organizations and foreshadowed the extensive purges of 1966–67.[8] An warned cadres at every level that "whatever [their] seniority, Party standing, and worthy service," they must all intensify their reeducation. Echoing Mao's insistence that "one divides into two," An declared that the party tended to divide into proletarian and bourgeois wings, and that those who represented the bourgeois standpoint should be identified and resisted.

As a first step in organizational rectification, the party began to restructure major governmental institutions during this period. The model presented for emulation was the PLA. Following the purge of Peng Dehuai in 1959, Minister of Defense Lin Biao had begun to rebuild the political organizations within the army with the aim of rejuvenating the army's political departments and reconstructing party branches down to the company level. In February 1964, Beijing established political departments in the governmental offices responsible for industry, commerce, trade, and finance, modeling them on the political departments of the PLA. Furthermore, these new supervisory units were staffed, to a large extent, by cadres dispatched from the army. The PLA, in short, was seen as a good model of political reliability, and other bureaucracies were ordered to "learn from the PLA."[9]

As for Luo Ruiqing, who as head of the PLA stood to benefit from the party center's attempt to make the PLA the vanguard of the party's assault on "revisionism," there is scattered and somewhat ambiguous evidence that he did not fully support the Maoist position on army affairs in 1964.

The fact that the evidence is ambiguous is not as surprising as it may seem. Although Luo is now considered to have been a military "professional," his appointment as chief of staff of the PLA in 1959 was interpreted at the time as an attempt by Mao and Lin Biao to place a loyal, reliable, politically oriented officer in a sensitive position. Luo had formed a close association with Lin during the Anti-Japanese War, when he had served as Lin's deputy, first at the Red Army College, and then at Kangda (K'ang-ta) (the Resist-Japan Military-Political University in Yanan [Yenan]). During the civil war, Luo fulfilled political assignments in the PLA, including that of deputy political commissar and chairman of the Political Department of the Shansi (Shanxi)-Chahar-Hopei (Hebei) Field Army in 1946–47, and chairman of the Political Department of the North China Military Region in 1948. Between October 1949 and his 1959 promotion to chief of staff, he served as minister of public security and commander of the Public Security Forces. During the next five years, Luo held additional positions of trust: vice-premier of the State Council, deputy minister of national defense, secretary of the Central Committee of the CCP, and secretary-general of the Military Affairs Committee.

Furthermore, Luo's public statements gave few indications that he was succumbing to the "professional standpoint." As late as December 1964, Luo reiterated his support of the Maoist position on the primacy of politics in the work of the PLA, declaring that the armed forces "should strengthen their military and political training, *particularly political training*. They should carry out all kinds of ideological and political tasks, raise the class consciousness of their members, and cultivate excellent work styles. On this basis, they should carry out painstaking training to master the skill of killing the enemy within 200 metres."[10] As Morton Halperin and John Lewis have pointed out, this statement by Luo indicated his acceptance of the so-called party position on military affairs, as opposed to the "professional standpoint," for Luo's reference to killing the enemy within 200 meters was indicative of an emphasis on "close combat," which, according to Halperin and Lewis, is "the highest political form of the art of military engagement. It is this form which shows that in war people are more important than weapons."[11]

On the other hand, Red Guard documents have consistently referred to a private dispute between Luo and the Maoists over the so-called military tournaments. According to the Red Guard accounts, Luo instituted a series of military competitions in January 1964 in the belief that a desire to perform well in the tournaments would encourage military units to improve their military skills. Luo's first mistake was to initiate the tournaments without consulting either Mao, Lin, the Central Committee, or the Military Affairs Committee; he apparently made the decision on his own authority. It is not clear when opposition to the tournaments began to arise. But the Maoists eventually decided that they distracted the troops' attention from political study and fostered a competitive—rather than cooperative—spirit among the soldiers. Cultural Revolution documents claim that at the "end of 1964" Lin issued a directive criticizing the tournaments (and by implication ordering their termination), and that Luo tried to distort and delay the directive. Luo allegedly continued to argue that because of the tournaments, military training in 1964 had been more successful than in any other year since 1949.[12]

Moreover, some of Luo's public statements on the proper relationship between political and military training appear to be ambiguous. In an article for *Zhongguo qingnian* [China's Youth], for example, Luo acknowledged the necessity for young soldiers to study political theory and Mao Zedong's thought, but he also said that "tempering in revolutionary struggle," which he defined as learning the regimen of the common soldier, was "even more important."[13] During the Cultural Revolution, Luo was criticized for making statements, like this one, that could be interpreted as placing equal emphasis on military and ideological training.[14] There is room, therefore, to speculate that Mao and Luo differed both publicly and privately over the doctrine of the "primacy of politics."

Another possible cause of tension between Luo and Lin Biao was Lin's poor health. The Red Guards have accused Luo of using Lin's illness to further his own ambitions. According to one of the more reliable accounts, Luo visited Lin sometime in late 1964 to request authority to oversee the operational affairs of the army. In effect, Luo was asking Lin to delegate to him all the day-to-day tasks of managing the PLA. When Lin refused, Luo is accused of having "exploded," saying, "A sick man should seek cure for his illness and should not concern himself with other things! A sick man should give his place to the worth! Don't meddle! Don't block the way!"[15] If true, this rather melodramatic incident would indicate both that Luo thought his own career was being obstructed by a man who was kept in office, despite ill health, largely because of his increasingly close relationship with Mao, and that the personal relations between Luo and Lin were seriously strained as a result. As Liu Shaoqi reportedly put it, "Lo Jui-ch'ing despises and fears Comrade Lin Piao."[16]

How, then, can we evaluate Luo's personal and political position at the beginning of 1965? It is possible, we believe, that Luo was more interested than Lin or Mao in the military duties of the PLA; there are also some indications of strong political ambitions on Luo's part and perhaps a personal rivalry between Lin and Luo. But Luo's position appears on balance to have been quite secure. Even the Red Guard documents are unable to make a strong argument that Luo followed an incorrect policy line during 1964.[17] Once the United States began to escalate its military operations in Vietnam, however, Luo's differences with Mao and Lin over China's strategic policy and defense posture, which may previously have been latent or compromisable, became points of conflict.

In summary, then, 1964 saw the intensification of a political, "protracted war"[18] that was aimed both at rectifying organizational and ideological deviations and at molding "revolutionary successors to the cause of the proletariat." The Maoists apparently considered the continued participation of the PLA crucial to the successful conduct of this struggle. As we have just indicated, the PLA was neither devoid of personal rivalries nor completely free of professionalism. Nonetheless, Lin Biao's efforts to improve the political reliability and ideological correctness of the PLA had been sufficiently successful for Mao to use the army as an organizational model for the party and state, and to dispatch cadres from the GPD to lead campaigns against revisionism in sectors of civilian society ranging from economics to the arts. The importance of these campaigns to the Maoists and the importance of the PLA to the campaigns was such that any proposal that would divert attention from domestic problems, restrict the army's performance of its domestic functions, or threaten to weaken the political fiber of the PLA would probably receive extremely critical scrutiny.

The Strategic Context

Vietnam. Prior to the Tonkin Gulf incidents, the Chinese communists' characterization of the Vietnam conflict, as well as their material commitment to the insurgents, was modest. The Chinese considered the revolution of the National Liberation Front (NLF) to be only one of several national liberation movements in the underdeveloped world, and not the most important.[19] China's public identification with the NLF consisted of sympathetic support and encouragement, which probably reflected the leadership's belief that a Vietnamese communist guerrilla war would eventually be capable of overwhelming the Saigon government without the need of major external assistance. Accordingly, during 1964 the P.R.C. became an increasingly important, but not the most significant, source of weapons for the NLF.

Although the Chinese leadership was confident about the outcome of the NLF revolution, it was apparently concerned about U.S. intentions, mainly, it seems, with respect to North Vietnam. In the summer of 1964, Beijing charged that the United States had violated Chinese territory and air space nineteen times during May and June, and said that such violations bore a "close relation" to U.S. "schemes" in Southeast Asia.[20] Perhaps in anticipation of new trouble, Foreign Minister Chen Yi wrote to Xuan Thuy, then North Vietnam's foreign minister: "China is the brotherly neighbor of the DRV, as closely related to it as the lips to the teeth. Any aggression against the DRV cannot expect [to find] the Chinese people sitting idly by doing nothing."[21] An editorial in *Renmin ribao* on July 9 noted recent American threats "to carry out a sea blockade and bombing of the DRV," actions that would be considered a threat to "China's peace and security." And Premier Zhou Enlai, in an unattributed interview published only days before the Tonkin incidents, referred to the possibility of direct Chinese intervention in Vietnam in response to a U.S. ground invasion of North Vietnam. Zhou warned that it was for the Americans to decide whether they wanted war with China, and if so, on what scale; but that if they decided on war, China would consider fighting a multifront war rather than "a second Korea."[22]

These pessimistic official Chinese statements reflected not only an attempt to deter U.S. escalation in Vietnam but also a reluctance to stake out in advance the range of China's commitment to Vietnam. In the aforementioned interview, for example, Zhou seemed—perhaps purposely—to contradict himself when he said at one point that China might become involved if North Vietnam were invaded, but at another point implied that Chinese involvement would depend on whether the United States attacked China.

The engagements in the Tonkin Gulf on August 2 and 4, 1964, and the first U.S. air raids against North Vietnamese targets did not lead the Chinese to augment their verbal or material commitments to North Vietnam substantially. While asserting through official statements and newspaper commentaries that "aggression against the DRV is aggression against China," the leadership seemed to distinguish between American *attacks* on North Vietnam (such as the air sorties of August 4), which called for China's "resolute support," and an American *invasion,* which might require a more direct Chinese response.[23] To meet the first contingency, China sent about fifteen MIG-15 and MIG-17 subsonic jets to North Vietnam in August, agreed to train Hanoi's pilots in China,[24] and completed or began to construct new jet-basing airfields in south China.[25] This last measure, as subsequent events would make clearer, was designed to provide sanctuary and repair and maintenance facilities for North Vietnam's jet fighters. It was also a minimum step, in the absence of accompanying air force redeployment, toward strengthening China's own air defense system. To meet the second contingency, Beijing appeared to rely more on the force of words than on action. Although large-scale close-range combat maneuvers reportedly took place in August in Guangdong and Fujian provinces,[26] no significant redeployments of PLA units occurred during the latter half of 1964.

When the Tonkin incidents were not followed by further U.S. air attacks or by increased American involvement in South Vietnam, whatever concern existed in China over U.S. intentions seems to have relaxed. No deployment of additional jet fighters or personnel to military facilities in south China appears to have occurred, for one thing. For another, the anxiety in Chinese statements about Vietnam that was noticeable in mid-1964 was greatly muted by the end of the year. The explanation for this can be found in Mao Zedong's interview with Edgar Snow in January 1965.[27] In that interview, Mao expressed confidence that the United States would not expand the war to North Vietnam (Secretary of State Rusk had said so); but in any event, he declared, Chinese forces would not fight beyond the border. In South Vietnam, the Viet Cong were proving quite capable of winning on their own; increased U.S. intervention would only strengthen the NLF materially and politically, so that the Americans could be expected, after another few years, to return home or try elsewhere. Mao did not even exclude the possibility of another conference in Geneva to discuss American withdrawal from Vietnam while U.S. forces were still there.

Sino-Soviet relations. Following the announcement on October 14, 1964, of Khrushchev's ouster, the Chinese Communists accepted Moscow's invitation to send a delegation to the October Revolution celebrations. Unquestionably, the main purpose of the delegation, led by Zhou Enlai, was to sound out the new leaders, Kosygin and Brezhnev, on the numerous issues in dispute. These included Khrushchev's long-delayed plan to hold an international Communist conference; peaceful coexistence with the United States; commitments to revolutionary movements; the Soviets' "revisionist" domestic programs; and the acceptability of Titoism. The Chinese found in the course of their visit (November 5–13) that nothing had really changed in the Soviet posture: Khrushchev's successors wanted an improvement in Sino-Soviet relations on terms that would silence Beijing's criticisms and limit competition in foreign policy, probably in return for the resumption of Soviet economic assistance.[28] The two Communist parties remained as far apart as ever. According to Peng Zhen's (P'eng Chen's) later account, the Chinese delegation "advised them [Brezhnev and Kosygin] to discard their [Khrushchev's] legacy and to put right their perverse attitude towards enemies and friends. They again refused to listen. They declared to our delegation's face that there was not a shade of difference between them and Khrushchev in their attitude toward enemies and friends."[29]

The possibility of a reconciliation was dimmed by the Moscow experience, but at least some Chinese leaders—to judge from Zhou's remarks in his "Report on the Work of the Government" (December 21–22, 1964)—still held out hopes for Sino-Soviet unity. Nevertheless, at the end of 1964 and into the new year, the Chinese press published a number of statements by other Communist parties, such as those of Japan and Albania, that were critical of the new Soviet leaders. Beijing resumed more direct polemics denouncing Khrushchev's policies, and this may have been responsible for the Soviet decision, late in November, to hold a preliminary conference of Communist parties the following March 1.[30] The first step had been taken toward a world conference that would, Beijing had long insisted, irrevocably split the communist movement.

Domestic Politics, Strategic Posture, and Foreign Policy at the Start of 1965

The first months of 1965 saw a major increase in the level of American involvement in Vietnam. On February 7, 9, and 11, American war planes raided installations in North Vietnam, supposedly in retaliation against NLF attacks on American barracks near Pleiku and in Quinhon. On March 1, the United States stopped claiming that its air strikes against the D.R.V. were reprisals for specific communist actions in South Vietnam and began a continuous air campaign against North Vietnam. For the Chinese, the situation in Vietnam had, in the space of a month, undergone a very ominous change.

In China, as in every nation, the three policy arenas we have been discussing—strategic, domestic, and foreign—are intimately interrelated. In determining their response to American escalation, therefore, China's leaders had to take into account the effects of a change in strategic posture or foreign policy on the domestic Chinese political situation. Those who advocated a major shift in China's strategic posture, for example, would have to justify the resulting cost to domestic political and economic programs. Conversely, those who wished to continue existing domestic policies would have to consider the implications of that decision for Chinese military preparedness and for the flexibility of Chinese foreign policy.

In reevaluating their policies in 1965, then, China's leaders almost certainly considered the interconnections among the various policy arenas.

Our discussion of China's domestic and international environments at the end of 1964 leads us to believe that the CCP probably took the following relationships into account.

The relationship between strategic and domestic policies. Given the extensive and critical role of the General Political Department of the PLA in several major domestic political campaigns, an intensification of military training or a redeployment of military units to meet strategic needs might have two effects. First, it might seriously hamper the continuation of the political campaigns begun in 1964. Second, greater emphasis on military training might lower the priority of political indoctrination programs within the PLA, and might therefore reduce the overall political reliability and ideological correctness of the army.

Economically, a decision to improve the combat posture of the PLA would require the diversion of economic resources from civilian projects into military programs. In addition, greater emphasis within the army on military activities might divert the army from its domestic economic functions, such as sideline production and public works.

Conversely, domestic political and economic requirements might be permitted to limit the kinds of military preparations and the level of military expenditures that the PLA could undertake. Strategic options might be selected that would maximize the PLA's participation in politics and minimize the army's share of the nation's economic resources.

The relationship between strategic and foreign policies. Chinese policy toward Vietnam would clearly exert considerable influence on the character of Chinese strategic policy, including the deployment of forces and the nature of military preparations. A decision to expand or restrict military expenditures and preparations would tend, respectively, to enlarge or diminish the flexibility of Chinese policies toward the Vietnam War.

China's policy toward the Soviet Union would affect the availability of certain types of sophisticated conventional weapons and a nuclear deterrent against the United States. Therefore, China's perceived need for an improved strategic posture might require a readjustment of its relations with Moscow.

The relationship between domestic and foreign policies. Since an aid program to North Vietnam might necessitate readjustment of domestic expenditure patterns, depending upon the amount and scarcity of the resources supplied, domestic economic requirements might put constraints on Chinese aid to North Vietnam.

Conceivably, the desire to improve China's economic conditions might encourage attempts to ameliorate relations with the Soviet Union.[31] On the other hand, China's continued use of conditions within the Soviet Union as a "negative model" domestically (consider the devastating critique of Soviet society contained in "On Krushchov's Phoney Communism") would severely restrict its ability to improve relations with Moscow, whether such an improvement were intended to increase Soviet trade and aid to China or to elicit Moscow's cooperation on assistance to North Vietnam.

These three interrelationships provide a background for analyzing the intraparty debate of 1965. By bringing into question the adequacy of the Chinese strategic posture, the rapid American escalation in Vietnam threatened to disrupt the balance established in 1964 among the three realms of policy. Proposals to alter China's strategic stance or its foreign policy would inevitably raise very touchy domestic political and economic questions. Beijing's leaders would have to determine the degree to which improvement or maintenance of their position in one policy arena would warrant sacrifices in the other two. And this decision in turn hinged upon another: whether domestic "revisionism" or American "imperialism" posed the greater threat to the Chinese state in 1965. In fact, as we will argue, it was the inability to decide which was the more serious threat that lay at the heart of the so-called strategic debate of 1965.

The Evolution of China's Vietnam Policy, February–November 1965

U.S. air strikes against North Vietnam in February 1965, and the March 1 announcement from Washington of the start of a continuous air campaign over North Vietnam, compelled Beijing to redefine its Vietnam policy and to consider the implications of that change for the rift with Moscow. By chronologically tracing Chinese policy formulations and Chinese actions, the groundwork can be laid for establishing whether, to what extent, and on what basis Luo Ruiqing differed with other leaders on Vietnam policy, Sino-Soviet relations, and China's strategic posture.

February

Chinese statements regarding the U.S. air strikes—including a speech by Luo Ruiqing—were quite consistent. Two points were stressed: first, that the D.R.V. now had the right to retaliate, and could expect continued Chinese political and material support; second, that China was prepared for a direct confrontation with the United States only if the United States "imposed" war on China. Contrary to the interpretations of some analysts, there is no evidence that at this juncture, unity with the Soviet Union (except on China's terms) was being advocated by any Chinese leaders.

As for the appropriate response to the U.S. attacks, the implication of various Chinese statements was that North Vietnam should step up the infiltration of men into South Vietnam. The D.R.V., said Liu Ningyi (a member of the CCP Central Committee and president of the All-China Federation of Trade Unions) on February 10, now had "the right to take the initiative and counterattack the U.S. imperialist aggressors." He expressed confidence that "the Vietnamese people" could cope with the Americans.[32] A Chinese government statement on February 13 proclaimed that the "DRV has secured the right to take the initiative in dealing counterblows to the South Vietnamese puppets."[33] China would play a supporting role in this undertaking. According to Liu Ningyi, "The 650 million Chinese people will definitely not ignore it [U.S. aggression] or stand idly by without helping." And in the words of Luo Ruiqing, "With respect to the struggle of the Vietnamese people against U.S. imperialist aggression, we will exert our greatest effort to support it."[34]

In promising China's "greatest effort," Luo does not appear to have been recommending a new P.R.C. commitment to Vietnam.[35] Actually, he seemed to hedge on China's commitment. He would say only that "with respect to U.S. aggressive action in expanding the war to the DRV, the Chinese people definitely cannot ignore it," and that it would "stir up the protests of Asian and the world's people." Luo was much less equivocal about the case where "U.S. imperialism singlemindedly dares to impose aggressive war on us," for then "we are prepared and understand how to deal with its aggression."

Such Chinese statements notwithstanding, renewal of the U.S. air attacks had belied Mao's optimistic forecast about American intentions and therefore must have raised questions about whether proclamations of Chinese attentiveness would be sufficient to deter further U.S. escalation. It has been suggested that at this time the position of some Chinese leaders, Luo Ruiqing among them, was that "while China was not prepared to change its basic position on the questions at issue with Moscow, it was prepared to strengthen the alliance in the face of the common danger."[36] Certainly, several (if not most) Chinese leaders, including Mao,[37] still accepted Sino-Soviet unity and the Sino-Soviet alliance in principle. None seemed prepared, however, to compromise on the issues in dispute— including support of the Vietnamese revolution and Soviet leadership in the world communist movement—in order to improve China's deterrent posture toward the United States, least of all at a time when the U.S. threat to *China* was still remote. It may also be questioned whether any Chinese leader could really have believed that the Soviets would give something for nothing—that is, would agree to reaffirm a commitment to China's defense while accepting continued Chinese criticism and ideological separatism.

On February 5, Kosygin's stopover in Beijing on his trip to Hanoi provided the occasion for Mao and his associates to confront the Soviet premier personally with their discontent. According to a later Chinese account,[38] Kosygin contended that the United States should be helped out of Vietnam through negotiations, but was told by the Chinese that it was time for resistance, not talking. The Chinese still resisted Kosygin's proposals for normalizing Sino-Soviet relations,[39] and in speeches after his departure, expressed continued suspicions about Soviet reliability. Guo Moruo, vice-chairman of the Sino-Soviet Friendship Association, and Foreign Minister Chen Yi both expressed their belief that Sino-Soviet unity still needed to be "consolidated and developed" (Guo) and "tested and tempered" in "concrete action" (Chen).[40] By the end of February, the Chinese felt that their position had been vindicated: as they would later charge,[41] no sooner had Kosygin returned to Moscow than he and his colleagues proposed to convene a new Indochina conference, based on President Johnson's call for "unconditional negotiations," and later urged that negotiations begin once the United States stopped bombing the D.R.V. "The dark spirit of Khrushchev has not dissipated," a biting *Renmin ribao* commentary asserted on February 26; the new Soviet leadership—"Khrushchevism without Khrushchev"—was as interested as ever in peaceful coexistence with the United States.

March

By the end of February, the Chinese position on aid to Vietnam had become fairly well established. To maintain the sanctity of their "principled stand" against imperialism and revisionism, Beijing's leaders would do nothing publicly that would imply acceptance of Soviet leadership in combating the threat to North Vietnam. On their own the Chinese would increase military and economic aid to Hanoi;[42] provide antiaircraft artillery units and instructors;[43] introduce PLA construction personnel (eventually numbering from 30,000 to 50,000)[44] to rebuild and defend damaged rail and road links and storage facilities in the area between the Chinese border and major D.R.V. cities;[45] assist in the construction or expansion of D.R.V. airfields and other defense facilities; and make southern Chinese airfields available as redeployment areas for North Vietnamese jets, which would otherwise be vulnerable to U.S. air attacks.[46] From Mao's viewpoint, it may be assumed, these steps were in keeping with the stated policy of self-reliance (since they would free North Vietnamese army personnel to assist the NLF); bolstered the D.R.V.'s defenses (and thus encouraged Hanoi's continued resistance); and minimized the risks and necessity of deeper Chinese involvement in the conflict. Tough-sounding Chinese statements during March[47] consequently seemed more relevant to the Sino-Soviet controversy than to actual Chinese policy on Vietnam.

Soviet activities, meanwhile, could only have decreased the likelihood that Mao's opposition to unity with Moscow would change, or that anyone in Beijing advocating unity would make headway. From March 1 to March 5, the Soviets held a nineteen-party "consultative meeting" (not attended by Hanoi) that prompted the most intensive Chinese criticism yet of Soviet policies.[48] During the conference (on March 4), Chinese students in Moscow staged a demonstration in front of the American Embassy, and Soviet authorities moved in to stop it, drawing a Chinese protest against their "ruthless suppression" (rejected by Moscow). At the end of the month, four of the students were ordered to leave the U.S.S.R., which again aroused Chinese protests.

Chinese polemics directed at Moscow, such as the March 23 commentary on the Moscow meeting, continued to support the principle of unity while discounting the prospects for it.[49] To be consistent in this position, Beijing at least had to agree to assist in the shipment of Soviet goods to North Vietnam. Kosygin had in fact received assurances of Chinese cooperation in February.[50] If the Chinese felt that the Soviets were not matching words with deeds on Vietnam—and there was evidence of Soviet foot-dragging[51]—Beijing could hardly resist both Soviet and North Vietnamese pressure for Chinese cooperation in facilitating the delivery of Soviet military aid. On March 30, two agreements were signed (but, probably at China's insistence, not publicized) regarding the transshipment of Soviet matériel to the D.R.V.: one between Beijing and Moscow; another between Beijing and Hanoi.[52] As would later become plain, however, the Sino-Soviet agreement did not guarantee that China would expedite Soviet deliveries and thus give the appearance of a rapid Soviet response to Hanoi's needs.

April

The limits of China's willingness to help the Soviet Union help North Vietnam were clearly set in April. In letters to Beijing on April 3 and 17, the Russians proposed holding trilateral (D.R.V.–U.S.S.R.–P.R.C.) talks on the coordination of aid. They further proposed, probably in the same two letters,[53] that China permit the Soviet Union to send 4,000 regular army personnel through Chinese territory to Vietnam; to have the use of one or two airfields in southwest China (probably Yunnan) for the air defense of North Vietnam; to garrison 500 men at such bases; and to establish an air corridor over Chinese territory.

The Chinese wasted little time in replying: judging from the context of a July 14 letter, the reply was delivered sometime between the Soviet letters of April 3 and April 17.[54] The Chinese rejected the proposal for trilateral talks on the grounds that they did not want to give either the West or other Communist nations the impression that when the conference was over the Soviet Union would be empowered to speak for China on Vietnam. Beijing probably feared that the Soviet leaders would exploit a trilateral conference to pursue their role as brokers trying to bring Hanoi and Washington together around a peace table. In the Chinese view, the Soviets would seize the opportunity afforded by the summit meeting to tie China to a Soviet- and American-composed Vietnam settlement that would bargain away the NLF's interests for the sake of world-wide détente.

At the same time, or within a few weeks, Beijing also spurned Moscow's proposals for the direct use of Chinese territory by Soviet military personnel. In the words of the July 14 letter of the CCP Central Committee, these proposals had "ulterior motives." "China is not one of your provinces," the Committee told the Soviet party leaders.

Beijing probably rejected the establishment of an air corridor because it would have allowed the Soviets to retain control over their aid deliveries through China. The Chinese would thus in some sense surrender authority over their own territory, and the opportunity to inspect Soviet shipments would be lost. The remaining proposals were probably even more unacceptable: they amounted to permitting the Soviets to maintain and garrison one or more bases that could be used to receive, assemble, repair, and refuel Soviet-built jets that would be flown by North Vietnamese pilots back and forth across the Chinese border. The Russians would thereby reap the credit for providing dramatic new military assistance to the D.R.V.—probably including late-model jets that China could not offer (see below)—and for seemingly winning Beijing over to "united action." Moreover, since the Soviets would have unfettered control over the disposition of the aircraft, China would run the risk of U.S. "hot pursuit" and retaliation—a risk that China so far had minimized by making its airfields available only for the deployment of North Vietnamese aircraft, not for their use in combat. The Chinese would have no opportunity to determine the missions of the jets (or to examine closely those models not in the Chinese arsenal). Finally, a Soviet base on Chinese soil would constitute a dangerous extraterritorial precedent, one that Beijing might have difficulty reversing if the base continued to function as the war dragged on.

In short, the Chinese—and unquestionably Mao—would have nothing to do with any measure that would allow the Soviets access to China. The transshipment of military cargo was agreed upon precisely because the Chinese controlled it—a fact that soon produced Soviet charges of Chinese tampering and deliberate delays. Moreover, the real meaning of Chinese criticism of Soviet aid to Hanoi—in a *Red Flag* commentary[55]—was that the Russians were reluctant to confront the Americans by sea (at Haiphong) and were willing to assist North Vietnam only in ways that would have the Chinese take all the risks.

May

Thus, in three respects, Beijing's policies had already been determined. Briefly, these were: (1) China would not permit the Soviet Union independent use of Chinese territory or air space to aid North Vietnam, because of the military risks and political costs involved; (2) support of the socialist revolution in South Vietnam would be based on the principle of self-reliance,[56] and would consist of the kinds of matériel and personnel that would benefit the communists, north and south, without creating undue risks for China; and (3) U.S. intentions to intensify the bombing of North Vietnam in order to blackmail Hanoi to the conference table (a strategy that Moscow was abetting) should be exposed and resisted.[57] Any high-ranking Chinese communist who might have wanted to propose a different Vietnam strategy would have had to consider that Mao had already made some basic policy choices.

Luo Ruiqing's major article commemorating V-E Day[58] offers interesting contrasts and similarities to a *Renmin ribao* editorial, published at about the same time,[59] which presumably reflected the views of Mao and Lin Biao. Luo and the editorial were in agreement that a distinction must be made between unity against imperialism (a united front on Chinese terms) and Soviet-style unity (which is not unity but socialist betrayal). They also agreed on the implications of the distinction for negotiations with imperialists: certain limited kinds of agreements have, correctly, been negotiated with the imperialists (in Korea and at Geneva); but peace agreements, especially when made from a disadvantageous military position, only encourage aggression. As Munich showed, imperialism cannot be appeased by making concessions.[60] Luo and the editorial were restating, undoubtedly for Hanoi's benefit, the Chinese case against negotiating with the Americans on Vietnam in order to make them stop the bombing.

Luo and the editorial differed somewhat in their assessments of U.S. strength and intentions. Whereas the editorial held that the United States was "in a much worse strategic position than was Hitler in his day," and hence that the possibilities for frustrating America's aggressive plans were greater than ever, Luo contended that American *ambitions* exceeded Hitler's, even though actual U.S. military capabilities were inferior to his.[61] Consequently, Luo's argument—one on which the editorial did not take a position—was that the danger of a new world war was sufficiently great to compel China's increased preparedness:

It makes a world of difference whether or not one is prepared once a war breaks out. Among all these preparations, political and ideological preparation must be given the first priority. Moreover, these preparations must be made for the most difficult and worst situations that may possibly arise. Preparations must be made not only against any small-scale warfare but also against any medium- or large-scale warfare that imperialism may launch. These preparations must envisage the use by the imperialists of nuclear weapons as well as of conventional weapons.

Was Luo, then, urging that China's preparations include reconciliation with the U.S.S.R. in order to be assured of having the Soviet nuclear deterrent, in which case concessions to the Soviets—perhaps along the lines of their April proposals—would have to be made?[62] His condemnation of the Soviet leadership and its line on united action argues otherwise, as does his statement, in accord with the editorial, that "new weapons" should not be preferred to proven revolutionary warfare methods. But Luo's remarks about preparations and his proposals for defending China may be interpreted as differing with the Maoist position in two important respects.

First, in emphasizing the need to prepare for all-out attacks by the enemy, Luo may have had in mind a surprise air attack against China's defense and industrial targets and military installations. Conceivably, his assessment was based on the conviction that Mao's program to aid North Vietnam risked U.S. retaliation, against which urgent preparations were necessary. Luo may therefore have been proposing faster improvements than were being made in China's air defense (jet fighters, SAMs, radar, and AAA), which would have required the redeployment of available equipment to southern China.[63] The Soviet Union, of course, was one possible source of late-model MIGs, sophisticated radar sets, and SAMs—all of which the North Vietnamese were receiving.[64] But even if the Soviets had been willing to provide these items,[65] the price was known and had been rejected; and it is difficult to believe that Luo was willing to risk political suicide by proposing that China deal with Moscow.

Second, in entertaining the possibility of a U.S. invasion of China, Luo proposed as the "only strategy" a version of active defense that seemed to involve a deployment of the PLA that was quite different from Mao's "people's war" concept. Citing Mao and the experience of the Soviet army, Lo said that China should defend against enemy penetrations, trade space for time, and *prepare to counterattack* with superior forces to destroy the enemy's remaining troops. Chinese ground forces should be able to pursue and destroy the invader "in its own lair," "in his nest."[66] Instead of "luring the enemy in deep" (the Maoist view), which would give a prominent defense role to the militia,[67] Luo's strategy apparently was to rely heavily on a conventional defense, relegate the militia to harassing the enemy's rear positions,[68] and deploy the PLA to defend fixed positions, carry on interior warfare, and be prepared for strategic pursuit.[69] After Luo's purge, the Maoists would charge that Luo had really advocated "passive defense," a strategy that Mao had opposed in the encirclement period of the civil war because it meant the defense of static positions, "the building of defensive works everywhere and [the] wide dispersal of forces to man them."[70] Luo's description (in his May article) of the Soviets' defense strategy during World War II indicates that he apparently did favor defending certain strategic "cities and other places" and establishing a "far-flung" defense line. But a review of his published statements leads one to the conclusion that he did not want to defend every city or installation; his position allowed for a fluid defense, but opposed the indefinite retreat of the PLA into the interior.

It was, of course, in Vietnam that a direct confrontation with the United States was most likely to occur. But Luo did not seem to favor commitments beyond those Mao had already dictated. He said that China was providing political, moral, and full material support, and was "also prepared to send our men [*renyuan;* more accurately, "personnel"] to fight together with the people of Vietnam when they need us," but consistent with previous pronouncements, he added that China would attack only when attacked, and that he thought the NLF forces were "daily approaching final victory."[71]

Summarizing Luo's position, our interpretation is that he (1) considered, or at least asserted, that the U.S. threat to attack China was imminent, more so than the Maoists were ready to concede; (2) advocated that China be better prepared for an attack by improving its air defense system in southern China and possibly also deploying additional ground forces there;[72] (3) as an alternative to reliance on the Soviet Union's protection, sought to deter a U.S. invasion by warning that Chinese ground forces might cross international frontiers (e.g., into Vietnam, Korea, Laos, or Thailand) if war were imposed on China; and (4) upheld the policy that the kinds of assistance the NLF and the North Vietnamese were receiving from China were appropriate and sufficient.

Luo's professed anxiety about the U.S. threat, and his strategy for dealing with it, seem to have received lukewarm support from the Maoists. Aside from the domestic political implications of redeploying forces and equipment and thus emphasizing the PLA's national-security functions, there remained the strategic question, Did American actions in Vietnam threaten to spill over into China? On this question, which arose anew when the United States resumed bombing North Vietnam after a one-week pause (May 13–19), Chinese commentaries remained cautious. A *Renmin ribao* editorial on May 20 predicted continued escalation in Vietnam but refrained from saying that the United States was preparing to extend the bombing closer to China.[73]

June, July, and August

Luo Ruiqing may have received additional support for his strategy recommendations when the air war over North Vietnam widened in the summer. Late in June, U.S. aircraft attacked targets north of Hanoi for the first time. The North Vietnamese industrial city of Nam Dinh was said to have been struck on July 2. The Chinese also charged that their air space over Yunnan was violated on July 11, when U.S. planes allegedly bombed the strategic Vietnamese border city of Lao Cai.

The new support for Luo's position seemed to be reflected in *Renmin ribao,* which now began to characterize U.S. actions in more threatening terms. On June 1 its "Observer" noted that American air strikes were moving steadily northward. A "dramatic change" in the scope of the fighting was taking place; was not "the Johnson administration . . . preparing to spread the war in Indochina to the rest of Southeast Asia, and even to China?" *Renmin ribao*'s "Observer" did not call for additional war preparations, but he did imply their advisability, and he also seemed to propose additional aid to enable the North Vietnamese to intensify their efforts in South Vietnam:

> Since the United States, ignoring repeated warnings from the Chinese people, has sent large numbers of its own troops and rounded up troops from some of its satellites and committed them to its aggression against Vietnam, a fraternal country of China, the Chinese people have thus acquired the right to do all in their power to aid the Vietnamese people in counter-attacking the American aggressors. . . . Now that U.S. imperialism has . . . threatened China's security in an increasingly serious manner, the Chinese people are all the more entitled to take every additional measure necessary.[74]

Reacting to the air incident of July 11, *Renmin ribao* went further, considering it "even more serious" than previous incidents: "This is planned, deliberate war provocation pure and simple," and is "another extremely dangerous threshold" in U.S. escalation. Again, however, the writer was ambiguous about the implications of escalation: "We have a full estimation of the madness of U.S. imperialism and are well prepared with regard to its war adventure plan. The Chinese People's Liberation Army now stands ready, in battle array. We will not attack unless we are attacked; if we are attacked, we will certainly counter-attack."[75] Luo Ruiqing's pithy formula had been quoted, but the PLA was said to be already fully prepared.

If these commentaries were meant to put pressure on Mao, they did not succeed. Not only did Mao apparently fail to order a quickening of the pace of development of China's air defenses (beyond airfield construction, which seems, however, to have been part of a long-term, nationwide program rather than a response geared exlusively to events in Vietnam). But through the army newspaper, whose increasing usefulness to Mao may have been related to *Renmin ribao*'s at least partial adoption of the professional military's (and perhaps the party dissidents') viewpoint,[76] Mao's concern was made known anew that "some people" in the army command, still holding to "bourgeois military thinking," were denigrating political training and party leadership in the armed forces. Politics had to remain "in command"; improvements in military training, the fulfillment of military tasks, and the practical (rather than the educational or ideological) use of political training were not what was meant by "politics in command." Only through increased political work in the PLA could party leadership be assured and revisionist and bourgeois trends of thought be eliminated.[77] Was the army command being warned here to cut out talk of war preparedness when the primary need of the army was to improve its political performance?

During June and July, too, criticisms of the Soviet Union continued. A joint newspaper editorial[78] re-covered old ground on Sino-Soviet differences and came up with the same conclusions: revisionism had to be combatted if China's revolutionary stance and anti-imperialist line were to be successful. Soviet aid to Vietnam was dismissed as "gestures." Similar statements were made by the Chinese delegate to the Helsinki World Congress for Peace, National Independence, and General Disarmament,[79] and by Liu Ningyi at an antibomb conference in Tokyo.[80] Most authoritative of the anti-Soviet diatribes was the CCP Central Committee's letter of July 14, which (as has already been discussed) denounced anew the Soviet proposals of April, thus indicating that Moscow was still trying to gain their acceptance.

As July ended, a new element was introduced into the Vietnam conflict with indications from Washington that additional ground forces would be dispatched to augment the existing U.S. troop strength of about 75,000. A pessimistic appraisal again came from *Renmin ribao*'s "Observer," who said that the Vietnam situation, like that in Korea in 1950, was escalating dangerously. He wondered whether President Johnson intended that "the 'ground war' will be expanded without limit? People can still remember clearly how the U.S. war of aggression in Korea was expanded. The Johnson administration is taking the same old road."[81] Once the president (on July 28) confirmed the troop increase—an additional 50,000 men— another article in *Renmin ribao* expressed surprise that Johnson would do "what Eisenhower and Kennedy dared not to do or refrained from doing"— that is, send large numbers of soldiers to fight a land war in Asia. The article contrasted the relatively favorable conditions for the United States in Korea with the insurmountable disadvantages in Vietnam. China, Washington was reminded, had taken part in the Korean conflict only one year after it took over the mainland; now China "is already 15 years old and has become much stronger than before."[82] The concern in Beijing clearly was that the United States might cross the demilitarized zone and, as it did in Korea, confront China with an invasion of a socialist ally. Yet, as before, no new commitments to the D.R.V. were offered or proposed; instead, the ongoing resistance of the NLF, with China's "utmost" support, was cited as the best way to "smash" American war plans.

Speaking on Army Day (August 1), Luo Ruiqing agreed with *Renmin ribao*'s estimate of the seriousness of the U.S. threat. Referring to Secretary Rusk's statement that "the idea of the sanctuary is dead," Luo said that the PLA was prepared for an American attack:

> If [the Americans] become blinded by their lust for power, miscalculate the strength and determination of the Chinese people, insist on spreading the war to the Chinese people, and force us to accept their challenge, then the Chinese people and the Chinese PLA, which has long since been well prepared and been standing in battle array, will not only resolutely take them on to the end, but moreover will welcome their arrival in great numbers.[83]

In stating that the PLA was *already* well prepared, however, and in going on to assert the primacy of political training and "the revolutionary spirit of men," Luo appears to have retreated from his May stance.

Perhaps Luo was responding to criticisms in the June 10 army newspaper editorial. Or perhaps it was the *Jiefangjun bao* editorial on August 1 that caused the retreat. While agreeing with Luo's May article that the United States was fully capable of spreading the Vietnam War to China, and that "full preparations" should be made for every contingency, the editorial sought to close the debate over the best kind of defense. People's war, as Lin Biao had said, constitutes the best defense; it negates the enemy's technological edge, does not depend on the size of the enemy's attack, and is just, revolutionary war. Moreover, people's war acts as a deterrent: "Imperialism's military experts and advisers cannot conceal their fear of people's war; they cannot but recognize that all China's people are troops, that they are 'an important force which frightens foreigners into not daring to invade,' 'a great sea formed by 700 million which no modern weapons can destroy.'" And nothing could change this doctrine:

> No matter whether past, present, or future, regardless of changes in the style or objectives of war, regardless of the appearance of nuclear weapons and how great the changes in technological conditions, this truth [that the masses are the greatest strength in war] that Chairman Mao has clearly pointed out *will never change*. At present, our weapons and equipment are becoming daily more modernized. Moreover, we have our own atomic bomb. When imperialism forces war upon us, we must as before rely on the masses to carry out people's war. Even if, in the future, destructive power and weapons are much greater, [our strategy] will still be this way and will forever be this way. *There cannot be the slightest doubt about this point.* [Italics added]

The editorial closed by reemphasizing Mao's instructions on militia building.

Mao's position on PLA doctrine and defense posture also received support from a senior army veteran in a third major Army Day statement. In an article that received wide coverage,[84] Huo Long (Ho Lung), a member of the Politburo and vice-chairman of the National Defense Council, wrote on the "struggle between two lines on army building." Huo asserted that conditions of modern warfare, far from being grounds for changing the system of democratic centralism in the armed forces, were all the more reason for retaining it. New equipment and techniques could be fully used only by "practising democracy, bringing the collective wisdom of the masses into full play and rallying the initiative and creativeness of the masses under the collective leadership of the Party committee." Huo reminded his readers that the PLA had long been a political, no less than a military, force: "The Marxist-Leninist line of the Chinese Communist Party, represented by Comrade Mao Tse-tung, and all the fine traditions of the Party were usually implemented first in the army." The clear implication of Huo's remarks was that no strategy or weapon could be used as a pretext for changing the organization, political regimen, or political purposes of the PLA.

September, October, and November

If Luo Ruiqing's Army Day speech was a retreat on the question of war preparedness, his speech on V-J Day (September 2) showed that the retreat was only temporary and perhaps tactical.[85] A comparison of his views with those of Lin Biao in the now-famous article "Long Live the Victory of People's War!"[86] leads to further speculations about differences in the Chinese leadership over U.S. intentions and China's defense.

That the United States was threatening China was no longer a matter of disagreement. But the nature of the threat was characterized differently by Luo and Lin. Luo drew analogies between the existing situation and the Korean War, in which China's involvement stemmed from the expansion of a nearby conflict, and World War II, in which Germany launched an all-out invasion of Russia without warning. Lin's analogy was to the Japanese invasion of China in the 1930s. Thus, whereas Lin held that "the U.S. imperialists are now clamouring . . . for another large-scale ground war on the Asian mainland" involving China, Luo asserted that the U.S. threat was twofold: Washington might "dare to send its troops to invade China," or it might, "in order to save itself from defeat, . . . go mad." Unlike Lin Biao, Luo did not rule out the possibility of an irrational escalation of the U.S. air war into China.

Implicitly, the imminence of the U.S. threat was also in dispute, for since Luo was concerned about a surprise U.S. attack, he also had to be concerned that such an attack might come sooner rather than later. As seems to have been the case earlier, Luo urged more attention to China's defenses against the various possible kinds of U.S. attacks. China, he said, "certainly must have sufficient plans and certainly must complete preparations for U.S. imperialism's spreading the war of aggression against Vietnam and for imposing the war on us. Preparations involve a thousand and one things." Lin Biao's article lacked the same note of urgency. His statement implied confidence that the United States would prefer not to invade China and get bogged down in a people's war:

> The Chinese people definitely have ways of their own for coping with a U.S. imperialist war of aggression. Our methods are no secret. The most important one is still mobilization of the people, reliance on the people, making everyone a soldier and waging a people's war. We want to tell the U.S. imperialists once again that the vast ocean of several hundred million Chinese people in arms will be more than enough to submerge your few million aggressor troops. If you dare to impose war on us, we shall gain freedom of action. It will then not be up to you to decide how the war will be fought.

Lin seemed more interested in *deterring* the United States than in mobilizing quickly for *defense;* and his statement suggests that, in his and Mao's view, China was already well organized to defend against an invasion if deterrence failed.[87] Luo, besides apparently believing that improvements in air defense were urgently required, may also have decided that even in ground defense, the leadership needed to do more and to do it quickly. He said that "the most important, the most fundamental," kind of readiness stemmed from preparing well "in all fields for making people's war in accordance with the demands of Chairman Mao Zedong's thoughts on people's war." As in previous months, Luo was mainly concerned about getting troops and equipment into position before it was too late, not about selling his superiors on the idea of dickering with the Russians for nuclear protection or new weapons.[88]

By September, the conflict between Mao and Lin's view of the PLA's role and mission and Luo Ruiqing's view probably began to become acute, for by that time, Mao's political program for reinfusing discipline and ending moral decay and corruption in Chinese society—the Socialist Education Movement—had floundered badly.[89] This weakening had developed in roughly two stages. In the first, from late 1964 to January 1965, basic-level rural cadres, placed under investigation by party work teams and supervised by peasant groups formed by party committees, became demoralized because of such harassment. Discipline and production in the villages apparently suffered instead of improving. In the second stage, beginning in January 1965, the program's emphasis shifted from rectification and "class struggle" to conciliation and indoctrination. Pressures against basic-level cadres and peasants were relaxed. Gradually, however, a new target took their place: party members "in authority who take the capitalist road." Two kinds of drives were launched to deal with these persons, one to "revolutionize" *xian*-("country-")level party committees, another to have the entire population "study and apply the thought of Mao Zedong."

Mao's appearance at a Central Committee meeting in September 1965 has been considered the first shot of the "Great Proletarian Cultural Revolution."[90] The available evidence suggests that Mao probably called the meeting because the latest phase of the Socialist Education Movement had failed to root out higher-level party dissidents. Mao was probably confirmed in his suspicions by the resistance to his authority encountered at that meeting.[91] With the benefit of hindsight, it would seem that Mao at that time (if not earlier) reached two decisions about the new course his rectification campaign would have to take: first, it would require more militant forms of struggle to expose and, if necessary, purge party members whose loyalty to his "thoughts" was flagging; second, since the party leadership was of doubtful reliability, the vehicle for carrying the revolution forward would have to be the army under Lin Biao, in particular its General Political Department.[92]

Yet "bourgeois thinking" existed in the army as well as in the party. If the army's political command was to replace the party as the vanguard of the revolution, Luo Ruiqing, whose insistence on war preparations would divert the PLA from political involvement, had to be dealt with first. Mao's counterattack against his opponents, beginning with Yao Wenyuan's article in the November 10 *Wenhui bao* on Wu Han's drama *The Dismissal of Hai Rui from Office* may thus have been more than an indirect criticism of Peng Zhen, Wu Han's superior as mayor of Beijing.[93] It may also have been a warning to Luo Ruiqing and others in the army leadership. This interpretation is supported by Mao's statement that Hai Rui represented the dismissed defense minister Peng Dehuai,[94] and by the fact that Yao's critique was reprinted and endorsed by the army organ *Jiefangjun bao* (on November 29), which had become Mao's principal news organ.

The possibility cannot be dismissed that in the fall of 1965, Mao and Lin genuinely believed that Luo, Peng Zhen, and two other senior party officials, Yang Shangkun and Lu Dingyi (Lu Ting-yi) (later labeled the "four-family village"), were the leaders of a conspiracy to usurp power in a military coup.[95] Peng Zhen may have managed to survive longer than Luo and Yang—he was not purged until May 1966—because the Maoists did not yet feel strong enough to move against someone of his stature and power, because they required further evidence to persuade themselves or others, or because events in Vietnam were still too uncertain to warrant declaring war on the party apparatus. In the light of these considerations, the effective purge of Luo, probably in early December,[96] served two purposes in addition to removing a potential obstacle to the PLA's full-scale involvement in politics. First, eliminating Luo and, at about the same time, Yang Shangkun, his colleague in the party Secretariat, disposed of two resistants *within the party* to a future move *against* the party.[97] Second, the removal of Luo and Yang was a way of warning and, indeed, of putting further pressure on Peng Zhen, a suspected coconspirator.

The leading role of the General Political Department in the evolving Cultural Revolution was not apparent to outsiders for some time. But to Beijing insiders, the handwriting may have been on the wall by the middle of November. Lin Biao's "five principles"—his early directive of November 15 on the tasks of the PLA for 1966, with its stress on "putting politics in the forefront" (*tuchu zhengzhi*) and regard for "the works of Chairman Mao Zedong as the highest instructions" in all work—may have been intended as the guidelines for determining the loyalty of party cadres.[98] A political work conference of the PLA's General Political Department, which lasted from December 30, 1965, to January 18, 1966, confirmed the PLA's priorities. Lin Biao's five principles were reported to be the main topic; and "putting politics in the forefront" was said to be important in modernizing the armed forces, revolutionizing the army, and defeating imperialism and modern revisionism.[99] The report of the head of the General Political Department, Xiao Hua (Hsiao Hua), recited Mao's warning of a counterrevolutionary comeback that would change the party unless politics remained in command. The army's role in preventing that "dangerous situation" would be critical; yet the army was vulnerable to "political degeneration" because, having been victorious and having enjoyed a long period of peace, it might relax its vigilance. Xiao's recommendation—to "make the army the most responsible tool of the Party and to put guns forever in the hands of the most reliable people"[100]—would not have to wait long before being implemented.

The Purge of Luo Ruiqing: Issues and Implications

In attempting to explain the purge of Luo Ruiqing, we will first identify the major policy issues on which Luo significantly differed from Mao Zedong and Lin Biao. We believe that these issues did not concern Sino-Soviet relations or the level of Chinese involvement in Vietnam so much as Chinese strategic doctrine on defense and its implications for domestic politics. In particular, we believe that the most important issue was Luo's insistence that the PLA reorder its priorities, reduce its domestic political activities, and make urgent preparations against an American attack. To the Maoists, these proposals involved unacceptable political and economic costs, and placed Luo's loyalty and reliability in serious question.

The Major Issues

Instead of being central issues, the two foreign-policy issues most often linked to the purge of Luo Ruiqing—China's relations with the Soviet Union and China's policy toward North Vietnam—seem to have provided the *context* for a debate over defense strategy and over the domestic political implications of alternative Chinese strategic postures. As for Sino-Soviet relations, it is not inconceivable that the Soviet proposals for united action found advocates in Beijing. Certain Chinese leaders might have found the Soviet package attractive on economic grounds or might have been sensitive to external pressures to cooperate more fully with Moscow on aid to North Vietnam. China's continued refusal to accept the Soviet initiatives had been disenchanting other Communist parties, which considered Chinese intransigence a significant aid to the American war effort.[101] Accepting the Soviet proposals would incur certain ideological costs, to be sure, but it would also bring economic benefits and might improve Beijing's chances of acquiring Soviet conventional weapons.

Our assessment, however, is that the question of united action played little part in the purge of Luo Ruiqing.[102] First of all, Luo's speeches were hostile to Khrushchev and his successors. More important, Chinese dissatisfaction with the new Soviet leadership reached the level of open criticism by February 1965; and in April, Beijing decided to reject the Soviet proposals, just weeks after their receipt. For Luo to have attempted to reverse this decision would have been tantamount to political suicide. Furthermore, since Kosygin apparently did not offer to resume military aid to China, Luo could not have been assured that China would receive sophisticated weapons in return for making concessions to the Russians. Finally, Luo, as army chief of staff, probably resisted Moscow's attempt to acquire extraterritorial privileges and air bases on Chinese territory. His personal authority would have been reduced, the risk of U.S. retaliation would have increased, and Chinese air force technicians would have been prevented from examining North Vietnamese MIGs flying to and from China.

On China's Vietnam policy, our conclusion is that Luo's position was consistent with that of other Chinese leaders. This position did contain ambiguities, however. On the one hand, Luo and others declared that China would not attack unless it were attacked first; on the other hand, by referring to the Korean analogy, and by offering to "send personnel" into North Vietnam, the same men seemed to threaten stronger action should the United States continue to escalate its level of action against North Vietnam.[103] There are several interpretations of these seemingly contradictory remarks. One is that China did not envisage sending combat troops into North Vietnam under any circumstances, and that the threatened "stronger action" would be limited to material and political aid and support personnel. Luo's formulation—"we are prepared to send our men to fight together with the people of Vietnam when they need us, [but] we will not attack unless we are attacked"—brought these two elements together. It described perfectly the construction troops and antiaircraft divisions sent to North Vietnam during 1965. Supplying defense support troops and technical assistance would enable Hanoi to increase significantly its defensive and offensive capabilities and would improve China's capacity to send aid to the North Vietnamese.

Another interpretation, which is not incompatible with the first, is that the Chinese were being deliberately ambiguous in order to deter the U.S. from escalating its attacks against North Vietnam while at the same time avoiding an irrevocable commitment to protect the Hanoi regime by armed intervention. Such a commitment would reduce Chinese flexibility at a time when the international and domestic situations were in a state of rapid flux.

Finally, a third possibility is simply that the Chinese had not decided what to do if the United States escalated the war, and that the somewhat contradictory statements reflected true ambivalence in the thinking of top Chinese leaders. Whichever interpretation proves correct, it is important to reemphasize that Luo's position was basically in accord with the position of other Chinese leaders. Neither Luo nor anyone else seems to have advocated measures such as the introduction of Chinese combat forces into North Vietnam or the widening of China's air defense perimeter to include the northern sectors of the D.R.V. Nor is there any firm evidence that Luo believed that the level of Chinese material aid, political support, or noncombatant manpower assistance to the D.R.V. was seriously deficient.[104]

While Luo apparently did not disagree with the content of Chinese policy toward the Soviet Union and North Vietnam, one of our major conclusions is that he did significantly disagree with Mao and Lin over the implications of Chinese policy in Vietnam for an adequate strategic posture. Luo seems to have argued that even with a relatively cautious policy toward Vietnam, China was running military risks that demanded a reevaluation of defensive strategy and an increase in defense preparations. The ensuing debate involved disagreements over the nature of the threat that the U.S. posed to China, the most appropriate Chinese strategy for responding to the threat, and the corresponding preparations necessary to implement that strategy.

As we have seen, Luo and Lin Biao agreed that the threat posed by the United States was not an overwhelming one, that the United States had certain critical weaknesses, and that therefore China could adequately deter or defend itself against an American attack. But Luo disagreed with Lin on two major points. First, Luo saw a broader spectrum of threats facing

China. While Lin (and Mao) believed that any hostile American action would inexorably lead to an American invasion, Luo warned of discrete and limited American actions of much lesser magnitude, such as air strikes (with either conventional or nuclear weapons) against Chinese military installations. Second, as compared with Lin, Luo saw not only a wider range of possible hostile American actions, but also a greater probability that the U.S. would initiate hostilities against China. Referring both to the ambitions (which Luo characterized as even greater than Hitler's) and the possible irrationality of the United States, Luo warned that China's deterrence posture was not as secure as the Maoists believed.

To meet these threats, Luo seems to have proposed a strategy that differed from Maoist prescriptions in at least three respects. First, Luo placed more reliance on the regular PLA forces (especially the infantry) than on either local forces or the militia. This is not to say that he advocated ignoring the militia, but rather that he saw China's militia playing a distinctly subordinate role in war. Second, Luo tempered the strategy of "luring deep" with calls for the establishment of prepared defensive positions fairly close to and covering sizable portions of the Chinese border. And third, because Luo saw limited American air strikes (unaccompanied by an invasion) as a real possibility, he advocated the rapid improvement of China's air defense in the south.[105]

To the Maoists, reliance on elaborate air-defense installations and on conventional ground forces meant competing with the United States in an area where the Americans had clear-cut superiority. It would be foolish indeed to try to meet the enemy on its own terms. Rather, China should rely on its strong points—vast superiority in manpower and large expanse of territory—and follow a strategy of irregular warfare after luring the enemy deep. Furthermore, the establishment of prepared defensive positions would provide American forces with clear targets for air attacks, and would require dispersal of Chinese forces to such an extent that the initiative would be lost.

Since Luo and the Maoists disagreed about the most effective strategies for coping with American threats to China, it is not surprising that they also disagreed on the types of defense preparations that China should undertake. Lin Biao's statements in 1965 reflect his conviction that China's preparations to wage people's war were already sufficient both to deter the United States from an invasion and to defend China in the unlikely event that the Americans did attack.[106] Luo, assigning greater probability to an American attack, and advocating significant changes in Chinese strategy, called for crash preparations for defense. Making immediate and urgent preparations, Luo argued, would be more realistic than either assuming that war was unlikely or concluding that China's defensive capabilities were already sufficient. Although some preparations and redeployments were made during the summer of 1965, Luo probably considered them inadequate.

Western news reports revealed shortages of equipment and ammunition, and troops being urged to use dummy weapons in training.[107] Despite the efforts of the summer, in his September speech Luo still warned that there were "a thousand and one things" to do to make China ready for war. While he did not spell out what preparations he had in mind, on the basis of our reconstruction of the strategy he advocated we believe that he sought (1) construction of additional defensive installations, especially antiaircraft sites, in south China; (2) a redeployment of China's air defenses—including jets, radar, and available SAMs—to the south; (3) a reemphasis on military, as opposed to political, training within the PLA; and perhaps (4) an increase in the number of regular troops.

Our main conclusion is that these proposed defense preparations, because they required a number of domestic policy decisions that were inconsistent with Mao's plans and the interests of other groups, represented the single most important issue behind Luo's purge.

In the first place, Luo's proposed defense preparations involved decisions on resource allocations that would have harmed sectoral and national-defense interest groups. Military and civilian cadres associated with the militia, with industrial and public works projects that relied on army cooperation and support, and with military regions that would be tapped to provide equipment and personnel for the south, could be expected to be skeptical and critical of Luo's proposals. The national program for research and development of advanced weapons was particularly threatened, Red Guard commentaries suggest.[108] Implicit in Luo's recommendations was the diversion of funds to the PLA—for training and additional equipment—at the expense of the budget, the experimentation program, and the production schedules of certain sectors of the defense industry.

The most telling criticism of Luo's proposals, however, was that they would have had a crippling effect on the crucial immediate political functions of the General Political Department and on the roles planned for the army in the future. Luo's program for military training would have placed political education in a subordinate position; as early as June 1965, the Maoists indirectly criticized Luo for using political training merely as a tool for boosting spirit and morale, and therefore for improving military efficiency. While admitting that good political work would be reflected in military performance, the Maoists warned against those "comrades" who viewed political work as a means, not as an end.[109] If political training were sacrificed for military training, then the political reliability of the PLA would suffer; and if security affairs came to demand more of the army's time, then the army's involvement in domestic political activities would be reduced. Moreover, Luo's programs were not only politically costly; they were also (given the Maoists' perceptions of the American threat outlined above) strategically unnecessary. The conjunction of disagreements over strategic estimates and domestic priorities added a significant element to the debate. If Mao and Lin had disagreed with Luo as to the proper defense strategy, but had agreed with him that the American threat was imminent, then Luo might simply have been accused of misjudgment. But since the Maoists saw no significant American threat to China that would warrant immediate and wide-ranging defense preparations, they could logically have concluded that Luo had ulterior motives for suggesting major adjustments in domestic priorities. They accused him of concocting an elaborate rationalization for proposals whose *real purpose* was to force the disengagement of the PLA from political activity, reduce its political reliability, and thus encourage the spread of revisionism in China: "Lo Jui-ch'ing dwelt considerably on 'war preparations,' and it *seemed as if* he was concerned over our country's security. *This is not true.* What he called 'war preparations' were in fact preparations for usurping the army leadership and opposing the Party."[110]

In short, Luo's position was probably criticized on two grounds. First, Luo was proposing a crash program of military preparations—a "quick-fix" of China's defense system—that would have necessitated a redistribution of economic resources among various sectors of Chinese society. Interest groups that would have suffered from this redistribution were probably a major component of the opposition to Luo's proposals. Second, the Maoists apparently feared that Luo was exaggerating the need for defense preparations in an effort to draw the army away from political activities, and thus to undermine its ideological reliability. The Maoists may even have believed that Luo intended, by disrupting and delaying party rectification activities, to support and protect high-level party officials who opposed Mao's efforts to "re-revolutionize" Chinese society.

Were the Maoists correct in their estimate that Luo was using strategic policy issues in a cleverly disguised effort to obstruct their "protracted" political war? Or were they misinterpreting what was actually an honest disagreement over the strategic implications of the Vietnam War? What, in other words, were Luo's motives in the Vietnam debate of 1965? Unfortunately, the available evidence does not permit us to answer these important questions adequately. But we can list briefly three possible interpretations of Luo's behavior. The first is that Luo sincerely disagreed with Lin and Mao about the risks that China was incurring by aiding North Vietnam. Luo's more pessimistic evaluation of the situation may, of course, have stemmed largely from his perspective as head of the General Staff Department of the PLA. As army chief of staff, Luo's primary concerns were the army's national-security functions and its preparedness for war. His role, in other words, demanded that he prepare for the worst possible contingency. As a result, he may have overestimated the dangers posed to China by the escalating American participation in the Vietnam conflict.

Mao and Lin Biao had a different set of concerns: internal security and the general political direction of Chinese society. Both of these concerns demanded that the PLA remain a reliable instrument of political authority. Just as the Vietnam War made questions of external security more crucial to Luo, so the Socialist Education Movement made the maintenance of the army's "proletarian standpoint" increasingly important to Mao and Lin. As the salience of these concerns increased for both sides and began to conflict, the Maoists came—mistakenly, if this first interpretation is correct—to equate Luo's honest professionalism with opportunism and bureaucratism. Luo, they felt, could not be trusted to help launch and sustain a Cultural Revolution purge of the party apparatus. He was considered unreliable at a time when reliability and loyalty were the qualities that Mao and Lin valued most.[111]

A second interpretation—one that is less charitable to Luo—is that he was using the Vietnam War as a justification for an attempt to improve his own political position, particularly vis-à-vis Lin Biao. Continued emphasis on the political role of the PLA, and on the preeminence of the GPD within the PLA, would mean continued priority for tasks that Lin, not Luo, would lead. Continued subordination to a man he had come to dislike may have seemed a rather gloomy future to Luo Ruiqing. On the other hand, the additional resources he was requesting—resources that were ostensibly needed to improve China's strategic posture— would have enhanced his personal authority, widened his area of responsibility, and increased the power of the General Staff Department. It may have been for reasons of bureaucratic politics, then, that Luo responded to the escalation of the Vietnam conflict with a request for intensification of defense preparations.

A third interpretation, which is not inconsistent with the second, is that Luo was attempting to protect his allies and patrons in the Politburo (particularly Peng Zhen and Liu Shaoqi), along with *their* clients and protégés in the lower party ranks, against what was becoming a widespread Maoist attack on the CCP. Publication of the "Twenty-three Articles" in January 1965 represented, according to Cultural Revolution accounts, Mao's personal repudiation of the alleged mismanagement of the Socialist Education Movement by Liu, Deng Xiaoping, and other party leaders. In addition to correcting the "errors" committed by Liu and Deng, the "Twenty-three Articles" also pointedly referred to the existence of "capitalist roaders" at all levels in the party, including the Central Committee. It is quite plausible that Luo and his civilian party allies were concerned about the new directions the Socialist Education Movement was taking, that they saw the escalation of the Vietnam conflict as an opportunity to divert attention from the task of exposing domestic "revisionist" enemies, and that they hoped that the time gained could be used to secure their own political positions.

The available evidence does not indicate which of these three interpretations is the most likely to be correct. But it does seem that the Maoists believed—whether correctly or not—that Luo's behavior was at the minimum an effort to improve his personal position and at worst an attempt to keep the army from supporting Mao's developing campaign against party revisionism. From the Maoists' viewpoint, Luo was not just mistaken, he was treacherous.

Had Luo occupied an uninfluential post in the governmental hierarchy, his fate might have been different. But this powerful, ambitious man held sensitive party and army positions that the Maoists feared he might use to sabotage policies with which he disagreed. As secretary of the Central Committee and secretary-general of the Military Affairs Committee, he played vital coordinating and policy-implementing roles. As a former minister of public security, he retained important connections with his former colleagues, and his influence in public security work probably remained great.[112] And finally, as chief of staff, he had considerable operational control over China's military forces. It was this combination of offices that contributed to Maoist suspicions that Luo—in collaboration with Peng Zhen, Yang Shangkun, and Lu Dingyi—had the power to carry out some kind of coup against Mao and his close supporters. From the Maoist standpoint, the concentration of potential power in Luo's hands made his purge even more essential.

A Balance Sheet

While Luo's position, as we have seen, aroused considerable opposition in Beijing, it probably attracted substantial support as well. Luo's supporters would have included other "professional" military men who either sincerely believed that his proposals were essential to China's military security or saw in his program an opportunity to further their own bureaucratic positions. Although Luo was ultimately purged, it appears that his supporters were powerful enough to arrange a compromise with Mao and Lin. The outcome of the strategic debate was attractive (though in different ways) to three main groups of participants: the Maoists, the military professionals, and Luo's opponents within China's defense industry.

The compromise involved rejection of the elements of Luo's program that were especially objectionable to major interest groups within the defense industry, including Luo's proposals to cut back on research and development in order to permit rapid expansion of production and the completion of defense preparations on a crash basis. On the other hand, there is evidence that some of Luo's other proposals for the improvement of China's air defense were ultimately accepted. Perhaps they were implemented more slowly (and geographically more widely) than Luo and his supporters had originally proposed, in accordance with Mao's preference for long-term national defense planning. But they were implemented nonetheless, and paeans to "people's war" notwithstanding, they represented a considerable victory for China's military professionals.

The Maoists, too, gained major benefits from the Luo Ruiqing affair. The purge itself, perhaps conducted with the acquiescence of some of Luo's own colleagues,[113] allowed the Maoists to (1) eliminate from sensitive bureaucratic positions a powerful and ambitious politician whose active opposition to Mao was suggested by his persistent public dissent on basic strategic and domestic policies, and who might have been allied with Mao's opponents in the party; and (2) warn party leaders that the rectification of the CCP was to continue and that any opposition on their part would be dealt with harshly. Perhaps most important, the Maoists were apparently thereby assured that the military professionals would not interfere with the continued involvement of the GPD in domestic political activity or with political training in the PLA.

6 The Sino-Soviet Border Clashes of 1969

Introduction

The March 1969 border clashes between the P.R.C. and the Soviet Union took place at a time when the Chinese leadership was confronting serious political and civil disorders caused by the violent power-seizure movements of the revolutionary masses in the Cultural Revolution. Armed clashes between rival political factions posed a threat to China's internal security. Primarily due to the Red Guards' and other rebels' indiscriminate attacks, large numbers of veteran party and government cadres were purged or suspended from their duties. The government apparatus also was disrupted. Paralysis of the national defense industry and institutes impaired arms production and thereby harmed China's overall military capability. Most senior Foreign Ministry personnel were being supervised and therefore became primarily concerned with their own survival. China's diplomacy remained inactive throughout the period of revolutionary turmoil at home. The armed forces were ordered to intervene in the Cultural Revolution, and had to carry out actively and massively numerous nonmilitary tasks, such as maintaining internal order, supporting the Left, supervising administrative and industrial organs, and propagating Mao Zedong's thought. Thanks to these tasks, army units, especially the main-force units, which were the backbone of China's national defense, became spread quite thinly across the nation to meet internal political needs rather than any strategic emergency, and were deprived of their training time. As a result, China's ability to reinforce war preparations in the event of an external crisis seemed to be severely weakened.

Despite domestic turmoil, however, the Chinese leadership continued to devote the nation's time and energy to the ongoing antirevisionist movement. At the same time, the leadership was obviously apprehensive that

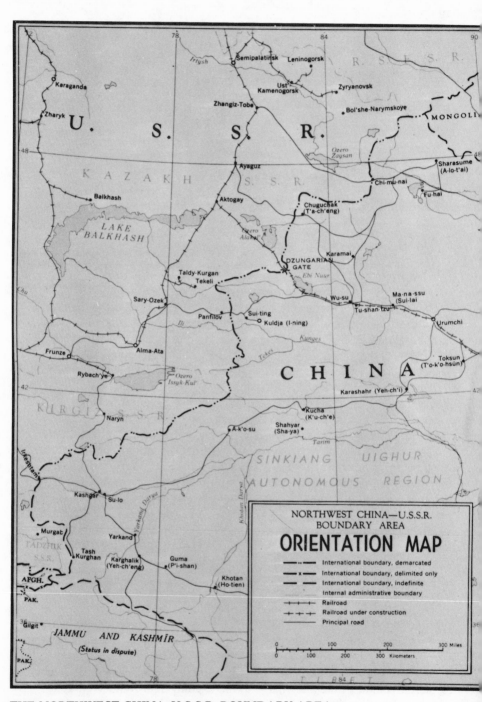

THE NORTHWEST CHINA–U.S.S.R. BOUNDARY AREA

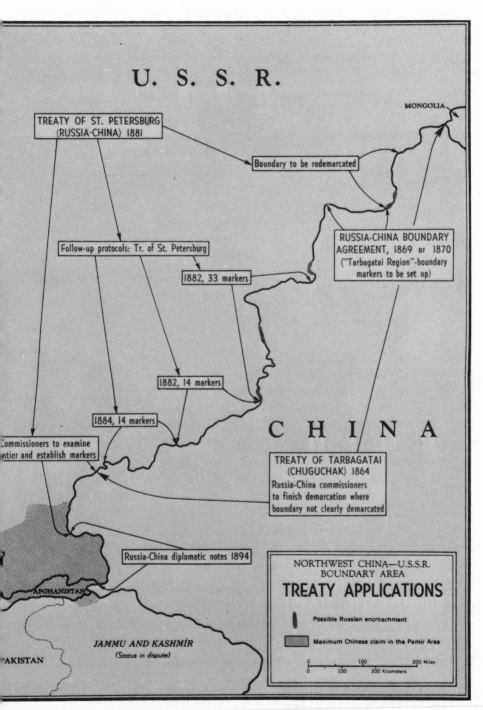

U. S. S. R.

MONGOLIA

TREATY OF ST. PETERSBURG
(RUSSIA-CHINA) 1881

Boundary to be redemarcated

RUSSIA-CHINA BOUNDARY
AGREEMENT, 1869 or 1870
("Tarbagatai Region"-boundary
markers to be set up)

Follow-up protocols: Tr. of St. Petersburg

1882, 33 markers

1882, 14 markers

1884, 14 markers

C H I N A

Commissioners to examine
frontier and establish markers

TREATY OF TARBAGATAI
(CHUGUCHAK) 1864
Russia-China commissioners
to finish demarcation where
boundary not clearly demarcated

Russia-China diplomatic notes 1894

NORTHWEST CHINA—U.S.S.R.
BOUNDARY AREA

TREATY APPLICATIONS

Possible Russian encroachment

Maximum Chinese claim in the Pamir Area

0   100   200 Miles
0   100   200 Kilometers

AFGHANISTAN

JAMMU AND KASHMIR
(Status in dispute)

PAKISTAN

TREATY APPLICATIONS IN THE NORTHWEST CHINA–U.S.S.R. BOUNDARY AREA

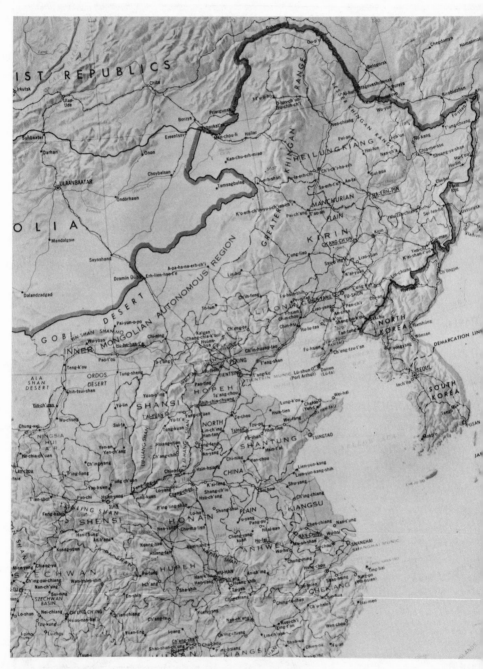

THE NORTHEAST CHINA–U.S.S.R. BORDER AREA

domestic weakness would become a constraint on China's foreign policy. Beijing perceived external threats from various sources. The Soviets' large-scale military build-up along the Sino-Soviet border, combined with increasing border incidents, and the Soviets' subversive activities in the border regions posed a growing and grave threat to China. The Soviet invasion of Czechoslovakia in late August 1968 increased the Beijing leadership's fear of a possible Soviet invasion of China. The Soviets' collaboration with the United States over global strategy, combined with Moscow's support of India's military pressure on the Sino-Indian border, added to Beijing's fear of a "ring of encirclement against China."

The interplay of domestic weakness and external threats led insecure Chinese leaders to have different policy priorities and to advocate different strategies for coping with domestic problems and external threats. In exploring the motives behind China's action on Zhenbao (Chen Pao) Island (Russian name: Damansky), we will begin, as in the other chapters, by describing the domestic and external situation that China faced at the time of the crisis, and conclude by discussing China's decision to engage in the border clashes.

The Domestic Situation

The Political Climate

In April 1969, one month after the Sino-Soviet border clashes on Zhenbao Island, in a keynote report to the Ninth CCP Congress, Lin Biao listed the objectives of China's Cultural Revolution. He stressed that "the fundamental question in the current revolution is the question of political power, a question of which class holds leadership,"[1] and that the Maoists' fundamental purpose in launching the Cultural Revolution had been to overthrow "those in authority [who were] taking the capitalist road," and thereby to consolidate the new revolutionary structure of power.[2] But as Lin revealed in the report, the power-seizure campaign had undergone "twists and reversals," producing extreme political turmoil in the struggle between the proletariat and the bourgeoisie.[3] Throughout 1967 and 1968 there had been widespread disorder and bloody clashes between rival political factions. Central and local parties were in complete chaos. As a result, the Chinese Communist party remained largely inoperative outside Beijing. Paralysis of the government apparatus caused administrative disintegration, which resulted in the disruption of policy planning and coordination among the various departments in the State Council.

Soon after the so-called January (1967) revolution in Shanghai, in which the revolutionary masses were authorized to "drag out" the "capitalist roaders" in the city and seize power through "struggle by force," the revolutionary storm spilled over into most of the provinces in China as violent struggles among various factions resulted in the seizure and counterseizure of power. That spring, fifteen of China's twenty-nine provinces were identified as "trouble areas," and all the provinces remained in turmoil until the summer of 1969, when the so-called ultraleftist phase of the revolution reached its peak. In the spring of 1967, university campuses, factories, railway depots, and farms became the scenes of bloody, pitched battles. Work stoppages in the factories and communes and disruption of transport severely impaired production.[4]

The violence and disorder worsened that summer when a radical faction in Beijing attempted to expand the power-seizure campaign to the PLA, which in January had been ordered to intervene in the revolution to maintain public order. Immediately after the Wuhan mutiny in July, during which a local commander disobeyed Beijing's orders and the army overtly suppressed mass revolutionary activities,[5] the revolutionary masses were encouraged to "drag out the handful in the army."[6] From then on, the revolutionary masses frequently raided military headquarters and seized weapons from soldiers and military warehouses. Armed clashes between the rebels and troops became widespread. In some extreme instances, entire cities or sections of cities were reported to be in flames as a result of local civil war.[7]

By the middle of 1968, partly because of the Maoists' efforts to curb the violent power-seizure movements through military control, and partly because of the formation of revolutionary committees in more than twenty provinces, the number of armed clashes in most provinces seemed to decrease. But they still remained at a level that was dangerous to internal security in some areas, especially in the border regions of Xinjiang, Tibet, Sichuan, Yunnan, Guangxi, and Fujian. For instance, in July 1968, Beijing's leaders reported that in Guangxi, "1,000 houses have been burned down," and that in Sichuan, "the fighting is real war"; each side of the revolutionary masses had "tens of thousands of men" armed with "rifles and cannons."[8]

Along with these serious civil disorders, the Beijing leadership faced a weakening of central and local party structure. Primarily due to the rebels' indiscriminate attacks, large numbers of veteran party cadres were removed from authority. By mid-1968, 99 out of a total of 136 active and alternate members of the Central Committee had been publicly criticized, "dragged out," or otherwise vilified by the Red Guard or other revolutionary groups. Top-ranking provincial party leaders appeared to suffer the same fate in 1967–68, when 23 of 28 leaders were purged outright or suspended from their duties.[9] Not only were the Communist party's local branches weakened by this "bombardment" by the revolutionary groups, but factional rivalry among the branches then probably delayed the formation of the new revolutionary committees.

The government apparatus was also paralyzed by the political turmoil. One-third of the 294 high-level government leaders who were mainly in charge of top-level policy making, planning, and supervising the operation of the economy seem to have been purged by late 1968.[10] Ninety-one senior members of the Foreign Ministry were being supervised and therefore were not in a position to carry out their duties during 1968.[11] In addition, despite Beijing's efforts to insulate the revolution from the departments related to national defense and science, top officials in those departments, like their colleagues in other organs, were victimized by the revolution. Vice-Premier Nie Rongzhen (Nieh Jung-chen), who headed the government's Commission of Science and Technology, and five vice-chairmen of the CST were attacked by several revolutionary organizations for building up an "independent kingdom," among other crimes. The Seventh Ministry of Machine Building, an agency of the State Council that had jurisdiction over the manufacture of airplanes, missiles, and related weapons systems, also was hit by the revolution.[12] It is safe to say that by mid-1968 the revolution's spillover into the national defense industry and the scientific and research institutes had adversely affected the production of military equipment and harmed China's overall military capability.

From the standpoint of national defense there was an even more serious consideration for Beijing's leaders. The breakdown of provincial parties and the disintegration of the administrative apparatus might undercut Beijing's ability to efficiently allocate or quickly shift resources to the military in the event of an external crisis. In a speech in February 1968, Premier Zhou revealed this weakness that the functional departments of the State Council had confronted in reinforcing their planning and war preparation efforts:

> We must step up war preparations, not only strengthening the national defense industries but also coordinating the industry and communications, finance and trade, and agriculture and forestry sectors which serve national defense needs. . . . To be sure, coordination is also needed between political and law and scientific research departments. . . . One of the crucial issues in the excellent situation concerns our functional departments. If it is said that last year we were busy setting up local provincial organs of power, the revolutionary committees, then now we must devote part of our strength to improve the work of the various ministries and commissions of the State Council.[13]

It was during the second half of 1968 that the Maoists attempted to terminate the Red Guard phase of the Cultural Revolution and consolidate its gains. In the summer of 1968, as the violence and armed clashes increased, Mao probably decided that "struggle by force" no longer contributed to the power-seizure movement, and instead was aggravating public disorder. At a meeting with five top-level Red Guard leaders on July

28, Mao condemned them for their failure to unite and for their persistent squabbling, and urged them to carry out "struggle by reason." Mao was quoted as saying, "First of all, we want cultural struggle, not armed struggle."[14] In August, Mao introduced a group called the "Worker-Peasant Mao Zedong Thought Propaganda Team" into the Cultural Revolution to further discipline the Red Guards.[15] A major campaign began during the winter of 1968/69 to transfer large numbers of students to rural areas and the border regions.[16]

In the meantime, the Maoists attempted to move the Cultural Revolution into a new stage of internal consolidation. A joint editorial by *People's Daily* and the *Liberation Army Daily* on September 7 hailed the establishment of revolutionary committees in all the provinces, stressing that "the whole country is red," and that in the future the revolutionary masses should devote their time and energy to the work of internal consolidation through a method of struggle-criticism-transformation.[17] The Twelfth Plenum communiqué of the Central Committee, adopted on October 31, as well as press editorials at that time, repeatedly emphasized that the central task of the Chinese people was internal consolidation: reconstruction of the party apparatus, purification of the class ranks, educational revolution, promotion of production, and simplification of administrative structures.[18]

In reconstructing the party apparatus, however, the Maoist leadership obviously worried about the revival of a false power seizure by the exploiting classes and their agents. In working to moderate the pace of the revolution, there was every reason for the Maoists to be concerned that internal class enemies might pose a threat to the leadership by infiltrating the new power structures and by sabotaging the process of struggle-criticism-transformation. On November 25 a joint editorial by *People's Daily, Red Flag,* and the *Liberation Army Daily* revealed this concern. It noted that "after the enemies with guns have been wiped out, there will still be enemies without guns," and warned that the people should guard against "attack with sugar-coated bullets by [the] bourgeoisie."[19]

In the months prior to the Sino-Soviet border clashes in March 1969, China's primary concern was internal consolidation—restoring public and civil order, exposing hidden revisionists, and rebuilding the party. Considering such domestic tasks, we may assume that China's leaders, in determining their response to external military pressure, had to take into account the effect of war preparedness on the domestic political situation. Those who preferred shifting their policy concerns from the home front to the external arena would have to justify the resulting price paid by domestic political programs. Conversely, those who wanted to continue existing domestic policies would have to consider the implications of those policies for China's military preparedness, which, as we will discuss next, was seriously weakened by the PLA's complicated role in the revolutionary turmoil.

The Military

For the Beijing leadership, 1965 was a critical year in the sense that it had to cope with two crucial problems that directly affected the PLA: internal security, which was being undermined by domestic revisionism; and the external threat brought on by U.S. escalation of the war in Vietnam. As the case of the purge of Luo Ruiqing indicates, these issues were intertwined: dealing effectively with one, Mao evidently decided (with Lin Biao's support), required giving the other a lower priority. Mao's decision was that internal security—preventing the restoration of capitalism in Chinese society—was a much more important priority than external security. By late 1965, the debate ended in victory for the Maoists.[20] The priorities in army building became political work over military training in the PLA; the strategy of "people's war" over the strategy based on conventional war to deter U.S. invasion of mainland China; and development of the most advanced science and technology on the basis of self-reliance in order to consolidate the national defense.[21]

During the Cultural Revolution, these priorities were further strengthened. But the Maoists' preference for the PLA's role in supporting the Left and maintaining public order, as well as the impact of the revolution itself, inevitably resulted in reducing the military establishment's strategic role, weakening China's overall military capability, and making the strategic outlook of military leaders cautious and defensive. Again, Maoist priorities in military politics caused differences in the Beijing leadership and among military leaders over the proper role of the PLA.

Military politics. After the mass demonstrations of the Red Guards in August 1966, the armed forces were ordered to give them limited support, such as short-term military and political training and logistical assistance. But soon thereafter, the PLA was ordered to intervene actively in the Cultural Revolution under the slogan "Three Supports and Two Militaries" —that is, support the Left, agriculture, and industry; exercise military control; and help with military and political training in the schools.[22] These tasks inevitably led the armed forces to become involved in nonmilitary functions directly and on a massive scale. As a result, the defense preparedness of the PLA was adversely affected, and central and regional military leaders became deeply involved in internal politics and factional struggles.

In 1967–68, the several political tasks assigned to the PLA caused its units to become organizationally scattered and subject to frequent relocation. Units were separated from their base camps and training areas and thus were deprived of training time. In addition, "Mao Zedong Thought Propaganda Teams" were formed in all units. It was reported, for instance, that in June 1968 some troops in north China organized 100,000 persons to spread Mao's thoughts, and that the troops in Lanzhou (Lanchow) sent 15,000 military party members in 500 propaganda teams to the villages of 110 counties.[23] Many military units took charge of politicizing and supervising industrial organs in at least twenty-three provinces.[24] Moreover, the PLA took over public security bureaus throughout the country and actually remained as a police force in 1967 and 1968.[25] Because of such different tasks, the PLA units changed location frequently. For instance, one regimental company stationed in the Guangzhou area reportedly moved fourteen times in 1968.[26]

More important was the fact that the army's task of "supporting the Left" affected not only the cohesion of regional forces but also the location of main-force army units, which were normally concentrated in important strategic areas in the coastal and northeastern provinces. In the early months of 1967, this political task had been assigned mainly to regional forces. The party center found, however, that regional forces alone were not adequate to carry out the job of "supporting the Left," mainly because of the tendency of regional forces to support conservative factions, in accordance with the orders of provincial parties rather than Beijing's orders.[27]

In the spring of 1967, the Beijing leadership appears to have decided to purge or transfer local military leaders and to dispatch centrally controlled main-force units to trouble spots in order to supervise the local army units in their "support-the-Left" work and to correct their mistakes. Commanders in five military regions (Chengdu, Inner Mongolia, Beijing, Xinjiang, and Lanzhou) and in seven military districts were removed or transferred.[28] High-level military leaders who held positions in the PLA's Cultural Revolution Group—including Xiao Hua, director of the General Political Department—were replaced by new members whose primary responsibility was national defense.[29]

For the purpose of supervising local armed forces, main-force units—called "central support-the-Left units"—were redeployed to areas either where revolutionary committees had not yet been established or where existing revolutionary committees faced political instability.[30] By mid-1968, more than twenty of the PLA's thirty-five army corps had been relocated in the trouble spots of at least eleven provinces. As a result, the centrally controlled main-force units were spread quite thinly across eighteen provinces to meet internal political needs and were no longer in a position to counter a strategic emergency. The eighteen provinces included four in east China (Anhui [Anhwei], Zhejiang [Chekiang], Jiangxi, Jiangsu [Kiangsu]); three in the northwest (Xinjiang, Shanxi [Shansi], Ningxia [Ningsia]); three in the northeast (Jilin [Kirin], Liaoning, and

Hebei); two in central-south China (Hunan and Henan); three in the southwest (Yunnan, Sichuan, and Tibet); and three in the south coastal region (Guangxi, Guangdong, and Fujian).[31] The PLA units were usually broken into their subunits, to the level of company or platoon, so that they could cover all the areas assigned to them and maintain extensive liaison with the masses. Main-force units directly controlled several military districts, took over administrative units at the county level, and provided preparatory groups for the revolutionary committees.[32]

During the Cultural Revolution, the Chinese military was not a cohesive group in carrying out revolutionary activities. Some regional and local military leaders, especially in the strategic border areas, not only resisted the active involvement of their units in "supporting the Left" but also contained disturbances or riots created by the revolutionary rebels, thereby stressing the restoration of public order and the critical nature of their standing defense missions. For instance, according to Radio Kunming on July 29, 1967, Yan Hongyan (Yen Hung-yen), first political commissar of the Kunming Military Region in charge of Yunnan Province's borders with Laos and North Vietnam, was condemned for "banning class struggle in Yünnan, under the pretext that Yünnan borders foreign countries."[33] General Wang Enmao, commander of the Xinjiang Military Region, likewise was criticized in numerous Red Guard tabloids for suppressing the rebels' upsurge in that province, and in November 1968 was relieved of his command. General Zhang Guohua (Chang Kuo-hua) in Tibet was also under attack from rebel groups backed by Beijing mainly because he favored restoration of order in Tibet and supported "conservative forces."[34] It is not accidental that the revolutionary committees in the five provinces of Yunnan, Fujian, Guangxi, Tibet, and Xinjiang—China's first line of defense—were not set up until the last phase of the Cultural Revolution, in April–September 1968, or that their formation in these provinces was guided and supported entirely by the centrally controlled military units.[35]

There is ample evidence to suggest that Premier Zhou, in charge of numerous government organs within the State Council, felt it was necessary to curb Red Guard extremism and favored an increased army role in the restoration of civil order and administrative control. On several occasions, Zhou is said to have blamed the Red Guards for industry's failure to meet the quotas for 1967, as well as for the disruption of defense-related agencies such as the Seventh Ministry of Machine Building and the Scientific and Technological Commission.[36] The premier obviously attempted to insulate China's defense industries from the Cultural Revolution. Commenting on the situation in northeast China on September 28, 1967, Zhou claimed:

It is now definitely decided that Peking's defense industries should organize their own alliance and should not exchange experience or establish ties with local industries and schools, otherwise it will be impossible for them to guarantee exact production. The Tank Works must not get involved in local affairs. The national defense industries of Liaoning must not join local organizations. . . . How many people of Harbin Military Engineering College are still in outside areas? (Answer: More than 2,000). So there are still more than 2,000 men in other provinces?[37]

Zhou's sensitivity to political disorder seemed to be occasioned by his fear that external enemies, in collaboration with internal enemies, would exploit China's domestic weakness. In the comment just quoted Zhou noted: "It [domestic disorder] tends to be utilized by enemies both inside and outside"; we should "prevent infiltration by U.S.-Chiang, Japanese, and British secret agents and Soviet, Mongolian, and Korean revisionists, who may sow seeds of dissension among us and fish in muddled waters."[38] In his instructions to "comrades from two factions' mass organizations in Kwangsi" on July 25, 1968, the premier urged the rapid setting up of a revolutionary committee with the reminder that "the U.S. imperialists, the Soviet revisionists and the Chiang gangsters every day say that we cannot set up revolutionary committees in border regions."[39] Premier Zhou is said to have done his best to defend regional military leaders from Red Guard attacks.[40]

It is safe to say that because of his sensitivity to external threat amid domestic turmoil, Zhou wanted the PLA to increase its internal security role *and* to maintain an adequate combat readiness. An order of September 5, 1967, issued by the central Military Affairs Committee and the State Council probably came in part as a response to Zhou's and the military professionals' concerns. In contrast to both the propaganda theme of the Chinese press, which continued to stress the "three support and two military" tasks of the PLA, and the program of redeployments for political needs, the order called upon all units to "be constantly on the alert against sudden attacks by imperialism, reactionaries of all countries, and modern revisionism. It must firmly stick to its fighting posts, strengthen war preparedness, and insure the perfect condition of its equipment, so that as soon as an order comes it may take action immediately."[41]

As vice-chairman of the Central Committee and concurrently minister of national defense, Lin Biao tended to be the chief conduit between the radicals in the Maoist leadership and the PLA. Lin took the position that the PLA should be secured from Red Guard attacks, but he did not want to reduce the army's political role in the middle of the Cultural Revolution.[42] Furthermore, as far as the primary role of the PLA in the Cultural Revolution was concerned, Lin was inclined to place more emphasis on the "support-the-Left" movement than on internal order. Soon after the hot summer of 1967, in which the ultraleft was responsible for many public disorders, Lin Biao made a speech to the military cadres in Beijing in which he accepted the necessity of instability: "The victories of the GPCR have been great. The cost has been very very small and victories very very great. Outwardly it appears as if there is a great chaos. . . . This confusion is necessary and normal. Without this confusion reactionary things cannot be exploded. . . . If under these conditions we do not expose them then when shall we expose them? Under the leadership of Chairman Mao we do not fear confusion."[43]

This evaluation of the domestic situation at that time contrasted sharply with an analysis made by the moderates, including Mao, who called the situation a "civil war" after his trip to central China in September 1967.[44] It seems unlikely that Lin would support an ultraleft upsurge, but it is plausible that he would feel it was necessary to keep exposing and purging the party's internal enemies who had collaborated with Liu Shaoqi and Deng Xiaoping, even at the risk of civil disorder. But the outcome of the power-seizure campaign in the first half of 1967 suggested that the revolutionary masses alone would not be strong enough to drag out the "capitalist roaders" in the local party and government, mainly because of resistance by the anti-Maoists, who created and used their own mass organizations, and because the rebels who supported the Maoists were themselves divided into factions. Lin Biao probably regarded a PLA that was organizationally well disciplined, ideologically pure, and loyal to Mao's line as a deterrent to the erosion of the revolution and wanted the PLA to give more vigorous support to the Left. Nevertheless, as the Wuhan mutiny indicates, for Lin, the army's correct role of supporting the Left was easily undermined by factionalism, sectarianism, "mountaintopism," and other problems within the PLA.[45] Probably for this reason Lin was much more concerned about the ideological and political attitudes of the military leaders, especially at the regional and local levels, than the moderates were, and thus was determined to give more prominence to political work within the PLA than to the initial stage of the revolution, when Luo Ruiqing was purged.

Numerous speeches made by Lin Biao to the PLA in 1967–68 centered on how to grasp revolutionary ideology and continue the revolution. In a speech in November 1967, Lin reminded his audience that "the chief task for the army is to rely on Mao Tse-tung thought to transform the face of China," and he reiterated the standard theme that "politics commands military affairs." He noted that "if political work is done well, training, production, internal solidarity will also be done well, and wars will be fought well."[46] In important directives to the army on April 6, 1968, Lin again revealed that his primary concern was politics in the army, noting that the engineer troops should be rotated for construction, production, and political training.[47] What bothered him more in mid-1968 than before were the deep rifts that had developed between regional military leaders and the centrally controlled units that were prevalent in numerous provinces, including Hebei, Shanxi, Tibet, Gansu, Hubei, Guangxi, Henan, and the Xinjiang Uygur Autonomous Region.[48] Growing friction and antagonism among the military leaders probably compelled Lin to consider seriously the ideological direction of army cadres. In referring to armed clashes between local and central army units in Shanxi, Lin is said to have claimed: "The Peking Military Region, the Shansi Provincial Military District, and the 69th Army should all be asked to make self-criticism and quickly correct their mistakes; the armed struggle in the army is due largely to the wrong ideological direction which they have taken."[49]

The above discussion suggests two interesting hypotheses about Lin's position. One is that by mid-1968, Lin's preoccupation with the ongoing Cultural Revolution led him to be concerned primarily about the internal struggle to weed out domestic revisionists and in turn to regard a revival of internal enemies as a more serious threat than any threat from external sources. The second is that Lin's concern about the correct ideological direction of the army made politics within the PLA his highest priority, with less emphasis being placed on the combat readiness of the PLA, despite the fact that the army was weakened by the turmoil of the revolution. In either or both cases, Lin appears to have stood in opposition to Zhou Enlai.

Conventional and strategic capabilities. By 1966, China's economy had completely recovered from the Great Leap Forward, and appears to have provided more funds for the country's defense industries. According to a U.S. estimate, the GNP of the P.R.C. in 1966 was $145 billion (an increase of 77 percent from 1961 [$82 billion]), and per capita income was 61 percent higher than it had been in 1961.[50] But the turmoil of the Cultural Revolution in 1967–68 reduced industrial production, which in turn lowered the GNP of the P.R.C. The GNP for 1967–68 decreased by about 6–7 percent from the level for 1966.[51] During these same years (1966–68), the ratio of defense expenditures to the GNP is estimated to have risen constantly from approximately 8.9 percent (1966) to 9.2 percent (1967) to 9.5 percent (1968).[52] Considering the decrease in the GNP for 1967–68, however, a net increase in defense expenditures during the same period was unlikely to be high.

Despite Beijing's emphasis on advanced technology and science, there is no hint that the conventional and strategic capabilities of the PLA were rapidly modernized with sophisticated weapons and equipment. In addition to the setbacks that occurred in the machine-building industry (mainly due to work stoppages and disruptions in transportation), two other factors may explain why. A shift in the defense budget in favor of advanced weapons, including nuclear warheads and delivery systems, could not be made without reducing funds for other programs—for instance, for China's ground forces—primarily because of restricted budget ceilings.[53] Beijing's policy of self-reliance in developing nuclear weapons, the requirement of a long lead time in research and development, and a general lack of technology probably all contributed to the delay in China's development of an advanced weapons program.[54] According to an evaluation by the International Institute for Strategic Studies, in 1967–68 the PLA still suffered greatly from an inadequate logistical support system and obsolete equipment. It had a high standard of tactical mobility, but was restricted at the strategic level in terms of air and seaborne, as well as motor-transport, mobility. Its bomber force—an important indicator of offensive capability— appeared to be composed mainly of IL-28 light bombers.[55] China was not believed to possess long-range strategic bombers and missiles. Despite several nuclear test explosions since October 1964, particularly the thermonuclear tests in June 1967 and December 1968, the P.R.C. was said to lack a delivery system for nuclear warheads and to remain highly vulnerable to preemptive attacks by either the United States or the Soviet Union.[56]

Putting the military weaknesses of the P.R.C. aside, it seems unlikely that in 1968 China possessed an emergency food reserve sufficient to feed its 750 million people in the event of prolonged hostilities. Grain production in China continued to increase from about 185 million metric tons in 1966 to about 195 million tons in 1969, but grain reserves appeared to be very limited.[57] During the Cultural Revolution, under the influence of "economism" in some places, many communes and production brigades reportedly consumed or divided up their reserves.[58] Several reports in *People's Daily* in July 1969 emphasized preparation against war and natural disaster by amassing reserves of grain in the commune and hinted that during 1967–68 the P.R.C. had confronted a shortage of grain reserves.[59] Not until the end of 1970, after a campaign to build up these reserves, did this circumstance change. Zhou Enlai is said to have told Edgar Snow that by that time China had accumulated 40 million metric tons of grain reserves above the commune level.[60]

Strategic outlook. The strategic outlook of the PLA was cautious and defensive. Lin Biao's article "Long Live the Victory of People's War!," with its emphasis on an orthodox Maoist defense, was originally published on September 3, 1965, but it reappeared in the Chinese press in 1967–68.[61] Chinese press reports on the country's two thermonuclear explosions were low key, concentrated on domestic implications,[62] and suggested that China's possession of thermonuclear weapons would not alter the defense doctrine or foreign-policy behavior of the P.R.C. The Chinese regarded their several nuclear tests after October 1964 as "necessary and limited ones," as defensive exercises, and as being ultimately aimed at "abolishing nuclear weapons."[63] In January 1968, despite China's acquisition of nuclear weapons, an article in *People's Daily* reiterated that China would firmly rely on "Mao's brilliant theory" of waging the people's war by fully mobilizing the masses if enemies should attack.[64] The P.R.C. continued to offer a "no-first-use" pledge on nuclear weapons and repeated its basic policy line regarding atomic bombs: "China will neither commit the error of adventurism nor the error of capitulationism."[65]

This defensiveness concerning strategic weapons was, if anything, reinforced by existing domestic political uncertainties and their effects on troop deployments. Regional military leaders, while they increased their leverage on the party center, were still under tight control of the central authority, which retained the power to transfer military leaders or dispatch centrally controlled main-force units. In the two critical years 1967–68, when the party center needed the loyalty of the regional military units to the Maoist leadership, the center appeared to operate on the basis of the requirement that it approve the movement of all troops within its jurisdiction. In September 1967, Deng Yongya (Teng Yung-ya), commander of the Tibet Military Region, reportedly asked for the movement of "two battalions and machine gun troops" to Lhasa to participate in a military parade but was turned down by the Cultural Revolution Group of the PLA. Huang Xinding (Huang Hsin-ting), the dismissed commander of the Chengdu Military Region, was charged with having moved troops on his own authority in late 1967.[66] The central and regional military leaders who survived the Cultural Revolution were highly sensitive to the maintenance of internal order as well as to the preservation of their status. In this regard, the military leaders were likely to have been far more concerned about accommodating their interests and safety in an unstable political situation than about expanding their influence abroad and taking adventuristic military action.

The Struggle in the Foreign Ministry and China's World Outlook

Like the impact of the power-seizure campaign on the party and military, the Cultural Revolution in the Foreign Ministry resulted in a struggle within the ministry over China's foreign policy making and implementation. In particular, in the spring and summer of 1967, when the Beijing leadership appeared to lose control over the Red Guards, the impact of the struggle became serious: most of the Foreign Ministry bureaucrats were being harassed by Red Guard criticism; the normal routine of the ministry had been disrupted; an ultraradical foreign-policy line was apparently being pursued without the knowledge and against the wishes of the Beijing leadership; and, to a certain extent, the revolution at home spilled over into China's foreign relations.

It should be noted, however, as several writers have argued, that the diplomatic incidents created by Chinese citizens in Burma, Cambodia, Nepal, and Ceylon were not prearranged in Beijing. They were uncalculated, unavoidable, and usually unauthorized activities that occurred when the influence of conservative Foreign Ministry bureaucrats was being held in check.[67] The anti-Soviet demonstrations in Moscow, the protest at the Soviet Embassy in Beijing, and the *Svirsk* incident followed a similar pattern in the sense that the Chinese leadership responded to incidents created by private Chinese citizens and Red Guards. For that reason, these incidents deserve our attention.

A group of Chinese students who had been called home arrived in Moscow en route to Beijing on January 25, 1967. Perhaps stimulated by the January revolution in China, the students were tempted to demonstrate their antirevisionist revolutionary spirit. They went to Lenin's tomb and staged a demonstration. Soviet police and soldiers clashed with the students, injuring more than nine of them.[68] A *People's Daily* editorial on January 27 reported the "shocking and bloody" incident and "the rabid provocation of the filthy Soviet revisionist swine."[69] Soon afterward, the Chinese Embassy in Moscow protested the Soviet action by displaying photographs of the incident in showcases mounted outside the embassy building near the street. When the Soviets demanded that the pictures be withdrawn, the embassy refused. The Soviet authorities then sent armed personnel to remove the showcases, after which Soviet hooligans allegedly invaded the Chinese Embassy in Moscow and beat up Chinese diplomatic personnel. On February 5, 1967, the Chinese government issued a serious warning concerning the incident.[70] Nationwide protests and demonstrations erupted. On February 11, a massive anti-Soviet rally was held in Beijing. The Soviet Embassy was seized, and Soviet diplomats were harassed by a hostile crowd of Chinese for more than two weeks in early February.[71] Under these circumstances, Moscow threatened Beijing that diplomatic relations would be severed if the Chinese broke into the embassy building. On February 9, the Soviet Foreign Ministry informed An Zhiyuan (An Chih-yuan), chargé d'affaires of the Chinese Embassy, that his government had scrapped the agreements of the two countries on the abolition of visas.[72] An East European source also revealed that in early February, the two governments exchanged secret notes and came very close to rupturing formal diplomatic relations.[73]

There is plausible evidence that during the anti-Soviet demonstrations the extremists wanted to use violent methods of struggle against the Soviet Union, but were overruled by the moderates, headed by Zhou Enlai. A *People's Daily* editorial on February 6 seemed to suggest a militant Chinese stand on Soviet activities in its claim that the Chinese people's responses of the past few days to the Soviet revisionists' fascist outrages had been quite restrained, and that this weakness would lead the Soviets to miscalculate China's strength.[74] But Zhou's speech at a Beijing rally on February 11 denounced the violent method of struggle against the Soviet authorities. "Showing facts and reasoning," Zhou demanded that the Chinese "expose all insidious plots and cunning tricks of the Soviet revisionist leading clique," but without "intruding into the Embassy." The premier added: "We have also permitted their diplomatic personnel to engage in normal activities." Citing Mao's famous dictum "We must slight the enemy strategically and take full account of him tactically," Zhou said: "This [method] is what we have been doing in the current struggle against the Soviet revisionist leading clique. But *this by no means illustrates that we are weak, on the contrary, this has precisely demonstrated our firm stand, great spirit, high degree of self-confidence. . . .* This method of struggle is a Leninist method of struggle, and also one of the great thoughts of Mao Tse-tung. We must persist in this method of struggle. We must master this method of struggle."[75]

Two days after Zhou's speech, the Red Guards' siege of the Soviet Embassy in Beijing was lifted. It is likely that the radicals responded to Zhou's moderate anti-Soviet line. However, neither the New China News Agency nor the daily press, both of which were controlled by the radicals of the Cultural Revolutionary Group, published Zhou's speech or even mentioned that he had spoken at the Beijing rally.[76] On July 7, one article in *People's Daily*, apparently written by one of the extremists, indirectly attacked the moderates' attitude toward the antirevisionist struggle. It noted that "during the Cultural Revolution, the top party person raised the evil flag of capitulationism" by arguing that "all conflicts must be solved peacefully."[77]

Another event in the Cultural Revolution that affected China's relations with the Soviet Union was the *Svirsk* incident. On August 11, Red Guards at Dairen damaged the Soviet merchant ship *Svirsk* and beat up its crew, who had allegedly directed insults at badges bearing Mao's profile. On August 13, the Chinese Foreign Ministry reportedly ordered the captain of the Soviet ship to hand over the offenders immediately for summons and trial.[78] The captain rejected the order. In a telegram to Zhou, Soviet Premier Kosygin warned that the Soviet Union would abolish the trade agreement between the two countries if China did not release the detained crew. The telegram noted that China's "arbitrary and lawless acts" were "placing in doubt the fulfillment of existing trade relations between the Soviet Union and China."[79]

Again, Zhou seemed to take the initiative in securing the release of the crew, and the radicals reacted to his decision. On August 14, the day after the *Svirsk* sailed and at the very time when ultraleftist revolutionary activism was at its zenith, a new Red Guard demonstration occurred at the Soviet Embassy in Beijing. The consular section of the embassy was raided and files were burned.[80] In the meantime, numerous articles in *People's Daily* hailed the new revolutionary diplomacy and stressed that in "a new era of a high tide of world revolution," the Chinese should not be afraid of being isolated by the resulting turmoil. These articles quoted Mao's dictum that "to be attacked by the enemy is not a bad thing but a good thing."[81] But in late August the Red Guards' siege of the Soviet Embassy was lifted.

Beginning in September 1967, diplomatic incidents such as the attacks upon embassies and foreigners ceased. The spillover of the Cultural Revolution into Chinese foreign affairs ended. In early September, Wang Li was purged and Yao Dengshan (Yao Teng-shan) lost power within the Foreign Ministry. Zhou Enlai reportedly issued a six-point directive that forbade the rebels from making trouble with foreigners.[82] The Chinese press officially denounced the "organizers and manipulators" of the "May 16 group" as a "conspiratorial and counter-revolutionary clique."[83] The Beijing leadership announced that it was prepared, much more than before, to defend senior officials of the Foreign Ministry, including Foreign Minister Chen Yi, from any effort by the ultraleft to overthrow them. Moreover, Beijing's interest in renewing friendly government-to-government relations revived. The P.R.C. soon resumed normal ties with Burma, Ceylon, Cambodia, Nepal, and Hong Kong, and made new commitments to provide economic and technical aid to Mali, Guinea, Tanzania and Zambia.[84]

But the Cultural Revolution appeared to leave the leadership divided over China's foreign policy. The radicals' view was that the United States was colluding with the Soviet Union against China, but that imperialism and modern revisionism were heading toward total collapse primarily because of difficulties at home and abroad, but also because of the rising revolutionary movement in the Third World. The radicals seemed to believe that any new anti-China "holy alliance," as well as the dream of "Soviet-U.S. cooperation for world domination," would be either torn by contradictions or smashed completely by the revolutionary peoples of the world. In this regard, the radicals seemed to advocate that as a powerful base for world revolution, the P.R.C. should actively support the revolutionary struggles of the proletariat and people of all countries.[85] As indicated in the anti-Soviet demonstrations and the *Svirsk* incident, the radicals downgraded any diplomatic method to ease tensions with the Soviet Union. Instead, they wanted to encourage the Chinese people to struggle against Soviet revisionism, even to the point of risking a Soviet counteraction. It seemed intolerable to the radicals that in mobilizing the revolutionary masses around an antirevisionist front at home, the party center should appease an adversary, either the United States or the Soviet Union, and thereby expose China's weakness to both domestic and foreign enemies.

The moderates, represented by Zhou Enlai, appeared to believe that the United States was not only "colluding" but also "contending" with the Soviet Union for world domination, and that the superpowers' domestic weaknesses did not entirely negate their military strength and aggressiveness. In a speech on February 2, 1968, Zhou noted that "strategically," American imperialism and Soviet revisionism were paper tigers, but that "tactically" they were capable of damaging China.[86] The moderates believed that excessive emphasis on confronting the two superpowers might strengthen their collaboration against China and risk an escalation of the struggle with them. They seemed to rely far more on diplomacy in dealing with future eventualities involving the United States and the Soviet Union.

But it is highly probable that in 1967–68, when the antirevisionist movement at home was heightened, Zhou and China's Foreign Ministry personnel were not in a strong position to advocate an active diplomatic line. Most senior officials of the Foreign Ministry were primarily concerned about their own survival. Nevertheless, despite China's diplomatic inactivity in the midst of the revolutionary turmoil, the Foreign Ministry did not disrupt its Warsaw talks with the United States. Two sessions took place in 1967, one in January 1968. As Kenneth Young indicates, although the moderate faction in Beijing did not move to use these talks to reduce tensions and seek accommodation on any international issues, including Vietnam, it did seem determined to "keep a channel open to Washington for future eventualities."[87] This moderate position seems to have been reinforced in mid-1968. On May 18, 1968, the Chinese Foreign Ministry announced that the one hundred thirty-fifth meeting of the Sino-U.S. ambassadorial talks scheduled for May 29 would be postponed "till the middle of November." The Ministry referred to China's domestic situation, among other circumstances, in stating that "the Chinese ambassador will not be able to return to his post."[88]

There is also evidence that at about the same time, China's Foreign Ministry seriously evaluated a Soviet proposal for border negotiations. In late April 1968, the Soviets reportedly proposed to the Chinese that a session concerning the problems of maintaining normal navigation conditions along border sections of the Amur and Ussuri rivers be held in Khabarovsk in May 1968. However, Beijing is said to have rejected this proposal in mid-August.[89] The delay of the Chinese response hinted that Foreign Ministry officials remained undecided about a proper response to the proposal, probably because of a debate of the question in Beijing or the ministry's unpreparedness for negotiations.

Lin Biao's position seemed to be complicated by the ambivalence between his world outlook, which was similar to the radicals', and his preference for the moderates' tactics. Like the radicals, Lin seemed to believe that the imperialists and revisionists would go on making trouble in collusion with each other, but that this adverse current would never become the main current, primarily because the United States and the Soviet Union were weak domestically.[90] Nevertheless, in dealing with the superpowers, Lin did not appear one-sidedly to emphasize "tit-for-tat struggle" against them, since such action could easily have escalated into a major confrontationn at a time when China's own military was weak. To some extent, Lin seemed to share the moderates' views on how to reduce tensions with the two powers.

We have no evidence of what Lin's position was at the time of the anti-Soviet demonstrations in Moscow and Beijing or the *Svirsk* incident, but we can infer it from his reaction to the Hong Kong incident. In mid-1967, civil disorders in Hong Kong escalated into an armed struggle between local Chinese rioters and the Hong Kong authorities. A British aircraft carrier and six warships, with support from a U.S. nuclear-powered submarine, appeared in the seas off Hong Kong to help local authorities in Hong Kong put down the Chinese rioters. In responding to this crisis, which peaked during the summer of 1967, Lin Biao was reportedly reluctant, as was Zhou, to send 400 specially trained Red Guards to Hong Kong to spearhead the violence—a move that the radicals in the Cultural Revolution Group supported.[91] Moreover, Lin evidently ordered the PLA units bordering Hong Kong to remain neutral during the crisis. He also seemed to favor negotiating with British officials in Hong Kong. In early August, secret talks between Hong Kong authorities and PLA officers reportedly led to agreements that eliminated the risks of escalation.[92]

In line with his moderate strategy in coping with the British (and indirectly the Americans) in Hong Kong, Lin Biao also seemed anxious not to thrust China into the position of directly opposing the Soviet Union. One piece of evidence is that in his position as minister of national defense of the P.R.C., Lin sent the Soviet Defense Ministry a cable on February 23, 1968, on the occasion of the fifty-ninth anniversary of the founding of the Soviet army. In that message Lin is said to have praised the "glorious history" of the Soviet army and to hold out hopes for greater unity between the Chinese and Soviet "peoples" and "armies." This positive reference to the Soviet Union, as Thomas Gottlieb argues, contrasted sharply with longstanding anti-Soviet themes in the Chinese press at that time. It also stood in opposition to Mao's instructions of March 20, 1966, that "in the future we will send greetings, but they will be addressed only to the Soviet peoples" rather than to the Soviet leaders.[93]

The above cases and our discussion of China's military politics suggest that in 1967 and early 1968, Lin shared the view of the radicals concerning how to maintain the revolutionary momentum needed to sieze power from domestic revisionists, but did not agree with them about the appropriate method for coping with U.S. imperialism and Soviet revisionism. He stressed that China should not take unnecessary risks that could turn a local conflict into a major confrontation with the United States or into an unnecessarily direct confrontation with the Soviet Union. Lin thus would have had China maintain cautious readiness in its border defense. Precisely what this position meant will be discussed after we consider how the Chinese leadership perceived the external threats posed primarily by the Soviet military on the Sino-Soviet frontiers and elsewhere.

The International Situation

The Sino-Soviet Border Dispute

Conflict over the Sino-Soviet border generally intensified in line with larger political and economic differences between the P.R.C. and the Soviet Union. In the early 1950s, Sino-Soviet relations were generally cooperative, and though they existed, border problems were not publicized. By the late 1950s and early 1960s, however, relations had worsened and moved into the public arena, and controversy over the border and old treaties became part of the polemical exchanges between the two governments. On two occasions that we know of, Chinese leaders sought to discuss border problems with the Soviet leaders. In 1954, Mao Zedong reportedly tried to discuss the status of Outer Mongolia with Khrushchev and Bulganin but failed to persuade them to negotiate. In January 1959, Zhou Enlai attempted to discuss with Khrushchev a wider range of territorial issues, but was unsuccessful.[94] It was during the early 1960s that the controversy over the border between the two countries became overt, when the P.R.C. publicly raised the question of old, unequal treaties.

The occasion was China's reply to a statement of the U.S. Communist party in January 1963 that had attacked China's position on the Cuban missile crisis and China's way of dealing with the Sino-Indian boundary dispute, thereby supporting the Soviets' stand on the two issues. An editorial in *People's Daily* on March 8, 1963, listed nine unequal treaties with imperialist powers, including three with Russia—Aigun (1858), Beijing (1860), and Ili (1881)—and commented that by virtue of these treaties a vast area of Chinese territory had been unfairly annexed to the Soviet Union. The editorial even described the unequal treaties as "outstanding issues," and revealed the stand the Chinese would take on border issues in the future: "When conditions are ripe, the outstanding issues should be settled peacefully through negotiations; pending a settlement, the status quo should be maintained."[95]

The publication of this editorial seemed to be a by-product of the polemics engaged in by the U.S., Soviet, and Chinese Communist parties in the wake of the Cuban crisis of October 1962 and other foreign-policy differences. Because of the growing rift, as early as 1959 the P.R.C. leadership was uneasy about the security of China's border with the Soviet Union. In May and June 1962, prior to China's border war with India, the Soviets interfered with tribal minorities in Xinjiang. A year later, in September 1963, China made public its charge against the Soviets for their activities in Xinjiang. In early 1964, one Chinese document vividly described the border incidents, which had allegedly arisen from Soviet-provoked activities, as follows:

> With the stepping up of anti-Chinese activities by the leaders of the CPSU in recent years, the Soviet side has made frequent breaches of the status quo on the border, occupied Chinese territory and provoked border incidents. Still more serious, the Soviet side has flagrantly carried out large-scale subversive activities in Chinese frontier areas, trying to sow discord among China's nationalities by means of the press and wireless, inciting China's minority nationalities to break away from their motherland, and inveigling and coercing tens of thousands of Chinese citizens into going to the Soviet Union.[96]

Shortly after the Chinese published their version of the Xinjiang incidents, the Soviet Union made its first public countercharges. On September 20, 1963, the Soviet government issued a long statement that rebuked the Chinese government for "using some ancient data and graves of their forefathers" in order to make territorial claims. The Soviet government admitted, however, that the two countries had a border problem that needed solving. It stated that "socialist countries, guided by the principle of proletarian internationalism in their relations, should show other peoples an example of friendly solution of territorial problems."[97] At that time the Soviet leaders were obviously well aware of the border incidents that had occurred. Early in 1964, high-level Soviet officials reportedly described the Sino-Soviet frontier as "the most unquiet border in the world."[98] By early 1964, Moscow and Beijing seem to have agreed that negotiations should be held to discuss the Sino-Soviet boundary problem.

On February 25, 1964, delegations representing the two governments met in Beijing. But the negotiations apparently broke down in the fall of the same year and did not resume until October 1969, when the March 1969 border clashes on Zhenbao Island, in the Wusuli River (Russian name: Ussuri), forced the two powers to meet again. During the border talks, the P.R.C. appeared to have two objectives. While it accepted the old treaties as the basis for determining the boundary between the two countries, China also wanted to replace these treaties with new ones that redefined the areas both sides had contested. In this regard, the Chinese seemed to want Moscow to recognize the old treaties relating to the Sino-Soviet boundary as unequal traties and to review comprehensively the definition of the entire border. Until the boundary question could be resolved, Beijing hoped that the status quo of the boundary could be maintained. But the Soviet Union would not agree to such an agenda, and contended that the negotiations should not concern the entire border. The Soviet view was that only minor adjustments were needed in those sections of the frontier where both sides disagreed.[99] The two sides faced an even more serious obstacle, however: defining the boundary set forth in the old treaties.

During the border talks of 1964, it seems that Beijing and Moscow disagreed mainly about two sectors of the boundary.[100] One sector extended about 20,000 square kilometers west of the Sarykal Range in the Pamir, which Russia had allegedly occupied since 1892. The other sector, which was relevant to the March 1969 border war, involved the Amur and Ussuri rivers. Both sides agreed that the two rivers themselves formed the boundary in the eastern sector, but disagreed over the proper mode of determining both river boundary lines in terms of ownership of river islands. The Soviet Union claimed that the boundary line in the Amur and Ussuri rivers ran along the "Chinese bank of the rivers," and thus should place within Soviet territory the several hundred islands of the river system. In support of their claim, the Soviets cited the map (on a scale of 1:1,000,000) attached to the 1860 Beijing Treaty.

The P.R.C. refused to recognize the Soviets' interpretation, however. Its delegates argued that the Beijing Treaty (Article 1) merely stipulated that the two rivers formed the boundary line between China and Russia, without showing the precise line in the rivers themselves. The Chinese claimed that the map attached to the treaty had been drawn up unilaterally one year before the signing of the treaty, and because of its scale (smaller than 1:1,000,000), failed to delineate the boundary line in the rivers. In Beijing's view, in the absence of an explicit treaty provision, the central line of the main channel—the Thalweg principle—provided a legal basis for delimiting the boundary in the two rivers. On this basis, Beijing claimed that 600 of the rivers' 700 islands—including Zhenbao Island on the Ussuri River, just 180 miles southwest of an important Soviet city, Khabarovsk—belonged to the P.R.C.

During the border talks, the Beijing leadership apparently became greatly agitated by Moscow's territorial claims. According to a later account, the leadership perceived that Moscow's insistence on the ownership of several hundred islands in the two rivers and of the Pamir region represented "new territorial claims in violation of the treaty stipulation"

that "even the old tsars dared not advance."[101] It may well be that faced with
the Soviet Union's new territorial claims in 1964, Mao felt compelled to let
it be known that if Moscow insisted on making these claims and discounting
czarist Russia's annexation of Chinese territory in violation of the old
treaties, China would reconsider its negotiating position—that is, China
would take the old treaties as the basis for delimiting the *entire* Sino-Soviet
border. In an interview with Japanese Socialist party members on July 10,
1964, Mao was quoted as saying: "About a hundred years ago, the area to
the east of [Lake] Baikal became Russian territory, and since then
Vladivostok, Khabarovsk, Kamchatka, and other areas have been Soviet
territory. We have not yet presented our account for this list."[102]

It seems highly probable that in making this statement, Mao was reacting
to new Soviet territorial claims rather than attempting to assert Chinese
claims to all the lost territories. Two years later, in an interview with Danish
journalists on May 24, 1966, Foreign Minister Chen Yi indicated that the
Soviet Union had insisted on "preposterous and unreasonable territorial
claims" and was "still occupying certain other areas" in violation of the
treaties. Chen Yi reminded the journalists that as a result of the "unequal
treaties," czarist Russia had annexed more than 1,540,000 square kilometers
of Chinese territory; but he clearly reiterated the official Chinese position of
February 1964, stating that China was willing to accept the so-called
"unequal treaties" as the "basis for settling the Sino-Soviet boundary
question" and "did not demand the recovery of Chinese territory annexed
by tsarist Russia."[103]

But Mao's comments on the territorial issue produced harsh reactions in
the U.S.S.R. Numerous articles and radio broadcasts in the Soviet Union
vigorously attacked Mao's statement. For instance, an editorial in *Pravda*
on September 2, 1964, examined Mao's view at length and condemned it as
a new version of "Lebensraum." It portrayed China's leaders as men like
Hitler and Tojo, who had advocated "an openly expansionist program with
far-reaching pretensions."[104]

Mao's statement, the break-up of the border talks, and the increasing
number of border incidents may have led Soviet leaders to consider that the
dispute over the ownership of certain uninhabited islands in the Amur and
Ussuri rivers could be exploited if either side wanted to cause trouble. Any
incidents or skirmishes on the Sino-Soviet border could escalate into a
major crisis. This possibility may account for the report that after the
ousting of Khrushchev in October 1964, the Soviet high command
reassessed the general requirements of the Soviet Union's ground forces,
including those in the Far East. In early 1965, the reappointment of
Marshal Matvei Zakharov, who had disagreed with Khrushchev on defense
policy and had been dismissed in March 1963, as chief of the Soviet
General Staff suggested that one trend in Soviet military thinking was to

consider the deployment of considerable nonnuclear forces (the stress being on amphibious and airborne operations) along the Sino-Soviet border.[105]

The first sign of efforts to improve the Soviets' military strength along the border was the conclusion of a new defense treaty with Mongolia in January 1966 which authorized the presence of Soviet troops on Mongolian soil. By early 1967, Moscow had moved nearly a hundred thousand men into the People's Republic of Mongolia.[106] It was also reported that beginning in early 1966, the Soviets continued to improve the capability of their far eastern forces by supplying them with sophisticated weapons such as missiles and surface-to-surface nuclear-tipped rockets. Meanwhile, from seven to eight Soviet divisions were moved from central Asia to a position east of Lake Baikal, bringing the total troop strength there to between 250,000 and 350,000 men.[107]

Soon after the Cultural Revolution officially started, the Soviet leadership formally reaffirmed a strongly anti-China stand in a communiqué of a plenary session of the Central Committee in December 1966. The communiqué referred to "recent events in China" as evidence that "the great power, anti-Soviet policy of Mao Tse-tung and his group has entered a dangerous new phase" and claimed: "The plenary session considers it necessary to unmask resolutely the anti-Leninist views and great-power nationalistic policy of the present Chinese leaders and to intensify the struggle to defend Marxism."[108]

This decision was fully supported by the Soviet military. On January 10, 1967, *Krasnaya Zvezda,* the Defense Ministry's newspaper, reported that the military leadership firmly endorsed the decision of the Central Committee on the China question, stressing the need to increase the country's vigilance.[109] In the meantime, Soviet political and military leaders, including Premier Kosygin, visited the border areas frequently, addressing the border troops and encouraging them to stand firm against China in this "new dangerous stage" of the Chinese revolution.[110] As part of the Soviet leadership's anti-China campaigns, Soviet troops were required to demonstrate their strength and readiness by engaging in exercises along the Sino-Soviet border. It was also reported that in 1967 and 1968, Soviet and Mongolian troops on several occasions conducted small- and large-scale military maneuvers and parades in the Sino-Mongolian and far eastern border areas.[111] In addition, the Soviet high command reportedly gave local commanders in the border region responsibility for handling border incidents, mainly because of the need for them to act rapidly in case of unexpected events.[112]

The Soviet military build-up and demonstrations along the Sino-Soviet border were obvious signals to the Beijing leadership and were noted with concern. At the beginning of the Cultural Revolution, Chen Yi for the first time mentioned a redeployment of Soviet troops. "The Soviets have 13 divisions at China's frontier, moved there from Europe," he said.[113] Mao himself appeared to worry about the increased number of Soviet troops along the border. In January 1967, Mao is reported to have said: "Soviet ground forces are on the move," and "Chinese troops in the north must be on guard and in a state of preparedness."[114] The Chinese leadership's awareness of Soviet military pressure on the Sino-Soviet border was further reflected in a January 28, 1967, directive of the Military Affairs Committee, which called the attention of all units of the PLA to the imperialists, revisionists, and reactionaries, who "are itching for stronger action and also want to avail themselves of [the] opportunity to launch raids."[115] In early 1967, at least one senior Chinese official expressed the belief that a border war between China and the U.S.S.R. would begin sooner than a war between China and the United States.[116]

Between July and November 1967, Soviet troops in Europe conducted nonnuclear military maneuvers that were coordinated with maneuvers in the far eastern region of the U.S.S.R. Large numbers of Soviet troops, including tank and missile units, were paraded publicly in Ulan Bator, the capital of Mongolia.[117] As a result, China's sensitivity to the Soviet threat seemed to heighten. For instance, a *People's Daily* article on September 13, 1967, noted that "tens of thousands of Soviet troops have been stationed in Mongolia."[118] On November 1, 1967, Radio Huhehaote urged the people and PLA units in Inner Mongolia to "suppress the agents of the Soviet and Outer Mongolia" and to turn the "northern frontier" into "a great wall of anti-revisionism."[119] Frequent references to Soviet "revisionist" activities in the border regions and exhortations to strengthen China's border defenses also appeared in the resolutions adopted by local authorities in Xinjiang and Heilongjiang (Heilungkiang) in January and February 1968.[120]

It seems probable that this large-scale Soviet military build-up along China's border was accompanied by intensive border patrolling and subversive activities by Soviets in the area. During the Cultural Revolution (1966–68), the Chinese hinted that the number of border incidents had increased. According to a later Chinese charge, from October 15, 1964, to March 1969 the Soviet Union provoked as many as 4,189 border incidents. This number was two and a half times that for the period 1960–64. According to the same document, the Chinese leadership regarded the Soviets' tactics as becoming "even more unbridled" and claimed: "The Soviet government directed Soviet frontier troops to push their patrol routes into Chinese territory, build military installations within Chinese territory, assault and kidnap Chinese border inhabitants, sabotage their production and carry out all sorts of provocative and subversive activities."[121]

In Beijing's view, these Soviet-provoked incidents increased mainly in the Amur and Ussuri rivers in the eastern sector and along the Xinjiang border in the western sector. During the winter months (November through April), Soviet border guards could drive multiton vehicles onto the Amur and Ussuri rivers' ice-bound islands. P.R.C. sources charged that Soviet troops repeatedly invaded Chinese-claimed islands in this way. One Red Guard document described the nature of conflict on the disputed islands. According to the document, from December 7 to December 25, 1966, five incidents between Chinese and Soviet border guards occurred on Hongqiling (Hung Ch'iling) Island in the Heilongjiang (Amur) River mainly because Soviet patrols onto the Chinese-claimed island interfered with the normal patrol and transit rights of Chinese frontier guards.[122] It seems likely that this kind of incident occurred frequently, leading both sides to engage in a vicious circle of "tit-for-tat" reprisals that escalated into more serious incidents involving bloodshed. Later, China's Ministry of Foreign Affairs gave the following account of armed incidents on and around Zhenbao Island:

> During the ice-bound seasons in the more than two years between January 23, 1967 and March 2 this year [1969], Soviet frontier guards intruded into Chen Pao island on 16 occasions, and on several occasions wounded Chinese frontier guards who were on normal patrol duty, and looted arms and ammunition. Between the end of November 1967 and January 5, 1968, the Soviet revisionists sent Soviet frontier guards on 18 occasions to intrude into the area of Chilichin island, north of Chen Pao island, disrupting Chinese people's production and on many occasions killing and wounding Chinese people engaged in productive labor. Soviet frontier guards also intruded into the area of Kapotzu island, south of Chen Pao island on many occasions.[123]

For the Beijing leadership, the Xinjiang border also was a sensitive area in terms of a direct military threat and potential Soviet subversion. Red Guard posters seen in August 1967 claimed that Chinese troops had annihilated a Soviet cavalry unit that had invaded the Ili area in Xinjiang. There were also unconfirmed reports from Hong Kong and from Japanese sources that during the summer of 1967, four additional incidents occurred involving violations of the Sino-Soviet frontier in the same area.[124]

Probably more important to the Chinese leadership were the Soviets' subversive activities in Xinjiang during the Cultural Revolution. As mentioned in Chapter 4, in mid-1962, tens of thousands of minority tribespeople in Xinjiang crossed the border into the U.S.S.R. at the peak of the P.R.C.'s domestic economic difficulties. Soviet authorities allegedly encouraged the exodus from Xinjiang by coercing the Moslems as well as by distributing Soviet passports to the Xinjiang rioters. The Cultural Revolution also appears to have stimulated Moslem dissension, especially when the Red Guards launched a new wave of political and religious persecution in Xinjiang, thus creating unrest and disorder in this sensitive province. In late 1966, several thousand Moslems fled from Xinjiang to Soviet territory. By late 1967, the factional struggles had intensified in Xinjiang. Numerous antirevolutionary groups had obtained machine guns, automatic rifles, and handgrenades; an unnamed national-defense highway had been seized; guardhouses on the border were being attacked frequently; and attempts to escape into the Soviet Union were on the rise.[125] According to an unconfirmed report from Hong Kong in January 1969, about 4,000 Uygurs (nomadic herdsmen) had clashed with Chinese troops near Yining, a town forty miles from the Sino-Soviet border.[126]

Moscow was apparently determined to take advantage of the turbulence in Xinjiang. Beginning in January 1967, broadcasts by Radio Tashkent in Uygur to Xinjiang were increased from one to two hours daily. From then onward, the Soviets beamed Tashkent's Uygur broadcasts at Xinjiang, providing lurid accounts of Chinese persecution of Moslem minorities, encouraging the Uygurs to revolt against Chinese rule, and offering refuge to the rebels.[127] In some instances, Moscow even encouraged Soviet-based Moslem guerrillas to raid Chinese frontier posts in Xinjiang. A refugee leader from Xinjiang is reported to have said that in 1966 alone, the Moslem refugee army supported by the Soviets made 5,000 guerrilla raids along the Xinjiang border.[128]

Soviet subversive activities in Xinjiang obviously added to the threatening signals the Beijing leadership was picking up. Beijing's sensitivity to Soviet subversion was well reflected in a series of defensive measures ordered in the first months of the Cultural Revolution. Local authorities reportedly ordered the civilian population to evacuate a strip of land 120 miles wide along the Mongolian and Xinjiang borders. Han Chinese immigrants were brought into the evacuated area to farm in 1966–68.[129] In early 1967, the P.R.C. reportedly denied Soviet airplanes overflight rights in Xinjiang and Tibet for security reasons.[130] Regulations governing public security work in January 1967, and an order published by the party center in September 1967, reflected China's fear that class enemies at home, in collaboration with foreign enemies, would take advantage of domestic turmoil to sow dissension among the people and carry out counterrevolutionary activities.[131] In March 1968, an important article by a *People's Daily* commentator again reminded the Chinese people that internal vulnerability might invite foreign subversion:

> For a long time, U.S.-led imperialism, modern revisionism with Soviet revisionism as its centre and the reactionaries of all countries have ceaselessly carried out subversive plots and sabotage activities against our country. In addition to collaborating with and making use of a handful of class enemies within China, they have continuously sent spies and secret agents . . . to carry out all kinds of criminal activities. *Particularly since the launching of China's great proletarian Cultural Revolution, the class enemies at home and abroad have feverishly intensified*

their espionage and sabotage activities. This is because they ... imagine this great Cultural Revolution to be an opportunity for them to fish in troubled waters.[132]

In summary, the threat perceived by the Chinese leadership resulted from three interrelated Soviet activities along the Sino-Soviet border: the increase in the number of Soviet border troops and weapons there; Soviet-created border incidents and intensified border patrolling; and Soviet subversive activities. A joint editorial by *People's Daily* and the *Liberation Army Daily* on March 4, 1969, summarized the Soviet threat as follows: "The Soviet revisionist clique has not only wantonly maligned and slandered China and unscrupulously conducted subversive and disruptive activities against China but also massed on the Sino-Mongolia and Sino-Soviet borders troops who repeatedly intruded into China's territory and air space, creating border incidents and posing military threats against our country."[133]

The Impact of the Soviet Invasion of Czechoslovakia

The other major reason for heightened Chinese concern at this time was the Soviet invasion of Czechoslovakia in the summer of 1968, out of which came the so-called Brezhnev doctrine. The invasion of Czechoslovakia coincided with deteriorating Sino-Soviet relations, increased border tensions, and an anti-China campaign that focused on the Soviets' criticism of the Cultural Revolution. Coming at such a juncture, the events in Czechoslovakia were most likely viewed by Beijing as part of a pattern of revived Soviet aggression that made the threat to China's northern and western borders even more immediate.

After the Moscow incidents and the anti-Soviet demonstrations in Beijing in late 1966 and early 1967, Sino-Soviet diplomatic relations had worsened considerably, and a series of "tit-for-tat" diplomatic reprisals had occurred. As a protest of anti-China reports from Moscow, and as a result of mounting Chinese suspicion of the Soviets, Beijing ordered *Pravda* correspondents to leave China in May 1967. Soviet Embassy personnel in Beijing were refused permission to travel in Yunnan, Harbin, Mukden, and Port Arthur—important cities along the Sino-Soviet and Sino-Vietnam frontiers. In June, the Chinese government cancelled an agreement on Soviet flights to Vietnam over Chinese territory.[134] During 1967, there was no session of the Soviet-Chinese Navigation Commission on the Amur and Ussuri Rivers, a group that had met regularly since 1958.[135] The year 1967 also marked the first time since 1949 that Beijing and Moscow failed to sign a new plan for trade, scientific exchange, and cooperation.

The worsening relations between Beijing and Moscow were further revealed in hostile propaganda campaigns launched by both sides. Each side accused the other of taking the capitalist road in collaboration with imperialists, of big-power chauvinism, and of seeking to disrupt the unity of the world communist movement. Moscow charged that Beijing had committed more than 200 provocative acts against Soviet institutions and representatives between mid-1967 and January 1968. According to Beijing's accusation, during the first half of 1967 the Soviets' anti-Mao campaign, which was aimed at vilifying the Cultural Revolution and undermining Chinese unity, continued to increase by means of Soviet radio broadcasts and a veritable flood of books and pamphlets.[136]

In the wake of aggravated Sino-Soviet relations, a hard-line faction against China was in the ascendant in the Soviet Politburo by the summer of 1967. This faction, represented by Mikhail Suslov, the Soviet Politburo secretary responsible for liaison with the international communist movement, believed that socialism was threatened by Mao and concluded that there was no possibility of restoring friendly relations with China without outside help or pressure. In this regard, Suslov attached great importance to the convening of a world communist conference without China.[137] Moscow succeeded in assembling a majority of the Communist parties in February 1968 at a preparatory meeting in Budapest, and at this meeting it was decided that a world conference would be convened in late 1968. In a speech at this meeting, Suslov is said to have stressed the impossibility of cooperation and unity with the Chinese communists. As he put it, "The Mao Tse-tung group demonstrably displayed its unwillingness to cooperate with communist parties."[138]

Suslov's address coincided with a flood of articles in the Soviet press that were aimed at China. Among them, in the first half of 1968, was a series of six articles on "events in China."[139] To judge from these six articles, the Soviet leadership seemed determined to support an anti-Mao faction within China either by itself or in collaboration with other communist leaderships. For instance, in an article entitled "The Cultural Revolution and the Mao Group's Foreign Policy," N. Kapchenko described the Chinese road to the Cultural Revolution as "an effort to establish a military-bureaucratic dictatorship," which in turn had led to reckless and adventuristic foreign policy, and pointed out that the anti-Soviet line had encountered resistance within the Communist party of China itself and among some of its leaders.[140] An article that appeared in *Kommunist* under the title "The Political Course of Mao Tse-tung in the International Arena" called for unmasking the foreign-policy course of Mao's group and for a "collective rebuff" of its provocations. The article emphasized the need to support more effectively the forces that opposed Mao inside China: "The struggle against Mao Tse-tung's group is the struggle for restoring friendship and cooperation with the Chinese communist party to the positions of scientific socialism. This is practical international aid to those forces in China who remain loyal to Marxism-Leninism and resist Maoism.[141]

This Soviet hard line against China was reaffirmed later at a plenary meeting of the Soviet Communist party in April and in Gromyko's foreign-policy report to the Supreme Soviet of the U.S.S.R. in June 1968. The resolution of the plenary meeting fully approved the results of the consultative meeting in Budapest and noted the Soviet leadership's expectation that the meeting would become a "landmark for the unity of the international communist movement."[142]

There is abundant evidence that by the middle of 1968, Moscow was fully aware of China's domestic vulnerability, and especially of the low morale of the PLA occasioned by the turbulent power-seizure campaign. For instance, in a message broadcast to China in Mandarin on June 26, 1968, Moscow informed the Chinese that the Cultural Revolution was destroying China's political system, hurting its economy, and damaging the strength of the PLA. In particular, the broadcast predicted a new round of purges of PLA officials:

> Commanders and political staff members who are stationed at different posts are discharged, reshuffled, or even arrested. . . . You should be aware that the constant reshuffle of commanders has seriously damaged the Chinese armed forces. It is only natural that they are opposed to Mao Tse-tung and his clique's policy. . . . In the course of this new purge, hundreds and thousands of military officials will be vilified, humiliated, and dismissed.[143]

The Beijing leadership naturally responded to these commentaries. The Chinese media in the first half of 1968 continued to condemn Suslov as "a chieftain of the Soviet revisionists" who was trying to restore a false unity within the communist movement on an anti-China platform.[144] Several articles in *People's Daily* charged that the Soviets were spreading anti-China rumors and were racking their brains to vilify China's great Cultural Revolution. However, these articles, and speeches made in the same period, did not reveal *immediate* Chinese concern about *armed* Soviet intervention in China.[145] Chief of Staff Huang Yongsheng (Huang Yung-sheng), for instance, in a speech at a PLA anniversary reception, did not single out the threat of war with the Soviet Union or of Soviet military intervention. Instead, he referred generally to efforts by U.S. imperialists, Soviet revisionists, and Indian reactionaries to "create border tension by frequently encroaching on Chinese territorial waters and air space."[146] It was not until the Soviet-led invasion of Czechoslovakia in late August that the Chinese leadership became acutely sensitive to the possibility of Soviet intervention in China and directly linked Soviet recklessness in Czechoslovakia to the Soviet threat to China's border areas.

Immediately after the Soviet-led military action against Czechoslovakia, a TASS statement published in *Pravda* and *Izvestia* on August 21 justified it in terms that sounded strangely similar to those that had been used to denounce China during the first half of 1968. The decision of the socialist countries to dispatch troops to Czechoslovakia, the TASS statement declared, was based on the belief that "the exacerbation of the situation in Czechoslovakia" not only posed a threat to the socialist system in Czechoslovakia but also affected "the vital interests of the Soviet Union and the security interests of all states in the socialist commonwealth."[147] A few days later a TASS communiqué and other articles further insisted that the decision to occupy Czechoslovakia was in complete accord with the right of all states to individual and collective self-defense as well as with the highest international duty of socialist countries to defend genuine socialism.[148]

The bold Soviet thrust into Czechoslovakia at the moment when the latter was advocating a more independent (though "liberal") road obviously deepened Chinese concern. In contrast to their past criticism of the "revisionist line" of the Czechoslovakian leader Dubček, the Chinese were now inclined to sympathize with him as a victim of Soviet, big-power chauvinism.[149] Soon after the New China News Agency reported on the invasion, numerous Chinese press correspondents and high-level Chinese leaders began to condemn the action.[150] On August 23, in a speech at Rumania's National Day reception, Zhou Enlai attacked the Soviet occupation of Czechoslovakia and for the first time called the Soviet leaders "a gang of social imperialists and social fascists," comparing events in Czechoslovakia to Hitler's aggression in 1938 and U.S. intervention in Vietnam.[151]

This Chinese sensitivity was surely further heightened by the proclamation of the Brezhnev doctrine, which linked Soviet military moves in Eastern Europe with Soviet actions along the Sino-Soviet border soon after the occupation of Czechoslovakia. Although initially aimed at justifying the Soviets' intervention in Czechoslovakia, the Brezhnev doctrine strongly implied that the Soviet Union would adopt military measures against *any* member of the socialist community if Moscow believed such action was necessary to defend socialism against its enemies inside or outside the member country. In other words, according to the doctrine, the sovereignty and the right of individual socialist countries to self-determination could be limited or counterposed to the interests of world socialism.[152] The proclamation of this doctrine was reinforced by Soviet military deployments throughout Eastern Europe, including Soviet troop activities on the borders of Austria, Czechoslovakia, and Yugoslavia, and reinforcement of the Soviet fleet in the Mediterranean close to Albania, China's main ideological ally in the Soviet sphere.[153]

The fact that China's leaders were by now apprehensive about Soviet military action along China's border is reflected in an official government protest. On September 16, *People's Daily* published a note sent by the

Chinese Foreign Ministry to the Soviet embassy in Beijing which strongly protested the intrusion of Soviet military aircraft into Chinese air space over Heilongjiang. "In the past year alone," the note alleged, "there were 119 cases of intrusion (a total of 131 sorties)." But "between August 9 and 29, 1968," the note stressed, "a succession of 29 sorties" into China's air space had occurred over the Donghua (Tunghua) area in Heilongjiang Province. The Chinese leadership called the latter intrusions a "fresh military provocation against China" in "an organized and planned way," and expressed its new fear that the Soviets would invade China as they had invaded Czechoslovakia:

> It is rare that within a short space of 21 days the Soviet side should have committed such concentrated, frequent, bare-faced, and flagrant military provocations over China's air space in one area. *In particular, it should be pointed out that these intrusions by the Soviet military aircraft took place around August 20 when the Soviet Union sent its troops for aggression against Czechoslovakia. And this is in no way accidental.* [154]

This fear was reinforced by Zhou Enlai in a speech on September 30 in which he pointed out: "While intensifying its aggression and threats against Eastern Europe, Soviet social imperialism is also stepping up armed provocations against China." Zhou further claimed that Moscow had stationed a massive number of troops along the Sino-Soviet and Sino-Mongolian borders, and at the same time was constantly creating border tension by frequently sending planes to violate China's air space. [155]

There was now every reason for the Beijing leadership to be concerned that the Soviets would interpret China's domestic instability as a sign of weakness and believe that they could deal with China as easily as they had dealt with Czechoslovakia. This concern was highly plausible, for during the Cultural Revolution China's leadership was sharply divided at the national and local levels—notably in the border provinces—and its national-defense position was extremely weak because of the deep involvement of PLA main-force units in the Cultural Revolution. A "stern warning" to Moscow, the Foreign Ministry note quoted above reflected this concern. It warned the Soviet government that "the 700 million Chinese people armed with Mao Tse-tung's thought are not to be bullied and China's territorial integrity and sovereignty absolutely brook no violation."

Several local reports from Xinjiang in the months following the Czechoslovakian invasion reiterated the Chinese people's determination to stand up against a possible Soviet move toward Xinjiang, despite local turbulence there. [156] A report by the Xinjiang People's Broadcasting Station on September 8 pointed out that during the Cultural Revolution, local nationalists had conspired with Soviet revisionists in various attempts to "break up the unity of the nationalities" and to "detach Sinkiang from the fatherland." But the report warned the Soviets that the Chinese would not be as easy to deal with as the Czechoslovakians had been: "As the occupation of Czechoslovakia has shown, Soviet revisionists are ready for every evil. . . . But if they dare to attack Sinkiang, the peoples of all nationalities in Sinkiang, tempered in a great Cultural Revolution, [will] annihilate them resolutely."[157]

China's Fear of "Encirclement" and the Vietnam Issue

During 1967 and 1968, Moscow and Washington held a series of talks—highlighted by those in Glassboro in mid-1967—to discuss and coordinate many international problems. After those meetings, a dominant theme in the Chinese press became fear of collaboration between Washington and Moscow to achieve world domination. The Chinese leadership faced external threats from India and Vietnam in addition to those on the Sino-Soviet border. Each event occurred separately, but in the eyes of the Beijing leadership, Soviet-U.S. diplomatic moves and other military pressure were linked as anti-China plots supported or coordinated by one or both superpowers in order to isolate, encircle, and threaten the P.R.C.

From Beijing's viewpoint, the Glassboro talks between Lyndon Johnson and Alexei Kosygin in late June 1967 marked the beginning of a new period of U.S.-Soviet collaboration for world domination and produced an overall coordination in their global strategy. The Chinese believed that through the Glassboro talks, Washington and Moscow would reach a common understanding about how jointly to deal with international issues like the Middle East, Vietnam, and nuclear weapons. Much more serious, in Beijing's view, was the existence of a common basis for the two powers' collusion at Glassboro—the fact that they both regarded the P.R.C. as their "number one enemy," and that in the future, both would support any forces that opposed China.[158] From then on, the Beijing leadership appears to have believed that the anti-China campaigns of Asian countries were instigated and supported by "back-stage managers" of the United States and the Soviet Union in an effort to isolate and encircle the P.R.C.[159]

During and after the Glassboro meetings, Washington and Moscow signaled jointly to Beijing that they would speed up cooperation on such issues as the nonproliferation of nuclear weapons, ballistic missile systems, and a balanced reduction of forces in Europe. The Chinese believed that this collaboration was at least partly aimed against China and would be harmful to China's security interests. To the Chinese leadership, the Treaty on the Nonproliferation of Nuclear Weapons, which was adopted by the UN General Assembly in June 1968, was a component of U.S.-Soviet anti-China plotting. In Beijing's view, the treaty meant not only that the two powers would maintain a nuclear monopoly, while carrying out nuclear blackmail of the P.R.C., but also that nuclear protection would be given to nonnuclear states like India (China's potential enemy) and other subscribing countries bordering China.[160] China's concern about U.S. and Soviet strategic collaboration against it was probably enhanced by U.S. and Soviet moves to deploy antiballistic missile systems aimed at China.[161]

For China, a still more serious aspect of U.S.-Soviet military collaboration was the possibility that while trying to relax tensions in Europe, Washington and Moscow might cooperate in shifting their military strength to the East, and at precisely the time when the P.R.C. faced the dual threat of the Vietnam War and the Sino-Soviet border dispute. This concern was probably heightened in December 1967 when a communiqué from a NATO ministerial meeting openly affirmed that "the threat from the Soviet Union to Western Europe is all but gone," and six months later when the NATO ministers called for a "balanced and mutual reduction of forces in Europe."[162] It is not unreasonable to argue that by mid-1968, Beijing may have perceived that Moscow and Washington had reached a tacit understanding on relaxing tensions in Europe and had already made anti-China military arrangements. Thanks to this "understanding," in Beijing's view, the United States could transfer several more army divisions from Europe to the Vietnam battlefield, while the Soviet Union would be able to shift its military strategy to the east, stepping up its disposition of troops along China's border.[163]

China's apprehension of Moscow's and Washington's anti-China military arrangements was probably abetted by what it regarded as the "Moscow-Tokyo axis," which developed from economic cooperation into political and military collusion. In mid-1967, the Soviet Union adopted a special nine-year economic plan for the development of Siberia.[164] In the summer of 1967, Japanese Foreign Minister Takeo Miki visited Moscow, and the Soviet leadership reportedly proposed opening Siberia to Japanese investment.[165] Reportedly, in August 1968, Moscow and Tokyo concluded a major new agreement on the joint development of Siberia.[166] At the same time, the Soviet Union seemed to step up political and military cooperation with Japan. In the course of their Moscow talks, Kosygin and Miki reportedly discussed Soviet-proposed preliminary measures that could lead to a peace treaty, as well as the question of strengthening peace and security in the Far East. In particular, it is known that during the talks, Kosygin implicitly endorsed, fully in line with the U.S. position, the idea that Japanese military strength was "a stable force in Asia," and proposed cooperation with the Sato government in the "organization of [a] counterattack against aggression."[167]

The Beijing leadership seems to have regarded the joint Soviet-Japanese development of Siberia as an effort to turn Siberia into a bastion against China. It equated the plan with a conspiracy by the Soviet and Japanese monopolists, in close collaboration with the United States, to "encircle" China on its northern flank.[168] Furthermore, the Chinese worried that along with a joint program of Siberian development, Soviet-Japanese military collaboration would develop into an extension of Soviet-U.S. collusion, thereby putting added pressure on China's northern border. "Instigated by the Soviet revisionist clique," a *People's Daily* commentator claimed on December 13, 1968, "the Japanese reactionaries gradually changed their emphasis in military deployment from Hokkaido, which is near the Soviet Union, to Kyushu, which is near China. There was a corresponding military deployment by the Soviet revisionists."[169]

Beijing's fear of an "anti-China ring of encirclement" was surely augmented by China's border dispute with India and by U.S. military activities in North Vietnam. In the summer of 1967, the number of border incidents between Chinese and Indian border guards seemed to increase.[170] But in early September, thirty-six Chinese frontier guards were reportedly killed or wounded in clashes with Indian frontier guards along the Sino-Sikkim border. Soon after these clashes, the Soviet Union expressed its support of India's action on the Sino-Sikkim border. In an anti-China statement issued on September 9 TASS reportedly encouraged India's forward deployment of troops in Sikkim, claiming that "Indian troops are staying on the territory of Sikkim to protect its borders."[171] On September 14, after making an anti-China statement, Indian Defense Minister Swanran Singh left New Delhi for Moscow.[172] It was also reported that before and after the September clashes, Moscow provided New Delhi with new military aid, including 170 Su-7 supersonic fighter-bombers, 100 tanks, and large numbers of long-range artillery pieces.[173]

The Beijing leadership termed these armed clashes a "grave armed provocation against China" and a "long-premeditated act of military adventure."[174] In particular, Beijing's concern was that either Moscow or Washington might utilize such border clashes to strengthen military pressure on the P.R.C. from India, which in turn might lead India to miscalculate the situation, as it did in the 1962 Sino-India border war.

Meanwhile, massive U.S. air raids were extended close to Chinese territory on the Sino-Vietnam border, reaching their peak in the summer of 1967. In addition, a group of U.S. warships, including a nuclear-powered submarine, entered the port of Hong Kong in July and stayed there until September, hinting that the U.S. was prepared to support the British in dealing with any eventuality in Hong Kong.[175] An article in *People's Daily* on September 13 accounted for the coincidence of India's provocation and U.S. and Soviet military pressure as follows: "It is by no means accidental that the Indian reactionary government is frantically stirring up large-scale military provocations at this particular time."[176] An article in *People's Daily* on September 14 linked India's military activities to Chinese apprehension that the border tension would be aggravated by the encouragement of Moscow or Washington, or both: "Immediately after the Indian reactionaries had launched their military provocations, the U.S. imperialists and Soviet revisionists turned on their propaganda machines to defend the Indian aggressors and attack China for allegedly aggravating the 'border tension.' Does this show clearly on whose orders the Indian reactionaries have acted?"[177]

This apprehension probably led the Chinese to be seriously concerned about an Indian miscalculation of China's strength. Thus, an article in the *Liberation Army Daily* on September 15 solemnly warned the Indian government: "You cannot last in a fight and your masters—U.S. imperialism and Soviet revisionism—are also not of great consequence"; so "do not err in judging the situation or miscalculate, and do not forget the lesson of the 1962 invasion of China."[178] In addition to this verbal deterrence, the Chinese leadership also engaged in diplomacy. Two days after China's warnings were published in *People's Daily* and the *Liberation Army Daily*, it was suddenly reported that the Chinese and Indian governments had agreed that China would hand over to an Indian representative the bodies of fourteen Indian soldiers together with their arms and ammunition. That agreement was carried out on September 16.[179] From then on, tension on the Sino-Indian border appeared to recede.

In 1967–68, the P.R.C. continued to perceive U.S. military pressure in the wake of the Vietnam War. In February 1967, the Johnson administration approved a "spring air offensive" that relaxed restrictions on air raids near Hanoi and Haiphong. In early August, President Johnson authorized American forces to bomb sixteen additional fixed targets in North Vietnam. "Nine targets out of them," according to *The Pentagon Papers,* "were located in the northeast rail line in the China buffer zone, the closest one eight miles from the border, and the tenth was a naval base within the China buffer zone."[180] By March 1968, U.S. air raids had been extended to the China-Laos border area, while U.S. and Thai ground troops were reportedly continuing to infiltrate Laos.[181]

Large-scale U.S. bombings right up to the Chinese border obviously alarmed Beijing. The Chinese leadership regarded the extension of U.S. bombing to North Vietnam and Laos as a grave escalation of the war for the purpose of implementing Johnson's brinkmanship policy and attempting to carry the flames of war to the whole of Indochina.[182] The Chinese stated that the United States posed a grave threat to China's security in the air and by sea. "In the past twelve months," the Chinese claimed in September 1967, "130 U.S. military planes intruded into China's air space on 73 occasions, while 31 U.S. warships illegally entered China's territorial waters on 42 occasions." During the same period, the PLA air force reportedly shot down nine U.S. planes and two U.S.-made Taiwanese planes.[183] In addition to fearing extension of the war throughout Indochina, China was equally concerned about the Soviets' collaboration with Washington in escalating the war in Vietnam. In Beijing's view, U.S. bombing was a tactic of the "peace talks" fraud that continued to be tacitly supported by the Soviet Union. The Beijing leadership appeared to believe that the spread of U.S. bombing to the vicinity of the Chinese border was "part of the new fraud jointly planned by the Soviet Union" and would lead to increased military pressure on China's northern frontier.[184]

President Johnson's decision of March 31, 1968, to partially stop the bombing and seek an end to the war through peace talks—a plan according to which nearly 80 percent of the territory of North Vietnam would no longer be subjected to U.S. bombing, the exception being the immediate vicinity of the DMZ—did not end China's vigilance and enmity against the United States.[185] Furthermore, the decision reinforced Beijing's suspicion of U.S.-Soviet collusion to sell out on the Vietnam question. On April 5, the Beijing leadership referred to Johnson's unilateral bombing halt as a tactic to gain "breathing space" on the Vietnam battlefield and as a "smoke-screen" for expanding the war. It added that the Soviets had increased their despicable role by becoming Johnson's number one accomplice in the program to induce "peace talks" through "a bombing halt."[186] The leadership reiterated China's position that "the Vietnam question can be solved only by completely defeating the U.S. aggressor on the battlefield and driving it out of South Vietnam."[187]

Despite Beijing's stress on armed struggle against the United States, Hanoi revealed its willingness to discuss the Vietnam question with the United States, and in May the Paris peace talks began. In late October 1968, after some twenty-six preliminary meetings in Paris, U.S. negotiating teams and the North Vietnamese appeared to reach certain understandings. On October 31, Johnson announced that the bombing of North Vietnam would cease, and Saigon was assured of a place at the conference table.[188]

The ongoing Paris peace talks added to China's suspicions of a Moscow-Washington collusion. Citing a UPI correspondent's report, the Chinese disclosed on October 19, 1968, that the Soviet Union was continuing to play a part in the talks in order to bring Hanoi and Washington closer together, and had even advised Hanoi that in return for Johnson's bombing halt, it should make some concessions, probably some restraint on military action in Vietnam.[189]

This Chinese sensitivity to U.S.-Soviet collusion was reinforced by the Soviet invasion of Czechoslovakia. In Beijing's view, the United States' tacit recognition of Eastern Europe as belonging within the sphere of influence of the Soviet Union would lead Moscow to accept a higher price in terms of U.S. demands on the Vietnam question.[190] Such a growing de facto U.S.-Soviet collaboration on a global level, China's leaders seemed to believe, decreased the opportunities to embroil Moscow with Washington, but increased the chances for both to act separately or jointly against China.

The most significant upshot of all these developments was that by the summer of 1968, the threat China perceived in Soviet military pressure on the Sino-Soviet border became intertwined with China's fear of being encircled as the result of U.S.-Soviet collaboration. An article in *People's Daily* on September 21, 1968, sought to document Soviet efforts—"in active coordination with U.S. global strategy, and in collusion with U.S. imperialism and the reactionaries of various Asian countries"—to rig up a "ring of encirclement against China," and linked them with the Soviet threat to China's border security: "Of late the Soviet revisionist renegade clique has been sending military aircraft to intrude into China's territorial air, aggravating tensions on the border, and unscrupulously carrying out military provocations against China. *These crimes of the Soviet revisionist renegade clique are organized and planned actions in accordance with its policy of ganging up with U.S. imperialism against China.*"[191]

The Border-War Decision

The Debate in Beijing

During the summer of 1968, as Beijing's leaders devoted their energy to the ongoing Cultural Revolution, the growing Soviet threat appeared to present them with a painful dilemma: To continue the Cultural Revolution would leave the P.R.C. exposed to outside aggression, while to terminate it would leave Mao's objective unfulfilled. China's initial response to the mounting Soviet threat appeared to be twofold. First, soon after the Soviets conducted large-scale military maneuvers along the Sino-Mongolian border in July 1968, Chinese troops were reportedly redeployed to the Sino-Soviet border, and several hundred heavy guns were removed from the coastal area opposite Quemoy Island, probably for deployment along the northern border.[192] Two months before the report of this troop redeployment, the Beijing leadership is said to have instructed the PLA units on the northern border to strengthen their defense work in desert areas and by late 1968 to have placed the Inner Mongolia Military District under the command of the Beijing Military Region.[193]

Second, Beijing attempted to stabilize the home front. Numerous instructions published by the party center called for the rapid restoration of order and law and for the termination of factional armed struggles. In addition, the Beijing leadership attempted to end the Red Guard stage of the Cultural Revolution and set forth a new stage, shifting emphasis to such tasks as party building, purification of class ranks, and educational revolution. The leading role in carrying out these tasks was assigned to the working class, which was also required to cooperate closely with the PLA.

To a certain extent, Beijing's leaders seemed to shift their policy concerns from domestic issues to the external arena. There is ample evidence that the radicals and moderates within the leadership developed different priorities on issue areas and advocated different policy alternatives to cope with pending domestic and external problems, thereby forming at least two competing policy coalitions.

The moderates were represented by Premier Zhou, who for the first time described the Soviet Union as a "social imperialist" country shortly after the Soviet invasion of Czechoslovakia. In their view, the P.R.C. was threatened more by the external revisionist, the Soviet Union, than by such internal revisionists as "China's Khrushchev"—Liu Shaoqi—and his followers. In early September 1968, in a speech at a Beijing rally of the revolutionary masses held to celebrate the establishment of revolutionary committees in twenty-nine provinces, Zhou pointed out that China simultaneously faced domestic and foreign enemies who were trying to stage a counterattack. But he depicted the foreign threat as the immediate one, and expressed concern that the internal success of the Cultural Revolution was vulnerable to external threat. Zhou claimed that "before the advent of victory, the enemies throughout the world will surely put up last-ditch struggles and launch a counter-attack."[194] In a National Day speech, Zhou expressed this belief more clearly, contrasting the excellent situation on the home front to the unfavorable external situation: "The bourgeois headquarters led by China's Khrushchev has been completely overthrown," but "U.S. imperialism and Soviet revisionism are capable of any evil."[195]

It seems natural that in responding to an immediate external threat, the moderates would emphasize internal consolidation for the purpose of stabilizing China's home front at a minimum and of transferring national energy from the home front to the external front at a maximum. This emphasis on internal consolidation logically led the moderates to be concerned about at least three policy issues: the rapid restoration of law and order; the reconstruction of party and governmental structures and increased coordination among them; and the extraction of the armed forces from their overcommitment to domestic politics so that they could increase their strategic role. However, those three problems were deeply interrelated because of the PLA's pivotal role in domestic politics, from which it could not withdraw without weakening law and order and the stability of party and administrative structures. Probably for this reason, Zhou, together with regional military leaders, advocated a much more moderate pace and more moderate methods for the Cultural Revolution, such as narrowing down "the target of attack" and opening up more party and government positions to old, experienced cadres. By rapidly restoring political and administrative stability, the armed forces could return to their strategic positions and strengthen all-round political and military mobilization.[196]

A sign of difference over domestic and foreign-policy issues between Lin and the radicals, on the one hand, and the moderates, on the other, appeared in the speeches made by Lin and Jiang Qing shortly after the Soviet invasion of Czechoslovakia. During the Beijing rally mentioned above, Jiang Qing also made a speech, but she did not refer to the international situation. Stressing the domestic tasks of party building and purifying the class ranks, she urged continuous "struggle" rather than "unity." She seemed to worry that in the future work of party building, internal class enemies would still pose a threat to the Maoist leadership. She declared: "We must not allow the few bad elements to make trouble, we must drag out these bad elements who sabotage struggle-criticism-transformation."[197] A similar tone was sounded in Lin Biao's National Day speech. In contrast to the attention paid by Zhou to the threat of Soviet revisionism to the P.R.C., Lin did not devote a single word to the Soviet invasion of Czechoslovakia or its future impact on China's security. As defense minister, Lin routinely called for the PLA to strengthen its war preparedness, but he seemed to be primarily concerned about how to carry the great Cultural Revolution through to the end: "At present, the central task confronting us, is to follow Chairman Mao's great teaching, that is, carry out the tasks of struggle-criticism-transformation conscientiously. That means to consolidate and develop the revolutionary committees, to do a good job of purifying the class ranks, of party consolidation and party building."[198]

Considering that the primary domestic tasks of party building and purifying the class ranks still required extensive political clean-up work in a continuous class struggle, Lin and the radicals may have worried that dramatization of the Soviet threat would divert the nation's time and energy away from these critical domestic problems. Excessive emphasis on leadership consolidation and national unity would undermine the ongoing work in the big political clean-up campaign and in turn was likely to bring about the restoration of the old cadres by narrowing the target of attack. This fear continued to appear in the Chinese media in late 1968 and early 1969.[199] For instance, in September 1968, a *Wenhui bao* commentator probably spoke for the radicals when he warned against the moderates' advocacy of a dampening down of the class struggle: "Some people said: 'the Red typhoon has already swept over the land several times and there is no need to get so excited over a few flies and bugs.' Yes, a few red typhoons were fanned up this year. This is needed for class struggle. Can class struggle be counted in terms of how often it occurs?"[200]

Another of the radicals' and Lin's concerns was that any move to stress war preparedness would encourage professionalism in the PLA. In turn the army's ideological and political work in the revolution would be hurt at a time when main-force units, together with regional forces, were deeply and massively involved in domestic politics, and when Lin was not entirely satisfied with the political role of the army, especially that of the regional forces. In addition, Mao's criticism of the army's political work in late July 1968,[201] coupled with the leading role the army could play in future party building, undoubtedly doubled Lin's sensitivity to the PLA's internal politics and moved him to prevent the rise of professionalism. Referring indirectly to the March border clashes, one provincial radio broadcast seemed also to express Lin's concern: "Some time ago, some PLA personnel failed to understand clearly the relationship between preparedness against war and the task of 'three supports and two militaries,' thinking that in the face of major enemies, these tasks should be suspended."[202]

There is reason to believe that Lin and the radicals also worried about a spillover of military professionalism into internal politics. A primary interest in war preparedness by regional military leaders who were supposed to play a critical role in future party building might lead them to be seriously concerned about the rapid stabilization of the home front and to act in favor of older, more experienced party and administrative officials, mainly to bring about a prompt reconstruction of party and administrative structures. It is by no means accidental that numerous criticisms of the PLA's role in party building were made at a time when the Beijing leadership was also concerned about the country's preparedness for war with the Soviet Union. A local newspaper in December 1968 condemned the notion that "to rectify the party, all you have to do is to eliminate a few," an idea it called a reflection of the "purely military viewpoint."[203] A March 1969 *Red Flag* editorial attributed the responsibility for failure to carry out Mao's directive, "Oppose the restoration of the old cadres," to the PLA representatives in the provincial revolutionary committees.[204]

Lin's fears concerning the domestic politics of war preparedness led him to resolve the PLA's two contradictory roles, political and strategic, by emphasizing the former. Wiping out the hidden enemies at home took precedence over the threat posed by the Soviet Union. Since mid-1968, Lin's instructions on "political frontier defenses" had been repeatedly emphasized in the Chinese press.[205] In opposing U.S. imperialism and Soviet revisionism, a New China News Agency report on February 21, 1969, interpreted Vice-Chairman Lin's instructions on "building frontier defenses into political frontier defenses" in the following way: "While standing guard with high vigilance in defence of the socialist motherland and the great Cultural Revolution . . . commanders and fighters of the PLA coastal and frontier units always take as their sacred task the work of propagating Mao Tse-tung's thought among the masses, of organizing and arming the masses with Mao Tse-tung's thought. . . . This has built China's coastal and frontier defence into an invincible great wall of steel."[206]

To Lin, "political frontier defenses" meant that in responding to any eventualities involving the Soviet Union, PLA border units should be armed primarily with Mao Zedong's thought, so as to be prepared politically and psychologically, and should consolidate the basis of the people's war by organizing the masses and arming *them* with Mao's thought. One advantage of Lin's line on "political frontier defenses" was that China's frontier defenses could be strengthened without reducing the army's political work or redeploying to the northern frontier the main-force units that were massively involved in domestic politics throughout the country. There are two indications that such a defense strategy was given priority. First, there is no hint that the border units reduced their political role and increased their strategic role in 1968. Instead, in accordance with Lin's instructions, all border units were urged to organize Mao Zedong thought propaganda teams and go to the rural and mountain areas to help "arm" the masses, an undertaking that would have forced them to leave their fighting posts and to decrease military training time. Indeed, in Inner Mongolia, the PLA units stationed on the border conducted 30,000 classes in Mao's thought, and "more than one million" attended the classes in 1968.[207] Second, during the winter of 1968/69, when Sino-Soviet border tensions were heightened, additional troops do not appear to have been redeployed in order to strengthen the northern frontier.

It should be noted, however, that Lin Biao's instructions on "political frontier defenses" seem to have excessively emphasized "politics" in the PLA at a time when the P.R.C. was believed to be in urgent need of war preparedness. The instructions, it was claimed, would hinder and delay regional commanders' efforts to arrange for adequate manpower at fighting posts, build entrenchements, and place minefields along the border area that was vulnerable to Soviet infiltration. After Lin was removed, the Chinese press charged him with overemphasizing "politics" at the expense of professionalism, negating the importance of military training, and weakening the PLA's fighting strength at the time when China needed an "early war preparedness." It also condemned his "incessant quest for perfection."[208]

It seems highly probable that Lin's lesser concern about war preparedness based on positional war and his awareness that the strength of China's border units was inferior to that of the Soviets' compelled him to minimize the risk of a full-scale Sino-Soviet military confrontation. In his effort to prevent "tit-for-tat" reprisals from developing into a large-scale war, Lin may have ordered Chinese border units to be restrained and nonprovocative. Evidence that this was his thinking is a later account that during the winter of 1968–69, the Soviets seemed determined to prevent Chinese patrols of Zhenbao Island by intensifying their own patrols. However, China's frontier guards were ordered to "keep their distance" from the Soviets and "not to return fire immediately," even after being attacked.[209]

Lin's orders would have eroded any Chinese border guard's psychology of "tit-for-tat" struggle against Soviet revisionism, which was Mao's famous standard. The orders would also have tended to undermine Mao's preferred strategy, based on positional war, to defend China against small-scale Soviet provocations along the border. A month after the March border clashes, Mao seemed to remind the party leadership of his standard—that is, "tit-for-tat" struggle depends upon the situation. He noted that "if it [the attack] is on a small scale, we will fight on the border."[210] Mao's comment suggested that in responding to the *kind* of threat the Soviet guards typically employed, the PLA should rely on positional war rather than, as Lin Biao believed, entirely on strategic withdrawal into the people's war. Lin's orders may not have been very popular with the troops either. Border guards at Zhenbao Island reportedly "recalled with anger the humiliation" of February 1969 when they obeyed Lin's orders "on five occasions." They were also quoted as saying that "the Russians mistaking restraint for weakness were more arrogant each time."[211]

The military option of self-restraint pressed by Lin Biao in response to the mounting Soviet threat on China's border could not be supported even by the radicals, who continued to maintain a coalition with him on most domestic issues. Considering their belief (as shown in the anti-Soviet demonstrations and the *Svirsk* incident in 1967) that any sign of Chinese weakness in waging struggle against the Soviet Union would whet the Soviets' aggressive appetite, the radicals were probably suspicious of Lin's alternative. They favored a show of Chinese resoluteness on the Sino-Soviet border—that is, waging "tit-for-tat" struggle against the Soviets. The charges later made in the Chinese media against Lin's defense line do not seem implausible. Acording to one Chinese document, in the face of an aggressive war from the North, "Lin and the like," without giving a "tit-for-tat" struggle and without waging a patriotic war of resistance, persisted in the old, invariably capitulated line and propagated defense literature that amounted to national betrayal.[212]

While Lin favored a cautious border-defense policy and relied heavily on the people's war to deter either a large-scale or a small-scale Soviet threat, the moderates appeared to support a diplomatic line that would defuse the Soviet threat. The moderates worried that in view of the staggering problems associated with stabilization of the home front, and considering China's inferiority to the Soviet Union in military armaments, China could not handle the military threat posed by the Soviet Union. It also seemed unbelievable to the moderates that the P.R.C. was in a position strong enough to confront the Soviet Union, which might be collaborating with the United States, or even to cope with the two superpowers simultaneously. The moderates appeared to prefer a diplomatic probe through U.S. channels to defuse the prospect of U.S.-Soviet collusion and dissuade Moscow from taking military action against China. In a speech at the Twelfth Plenum, Mao is reported to have claimed that "the Soviet Union represented a greater threat to China than [the] weary paper tigers of American imperialism."[213] In addition, the United States' declaration of its intention to deescalate the Vietnam War and enter into peace talks in late 1968 may have reinforced the moderates' support of a reconciliation with Washington.[214]

On November 25, a Chinese proposal to hold a new session of the Sino-U.S. ambassadorial talks in Warsaw was issued by a spokesman for the Information Department of the Chinese Foreign Ministry. In the statement, the spokesman proposed that the two sides meet on February 20, 1969, and suggested for the first time since 1964 that China would be willing to discuss a peaceful-coexistence pact based on the Five Principles. The precondition for such a meeting was that the U.S. remove its military forces and installations from Taiwan and the Strait area, a requirement which suggested that the P.R.C. was not in a rush to conclude the pact.[215] But the suggestion was also made that China's diplomacy should be so flexible as to negotiate with one's enemy under certain circumstances. To judge from China's media, the moderates were searching for a way to justify such an initiative theoretically. One day before the release of the MFA's statement, *People's Daily* republished Mao's report to the Second Plenary Session of the Seventh Central Committee dated March 5, 1949. One paragraph of the report was quoted as follows: "We should not refuse to enter into negotiations because we are afraid of trouble and want to avoid complications, nor should we enter into negotiations with our minds in a haze. We should be firm in principle, but should also have all the flexibility permissible and necessary to carry out our principles."[216]

The moderates' initiative in seeking negotiations with the United States appears to have been opposed by the radicals and by Lin Biao. To them, any move to relax tensions with China's capitalist enemy would not only erode the people's vigilance, especially that of the PLA, and spread feelings of national capitulation among them; it was also likely to undermine the achievements of the Cultural Revolution power-seizure campaigns of the past two years. An article in *People's Daily* on December 3, 1968, indirectly denounced bitterly any diplomatic engagement with U.S. imperialists. It cited Lin Biao's warning to army cadres "not to put any faith in the so-called new stage of peace and democracy and not to spread it to the army."[217]

In addition to this domestic opposition to their initiative, the moderates would face international complications in the winter of 1968–69. In the months after his inauguration, President Nixon did not indicate a fresh and conciliatory approach in response to China's November initiative. In his first press conference (on January 27, 1969), Nixon expressed interest in the Sino-American meeting in Warsaw, provided the Chinese showed a different attitude on major issues. Stressing the Chinese threat to world peace and revealing his desire to maintain closer relations with Moscow, Nixon stated that the United States would continue to oppose Beijing's admission to the United Nations, and supported Moscow's January 24 proposal to being talks on antiballistic missile (ABM) systems.[218] Another event probably further discouraged the moderates. On January 24, the Chinese chargé d'affaires in the Netherlands, Liao Heshu (Liao Ho-shu), defected from the Chinese Embassy in The Hague and took refuge in the American Embassy.[219]

Growing Sino-Soviet border tensions in early 1969 provided another reason for the Chinese leadership to review its alternatives for responding to the military threat posed by the Soviet Union. In early December 1968, *Izvestia* had quoted General O. A. Losik, Soviet Far Eastern Military District commander, as saying that military maneuvers had taken place in the eastern part of the Soviet Union. It had also quoted General Losik's reference to the Sino-Soviet border conflict of 1929 and his claim that should a similar incident take place again in the future, the Soviet army would relentlessly crush the enemy.[220] In January and February 1969, according to Chinese accounts, the Soviets intensified their efforts to prevent Chinese patrolling of Zhenbao Island. Soon after the ominous incident that occurred on the island on January 23, the number of incidents along China's northeastern border swelled significantly, and the likelihood of low-level skirmishes turning into a major confrontation greatly increased.[221]

Under such circumstances, the Beijing leadership seems to have accepted Mao's line of deterring the Soviet threat by means of a policy of self-reliance. Putting aside Nixon's nonconciliatory attitude toward the P.R.C. and his clear intention of working with Moscow, most leaders in Beijing probably believed that the option of improving Sino-American relations as a counterweight against the Soviet threat, even if successful, could only defuse the two powers' ambition to contain and isolate the P.R.C., but would do little to deter the *kind* of Soviet military threat that existed on the Sino-Soviet border.[222] The Chinese therefore apparently decided to oppose the Soviet Union *without* compromising with the United States. Beginning with an attack on Nixon's inaugural address, the Chinese press vehemently condemned the U.S.-Soviet "plot" against China and depicted the two superpowers as the "ferocious enemies" of China.[223] On

February 19, one day before the scheduled Warsaw talks, the Chinese Foreign Ministry issued a statement cancelling the meeting.[224]

In the meantime, China had begun to emphasize a militant line in standing up to Soviet military pressure. A January 25 rally attended by some 40,000 "revolutionary fighters" of the PLA was probably intended to signal to Moscow that a strong and unified PLA was fully prepared to carry out the sacred duty of defending the nation. During the rally, the PLA was called upon to follow Chairman Mao's great strategic plan in defeating the enemy and to heighten its preparedness for war.[225] Beginning in late January, Chinese border-patrol practices were reportedly modified to permit a second patrol to cover every patrol sent to the river ice around Zhenbao Island.[226] This suggests that the Chinese were enhancing their readiness to respond immediately to small-scale Soviet provocations in accordance with Mao's standard. A week before fighting broke out on March 2, Radio Beijing issued a warning of forthcoming Soviet military maneuvers in Heilongjiang and signaled that the worsening situation along the Ussuri might erupt into a large-scale border war.[227]

China's Motives and Objectives

China's decision to take preemptive action against the Soviets in March 1969 reflected domestic and international events, but was not an expression of external adventure for the sake of internal manipulation. An analysis of the internal and external environment in which the Chinese leadership made the border-war decision suggests that the main motive behind the action was not, contrary to some Western interpretations, the need to consolidate the unity of the Chinese leadership or to divert the people's attention from domestic problems to the international arena. Rather, China's primary concern was to defuse or deflect the increasing Soviet threat against its territory so that its insecure leadership could wind up the Cultural Revolution. The P.R.C. thus decided to undertake a low-risk, preemptive military action that had two main objectives: first, to deter future Soviet encroachments on China's territory, while at the same time preventing a full-scale war; second, to punish the Soviets for their military actions in Chinese-claimed territory, thereby impelling them to reassess their border policy and bring the border question back into the diplomatic arena.

During the Cultural Revolution, the continued Chinese concern about a growing Soviet threat derived mainly from three interrelated Soviet activities along the Sino-Soviet border: the Soviets' large-scale military build-up; increasing border incidents combined with intensified border patrolling; and Soviet subversive activities. In the summer of 1968, the Soviet invasion of Czechoslovakia catalyzed the increasing fears and hostility of the Beijing leadership. That event was paralleled by an increase in the number of Soviet intrusions into China's air space and by Soviet-inspired subversive activities along the Sino-Soviet border, especially in Xinjiang. During the winter of 1968–69, moreover, border incidents occurred more frequently on Zhenbao Island. The Chinese believed that these incidents derived mainly from more aggressive Soviet techniques of border patrolling.

Under these circumstances, China's leaders felt compelled to defuse the mounting Soviet military threat by launching a limited, preemptive military action. Such a strategy might serve China's territorial objective by halting Soviet provocations on the Chinese-claimed island of Zhenbao, at a minimum, and by securing the island, at a maximum. It might also serve China's larger, security interest in preventing small-scale skirmishes from turning into a full-scale border war. These two objectives were given ample coverage in the Chinese press. Soon after the March border clashes, the Chinese media concentrated their protests on Chinese ownership of Zhenbao Island and on the Soviets' aggressive designs. A joint editorial by *People's Daily* and the *Liberation Army Daily* on March 4, and a Chinese note to the Soviet Embassy in Beijing on March 3, began their protests by claiming that "Chen Pao island has always been Chinese territory" and recalling that the Soviets had repeatedly encroached upon China's territorial integrity and sovereignty.[228] According to a later account, during and after the fighting, the island was under Chinese control except when the Soviets returned to collect their dead and wounded.[229]

China's fear of a major war with the Soviet Union was revealed in its statements that the Soviets were capable of the "worst crime" and in its emphasis on preparedness for all possible contingencies beyond a small-scale border war. For instance, on April 1, in a political report to the CCP's Ninth Congress, Lin Biao stressed "full preparations" against "a conventional and nuclear war, a big war, and a war at an early date."[230] Thereafter, a predominant theme in the Chinese press was deep concern that the worst situation would come about.[231] China feared not merely the Soviet threat in the disputed border area, but the larger threat to its security, which, in the manner of the Soviet invasion of Czechoslovakia, would be both politically and strategically motivated.

To secure its territorial and security objectives, China opted for a preemptive action. Considering the Soviets' military superiority, China's unpreparedness for conducting a large-scale war with the Soviet Union, and the absence of a U.S. counterweight to Soviet ambitions, the Chinese may have believed that only a preemptive action against the Soviets could serve China's territorial and security interests without significantly risking the large-scale war that otherwise seemed imminent. The P.R.C. was set to follow Mao's standard behavior in dealing with external crises—that is, to struggle against foreign enemies without engaging in either capitulationism or adventurism. In this regard, a Soviet charge that Chinese soldiers ambushed Soviet patrols on Zhenbao on March 2 seems quite plausible.[232]

Another important Chinese objective was punitive in nature. By either firmly standing up to Soviet military pressure or giving a stunning blow to Russia's aggressive border patrolling, Beijing would instruct Moscow that China would not be weakened or bullied by Soviet military pressure. Moreover, such action would force Moscow to reconsider its border policy and seek to resolve the border dispute by diplomatic means.

There are indications that China's motives indeed included a punitive element. According to a Soviet account of the March 2 fighting, the Chinese set up an ambush of a group of Soviet patrols approaching Zhenbao Island, which suggests that the Chinese were prepared to attack the island by surprise. About three hundred Chinese border guards were involved in the fighting, which lasted only two hours and did not involve reinforcements to the island or the use of air power. The Chinese reportedly inflicted heavy casualties on the Soviet patrols, but did not chase them beyond the island, and allowed them to return to collect their dead shortly after the battle.[233] Following the small-scale, limited fighting of March 2, China's cautious approach to the Soviet Union also suggested that while skirting the risk of escalation the P.R.C. had used a limited military action to affect future policy toward the Sino-Soviet border question. During the week after the March 2 clash, Chinese protest rallies were launched throughout the nation. But in a Beijing rally, not one of China's high-level leaders, not even Premier Zhou, spoke.[234] Formal Chinese protests at that time took the form of notes sent to the Soviet Embassy, and numerous Chinese statements were published by the Information Department of the Foreign Ministry rather than at the level of foreign minister or premier. China's Defense Ministry did not issue a statement.[235] On April 4, several days after Lin Biao's report, it was formally announced that the Beijing leadership was considering a reply to the proposal for border negotiations that Premier Kosygin had presented by telephone on March 21 and that the Soviet government had made formally in a statement on March 29.[236]

The argument is sometimes made that the first Ussuri clash was a product of Chinese bellicosity or adventurism and was probably aimed at encouraging the neo-Stalinists in Moscow to rise up against the ruling revisionists by humiliating the Brezhnev-Kosygin regime, and at frustrating Moscow's plan for the development of Siberia by frightening away thousands of Soviet pioneers in the far east.[237] One might attribute this adventurism to an overflow of domestic radicalism into China's foreign affairs during the Cultural Revolution. But the argument is weakened by the fact that despite the revolutionary upsurge in 1967 and 1968, which was accompanied by heightened Chinese antiimperialist and antirevisionist zeal, China's behavior in dealing with external troubles was very cautious and restrained. As demonstrated in the *Svirsk* incident with the Soviet Union, in the border incidents with India, and in the Hong Kong crisis, the P.R.C. attempted to prevent the incidents from turning into major confrontations. Actually, throughout the Cultural Revolution, as the entire Chinese political system was disrupted and civil disorders occurred nationwide, and as the Foreign Ministry was attacked and its most experienced officers were inactivated, Beijing seemed determined to put foreign affairs in a state of suspended animation rather than undertake new initiatives.

Far from being in an adventuristic mood in the months prior to the Sino-Soviet border clashes, China's leaders seemed worried that Soviet moves to encircle China in collaboration with the United States, Japan, and India might convince Moscow that China was isolated and therefore even more vulnerable to Soviet military pressure on the border. This self-perceived weakness probably reinforced Beijing's fear that any restraint the P.R.C. exercised in dealing with the Sino-Soviet border dispute would be mistaken by the Soviets for weakness and would only whet their aggressive appetite. In this regard, Beijing's hope to correct this kind of Soviet miscalculation may have enhanced China's punitive objective. Such an attitude was revealed in the Chinese warnings that were repeatedly issued after the clashes.[238]

There is no convincing evidence that China's action was prompted by a domestic need to strengthen antirevisionist sentiment at home and to divert dissent, derived mainly from the nationwide power-seizure campaigns, to an external issue.[239] To judge from statements in the Chinese media, Beijing sought to draw a clear line between the purpose of domestic mobilization and that of underlining its fear of war with the Soviet Union. During the Cultural Revolution, the Chinese press continued to criticize everything in the Soviet system, describing it as "a teacher by negative example."[240] This propaganda was obviously intended for domestic consumption to educate and mobilize the Chinese masses around an antirevisionist front by leading them to be fully aware of and to refute Soviet revisionist thinking and practices. It should be noted, however, that the Chinese press did not regularly propagate or dramatize the threat of war with the Soviet Union. As studies of the P.R.C.'s perception of external hostility in 1967–69 indicate, the Chinese press expressed hostility toward the Soviet Union only in response to particular events and developments that from the Chinese perspective seemed threatening. In 1967–68, for instance, following the announcement of U.S.-Soviet ABM planning and collaboration on a nonproliferation treaty that came out of the Glassboro talks, the theme of an anti-China alliance between the United States and the Soviet Union began to receive great emphasis in the Chinese media. After the invasion of Czechoslovakia, China's anti-Soviet perceptions intensified.[241] Until the March fighting occurred, the border issue remained peripheral news, and not a single nationwide or local rally was launched to protest Soviet activities along the border.

Instead, during the second half of 1968 most Beijing leaders deliberately attempted to keep the war problem away from national attention, primarily because of domestic considerations. At a time when China's priority was internal consolidation through class struggle to wipe out hidden enemies, Beijing may have worried that a widespread war scare might divert attention to external problems, thereby delaying and hampering the political clean-up movement and the educational revolution. Even though a war scare might have contributed to domestic mobilization for national unity, it might also have seriously undermined some of the primary programs relevant to internal consolidation.

By the same logic, we are not persuaded that the Maoists manufactured a border clash in order to reinforce Mao's image and strengthen their leadership in the midst of factional struggles and with the Ninth CCP Congress approaching.[242] Despite a lack of evidence to counter this hypothesis, circumstances suggest its weakness. Throughout the Cultural Revolution, Mao remained firmly in command, initiating or at least approving all changes in policy concerning any sudden retreat or upsurge in revolutionary activities. Mao's cult was unprecedentedly established in Chinese society. As the Twelfth Plenum communiqué indicates, after smashing the bourgeois headquarters represented by Liu Shaoqi and completing the formation of revolutionary committees in twenty-nine provinces, the Maoist leadership was ready to convene the Ninth National Congress under "ample ideological and organizational conditions."

Were the border clashes a product of intraparty bickering based on bureaucratic parochial interests? Roger Brown supposes a high likelihood that Mao and Zhou, who preferred to relax tensions with the United States, engineered the border clash on March 2 in order to undermine the political power of Lin Biao and his supporters, who stood for the improvement of Sino-Soviet relations. Brown postulates that Mao and Zhou circumvented the normal chain of command and ordered Chen Xilian (Ch'en Hsi-lien), commander of the Shenyang Military Region, to attack the Soviet border patrol.[243] Harvey Nelsen expresses doubt that Mao and Zhou could circumvent the PLA's normal channel of command, since Lin held such a strong position in China's defense structure as vice-chairman of the MAC and as defense minister. Instead, Nelsen suggests that Lin may have set up the ambush and provoked a war scare in order to perpetuate military hegemony at a time when the party center was preparing to restore normal Communist party control.[244] In any case, both arguments are based on the common assumption that the primary motives in the border decision were bureaucratic interests behind power politics.

As has been discussed, Lin and Zhou did differ over how to solve domestic and international problems, and presented different alternatives with different motives. However, it is our understanding that neither Lin nor Zhou was in a position to advocate a militant Chinese response to the threat posed by the Soviet Union. Rather, in the months prior to the March fighting, the contending alternatives raised by Lin and Zhou were absorbed into Mao's line of opposing the United States and the Soviet Union simultaneously and defusing the growing Soviet threat by means of a limited, preemptive military action without sacrificing the domestic priorities of the P.R.C. There was no hint until the Ninth Party Congress that Lin and his aides had a grand design to take over political power from the party organization and that Mao was suspicious of Lin's mounting power. Lin was formally designated Mao's successor during the Ninth Party Congress. The political rise of Lin, like that of the PLA, as Ellis Joffe puts it, was more the product of unforeseen circumstances than the result of long-range planning and preparation.[245] If they affected China's border decision, bureaucratic interests would have concerned the tactics the P.R.C. chose to deal with the U.S. and the U.S.S.R. simultaneously rather than the basic policy response itself.

So far as the linkage between domestic politics and foreign policy is concerned, our interpretation is that China's domestic instability affected its leaders' perception of the Soviet threat and their policy choice in response to it. Domestic weakness and external threat were again linked in the Sino-Soviet border clashes as they had been in the Sino-Indian border war. In 1967 and 1968, Chinese politics were highly unstable due to political turmoil and civil disorders. Thus, the Soviets' growing vilification of the Chinese path to socialism as well as their verbal and actual support of subversive activities, especially in Xinjiang, probably led Beijing's leaders to believe that domestic weakness might invite foreign intervention. A mounting Soviet threat on the Sino-Soviet border appeared to them to be neither accidental nor independent of China's domestic fragmentation. In this regard, those who favored a militant Chinese reaction probably took into account the consideration that a weak stand toward the Soviet revisionists' threat might well encourage class enemies at home to resist the Cultural Revolution. In early 1966, when Mao started the Cultural Revolution and refused to attend the Twenty-third Congress of the CPSU, he revealed how Beijing's stand on Moscow would affect Chinese politics in the future. He noted that "if we wish people to stand firm, we ourselves must first be unwavering. We shall not go. The leftist faction has stiffened its back, the middle faction is leaning toward us."[246] He reinforced this belief in his speech at the First Plenum of the Ninth Central Committee on April 29, 1969, in which he reminded the party leadership that class enemies at home were dangerous to China when foreign enemies were preparing to attack it. He urged preparations against any evil plan made by the class enemies at home: "That lot [landlords, rich peasants, counterrevolutionaries and bad elements] would be happy to see the imperialists and revisionists attack us. If they attacked us these people suppose that this would turn the world upside down and they would come out on top. We should also be prepared on this score."[247]

A more important aspect of the link between domestic politics and foreign policy is the fact that a primary concern for domestic affairs would restrict the *kind* of strategy Beijing chose in coping with the Soviet threat. Zhou's concern about China's unpreparedness for war with the Soviet Union led him to suggest a diplomatic probe seeking negotiations with the United States as a counterweight against the mounting Soviet threat. Lin's preoccupation with the ongoing antirevisionist campaign and with the domestic ramifications of war preparedness led him to overemphasize a "political frontier defense" and to order border units to use passive and restrained patrolling. The strategy Beijing chose was obviously influenced by domestic factors such as the status of the PLA, the state of the economy, and bureaucratic political perspectives. The limited, preemptive military action that was eventually chosen seems to have been prompted by several domestic considerations—among them, the fact that the P.R.C. was not in a position to wage a prolonged war against the U.S.S.R., primarily because of the PLA's massive commitment to domestic politics and internal security, but also, to some extent, because of the economic costs of such a war. In the months after the March battles, the Chinese press repeatedly emphasized war preparedness against all eventualities, but there was still no hint that the PLA had been ordered to reduce its political role. It was not until August 1969 that the number of troops stationed along the Sino-Soviet border was reduced, but this was accomplished without suspending the PLA's role of "three supports and two militaries."[248] Beijing was not in a position to pour additional resources into rapid war preparations because of the status of the economy, which was in stagnation amid the revolutionary turmoil. In his talk at the First Plenum of the Ninth Central Committee, Mao stressed that "material preparation" should be made "year after year" and on the basis of decentralization: "Don't expect the centre to distribute materials even for the manufacture of hand-grenades. Hand-grenades can be made everywhere, in every province. Each province can even make rifles and light weapons."[249]

It should be noted, however, that China's preemptive action against the Soviet Union also demonstrated that domestic needs would not prevent a forceful response to an external threat. Despite domestic constraints and despite the fact that the international situation was unfavorable to China, the Sino-Soviet border case gives evidence that the P.R.C. will respond to any threat that is perceived by its leaders to seriously undermine its national security. Indeed, the March border clashes remind us that Beijing's decision was made in accordance with another of Mao's well-known standards, one that had appeared in the Chinese press throughout the Vietnam War: "We will not attack unless we are attacked, but if we are attacked, we will certainly counterattack."

7 Politics and Foreign Policy

The Security of China

Looking back on the last one hundred fifty years of China's history, we are struck by the powerful connection that has existed between every leadership's concept and practice of politics and economics, on the one hand, and its foreign-policy decisions and perceptions, on the other. Whether the leadership represented the Qing (Ch'ing) dynasty, the Guomindang, or the Chinese communists, China's external behavior has been molded in significant ways by the character of its domestic affairs. Its place in the world, more so perhaps than that of any other great power, has depended mainly on the strength of Chinese institutions and consensus among its leaders on ideological issues. So long as the country has been domestically sound, its leaders have faced the world with confidence.

Such occasions have been infrequent, however. China has almost always been in turmoil as its leaders have pondered and clashed over the appropriate strategy for producing popular unity and economic growth while fending off imperialism's interventions. Domestic instability has increased China's vulnerability to foreign penetration, thereby further contributing to political disputes and economic difficulties. "Internal chaos" and "external calamities" have indeed reinforced one another in cyclical fashion. Therefore, no Chinese leader can ignore either the foreign-policy implications of domestic decisions or the domestic political implications of foreign-policy decisions. In both cases the security of the Chinese way of life is at stake.

Every crisis studied here reveals the central leadership's concern about China's security. Of particular note is the change in China's understanding of what was being threatened. In 1950, U.S. intervention in the Korean civil war threatened the survival of the P.R.C. only months after its establishment. Imperialism was again at China's throat; hence the primacy of the Asian impulse over domestic (or foreign) revolution. By the late 1950s (the

Taiwan Strait crisis) and early 1960s (the border war with India and the Vietnam War), however, the threat had changed: China's borders were being threatened, but the security of the country as a whole was not in jeopardy. These were times of radical economic and social transformation in China, times when external threats were seen by Mao and his supporters as efforts to hit China while the country was least able and could least afford to counter them. Such remained the case right up to the Sino-Soviet border clashes of 1969, as the Great Proletarian Cultural Revolution was being closed out. The contradiction between the revolutionary impulse and the Asian impulse was resolved in Chinese initiatives to deter and diminish external threats without retreating from domestic economic priorities.

Thus, although the threatening behavior of the two superpowers defined each crisis, it was Chinese domestic politics that largely determined China's response. For the leadership, the crisis was not exclusively a matter of losing territory or strategic advantage. By themselves, these might not have been considered disastrous losses. What made each threat a critical matter was the potential domestic cost of a foreign-policy defeat—that is, passivity in the face of an external threat. On the Right, the revisionists and opportunists could blame Mao's restricted conception of self-reliance for isolating China internationally, forcing China simultaneously to confront two hostile superpowers and keeping its economy and military establishment "backward." Mao's insistence on continuous revolution could be criticized for impairing China's political unity. From the Left—the dogmatists and adventurists—Mao risked being accused of softness in the face of imperialist pressure, and of emphasizing professional (military and economic) interests over politics (permanent class struggle at home and abroad).

Within this probably intense political environment, Mao had to devise a cost-effective strategy that would neutralize or help deter an immediate or potential threat to China *without* worsening the threat, causing dislocations of economic plans, or upsetting the structure of political life. This was no small agenda. His successors, faced with a hostile Soviet Union and Vietnam, must address similar problems.

The Politics of Strategy and Diplomacy

With these introductory remarks, we can return to the propositions set down at the outset of the study. The five cases enable us to refine and enlarge upon the propositions, which get us to the heart of politics and foreign policy making. How useful the propositions are in interpreting China's foreign policy in the 1970s is a topic we will explore in the final section of this chapter.

Our first three propositions define China's international relations and national security in terms of domestic affairs:

1. The chief purpose of foreign policy in China is to protect and promote the radical socialist revolution at home.

2. A quiescent (nonthreatening) international environment is the optimum condition for radical socialist development.

3. Economic performance is considered by Chinese leaders to be the key to national security and international legitimacy.

We have commented on the strong tendency in the literature on China's foreign policy to explain crisis behavior in terms of Chinese ideology (communist expansionism), guerrilla strategy, and intractable domestic problems. Regarding the latter motive, we have often been informed that the Chinese leadership made a bold—even aggressive—foreign-policy move in order to turn attention away from domestic affairs, mobilize the masses, alleviate political factionalism or economic trouble, or promote parochial military interests. In this view, a victory abroad would offset failures at home.

The case studies decisively refute this interpretation of Chinese motives. External threats were not created for domestic political exploitation. China acted because each threat was real, as we have tried to establish. There were differences within the leadership about the imminence of the threat and the best means to confront it. Whether these differences reflected bureaucratic concerns or strategic calculations, the debates do not point to a leadership in search of an external solution to domestic problems. In three instances— during the Korean War, the Vietnam crisis, and the border clashes with the U.S.S.R.—foreign conflicts were used domestically to encourage popular unity. But this happened *after* the conflicts had broken out; and there is no evidence that the conflicts were prolonged for their domestic propaganda value. Moreover, the other two cases—the Taiwan Strait crisis and the Sino-Indian border war—show that major external confrontations will often be shielded from the Chinese public even though they have the potential to be used to promote unity.

Actually, the cases appear to demonstrate that throughout the 1950s and 1960s, China's leaders time and again tried to avoid international confrontations. They "needed" a nonthreatening external environment, not a crisis. Continuous class struggle at home against revisionist thoughts and practices required that China avoid becoming absorbed in a foreign conflict. It was precisely because Beijing could not rely on the Soviet Union for deterrence of threats that by 1958, self-reliance in domestic and foreign policy became critical to Mao. Defense of the ongoing revolution at home, not promotion of it abroad, was Mao's preeminent concern.

Economic self-reliance was central to foreign-policy independence: It would create a self-sustaining economy and defense that would enable China to be free of foreign debts and dependence on foreign advisers, technology, and development models. China's experience of dependency in the nineteenth and early twentieth centuries was surely reinforced, in the minds of Mao and his supporters, by the inequities of "leaning to one side" (that of the U.S.S.R.) in the immediate aftermath of liberation. The Soviets' interest in using Chinese territory for military purposes, as expressed in 1958 and 1965, undoubtedly contributed to Mao's determination not only to acquire an independent nuclear capability but also to speed up agricultural growth, ensure revolutionary continuity in succeeding generations, and decentralize much of the economic and political decision-making process.

At stake was not only the leadership's own estimation of China's strength but also foreign governments' estimations. The country could not afford to be weak or be perceived as being weak; in either case it would be vulnerable to external threats and pressures. Hence our fourth proposition:

4. Chinese sensitivity to external threat is highest at times of domestic political weakness or conflict.

"Weakness" covers a wide range of circumstances: leadership reorganization, factional disputes, economic transition or breakdown, bureaucratic rivalry, and intramilitary dissension, among others. The greater the number of these circumstances that pertained, the more acute was China's sensitivity to nearby events of a potentially threatening nature. The fighting in Korea, with India, and with Soviet border guards illustrates this conclusion well. In each case the P.R.C. leadership seems to have been troubled by the apparent "coordination" of external threats with serious domestic difficulties in China. The leadership was anxious to deflect the threats in a way that would, among other things, convince the opponent that China was not too weak to act decisively in the name of self-protection.

Were Mao and his colleagues "realistic" in their assessment of the threats posed to China's security? For one thing, threat perception may reflect an official's bureaucratic position (see the discussion under proposition 5, below). For another, it may depend on the stability of politics at any particular time. We are all aware of the consistent tendency of government officials everywhere—for example, U.S. policy makers during the Vietnam War—to magnify the threatening aspects of events abroad, to think in terms of the "worst case," and then to overreact in the use of force. The Chinese, our studies suggest, are not immune to this phenomenon, which probably relates to their historically based sensitivity to foreign threats at times of substantial domestic weakness. We therefore offer this corollary to proposition 4:

4.a. Domestic weakness magnifies external threats and may lead to misperceptions or miscalculations of the opponent.

That there were real threats to China in all the cases we studied is, to repeat, clear enough. Moreover, the leaders of China's *opponents* often asserted publicly that China was weak and, by strong implication, vulnerable. The reality of the threats, and the threatening implications of comments from abroad, were sufficient by themselves to make Beijing's leaders apprehensive, and all the more so if they were having to deal with domestic instability. Their perception of foreign threats may have become distorted in the direction of exaggerating them. Although direct evidence is lacking, such misperception may have been an important factor in China's behavior in 1950, 1962, and 1969.

If there were miscalculations of the opponent's response, and misperceptions of the opponent's domestic circumstances, these were shared by *both* sides in the crisis. In 1950, it should be recalled, U.S. leaders believed China was weak and on the verge of collapse. In 1958, the U.S. State Department considered that "dissatisfaction and unrest" on the mainland made communism only a "temporary phase." In 1962, India's leaders seemed to think that China's deep economic troubles would weaken Beijing's response to border issues, while by 1969 the Cultural Revolution had surely given Soviet leaders grounds for unwarranted optimism that the build-up of their border forces would not be contested. China's leadership had reason to assume that foreign leaders who were hostile to China, and who believed that China was weak, would try to test and take advantage of that weakness. This was not always true; in 1958 and 1965 the U.S. government did not want a conflict with China. But foreign leaders were consistently insensitive to the way the Chinese looked at the world, and in particular to their heightened sensitivity about national security at times of domestic weakness.[1]

We proposed in the introductory chapter that an external threat assumes major proportions for the Chinese leadership because of domestic enemies who may be in league with the threatening government.

4.b. The most dangerous aspect of external threat is its subversive influence on revisionist elements within the country.

In 1950 these enemies were pro-Guomindang spies and remnant forces, as well as non-Chinese minorities. During the Taiwan Strait crisis eight years later, the leadership was concerned not only about Guomindang elements but even more so about followers of a revisionist model of economic development who opposed the Great Leap Forward. The border war with India coincided with the ongoing debate in Beijing about economic policy, a debate in which some high-level officials apparently promoted "capitalist" practices at home (*sanze yibao*) while also advocating a moderation of tensions with the superpowers (*sanhe yishao*). In 1965, Luo Ruiqing's proposals in response to U.S. escalation of the Vietnam War were regarded by Mao as a political threat, not only because Mao was contemplating a cultural revolution, but also, perhaps, because Luo's position was perceived as an attempt to draw attention away from those high-level officials Mao suspected of disloyalty. Finally, in the late 1960s, the Chinese leadership was very much aware that in adopting a menacing posture on the border, Soviet leaders hoped to influence the outcome of the Cultural Revolution in favor of the anti-Maoists.

Given the history of foreign meddling in China, Chinese officials are always going to be suspicious of outside interference in their politics. Foreign military threats upgrade those suspicions sharply: The threatening power and its allies may be seeking to influence the distribution of political power in China, and may have the help of Chinese revisionists and reactionaries in doing so. Much more than a commanding power of one faction over another is at stake, however. At bottom is the power to use domestic *resources* to promote a particular pattern of socialist development. Here is where ideology, modernization, and foreign policy come together, for as Chinese communist analysts have interpreted their party's history, a "struggle between two lines" of development—revisionist (protocapitalist) and radical—has been central to all internal party debates. In the various debates over the appropriate strategy and diplomacy for dealing with foreign threats, the core issue has always been How should China's resources—financial, military, labor, technical—be distributed so as to promote socialist development and a radical foreign-policy line? The issue is expressed in proposition 5:

5. *Foreign policy becomes a domestic political issue by addressing economic or political choices that are under debate.*

The appearance of an external threat adds measurably to the urgency of reaching decisions on resource allocations, as all the case studies show. It is here that bureaucratic politics enter the picture. If the threat is commonly perceived by the leadership to be imminent, there is likely to be general agreement on the need to mobilize the country's resources for national security. The Asian impulse predominates. But if agreement does not exist, the likelihood is that there will be a scramble for resources, in which case *perceptions of the immediacy of the threat, and of the PLA's readiness for it, may reflect bureaucratic interests as well as, or possibly more than, the national interest.* The revolutionary or socialist impulse may, in our framework, prevail over the Asian impulse. Thus, perception of a foreign threat may be magnified by domestic insecurity, as suggested by proposition 4.a, or it may be given greater or lesser credence on the basis of an official's bureaucratic position and others' assessments of that person's personal and bureaucratic power. Although in our view the competition for influence among bureaucratic leaders takes place within and not apart from an ideological consensus,[2] there are contradictions between the impulses that create contention. Alignments with or against an official's assessment of a foreign threat *may* depend on whether one stands to gain or lose influence—for oneself and for one's administrative domain—from that official's assessment.

Consider again the 1950, 1958, 1965, and 1969 crises. In the first one, some generals viewed the intention of the Americans as less dangerous and imminently threatening than that of the Japanese in the 1930s. But Mao disagreed and preferred to intervene early in the Korean conflict. In 1958, Mao perceived an immediate threat to China's security from Taiwan; but Peng Dehuai would not agree to deal with it (and may even have disagreed with the immediacy of it), the PLA was not adequately prepared to meet it, and the P.R.C. did not have the Soviet Union as a reliable deterrent. In 1965 it was Luo Ruiqing who saw an imminent U.S. threat, and it was Mao who disagreed. And in 1969, while all the major Chinese leaders perceived a Soviet threat, there evidently was considerable disagreement about the best way to handle it. The "best" way may have depended principally on bureaucratic position. Lin Biao's advocacy of a "political frontier defense" may have been influenced by his concern that the PLA maintain the critical political power it had acquired during the Cultural Revolution, and that it continue to emphasize politics over professional interests. Zhou Enlai, as head of the State Council, may have exaggerated the Soviet threat so as to promote the restoration of popular unity and order and get the PLA *out* of politics. Somewhere between them stood Mao, intent on combatting the Soviets, but quite possibly, as in 1965, worried about enhancing the PLA's strategic role.

In these and other cases, all sides believed they spoke for China's national interests. But Mao perceived that Peng and Luo (and perhaps even Zhou) assessed the U.S. threat from a narrowly professional vantage point, one that would have required unacceptable new commitments of resources and major foreign-policy reorientations. Was he right? While each official's estimate of the threat may have been influenced by his bureaucratic position, the threat was certainly credible. It was a question of judgment: How *imminent* was the threat? There were sound reasons for urging *either* more or less military preparedness, bargaining or not bargaining with Moscow, changing or not changing the PLA's training regimen and strategic role. Deciding whether or not Mao's perception was correct points up the problem of determining whether or not bureaucratic politics were at work. One of the biggest problems with the bureaucratic-politics approach is that it does not provide a means of testing for its presence or absence.

Whether in times of crisis or not, the quality of domestic political life in China will have important effects on the resources the leadership can bring to bear in foreign affairs. As our sixth proposition states:

6. Domestic stability promotes conditions that are favorable to foreign-policy initiatives.

6.a. Domestic instability discourages foreign-policy initiatives.

The greater the instability or weakness, the more likely it is, we assume, that the leaders' energies will be directed inward. In all the cases we studied, domestic instability was an important factor that had to be taken into account as the external environment grew more threatening. In two instances—the crises of 1958 and 1962—Mao effectively dealt with political opponents and faced foreign threats with a reasonably unified leadership. But the economic situation was precarious.

At a time of foreign crisis, competition for national resources probably intensifies, as we have said. But as much as that competition may add to an already unstable domestic scene, a foreign-policy initiative—diplomatic or military—is not precluded. Options are constrained, but initiatives are not foreclosed. When a majority of the leadership (meaning Mao and his supporters) determined the existence of a threat to China, a response occurred, *regardless* of China's domestic circumstances. Mao's watchword, "We will not attack unless we are attacked; if we are attacked, we will certainly counterattack," was meant to convey to opponents that they should not mistake instability for incapacitation. The state of the economy, political authority, and the military—not just the opponent's strength—dictated the nature of China's response.

In keeping with his experiences before 1949, Mao's preferred military strategy was defensive. In 1969 he formulated the "general rule" that Chinese troops would never be sent outside Chinese territory to fight.[3] "Luring deep" rather than "fighting beyond the gates" was his model both for deterring and, if necessary, defeating an invading enemy. But he also favored "tit-for-tat" retaliation in the event China was subjected to threats. This took the form of a preemptive attack in all four cases in which China alone was under threat: an initial large-scale counterintervention against U.S.-UN forces in Korea, followed by a three-week disengagement; a two-front border offensive against Indian troops, followed by a disengagement; an artillery offensive against Quemoy and Matsu, followed by a call for talks with the United States; and an attack on Soviet border guards that months later culminated in the Kosygin-Zhou talks. Even the 1965 Vietnam case falls within the scope of preemption, since the dispatch of engineering, construction, and antiaircraft troops to assist the D.R.V. was probably meant to help deter further U.S. escalation in China's direction.

Mao's desire clearly was to deter or punish the intruder; and except in Korea, where a friendly government's survival (and conceivably China's as well) was on the line, the Chinese used measured force. There was no all-out mobilization of the society, because domestic programs had top priority.

Limited use of force was intended to defuse a crisis and not to win it or expand it. "Tit-for-tat" measures were designed to discourage the aggressor, bring it to its senses, and teach it respect. Therefore, to China's leaders, using force on a small scale not only was in keeping with Mao's domestic concerns but also was necessary to prevent escalation. Such a policy was in every way economical and politically motivated.

The Politics of "Three Worlds"

Our analysis of China's foreign policy has made use of the argument employed by Chinese Marxists that foreign policy is an extension of a country's domestic politics. The contradictions between the "two roads" of socialist development in China, and their reflection in party debates on economic, social, military, and related policies, will in this perspective be manifested in the P.R.C.'s foreign-policy decisions. By the same token, foreign-policy decisions will affect the "two roads" debate and the domestic programs that flow from it. This approach is helpful in understanding not only past crisis behavior but also Chinese foreign policy since Mao's death in September 1976. The "theory of the differentiation of the three worlds" can be regarded not merely as a reflection of China's strategic circumstances but also and more fundamentally as the external aspect of the "four modernizations."

We are asserting that global factors such as Soviet military strength and the increased political influence of Third World countries cannot in and of themselves explain why today China's leaders structure world politics the way they do. Internal factors are at least as important.[4] The U.S.S.R. is the focal point of China's concern, not only because of the military threat it continues to pose to China, but also because it remains a political threat to Chinese-style socialism, even given all the recent changes that have occurred in the content of that socialism. Contrariwise, the threat of the United States has diminished in China's eyes, not only because its power has receded (or so Chinese leaders assert) in Asia and world-wide, but also because its and its allies' technical achievements and capital are now considered essential to China's development. For the current Chinese leadership, as for all previous ones, foreign-policy choices are to a significant extent dictated by the *kind* of socialism being practiced. *Any* socialist program requires some degree of involvement with the outside world. The crucial issue has always been how to define self-reliance—either making foreign participation in China's economy a priority, as Vice-Premier Deng Xiaoping wants, or, at the other extreme, isolating China from all but the most minimal level of foreign trade and depending overwhelmingly on the country's own resources, as the "Gang of Four" wanted. This issue is, of course, the same one that all Third World governments face, whether socialist or not.

As in the past, China's domestic stability is still believed to require international peace, and the strength of China's economy continues to be the key to its national security. But at the risk of overstating developments that are still in flux, the content of these linkages is significantly different now from what it was under Mao. The party and military center is dominated by a modernizing vision—Deng's much more than Hua Guofeng's[5] —that seems to be departing in fundamental ways from Mao's political values and practices.[6] Deng's politics stress centralization of authority; higher output and efficiency in production; material as well as moral incentives to produce; large outlays of state funds for technology and scientific training; specialization (hence, the potential for elitism) in education and labor; scientific management; and renewed invitations to former capitalists and intellectuals to participate in the modernization. The pace for pursuing these objectives, the methods used, and, above all, the political consequences of the objectives—in particular, the deemphasis of class struggle, voluntarism, and mass-line democracy, along with slightly more openness to dissent by individuals—cannot help but have found expression in China's foreign policy.

The "three worlds" theory, we are told, originated with Mao in 1974.[7] At one level the theory—or more accurately the framework—is clearly Maoist. As in past Chinese conceptualizations of world politics, the "three worlds" theory projects class concepts of the 1930s and 1940s into the international arena. The "first world"—that of the superpowers—consists of the big capitalists; the "third world"—the developing states—represents the oppressed peasant masses; and the "second world"—that of other developed socialist and capitalist states—is the national bourgeoisie, a class that both exploits and is exploited. For the present Chinese leadership, as for Mao, the main contradiction in world politics is between imperialism (the "first world") and the Third World. The Asian impulse therefore remains a significant strand in Chinese foreign-policy thinking. Beyond these similarities, however, lie more important differences, which reflect not merely changes in China's strategic environment but also changes in its domestic political values and goals.

For Mao, class struggle to eliminate revisionism in China meant emphasizing class struggle internationally. The revolutionary impulse was a major one; revolution was the main form of struggle by which to resolve antagonistic contradictions. Domestically, this meant that workers, peasants, and others committed to radical socialism would unite against intellectuals, former landlords, and other groups or individuals who were "following the capitalist road." Internationally, Mao pressed for a united front (from below) of anti-imperialist revolutionary movements and parties. Beijing made clear in Mao's time that it would not cultivate relations with capitalist "second world" governments at the expense of revolutions in their colonies and semicolonies, nor would it accept relations with Third World governments that were dependent on and militarily tied to a superpower. The prospects for peaceful coexistence between the socialist and imperialist countries were consequently considered very slight, as were the prospects for peaceful transition to socialism in Third World countries. China established diplomatic relations with regimes of various political persuasions that it considered were truly independent; but for both national-security and domestic political reasons,[8] the Maoists opposed peaceful transition as a general strategy of the international communist movement. For Mao, antiimperialism meant active resistance against *both* superpowers, even when, in 1968, the U.S.S.R. became the primary military threat to China, forcing its leaders to reach out to the United States for contact.

Today, the strongest impulses influencing the Beijing leadership are socialist and Asian, with the socialist modernizing impulse dominating as China experiences less immediate physical danger to its security than at any time since 1949. The domestic united front has been opened to former landlords, rich peasants, and intellectuals with valued skills—a potential new national bourgeoisie. Class struggle has ceased to be a major issue at home—indeed, class analysis has largely vanished, and Mao's foremost opponents of the past (including Liu Shaoqi, Peng Dehuai, Deng Xiaoping, and Luo Ruiqing) have been rehabilitated. Many radical innovations of the Cultural Revolution period that relied on the spontaneity and enthusiasm of the masses have been abandoned or significantly revised. Abroad, China's efforts now center on the protection of state sovereignty against Soviet inroads, not on class contradictions or the seizure of power.[9] China's active support of revolution is confined to South Africa. United-front politics are now "from above," as is true domestically. The front has come to include a new partner, the United States, on the basis that rivalry, not collusion, characterizes U.S.-Soviet relations. For the first time since the early 1950s, China is actively cooperating and coordinating policy with one superpower against another, as shown, for example, in Zaire in 1978 (China's support of the U.S.-backed French and Moroccan intervention in Shaba Province); Vietnam in 1979 (discussed below); and Afghanistan in 1980 (when China and the United States, both before and after the Soviet invasion and occupation, supplied Moslem insurgents with arms, directly and via Pakistan).

Rapid industrialization, agricultural mechanization, and military modernization have stretched the concept of self-reliance beyond the point of recognition. Although lip service is still being paid to self-reliance, in practice Chinese leaders are now prepared to rely heavily on the capitalist world for sophisticated technology, technical expertise, capital, and the education of a scientific elite. The United States and Japan are looked upon as models of corporate efficiency and technological achievement. In the manner of so many Third World countries, China is exchanging raw materials (oil and coal in particular) for technology and investments. The P.R.C.'s trade and credit patterns have changed drastically since 1976: from a balance of imports and exports to an unfavorable balance caused by capital imports from the West, and from nonindebtedness to increased indebtedness as credit requirements expand. The Hua-Deng group believes it can absorb the best capitalism has to offer without witnessing an erosion of socialist institutions and values.[10] But it runs a substantial risk of making China dependent on a world economy dominated by international capitalism (the multinational corporations and financial institutions).

China's military establishment also benefits from the "three worlds" conceptualization. Under Mao and Lin Biao, "politics" was preeminent in the PLA: political rectitude was considered more important than military sophistication, and the PLA's role in domestic affairs outweighed its strategic functions. Early in the 1970s, when it became apparent that a major Sino-Soviet war was not imminent, the PLA's level of procurement of modern weapons and defense systems dropped considerably. The defeat of the "Gang of Four" was a boon to the PLA, whose support was essential to the triumph of Hua and Deng. That support gives the PLA added power to claim a larger share of the budget for modernization. Moreover, with so much stress being put on Soviet "hegemonism," and with the planned build-up of industry in the northeast and elsewhere, military leaders (who for a time included Deng Xiaoping as chief of staff) have "hard" strategic arguments for more money and weapons, particularly for air defense. Supporters of the "professional viewpoint," who once called for acquiring new weapons from the Soviet Union, can now urge getting them from the capitalist world. China cannot yet obtain weapons directly from the United States, but U.S. leaders have clearly encouraged West European military sales to China and possibly even Japanese military contacts with the PLA hierarchy. Judging from Deng's remarks on his visit to the United States in January 1979, China would prefer that these arrangements be strengthened in some kind of anti-Soviet alignment among the United States, Japan, Western Europe, and the P.R.C.[11]

These developments illustrate two sides to the proposition offered earlier that political stability lends itself to foreign-policy initiatives. On the one hand, the leadership is free to explore every avenue for modernizing the country and blocking Soviet advances. On the other hand, it will have to deal with demands from many sectors of the military, the economy, and society, all of which want a "part of the action." There may also be an external price to pay. To the extent that China must rely on foreign sources of technology, credit, and possibly security, its leaders may have to make concessions to other governments' foreign-policy interests that it would not otherwise make or even have to consider. For example, normalization of relations with the United States has occurred at the price of the continuation of U.S. arms deliveries to Taiwan. Chinese criticism of "U.S. imperialism" generally, and of particular U.S. policy moves such as those in the Middle East, have needed to be soft-pedaled. Aid to revolutionary groups such as the Palestinians is likely to be reduced, and diplomatic relations with Israel may be in the offing. The dispute with Japan over oil drilling in contested waters is bound to be affected by China's need of Japanese credit and technology. In short, the P.R.C. leadership now has less leverage in dealing with the capitalist world because of its vastly expanded domestic "needs" that only capitalism can satisfy. Were these needs to change again, the entire structure of China's relationship with the West would change as well—*regardless* of the state of Sino-Soviet relations.

We can illustrate the impact of domestic events on China's foreign policy by taking a closer look at changes in China's relations with Yugoslavia and Vietnam.

Since the mid-1950s, Chinese officials and commentators had engaged in vitriolic attacks on Yugoslavia's social system. In fact, until the Sino-Soviet dispute went public, the Chinese had looked upon Titoism as the symbol of revisionism. They had charged the Yugoslavs with neglecting class struggle and instead pursuing state capitalism under a dictatorship of the bourgeoisie.[12] In the Maoists' view, Yugoslavia's development directly challenged China's emerging commune-based system of the late 1950s and early 1960s, for it was shortly after the Great Leap Forward had begun to falter that the Chinese economy showed signs—such as in the use of material incentives and expanded private plots—of resembling Yugo-slavia's market socialism.[13] (Indeed, the widespread use of "capitalist" practices with the apparent endorsement of Liu Shaoqi and Deng Xiaoping was one reason Mao decided to launch the Cultural Revolution.) In the prevailing Chinese view, Yugoslavia's domestic system *explained* its "foreign policy of praising the United States and slandering the Soviet Union."[14] Yugoslavia was a leading member of the nonaligned movement that had rejected Chinese proposals for strongly supporting revolutionary movements—such as that in Vietnam—against U.S. imperialism.

In 1977, however, Tito made a state visit to Beijing, and in 1978, Hua Guofeng went to Belgrade, at which time the Chinese press heaped lavish praise on Yugoslavia's social and economic systems.[15] Although the beginnings of the Sino-Yugoslav rapprochement can now be traced to the early 1970s, when the Chinese leadership was searching for new allies against the Soviets, it was only after Mao's death and the purge of the "Gang of Four" that the relationship accelerated in terms of tangible ties and mutual appreciation.[16] (The reverse can be said of China's relations with Albania. Once China's closest ally ideologically and in foreign policy, Albania became an outcast in 1977 when its leaders challenged the "three worlds" thesis.) Did Hua's closeness to Tito develop only because of convergent attitudes on Soviet foreign policy and, by then, the nonaligned movement's criticisms of (Soviet) "hegemony"? We would contend that, additionally and especially, changes in China's political economy after 1976 brought the Hua-Deng leadership to view Yugoslav politics (domestic and international) in a new and favorable light.

Tito's domestic policies began to look good to the new Chinese leaders because the efficiency, productivity, and profitability that were said to mark Yugoslav industries had become one of China's central concerns. Although it seems premature to characterize the P.R.C.'s economy as market socialism on the Yugoslav model, Chinese modernization shows numerous signs of adopting some of that model's key features. As one of China's leading economists wrote late in 1979, the time has come to move from centralized planning to enabling enterprises to fix their own production targets and control their own finances. Market forces (supply and demand) and policies (such as government taxation and price manipulation) will determine output and ensure quality.[17] In essence, profitability and efficiency are becoming the chief criteria of a firm's (and a commune's?) contributions to socialism—criteria the Chinese used to call revisionist and now call the basis of scientific management.

The Chinese and Yugoslav Communist parties still have not established relations, and privately Chinese leaders remain critical of the Yugoslav party's departures from Marxism-Leninism.[18] Evidently some Chinese comrades disagree more fundamentally with the sudden burst of affection for Tito.[19] But their leaders interpret the country's domestic modernization and international anti-Sovietism as necessitating a Sino-Yugoslav rapprochement, their argument being that such alignments are temporary but expedient ways of delaying the coming of another world war.[20] How credible that argument is remains to be seen.

The dramatic improvement in China's relations with Yugoslavia is matched by the extraordinary transformation of the Sino-Vietnamese relationship from one of wartime allies to that of military rivals. In explaining this far-reaching reversal, most commentators have cited a number of issues in bilateral relations that emerged either during or soon after Vietnam's war with the United States—for instance, different wartime strategies, the question of Cambodia's (now Kampuchea's) political future, the Sino-Vietnamese border, the overseas Chinese in Vietnam, and ownership of Xisha (Paracel) and Nansha islands. To these surely must be added the two governments' divergent international partnerships: China's decision under Mao, with the Vietnam War still raging, to begin normalizing relations with the United States (which Washington subsequently denied to Hanoi); and Vietnam's decision, as it faced massive postwar reconstruction problems, to expand relations with the Soviet Union. The tensions caused by these developments culminated in Vietnam's invasion of Kampuchea in December 1978; the replacement of a Kampuchean regime friendly to Beijing with one dominated by Hanoi; a series of warnings by Chinese official sources of impending "punishment" of the Vietnamese;[21] and, finally, in February 1979, China's invasion of Vietnam.

Our preliminary assessment of the available evidence leads us to two conclusions about the Chinese action. First, strategic and tactical considerations alone are insufficient to explain it, although they certainly provide important background to understanding it. Political and economic developments inside China are critical elements of the story. Second, when we compare China's invasion of Vietnam with the other cases studied in this volume, we find substantial *continuity in Chinese crisis behavior,* but *discontinuity in the P.R.C.'s foreign policy* before and during the crises.

On the domestic side, the Chinese leadership evidently perceived the escalating number of border incidents and the Vietnamese invasion of Kampuchea as deliberate provocations designed to upset the timetable of modernization. As one editorial put it: "A stable and powerful China irritates both the Soviet Union which is out to seek world hegemony and the Vietnamese authorities who wish to gain hegemony in Southeast Asia. Both feel the need to create difficulties for China. Both seek to disrupt its stability and unity and impede its advance towards the four modernizations by creating border incidents and threatening war."[22] The Chinese may therefore have concluded that they needed to act to alter Vietnamese and Soviet perceptions that the P.R.C. was too preoccupied with domestic affairs to defend its presumed security interests decisively.

Exhibiting strength to dispel perceptions of weakness was consequently an important Chinese motive—as we have seen was the case with India in 1962. At the start of the crisis with Vietnam, the New China News Agency asserted that Vietnam had mistaken "China's restraint and desire for peace as a sign of weakness." As the crisis subsided, a *People's Daily* editorial returned to this theme: "No provocations or intimidations . . . can cow the great Chinese people into submission. The Chinese people are not weak-nerved."[23] In short, at least insofar as Beijing's leaders were concerned, the Soviet threat to China, directed through its "proxies," the Vietnamese, went beyond military and political challenges—for instance, by means of the U.S.S.R.-Vietnam friendship treaty of August 1978 and expanded Soviet influence in Southeast Asia throughout the 1970s—to attempting to destabilize Chinese society.

China's leaders *could* have responded to perceived provocations as they had before the border war with India—by continuing the search for a negotiated resolution of outstanding issues, a search based on the principles of proletarian internationalism and the peaceful settlement of disputes. That they did not may best be explained by considering two related sets of interests—one having to do with the PLA and the other with Sino-U.S. relations—that may have tied socialist modernization to foreign-policy activism. The Vietnam decision, after all, came amid well-known internal debate over modernization philosophy and priorities.[24] Surely there were high-level officials who argued against a new external involvement on the basis that it would take resources away from modernization—as Mao had evidently argued in 1965 during another Vietnam crisis—and (an unprecedented consideration) would risk rankling China's capitalist partners. This viewpoint carried implications that countered Deng's argument that China should "punish" Vietnam on the grounds that its provocations were preventing Chinese modernization from moving forward. If such an internal dialogue took place, the military's vote was undoubtedly crucial.

We have already pointed out how the PLA stands to benefit from the new course of modernization. Military modernization is one of the "four modernizations." Its realization is dependent on friendly relations with the United States, through which military sales and contacts with NATO and Japanese officials, and the direct receipt of technology with military applications, become possible. While it is far from certain that the Chinese military *as a group* supported Deng's determination for war, it is reasonable to suppose that influential figures in it agreed with Deng, on the basis either of "national security" or of the PLA's potential benefits from showing the Americans—as Deng would later imply in Washington[25]—the proper way to handle threats by the "hegemonists."

It is at this juncture that China's "American connection" comes into the picture. Deng had to make sure, both for himself and for his perhaps reluctant colleagues in the Politburo, that U.S. leaders *would not oppose* (if they could not be made to support) China's decision to intervene. His visit to Washington provided the perfect occasion for sounding out U.S. leaders. Deng found that their opposition was not strong, and specifically that they would not "penalize" China for invading Vietnam.[26] Subsequently, the

Chinese leadership did find that there were some external prices to pay for the invasion—the U.S. Congress decided to tie U.S. protection of Taiwan to normalization of U.S.-P.R.C. relations, and a few West European governments expressed concern about continuing to provide China with military technology—but these were modest in comparison with the potential denial or cutting back of capital and industrial technology.

The important fact remains, however, that the views of another power were taken into account in China's decision making during the 1979 Vietnam crisis. Thus the United States, in the Vietnam invasion and therefore quite possibly in future P.R.C. foreign-policy decisions, has become a quasi-ally whose attitude needs to be determined in advance, even if not precisely followed. There are opportunities here for the kind of strategic partnership that Deng talked about in Washington, that some PLA leaders surely find enticing, and that a few U.S. military and civilian officials have (in the context of direct U.S. military aid to China) discussed positively. Should that partnership materialize, however indirectly—and some analysts would say it has already materialized because of Vietnam— the PLA's primary role, which has traditionally been to perform domestic political and economic functions, would change to emphasize its strategic tasks. Deployment of the PLA beyond China's borders, which in the past was confined to only the most dire circumstances, might then be far less constrained by Maoist defense doctrine and limited material capabilities.

In the case of Vietnam, then, domestic considerations, which in the past had restrained China's foreign-policy initiatives, seem to have been instrumental in promoting them. Yet the tactics employed were thoroughly Maoist. The leadership warned the Vietnamese of impending retaliation. The force it deployed was sufficient to substantiate China's strength and teach the lesson it said needed to be taught; but it was coupled with assurances that China did not "want a single inch of Vietnamese soil," only "a peaceful and stable frontier."[27] Beijing then proposed that the two sides "speedily hold negotiations," but its subsequent behavior made plain that any negotiations would have to await completion of the punishment. The fighting was costly to China, as it was to Vietnam; yet China's tactics reflected anew the ability to avoid a prolonged war, which would damage the P.R.C.'s development plans, while also demonstrating the Maoist dictum that all "aggressors" are paper tigers, outwardly strong but inwardly weak.

In its 1964 attack on Soviet revisionism, "On Kruschov's Phoney Communism and Its Historical Lessons for the World," the CCP Central Committee pointed to the strength of capitalist, elitist, and bureaucratic tendencies in Soviet society in order to explain Soviet foreign-policy moves that were inimical to the interests of China and Third World revolutionaries.[28] The implication was that a state dominated by an elite of the Soviet type was bound to want stability, order, and balance in international affairs. China, by contrast, could ensure the continuation of a revolutionary foreign-policy line by keeping to mass-line politics and preventing the rise of a scientific and bureaucratic "new class." Today, sixteen years later, is that critique applicable to Mao's successors?

Notes

Chapter 1

1. Soviet rather than Chinese studies have benefited most from recent research into the policy-making process, although in both instances the case studies have mostly concerned domestic rather than foreign-policy issues. For a concise review of the literature on U.S. and Soviet foreign-policy-making processes, together with suggestions for a general paradigm, see William Zimmerman, "Issue Area and Foreign-Policy Process: A Research Note in Search of a General Theory," *American Political Science Review* 67 (1973): 1204–12.

2. A pioneering work on the general issue of domestic–foreign-policy "linkages" is James N. Rosenau, "Toward the Study of National-International Linkages," in Rosenau, ed. *Linkage Politics: Essays on the Convergence of National and International Systems* (New York: Free Press, 1969), chap. 3.

3. In 1958 Mao was referring to the NATO alliance, and was saying that while publicly the leadership should speak of NATO as an offensive-minded organization, privately NATO should be considered a defense against socialism. See U.S., Department of Commerce, Joint Publications Research Service (JPRS), *Miscellany of Mao Tse-tung Thought (1949–1968)* (Washington, D.C.: Government Printing Office, 1974), 1: 136.

4. See, in particular, John Gittings, *The World and China, 1922–1972* (New York: Harper and Row, 1974); Peter Van Ness, *Revolution and Chinese Foreign Policy: Peking's Support for Wars of National Liberation* (Berkeley: University of California Press, 1970); Ishwer C. Ojha, *Chinese Foreign Policy in an Age of Transition: The Diplomacy of Cultural Despair* (Boston: Beacon Press, 1969); A. Doak Barnett, *China and the Major Powers in East Asia* (Washington, D.C.: Brookings Institution, 1978); David P. Mozingo, *China's Foreign Policy and the Cultural Revolution,* International Relations of East Asia Monograph (Ithaca, N.Y.: Cornell University, March 1970); and Wang Gungwu, *China and the World since 1949: The Impact of Independence, Modernity, and Revolution* (New York: St. Martin's Press, 1977). These works are quite different in scope, depth, and methods, not to mention conclusions; and none of them achieves the kind of synthesis of internal and external elements we have in mind.

5. The translation used here is from Stuart R. Schram, ed., *The Political Thought of Mao Tse-tung,* rev. ed. (New York: Praeger, 1969), pp. 180–90.

6. This essay is most conveniently found in *Selected Readings from the Works of Mao Tse-tung,* hereafter cited as *Selected Readings* (Beijing: Foreign Languages Press, 1971), pp. 65–84.

7. Ibid., pp. 85–133.

8. "Talks at the Yenan Forum on Literature and Art," May 1942, ibid., p. 257.

9. Editorial Department of *Renmin ribao* [People's Daily], *Chairman Mao's Theory of*

the Differentiation of the Three Worlds Is a Major Contribution to Marxism-Leninism (hereafter cited as *Three Worlds*) (Beijing: Foreign Languages Press, 1977), p. 17.

10. Franz Schurmann, *Ideology and Organization in Communist China,* 2d ed., enl. (Berkeley: University of California Press, 1971).

11. See Lin Biao, "Long Live the Victory of People's War!," *Peking Review,* September 3, 1965, pp. 25–27.

12. Lin Biao, speech to the Ninth Congress of the Chinese Communist party, April 1, 1969, ibid., April 30, 1969, p. 31.

13. See, for example, Shi Jun, "On Studying Some History of the National Liberation Movement," ibid., November 10, 1972, p. 8.

14. *Three Worlds,* pp. 20–21.

15. Shi Jun, "Why It Is Necessary to Study World History," *Peking Review,* May 26, 1972, p. 8.

16. Those Chinese who fail to read the historical dialectic accurately are considered either left-wing or right-wing opportunists, depending on whether they underestimate or overestimate the opponent. Such people do not "know that small and big, weak and strong, defeat and victory, and darkness and brightness were all two contradictory aspects, each of which, in given conditions, would transform itself into its opposite." Writing Group of Yunnan Province Party Committee, "Restudying 'A Single Spark Can Start a Prairie Fire,' " *Honqi* [Red Flag], no. 13 (1971), ibid., February 25, 1972, p. 12.

17. Ibid., p. 24.

18. Probably the single best document that illustrates how revolutionary dialectics guides policy making is Mao's "On Policy," written in December 1940. See *Mao Zedong xuanji* [Selected Works of Mao Zedong] (Beijing: People's Publishing House, 1967), 2: 720–28. Subsequent citations in this chapter are to *Selected Works* (Chinese) unless otherwise noted.

19. Mao, "Talk with the American Correspondent Anna Louise Strong," August 1946, in *Selected Readings,* p. 349; italics added.

20. A Chinese folk saying used by Mao in a speech in Moscow, November 6, 1957, in Stuart R. Schram, ed., *Quotations from Chairman Mao Tse-tung* (hereafter cited as *Quotations*) (New York: Bantam Books, 1967), p. 41; italics added.

21. Mao, "Cast Away Illusions, Prepare for Struggle," August 1949, in *Selected Works* (English), 4: 428; italics added. In the remainder of the quotation, Mao says it is a "Marxist law" that imperialists make trouble to their doom, and that it is another "Marxist law" for the people to fight until victory.

22. Mao, "On Contradiction," in *Selected Readings,* p. 120; italics added.

23. *Selected Works* (Chinese), 5: 291.

24. Mao, "The Turning Point in World War II," October 1942, in *Selected Works* (English), 3: 103; italics added.

25. Mao, in a speech in Moscow, November 18, 1957; see *Quotations,* p. 43. See also his "Problems of War and Strategy," November 1938, in *Selected Works* (Chinese), 2: 506–21; italics added.

26. Speech by Mao at a meeting of the Chinese Communist party's Politburo, in *Quotations,* p. 40.

27. Mao, "To Be Attacked by the Enemy Is Not a Bad Thing but a Good Thing," May 1939, in *Selected Readings,* p. 161; italics added.

28. Mao, "On the Correct Handling of Contradictions among the People," February 1957, in *Selected Readings,* p. 473; italics added.

29. This expression, in different words, seems to have been first used by Mao during the civil war with the Guomindang in the mid-1940s. See *Quotations,* p. 45. Mao's most extensive treatment of the "we will not attack" theme came in a speech to the Supreme State Conference on September 5, 1958, during the Taiwan Strait crisis. A good translation of the main points of

that speech is in Allen S. Whiting, "Quemoy 1958: Mao's Miscalculations," *China Quarterly*, no. 62 (June 1975), p. 268.

30. See, for instance, Mao's "Conclusions on the Repulse of the Second Anti-Communist Onslaught," May 1941, in *Selected Military Writings of Mao Tse-tung* (Beijing: Foreign Languages Press, 1968), p. 289.

31. See *Selected Readings*, p. 74; and from a military perspective, "Problems of War and Strategy," *Selected Works* (Chinese), 2: 506–21.

32. *Three Worlds,* p. 50.

33. Mao, "On the Policy Concerning Industry and Commerce," February 1948, in *Selected Works* (English), 4: 204.

34. Mao, "Speech at a Conference of Cadres in the Shanxi-Suiyuan Liberated Area," April 1948, ibid., p. 238. For further discussion of the distinction between line and policy, see Schurmann, *Ideology and Organization in Communist China* (1971), p. 18.

35. Mao, "Analysis of the Classes in Chinese Society," March 1926, in *Selected Readings*, p. 11.

36. Speech to the Eleventh CCP Congress, *Peking Review*, August 26, 1977, p. 43.

37. Mao, "A Single Spark Can Start a Prairie Fire," January 1930, in *Selected Military Writings of Mao Tse-tung,* pp. 65–76; italics added.

38. Quoted in Gittings, *The World and China,* p. 225.

39. Mao, "On Protracted War," May 1938, in *Quotations*, p. 32; italics added.

40. *Peking Review*, special issue, May 23, 1970, p. 9.

41. Mao, "The Situation and Our Policy after the Victory in the War of Resistance against Japan," August 1945, in *Quotations*, p. 110.

42. Shi Jun, "On Studying Some History of the National Liberation Movement," *Peking Review*, November 10, 1972, pp. 8–9.

43. Mao, "On the Chungking Negotiations," October 1945, in *Quotations,* p. 111; italics added.

44. Mao, "On the Correct Handling of Contradictions among the People," February 1957, in *Selected Readings*, p. 472; italics added.

45. *Miscellany of Mao Tse-tung Thought*, 1: 99–100.

46. The 1956 speech is in *Peking Review*, January 1, 1977, pp. 10–25; the 1957 speech is in *Selected Readings*, pp. 432–76; and the 1962 speech is in Stuart R. Schram, ed., *Chairman Mao Talks to the People: Talks and Letters, 1956–1971* (New York: Pantheon Books, 1974), pp. 159–87.

47. Possibly the clearest Chinese statement on the interconnectedness of domestic politics and foreign policy is the lengthy ninth letter of the Chinese Communist party's Central Committee to its Soviet counterpart in 1964. See "On Kruschov's Phoney Communism and Its Historical Lessons for the World," *Peking Review*, July 17, 1964, pp. 7–27. The gist of the letter is that Soviet foreign-policy collaboration with the United States can only be explained with reference to the revisionist character of Khrushchev's rule.

48. Of the many that might be cited, see Mao's "The Chinese Revolution and the Chinese Communist Party," 1939, and "On New Democracy," in *Selected Works* (Chinese and English), vols. 2 and 4 respectively.

49. Ibid. (Chinese), 5: 3–7.

50. *Peking Review*, November 19, 1971, p. 6.

51. In adition to the previously cited books by Gittings and Van Ness, see David P. Mozingo, *Chinese Policy toward Indonesia, 1949–1967* (Ithaca, N.Y.: Cornell University Press, 1975); and Melvin Gurtov, *China and Southeast Asia—The Politics of Survival: A Study of Foreign Policy Interaction* (Baltimore: Johns Hopkins University Press, 1975).

52. *Peking Review*, October 16, 1970, p. 9.

53. "Our country is both poor and blank. Those who are poor have nothing to call their

own. Those who are blank are like a sheet of white paper. To be poor is fine because it makes you inclined to be revolutionary. With blank paper many things can be done. You can write on it or draw designs. Blank paper is best for writing on." From Mao's speech of January 28, 1958, to the Supreme State Conference, in Schram, ed., *Chairman Mao Talks to the People,* p. 92. For an earlier statement by Mao on the virtues of being "poor and blank," see his speech "On the Ten Great Relationships," April 1956, in *Selected Works* (Chinese), 5: 288.

54. The theme that China is a Third World country and "will never be a superpower" may be found, for instance, in a *Renmin ribao* (Beijing) editorial of January 23, 1971, in *Peking Review,* , January 29, 1971, p. 7; in a speech by Vice-Premier Deng Xiaoping (Teng Hsiao-p'ing) before the U.N. General Assembly, ibid., April 19, 1974, p. 11; and in *Three Worlds,* p. 51.

55. John Cranmer-Byng, "The Chinese View of Their Place in the World: An Historical Perspective," *China Quarterly,* no. 53 (January–March 1973), pp. 67–79.

56. In addition to the works cited in n. 4 above, see Bruce D. Larkin, *China and Africa* (Berkeley: University of California Press, 1971); Daniel Lovelace, *China and "People's War" in Thailand, 1964–69* (Berkeley: Center for Chinese Studies, University of California, 1971); and J. D. Armstrong, *Revolutionary Diplomacy: The United Front in Chinese Foreign Policy* (Berkeley: University of California Press, 1977).

57. Zhang Wentian (Chang Wen-t'ien), "Forty Years of Struggle for Peace," *Renmin ribao,* November 2, 1957, p. 2.

58. This is how Chinese analysts explained, for example, Eisenhower's dispatching of marines to Lebanon in 1958 (during a severe economic recession), Nixon's "Vietnamization" of the war and decision to invade Cambodia (at the height of the antiwar movement), the Soviet invasion of Czechoslovakia (when the government was militarizing the economy), and the 1969 border clashes of Chinese and Soviet troops (when Moscow was "beset with difficulties at home and abroad"). Among the many Chinese sources that pursue the theme of imperialism's "need" for foreign crises to offset domestic difficulties, see Xin Feng, "Mighty Ideological Weapon in the Struggle against Revisionism: A Study of Lenin's 'Imperialism, the Highest Stage of Capitalism,' " *Hongqi,* no. 3 (1974), in *Peking Review,* May 17, 1974, pp. 15–18. Here we have a classic example of the mirror image, since Soviet and U.S. analysts have likewise assumed and contended that instances of Chinese "aggressiveness" and "expansionism" could be explained by the P.R.C.'s domestic problems.

59. See, for example, Mao's statement in September 1955, quoted in Gittings, *The World and China,* p. 223; Liu Shaoqi's (Liu Shao-ch'i's) report to the Eighth Party Congress a year later, ibid., p. 206; Mao's speech "On the Ten Great Relationships," in *Selected Works* (Chinese), 5: 270; and Mao's speech at a party conference on propaganda work in March 1957, in *Quotations,* p. 15.

60. Most recently in the major statement in *Three Worlds,* p. 65: "Faced with the gigantic task of speeding up our socialist construction and modernizing our agriculture, industry, national defense and science and technology, we in China urgently need a long period of peace."

61. George F. Kennan, *The Cloud of Danger: Current Realities of American Foreign Policy* (Boston: Little, Brown, 1977), p. 26.

62. See the quotations in Gittings, *The World and China,* p. 229; and JPRS, *Miscellany of Mao Tse-tung Thought,* 1: 115. "It's only a matter of time," Mao said in 1958, but not to be recognized "is better; it allows us to produce even more steel, six or seven million tons. Then they'll all want to recognize us." *Mao Zedong sixiang wansui* [Long Live the Thought of Mao Zedong] (Beijing, 1969), p. 236.

63. From a directive of April 25, 1961, published in J. Chester Cheng, ed., *The Politics of the Chinese Red Army: The Bulletin of Activities of the PLA* (hereafter cited as *The Bulletin of Activities of the PLA*) (Stanford: Hoover Institution, 1966), p. 487.

64. Quoted in Gittings, *The World and China,* p. 235.

65. This concern is typified by a popular slogan of China's first nationalist movement in 1919: *wai zheng guo quan; nei zheng guo zei* ("externally, struggle for national sovereignty; internally, struggle against traitors").

66. "Address to the Preparatory Committee of the New Political Consultative Conference," June 1949, in *Quotations,* p. 38.

67. *Renmin ribao,* March 13, 1967, in U.S., Consulate General, Hong Kong, *Survey of China Mainland Press* (hereafter cited as *SCMP*) no. 3900 (March 16, 1967), p. 30.

68. Zhou Enlai, "Report on the Work of the Government," Third National People's Congress, First Session, December 21–22, 1964, in *Peking Review*, January 1, 1965, pp. 12–13.

69. Editorial departments of *Renmin ribao, Hongqi,* and *Jiefangjun bao* [Liberation Army Daily], "Commemorate the 50th Anniversary of the Communist Party of China," ibid., July 2, 1971, p. 15.

70. Ji Ping, "The Laws of Class Struggle in the Socialist Period," *Hongqi*, no. 8 (1972), ibid., August 18, 1972, p. 8.

71. See ibid.; and Mao, "On the Correct Handling of Contradictions among the People," in *Selected Readings*, pp. 437–41.

72. See, in particular, Wang Jiaxiang, "In Refutation of Modern Revisionism's Reactionary Theory of the State," *Peking Review,* June 24, 1958, pp. 6–11.

73. Editorial departments of *Renmin ribao* and *Hongqi,* "Is Yugoslavia a Socialist Country?," ibid., September 27, 1963, p. 26; italics added. As China's domestic and foreign policies changed in the post-Mao years, however, Yugoslavia's economic programs drew effusive praise from Beijing. The "lesson" of the 1950s and 1960s was shelved.

74. For the text of the letter, see ibid., July 17, 1964, pp. 7–27; the quotation is on p. 9.

75. An Ziwen, "Training Successors for the Revolution Is the Party's Strategic Task," *Hongqi,* nos. 17–18 (1964), in *Training Successors for the Revolution Is the Party's Strategic Task* (Beijing: Foreign Languages Press, 1965), pp. 1–32.

76. "Training Successors—A Long-term Plan for the Revolutionary Cause," *Hongqi,* no. 14 (1964), ibid., pp. 46–47. A parallel campaign in 1964 focused on the philosophy of Yang Xianzhen, who taught in the Beijing Higher Party School. His concept that "two combine into one," thus stressing the reconcilability of contradictions rather than the struggle between them, was attacked for its unacceptable domestic and foreign-policy implications. See, for example, "New Polemic on the Philosophical Front," *Peking Review,* September 11, 1964, p. 12.

77. *Renmin ribao,* March 13, 1967, in *SCMP,* no. 3900 (March 16, 1967), p. 29.

78. "Observer," *Renmin ribao,* June 4, 1967, ibid., no. 3954 (June 7, 1967), p. 19; italics added.

79. Melvin Gurtov, "The Foreign Ministry and Foreign Affairs in China's 'Cultural Revolution,' " in Thomas W. Robinson, ed., *The Cultural Revolution in China* (Berkeley: University of California Press, 1971), pp. 313–66.

Chapter 2

1. Chen Yun's report to the Central People's Government Council at its seventh session, April 13, 1950, in *People's China* (hereafter cited as *PC*), May 16, 1950, pp. 5–6.

2. Yang Peixin, "China Tackles Her Financial Problems," ibid., February 1, 1950, p. 5. This view also appeared in Vice-Premier Dong Biwu's (Tung Pi-wu's) report "Political and Legal Work," *Current Background* (hereafter cited as *CB*), October 7, 1950, p. 1, and in Chen Yun's report in *PC*, May 16, 1950, p. 26.

3. John Gittings, *The Role of the Chinese Army* (London: Oxford University Press, 1967), p. 27.

4. JPRS, *Miscellany of Mao Tse-tung Thought,* 1: 2–3.

5. *Selected Works of Mao Tse-tung* (Beijing: Foreign Languages Press, 1977), 5: 30.

6. Ge Jialong, "Manchuria's Economic Victories," *PC,* June 11, 1950, pp. 7–8.

7. Gao Gang's report in *CB,* August 23, 1950, pp. 1–22, esp. p. 2.

8. Richard C. Thornton, *China, the Struggle for Power, 1917–1972* (Bloomington: Indiana University Press, 1973), pp. 225–26; and NCNA, "Finance and Economics in China, October 1949–September 1950," September ?, 1950, in *CB,* October 25, 1950, pp. 2–3.

9. Kenneth Lieberthal, "Mao versus Liu? Policy towards Industry and Commerce, 1946–49," *China Quarterly,* no. 47 (July–September 1971), pp. 494–520; and Han Suyin, *Wind in the Tower: Mao Tse-tung and the Chinese Revolution* (Boston: Little, Brown, 1976), pp. 24–53.

10. Ibid., pp. 43–44.

11. *Selected Works of Mao Tse-tung* (1977), 5: 30.

12. Gittings, *The Role of the Chinese Army,* p. 27.

13. Allen S. Whiting, *China Crosses the Yalu: The Decision to Enter the Korean War* (Stanford: Stanford University Press, 1968), p. 23.

14. Gittings, *The Role of the Chinese Army,* p. 26.

15. Samuel B. Griffith, *The Chinese People's Liberation Army* (New York: McGraw-Hill, 1967), p. 106.

16. Gittings, *The Role of the Chinese Army,* p. 26.

17. Whiting, *China Crosses the Yalu,* p. 23.

18. Chen Dan, "The People's Army Turns to Production," *PC,* May 16, 1950, p. 17.

19. Ibid., p. 18.

20. Mao's report of June 6, 1950, pp. 27–29; Dong Biwu, "Several Important Aspects of Political and Legal Work in the Past Year," NCNA (Beijing), October 7, 1950, in *CB,* October 19, 1950, pp. 2–3; and Gittings, *The Role of the Chinese Army,* pp. 33–34.

21. Li Shiying, director of the Public Security Department of East China, report given at the Third Plenary Session of the East China Military and Administrative Commission in Shanghai, March 10–16, 1951, in *CB,* June 11, 1951, pp. 1–5.

22. Ye's report to the Joint Conference on City, Labor Union, and Financial-Economic Work in South China, April 9, 1950, appeared in *Nanfang ribao,* May 1, 1950, and in *Review of Hong Kong Chinese Press* (hereafter cited as *RCP*), May 2, 1950, p. 2.

23. Whiting, *China Crosses the Yalu,* p. 20.

24. Gittings, *The Role of the Chinese Army,* p. 37.

25. General Su Yu, "Liberation of Taiwan in Sight," in *PC,* February 16, 1950, pp. 8–9.

26. *Huaqiao ribao* [Overseas Chinese Daily] (Hong Kong), August 17, 1950, in *RCP,* August 17, 1950, pp. 1–2.

27. Cited in Whiting, *China Crosses the Yalu,* p. 21.

28. Cited in *People's China* editorial, *PC,* May 16, 1950, p. 4.

29. *PC,* May 1, 1950, p. 22.

30. In *RCP,* April 16–17, 1950, pp. 1–2.

31. One clue that modernization of the PLA was forthcoming, however, is that the central government assigned Xu Xiangqian (Hsu Hsiang-ch'ien) and Nie Rongzhen (Nieh Jung-chen), both of whom were Russian-trained professional military leaders, to be the first chief and deputy chief of the General Staff in the winter of 1949/50. William W. Whitson, *The Chinese High Command: A History of Communist Military Politics, 1927–71* (New York: Praeger, 1973), pp. 91–93.

32. Ibid., pp. 506, 524.

33. Gittings, *The Role of the Chinese Army,* pp. 269–71.

34. *Selected Works of Mao Tse-tung* (1977), 5: 26.

35. Whiting, *China Crosses the Yalu,* pp. 6–8; and John Spanier, "The Choices We Did Not Have: In Defense of Containment," in Charles Gati, ed., *Caging the Bear: Containment in the Cold War* (Indianapolis: Bobbs-Merrill, 1974), pp. 128–58.

36. *People's Daily,* October 8, 1949, cited in Robert R. Simmons, *The Strained Alliance: Peking, P'yongyang, Moscow, and the Politics of the Korean Civil War* (New York: Free Press, 1975), p. 69.

37. Mao, "The Momentous Change in China's Military Situation," November 14, 1948, in *Selected Works of Mao Tse-tung* (Beijing: Foreign Languages Press, 1961), 4: 287–88.

38. *China Digest* editorial, "Dewey's Defeat," in *Chinese Press Survey* (Shanghai) (hereafter cited as *CPS*), November 16, 1948, pp. 10–11.

39. Gittings, *The World and China,* p. 150, and Simmons, *The Strained Alliance,* p. 55.

40. For the Chinese Communists' debate, see Zhang Mingyang, "Why We Must 'Lean to One Side,' " *World Knowledge,* August 5, 1949, in *CPS,* August 11, 1949, pp. 106–9. Mao took a liberal position in the mid-1940s; see John Service, *The Amerasia Papers,* (Berkeley: Center for Chinese Studies, University of California, 1971), pp. 162–92.

41. Ye Jiashu, "Since Acheson Became U.S. Secretary of State," *World Knowledge,* January 22, 1949, in *CPS,* February 2, 1949, pp. 137–38; Wu Renzhi, "The Watch-and-Wait Policy of the United States," *World Knowledge,* January 22, 1949, ibid., pp. 139–40.

42. Wu Renzhi, "The Watch-and-Wait Policy of the United States," p. 140.

43. Lin Shifu, "China's National Independence and Sovereignty and Her Foreign Relations," *CPS,* May 11, 1949, pp. 40–43, esp. p. 40.

44. For excerpts of that document, see Robert M. Blum, "Secret Cable from Peking," *San Francisco Chronicle,* September 27, 1978, p. F-1; and *San Francisco Examiner and Chronicle,* August 13, 1978.

45. Zhou described the opposition as "the radicals" and said that Mao took a middle road between the two groups. Ibid.

46. Blum, "Secret Cable."

47. Seymour Topping, *Journey between Two Chinas* (New York: Harper and Row, 1972), pp. 81–83.

48. Ibid., p. 83; italics added.

49. Gittings, *The World and China,* pp. 165–66.

50. Topping, *Journey between Two Chinas,* p. 84.

51. On June 24, 1949, sixteen Republican and six Democratic senators asked the president not to contemplate recognition of the Communist forces. Tang Tsou, *America's Failure in China, 1941–50* (Chicago: University of Chicago Press, 1963), pp. 514–15.

52. *CPS,* July 11, 1949, pp. 25–44.

53. Jin Zhonghua, "China's Liberation and the World Situation," *CPS,* June 21, 1949, pp. 176–77.

54. Ibid., October 1, 1949, p. 101.

55. Zhang Mingyang, "New Designs of American Imperialism in the Pacific," *CPS,* July 1, 1949, pp. 14–15.

56. Ibid., p. 15.

57. *Selected Works of Mao Tse-tung* (1961), 4: 415–17.

58. Ibid., p. 416.

59. For instance, Zhang Mingyang, "The Foreign Policy of New China," *World Knowledge,* October 21, 1949, in *CPS,* November 1, 1949, pp. 10–12.

60. Zhou Zhenwen, "The Significance and Effects of the Sino-Soviet Barter Agreement," *Jingji zhoubao* [Economics Weekly] (Shanghai), August 11, 1949, in *CPS,* August 21, 1949, pp. 144–45.

61. See the extracts from Acheson's letter in Roderick MacFarquhar, ed., *Sino-American Relations, 1949–71* (New York: Praeger, 1972), pp. 67–69.

62. *New China News Agency Daily News Release* (Beijing) (hereafter cited as *DNR*), January 18, 1950, p. 74.

63. Ibid., January 20, 1950, p. 83.

64. Tsou, *America's Failure in China,* p. 525.

65. Ibid., p. 529.

66. MacFarquhar, ed., *Sino-American Relations,* p. 75.

67. Ibid., p. 70.

68. Si Mu, "American Policy of Aid for Taiwan and British Desire to Establish Relations with China," *World Knowledge,* January 13, 1950, in *CPS,* January 21, 1950, p. 61.

69. *DNR,* January 4, 1950, pp. 11–12.

70. *PC,* January 16, 1950, p. 4.

71. NCNA (Beijing), February 8, 1950, and NCNA (Shanghai), February 8, 1950, in *DNR,* February 9, 1950, p. 43.

72. NCNA (Beijing), March 2, 1950, ibid., March 3, 1950, pp. 11–12.

73. Ibid., March 1, 1950, pp. 1–2.

74. George F. Kennan, *Memoirs, 1925–50* (Boston: Little, Brown, 1967), chap. 16, esp. pp.375–76.

75. John W. Dower, "Occupied Japan and the American Lake, 1945–50," in Edward Friedman and Mark Selden, eds., *America's Asia: Dissenting Essays on Asian-American Relations* (New York: Vintage Books, 1971), pp. 173–97.

76. In *CPS,* July 1, 1949, pp. 12–13.

77. Ibid.

78. Herbert P. Bix, "Regional Integration: Japan and South Korea in America's Asian Policy," in Frank Baldwin, ed., *Without Parallel: The American-Korean Relationship since 1945* (New York: Pantheon Books, 1973), pp. 183–93.

79. Li Chunjing, "The Problem of the Peace Treaty with Japan," *World Knowledge,* February 3, 1950, in *CPS,* February 11, 1950, pp. 117–18.

80. *Dagong bao,* January 6, 1950, in *DNR,* January 7, 1950, p. 26; *People's Daily,* "U.S. Imperialist Design of Turning Japan into a Military Base for Aggression," in *CPS,* May 21, 1950, pp. 57–59, and *People's China* editorial, "Japan's People Rise in Anger," in *PC,* June 16, 1950, p. 3.

81. *PC,* February 1, 1950, p. 3.

82. *CPS,* May 1, 1950, p. 2.

83. *People's Daily* editorial, "American Lies and the Truth about Asia," March 18, 1949, in *CPS,* April 11, 1950, pp. 97–98; "America's New Aggressive Moves in Asia," *World Knowledge,* March 17, 1950, ibid., pp. 102–5; "Bankruptcy of America's New Policy in the Far East," *World Knowledge,* April 28, 1950, ibid., July 11, 1950, pp. 34–35; and Lin Tienmo, "MacArthur's Intrigues," *World Knowledge,* n.d., ibid., July 11, 1950, pp. 34–36.

84. "America's New Aggressive Moves in Asia," *World Knowledge,* ibid., April 11, 1950, p. 103.

85. Li Youhui, "An Exposure of Imperialist Intrigues for the Aggression of Tibet," *New Reconstruction,* September 22, 1949, ibid., October 11, 1949, pp. 126–31; Hu Jin, "Liberate Tibet to Smash the Diabolical Schemes of the Imperialists," *World Knowledge,* December 9, 1949, ibid., December 21, 1949, pp. 62–64; and *Progress Daily* (Tianjin), February 27, 1950, ibid., March 11, 1950, pp. 35–37.

86. NCNA (Beijing), January 20, 1950, in *DNR,* January 21, 1950, pp. 90–91; and NCNA (Beijing), January 30, 1950, ibid., January 31, 1950, p. 139.

87. Hu Jin, "Liberate Tibet," p. 62.

88. In particular, see Simmons, *The Strained Alliance,* chap. 5.

89. Raymond L. Garthoff, ed., *Sino-Soviet Military Relations* (New York: Praeger, 1966), pp. 83–84; Donald S. Zagoria, "Choices in the Postwar World: Containment and China," in Gati, ed., *Caging the Bear,* pp. 115–16.

90. Gittings, *The World and China,* p. 149.

91. "Interviewing Soviet Ambassador Roschin," *Newsweek* (Shanghai), in *CPS,* May 21, 1949, p. 82.

92. Simmons, *The Strained Alliance,* p. 65.

93. Schram, ed., *Chairman Mao Talks to the People*, p. 191.

94. Harrison E. Salisbury, *War between Russia and China* (New York: W. W. Norton, 1969), pp. 93–98; Oliver Edmund Clubb, *China and Russia: The Great Game* (New York: Columbia University Press, 1971), pp. 399–407.

95. Clubb, *China and Russia*, p. 406.

96. Schram, ed., *Chairman Mao Talks to the People*, p. 191.

97. *DNR*, January 4, 1950, p. 11.

98. Gittings, *The World and China*, pp. 153–54.

99. David Floyd, *Mao against Khrushchev* (New York: Praeger, 1963), p. 12.

100. Ibid., pp. 11–16.

101. Fei Xiaotong, "On the Distinction between New Patriotism and Nationalism," *Dagong bao*, January 29, 1950, in *CPS*, February 11, 1950, pp. 109–10.

102. *CPS*, March 11, 1950, pp. 33–34.

103. NCNA editorial, "New Era of Sino-Soviet Friendship," February 15, 1950, in *PC*, March 1, 1950, pp. 30–32; and articles by Zhu De, Deputy Chief of Staff Nie Rongzhen, and Guo Moruo on the commemoration of the founding of the Soviet Army, *DNR*, February 24, 1950, pp. 115–17.

104. Cited in Gittings, *The World and China*, p. 155.

105. See Whiting, *China Crosses the Yalu*, p. 43–44; and Simmons, *The Strained Alliance*, pp. 102–30.

106. For instance, see the *People's China* article "An Armed People Opposes Armed Counter-Revolution," *PC*, July 1, 1950, pp. 11–13.

107. Nikita S. Khrushchev, *Khrushchev Remembers: The Last Testament*, ed. and trans. Strobe Talbott (Boston: Little, Brown, 1970), p. 401.

108. Cited in Edward Friedman, "Problems in Dealing with an Irrational Power," in Friedman and Selden, eds., *America's Asia*, p. 216; see also NCNA commentary, January 25, 1950, "Armed Struggle of South Korean People Enters New Phase," in *DNR*, January 26, 1950, p. 119.

109. For an extract of Truman's statement on the mission of the Seventh Fleet in the Formosa area, see MacFarquhar, ed., *Sino-American Relations*, p. 83.

110. U.S., Department of the Army, *Korea: 1950* (Washington, D.C.: Government Printing Office, 1952), pp. 13–20; and Whiting, *China Crosses the Yalu*, pp. 47–48.

111. Whiting, *China Crosses the Yalu*, pp. 53–57.

112. *PC*, July 16, 1950, p. 4.

113. NCNA (Beijing), June 30, 1950, in *DNR*, July 1, 1950, p. 1; and NCNA (Beijing), July 3, 1950, ibid., July 4, 1950, pp. 21–22.

114. *PC*, July 16, 1950, p. 26.

115. Kavalarm M. Panikkar, *In Two Chinas: Memoirs of a Diplomat* (London: George Allen and Unwin, 1955), pp. 103–4.

116. *PC*, July 16, 1950, p. 26.

117. *DNR*, July 21, 1950, pp. 135–36.

118. *Xingdao ribao* correspondent in Guangzhou, July 8, 1950, in *RCP*, July 9–10, 1950, p. 2; *Xingdao ribao*, July 13, 1950, ibid., July 13, 1950, p. 2; and *Huaqiao ribao*, July 27, 1950, ibid., n.d., p. 3.

119. Whiting, *China Crosses the Yalu*, pp. 64–65.

120. *Huaqiao ribao*, August 15, 1950, in *RCP*, August 15, 1950, p. 3.

121. Whiting, *China Crosses the Yalu*, pp. 68–71.

122. *DNR*, August 13, 1950, p. 89; ibid., August 17, 1950, p. 119.

123. *PC*, September 1, 1950, p. 4.

124. Whiting, *China Crosses the Yalu*, p. 84.

125. For China's protests to the U.S. government, and Zhou Enlai's first and second messages to the UN, see *PC*, September 1, 1950, pp. 26–27.

126. *DNR,* August 30, 1950, pp. 205–6.

127. *PC,* September 1, 1950, p. 3.

128. U.S., Department of the Army, *Korea: 1950,* pp. 147–51.

129. Zhou Enlai's cable to Sir Gladwyn Jebb, president of the UN Security Council, September 16, 1950, in *DNR,* September 17, 1950 p. 107; and Harold C. Hinton, *Communist China in World Politics* (Boston: Houghton Mifflin, 1966), pp. 212–13.

130. Panikkar, *In Two Chinas,* p. 108.

131. *CB,* October 5, 1950, p. 6.

132. Panikkar, *In Two Chinas,* p. 110.

133. U.S., Department of the Army, *Korea: 1950,* p. 151.

134. *Selected Works of Mao Tse-tung* (1977), 5: 43.

135. U.S., Department of the Army, *Korea: 1950,* pp. 152–53.

136. Whiting, *China Crosses the Yalu,* pp. 148–49.

137. Griffith, *The Chinese People's Liberation Army,* p. 134.

138. Friedman, "Problems in Dealing with an Irrational Power," pp. 233–34.

139. *SCMP,* no. 8 (November 10–12, 1950), p. 22.

140. Whiting, *China Crosses the Yalu,* pp. 148–49; and Panikkar, *In Two Chinas,* p. 115.

141. Khrushchev's memoirs do not indicate a precise date for Zhou's visit to Moscow, only that it was made shortly after UN forces landed at Inchon. See Talbott, ed. and trans., *Khrushchev Remembers,* p. 405.

142. Huang Hua, "Report on the World Situation" (July 30, 1977), *Issues and Studies* (Taibei) 14 (January 1978): 113.

143. The Soviet press in November and December hinted that the Chinese offensive was timed by Mao and was primarily a Chinese affair. See Max Beloff, *Soviet Policy in the Far East, 1944–51* (London: Oxford University Press, 1953), pp. 194–95.

144. Clubb, *China and Russia,* p. 391.

145. Simmons, *Strained Alliance,* pp. 180–81.

146. For various accounts of Soviet passivity to U.S. action in spreading the war to North Korea and the areas bordering China and the Soviet Union, see ibid., pp. 149–60, 164–68, and 176–82.

147. General Ye Jianying's speech, October 6, 1950, in *CB,* December 18, 1950, p. 5; and Liao Kailong, "Smash the U.S. Imperialist Intrigue of War Expansion," *Observer,* no. 9 (n.d.), in *CPS,* November 21, 1950, pp. 75–76.

148. *SCMP,* no. 17 (November 26–27, 1950), pp. 21–22.

149. Chow Ching-wen, *Ten Years of Storm* (New York: Holt, Rinehart, and Winston, 1960), p. 117.

150. Gittings, *The World and China,* p. 183. The document is ambiguous about the time when Chen Yun made his argument—before or after China's entry into the war. We assume he held that position throughout 1950, and possibly later.

151. *SCMP,* no. 5 (November 7, 1950), pp. 4–5.

152. "Red Guard Paper," February 1967, in *Far Eastern Economic Review,* October 2, 1969, p. 25; and James C. Hsiung, *Ideology and Practice: The Evolution of Chinese Communism* (New York: Preager, 1970), p. 172.

153. *People's Daily* editorial, November 6, 1950, p. 5.

154. He Sheng, "Aid to Korea Necessary to Resist U.S.," *World Knowledge* 22, no. 19 (n.d.), in *CPS,* December 1, 1950, pp. 100–101.

155. "Why is U.S. Aggression in Korea Intolerable to Us?," *People's Daily,* November 5, 1950, in *CPS,* November 21, 1950, p. 171.

156. *CB,* December 18, 1950, p. 3.

157. Cited in Whiting, *China Crosses the Yalu,* p. 141.

158. For instance, *Dagong bao* said on November 27: "With the military might of the Soviet Union as powerful as it is, the problem in Korea should be easily settled with the

dispatch of Soviet forces," but "Chinese security was more threatened than the Soviets were." See *SCMP,* no. 17 (November 26–27, 1950), p. 21.

159. Lu Dejun, "An Account of the U.S. Seventh Fleet and American Imperialist Designs on Taiwan," *New Observer* 1, no. 2 (n.d.) in *CPS,* August 11, 1950, pp. 140–43; and "Oppose New Aggressive Plot against Taiwan," *World Knowledge* 22, no. 15 (n.d.), ibid., November 1, 1950, pp. 4–6.

160. Lin Tianmo, "Korean War and Japan," *World Knowledge* 22, no. 4 (n.d.), ibid, August 11, 1950, pp. 135–39; Wei Zhen, "The Japanese Peace Treaty and U.S. Imperialism's Plot," *World Knowledge* 22, no. 16 (n.d.), ibid, November 11, 1950, pp. 33–37; and *PC* editorial of December 16, 1950, *PC,* December 16, 1950, pp. 3–4.

161. *SCMP,* no. 8 (November 10–12, 1950), p. 23.

162. J.D. Simmonds, *China's World: The Foreign Policy of a Developing State* (New York: Columbia University Press, 1970), pp. 20–21.

163. *People's Daily* editorial, December 23, 1950, in *CB,* July 24, 1951, pp. 7–8.

164. Chen Yi's speech, October 29, 1951, ibid, November 27, 1951, p. 6.

165. Ezra Vogel, "Land Reform in Kwangtung, 1951–53: Central Control and Localism," *China Quarterly,* no. 38 (April–June 1969), pp. 34–35.

166. Whitson, *The Chinese High Command,* pp. 94, 524.

167. *The Case of P'eng Teh-huai: 1959–1968* (Hong Kong: Union Research Institute, 1968), p. 153.

168. Alexander L. George, *The Chinese Communist Army in Action: The Korean War and Its Aftermath* (New York: Columbia University Press, 1967), p. 164.

169. "How to Understand the United States," *Shishi shouce* [Current Events Handbook], November 5, 1950, in *CB,* November 29, 1950, p. 3.

170. *Guangming Daily* editorial, November 2, 1950, in *SCMP,* no. 3 (November 3–4, 1950), p. 10.

171. NCNA (Mukden), October 31, 1950, ibid, no. 1 (November 1, 1950), pp. 15–16.

172. On Chinese and American misperceptions before and during the Korean War, see John G. Stoessinger, *Nations In Darkness: China, Russia, and America* (New York: Random House, 1971), chap. 4.

173. A joint proclamation by the Southwest Military and Administrative Committee and the PLA's Southwest Military Command, November 9, 1950, in *PC,* December 1, 1950, p. 9; NCNA (Chongqing [Chungking]), October 24, 1950, in *DNR,* October 25, 1950, p. 187.

174. Gittings, *The World and China,* p. 183.

175. NCNA (Beijing), July 20, 1950, in *DNR,* July 21, 1950, pp. 136–37.

176. General Liu referred to the main tasks for Southwest China as the liberation of Tibet, the rehabilitation of the war-wrecked economy, and a balanced budget. As he stated, "Part of the PLA in the Southwest is to be demobilized in order to cut down government expenditure" (*DNR,* August 12, 1950, p. 84).

177. *People's Daily,* March 28, 1951, in *CB,* July 12, 1951, p. 4. A New Year's Day editorial of *People's Daily* stated that in 1951, "the Chinese people must regard as their primary tasks consolidation of national defense and development of struggle against imperialism, and must couple this task with tasks of economic construction so that they mutually help each other" (*SCMP,* no. 40 [January 1–3, 1951], p. 2).

Chapter 3

1. Richard H. Solomon, *Mao's Revolution and the Chinese Political Culture* (Berkeley: University of California Press, 1971), pp. 351–56.

2. *Documents of the Chinese Communist Party Central Committee, September 1958–April 1969* (Hong Kong: Union Research Institute, 1971), 1: 47–69.

3. Solomon, *Mao's Revolution,* pp. 357–58.

4. Speech to the Supreme State Conference, January 28, 1958, in *Chinese Law and Government* 1, no. 4 (Winter 1968/69): 10–12.

5. Jerome Ch'en, ed., *Mao Papers: Anthology and Bibliography* (London: Oxford University Press, 1970), pp. 57–76.

6. *Peking Review,* March 4, 1958, pp. 8–11.

7. Michel Oksenberg, "Policy-making under Mao Tse-tung, 1949–1968," *Comparative Politics* 3, no. 3 (April 1971): 329–30.

8. U.S., Department of Commerce, Joint Publications Research Service (JPRS), no. 49,826 (*Translations on Communist China,* no. 90), February 12, 1970, p. 50.

9. Solomon, *Mao's Revolution*; and Roderick MacFarquhar, "Communist China's Intra-party Dispute," *Pacific Affairs* 31, no. 4 (December 1958): 323–35.

10. Ch'en, ed., *Mao Papers,* p. 75.

11. *Documents of the Chinese Communist Party Central Committee,* 1: 305–9.

12. In December 1958 at the Wuchang Central Committee Plenum; see JPRS, *Miscellany of Mao Tse-tung Thought,* 1: 140.

13. MacFarquhar, "Communist China's Intra-party Dispute," pp. 328–32.

14. Gittings, *The Role of the Chinese Army,* pp. 167–69; Ellis Joffe, *Party and Army: Professionalism and Political Control in the Chinese Officer Corps, 1949–1964* (Cambridge Mass.: Harvard University Press, 1965).

15. NCNA (Beijing), October 19, 1958, in *SCMP,* no. 1881 (October 24, 1958), p. 8.

16. *Jiefangjun bao* editorial, July 1, 1958, ibid., pp. 3–5.

17. Gittings, *The Role of the Chinese Army,* p. 167.

18. Statistics are from ibid., p. 305, and the budget report of Li Xiannian on June 29, 1957, is in *CB,* July 5, 1957, pp. 1–31.

19. Gittings, *The Role of the Chinese Army,* p. 305.

20. *Renmin ribao,* August 1, 1957, in *SCMP,* no. 1596 (August 22, 1957), pp. 11–16.

21. For example, see Marshal Zhu De's speech for Army Day, NCNA (Beijing), July 31, 1958, in *CB,* August 6, 1958, p. 2.

22. *Jiefangjun bao* editorial, April 9, 1958, in *SCMP,* no. 1786 (June 6, 1958), pp. 9–10.

23. Gittings, *The Role of the Chinese Army,* p. 181.

24. NCNA (Chongqing), May 22, 1957, in *SCMP,* no. 1539 (May 28, 1957), p. 10.

25. *SCMP,* no. 1786 (June 6, 1958), p. 5. For evidence of protests against this policy by military professionals, see Joffe, *Party and Army,* pp. 85–87.

26. Gittings, *The Role of the Chinese Army,* pp. 208–09.

27. Ibid., pp. 202–3, 212; and Joffe, *Party and Army,* pp. 87–91.

28. Alice Langley Hsieh, *Communist China's Strategy in the Nuclear Era* (Englewood Cliffs, N.J.: Prentice-Hall, 1962), pp. 142–44.

29. Ibid., pp. 144–46; and Joffe, *Party and Army,* p. 85.

30. January 1962 speech to 7,000 party cadres; see U.S., Department of Commerce, Joint Publications Research Service (JPRS), no. 50,792 (*Translations on Communist China,* no. 109), June 23, 1970, p. 52.

31. Speeches of June 28, 1958, in *Chinese Law and Government* 1, no. 4 (Winter 1968/69): 15–21.

32. Joffe, *Party and Army,* p. 110.

33. *Jiefangjun pao* editorial, August 1, 1958, in *SCMP,* no. 1881 (October 24, 1958), pp. 1–3. See also the Army Day speeches of Zhu De, NCNA (Beijing), July 31, 1958, in *CB,* August 6, 1958, pp. 1–4, and of He Long, *Renmin ribao,* August 8, 1958, ibid., pp. 5–6.

34. See the speeches in *CB,* August 8, 1958, pp. 7–14.

35. Hsieh, *Communist China's Strategy in the Nuclear Era,* pp. 26, 34ff.

36. Ibid., pp. 108, 111–12.

37. Ch'en, ed., *Mao Papers*, p. 84.

38. *The Case of P'eng Teh-huai*, pp. 7–13, 40, 147, 164–65, 198ff.

39. See his 1959 article for the party journal *Hongqi*, reprinted in Center for Research on China Problems, ed., *Lin Biao quanji* [Collected Writings of Lin Biao] (Hong Kong: Zelian Chubanshe, 1970), pp. 150–51. In May 1958 Lin was elected a CCP Central Committee vice-chairman and a member of the Standing Committee of the party's Politburo.

40. Speech of March 12, 1957; see *Quotations*, p. 15; italics added.

41. Talbott, ed. and trans., *Khrushchev Remembers.*

42. JPRS, *Miscellany of Mao Tse-tung Thought,* 1:56.

43. Editorial departments of *Renmin ribao* and *Hongqi,* "The Origin and Development of the Differences between the Leadership of the CPSU and Ourselves," *Peking Review,* September 13, 1963, p. 12.

44. Morton H. Halperin, "Sino-Soviet Nuclear Relations, 1957–60," in Halperin, ed., *Sino-Soviet Relations and Arms Control* (Cambridge, Mass.: MIT Press, 1967), p. 121.

45. On Khrushchev's thinking, see ibid., pp. 122–23.

46. "The Origin and Development of the Differences between the Leadership of the CPSU and Ourselves."

47. Talbott, ed. and trans., *Khrushchev Remembers,* pp. 258–59.

48. Halperin, ed., *Sino-Soviet Relations,* pp. 124–28.

49. Ibid., pp. 128–30.

50. Talbott, ed. and trans., *Khrushchev Remembers,* pp. 273, 276.

51. Tang Tsou, "Mao's Limited War in the Taiwan Strait," *Orbis* 3, no. 3 (Fall 1959): 335–36; Oliver Edmund Clubb, "Formosa and the Offshore Islands in American Policy, 1950–1955," *Political Science Quarterly* 74, no. 4 (December 1959): 517–31.

52. Tang Tsou, "The Quemoy Imbroglio: Chiang Kai-shek and the United States," *Western Political Quarterly* 12, no. 4 (December 1959): 1075, 1077; Dwight D. Eisenhower, *Waging Peace, 1956–1961* (Garden City, N.Y.: Doubleday, 1965), p. 293.

53. Tsou, "The Quemoy Imbroglio," p. 1075, n. 2.

54. Leon V. Sigal, "The 'Rational Policy' Model and the Formosa Strait Crisis," *International Studies Quarterly* 14, no. 2 (June 1970): 134.

55. See, for example, ibid., p. 126.

56. U.S., Department of State, *Department of State Bulletin,* vol. 37, no. 942 (July 15, 1957), pp. 91–95.

57. Ibid., no. 935 (May 27, 1957), pp. 854–55.

58. *New York Times,* May 7, 1957, pp. 1, 5.

59. Ibid., January 4, 1957, p. 9.

60. Ibid., May 3, 1958, p. 4.

61. Hinton, *Communist China in World Politics,* pp. 263–64.

62. Kenneth T. Young, Jr., *Negotiating with the Chinese Communists: The United States Experience, 1953–1967* (New York: McGraw-Hill, 1968), chap. 4 and app. C.

63. Ibid., chap. 5.

64. *New York Times,* March 6, 1957, p. 11.

65. Tsou, "The Quemoy Imbroglio," p. 1078.

66. Eisenhower's memoirs (*Waging Peace,* pp. 298–99) reveal an awareness of Chiang's strategy, as in the statement that Chiang's "concern over Quemoy's vulnerability to blockade [and his request for a commitment of full U.S. power to defend the island] seemed totally inconsistent with his earlier insistence on loading down the offshore islands with far more troops than were necessary for defensive purposes."

67. Ibid., p. 296.

68. Ibid.

69. *Zhongyang ribao* [Central Daily News] (Taibei), July 11, 1958.

70. U.S., Department of State, *Department of State Bulletin,* vol. 39, no. 1002 (September 8, 1958), pp. 385–90.

71. Morton H. Halperin and Tang Tsou, "The 1958 Quemoy Crisis," in Halperin, ed., *Sino-Soviet Relations,* p. 275; and Allen S. Whiting, "Quemoy 1958: Mao's Miscalculations," *China Quarterly,* no. 62 (June 1975), p. 266. Whiting reports that "jet fighters occupied airfields in Fukien [Fujian] and Chekiang [Zhejiang] which had been completed more than a year earlier but never regularly utilized."

72. *Zhongyang ribao,* March 9, 1958.

73. Eisenhower, *Waging Peace,* p. 292; italics added.

74. Joyce Kallgren, "Nationalist China's Armed Forces," *China Quarterly,* no. 15 (July–September 1963), p. 38.

75. *New York Times,* March 17, 1958, p. 10; *Zhongyang ribao,* May 17, 1958.

76. *Zhongyang ribao,* January 21, 1958.

77. See, for example, NCNA (Beijing), English-language broadcast of April 5, 1958; Radio Beijing, in Mandarin, May 2, 1958; Radio Beijing, in Mandarin, broadcast of a "Commentator" article in *Renmin ribao,* May 2, 1958; *Renmin ribao,* May 3, 1958, p. 5; and Radio Beijing, Mandarin broadcast of a *Renmin ribao* article, July 14, 1958.

78. See, for example, "Commentator," *Renmin ribao,* April 11 and May 3, 1958, p. 5.

79. NCNA (Beijing), May 29, 1958, in *SCMP,* no. 1781 (May 29, 1958), p. 45; and Xiao Yi, "U.S. Imperialists Get Out of Taiwan!," *Shijie zhishi* [World Knowledge], August 5, 1958, pp. 11–13.

80. Announcement of the Chinese Ministry of Foreign Affairs, April 12, 1958, in *Zhonghua renmin gongheguo duiwai guanxi wenjianji* [Documents of the Foreign Relations of the P.R.C.] (hereafter cited as *Duiwai guanxi*), Vol. 5 (1958) (Beijing: Shijie zhishi Chubanshe, 1959), pp. 88–89.

81. Ibid., pp. 138–40.

82. Young, *Negotiating with the Chinese Communists,* p. 140.

83. *Duiwai guanxi,* pp. 140–41.

84. See, for example, the Chinese government statement in NCNA (Beijing), May 15, 1958, in *SCMP,* no. 1775 (May 29, 1958), pp. 33–34.

85. Neville Maxwell, *India's China War* (Garden City, N.Y.: Doubleday, Anchor, 1972), p. 100; *New York Times* Staff, *The Pentagon Papers* (New York: Bantam Books, 1971), p. 137.

86. George N. Patterson, *Tibet in Revolt* (London: Faber and Faber, 1960), p. 153.

87. *Duiwai guanxi,* p. 235.

88. P.R.C. government statement as reported by NCNA (Beijing), July 16, 1958, in *SCMP,* no. 1816 (July 22, 1958), p. 1.

89. NCNA (Beijing), July 17, 1958, ibid., no.1817 (July 23, 1958), pp. 23–24.

90. Xiao Yi, "U.S. Imperialists Get Out of Taiwan!," pp. 11–13.

91. *Peking Review,* September 9, 1958, p. 16.

92. In *SCMP,* no. 1829 (August 11, 1958), pp. 43–44.

93. See Chen Yi's statement of September 20, 1958, in Chinese People's Institute of Foreign Affairs, ed., *Oppose U.S. Military Provocations in the Taiwan Strait Area* (Beijing: Foreign Languages Press, 1958), p. 10; Peng Zhen's speech of September 7, 1958, ibid., pp. 27–28; "Observer," *Peking Review,* September 23, 1958, pp. 7–8; and Peng Dehuai's message of October 6, 1958, to compatriots on Taiwan, ibid., October 7, 1958 (supp.), p. 1.

94. Tsou, "Mao's Limited War in the Taiwan Strait," p. 340.

95. *New York Times,* August 29, 1958, p. 3.

96. Ibid.

97. Tsou, "Mao's Limited War in the Taiwan Strait," pp. 339–40; Tang Tsou, *The Embroilment over Quemoy: Mao, Chiang, and Dulles* (Salt Lake City: Institute of International Studies, University of Utah, 1959), pp. 10–11.

98. *Duiwai guanxi,* pp. 8–24.

99. Ibid., p. 223.

100. JPRS, *Miscellany of Mao Tse-tung Thought,* pp. 100, 108.

101. Indeed, many articles in Chinese publications of that time struck the same note: The American economic recession was rupturing the capitalist system, weakening the Western camp, but was also propelling it toward "exporting crises" and intervention in the Third World. See, for example, Ji Long, "The International Situation of Developing Struggle," *Shijie zhishi,* July 5, 1958, pp. 6–8.

102. JPRS, *Miscellany of Mao Tse-tung Thought,* p. 115.

103. See Hsieh, *Communist China's Strategy in the Nuclear Era,* chaps. 2–3.

104. Talbott, ed. and trans., *Khrushchev Remembers,* p. 262.

105. John R. Thomas, "Soviet Behavior in the Quemoy Crisis of 1958," *Orbis* 6, no. 1 (Spring 1962): 40.

106. Talbott, ed. and trans., *Khrushchev Remembers,* pp. 257–58.

107. In *Chinese Law and Government* 1, no. 4 (Winter 1968/69): 88; and in JPRS, *Miscellany of Mao Tse-tung Thought,* p. 135.

108. "The Origin and Development of the Differences between the Leadership of the C.P.S.U. and Ourselves."

109. Talbott, ed. and trans., *Khrushchev Remembers,* pp. 258–59.

110. Ibid., p. 262.

111. Speech of September 24, 1962, in *Chinese Law and Government* 1, no. 4 (Winter 1968/69): 88.

112. *Duiwai guanxi,* pp. 144–47.

113. Thomas, "Soviet Behavior in the Quemoy Crisis of 1958," pp. 41–42; *Pravda's* "Observer," in *Renmin ribao,* September 1, 1958, p. 4.

114. Thomas, "Soviet Behavior in the Quemoy Crisis of 1958," pp. 41–42.

115. Ibid. A Soviet government specialist on Asian affairs, M. S. Kapitsa, told an American writer of a meeting he and Soviet Foreign Minister Andrei Gromyko had had with Mao and the Chinese Politburo in Beijing on September 6. Gromyko was reportedly disturbed by Mao's remarks deprecating the possibility of nuclear war, and accordingly may have restated the limits of Soviet support. Zhou Enlai's statement the same day, and Khrushchev's letter to Eisenhower the next day, may thus have emerged from the Mao-Gromyko exchange. So, too, no doubt, did Soviet determination not to proceed with nuclear aid to China. Kapitsa's story appears in Barnett, *China and the Major Powers in East Asia,* pp. 344–45.

116. Statement of September 6, 1963, in Halperin and Tsou, "The 1958 Quemoy Crisis," p. 295.

117. *The Case of P'eng Teh-huai,* p. 202.

118. Among the accusations made against Peng during the Cultural Revolution (see *The Case of P'eng Teh-huai,* p. 165) is one that may be relevant to the Strait crisis. It is said that "he adopted the opportunist attitude that 'no fighting would break out' and that 'war was unlikely.' " Peng is thus said to have "adopted a completely passive attitude towards preparations for dealing with U.S. imperialist aggression."

119. Whiting's article "Quemoy 1958," pp. 267–68, offers persuasive evidence that Mao's views on the low risk of war with the United States in the Strait were disputed by other leaders. Mao believed that while both sides feared war, the United States feared it more than China did. But if the United States chose to fight, Mao argued, China would fight. This perspective was perfectly in accord with his dialectic we noted earlier that "we will not attack unless we are attacked; if we are attacked, we will certainly counterattack."

120. See *Quotations,* pp. 42–43; and *Renmin ribao,* October 31, 1958.

121. "Minutes of Speeches before the Supreme State Conference," September 5, 1958, in *Mao Zedong sixiang wansui,* p. 233.

122. As Mao reminded his colleagues in 1959, comparing the problems of liberating Taiwan and Tibet, Taiwan had a military treaty with the United States. See Whiting, "Quemoy 1958," p. 267.

123. Tsou, *The Embroilment over Quemoy,* p. 35.

124. *Peking Review,* October 7, 1958 (supp.), p. 1; ibid., October 14, 1958 (supp.), p. 1; ibid., October 28, 1958, pp. 5–6.

125. Tsou, *The Embroilment over Quemoy,* pp. 32–33; *Renmin ribao,* October 30, 1958, p. 1.

126. Robert W. Barnett, "China and Taiwan: The Economic Issues," *Foreign Affairs* 50, no. 3 (April 1972): 452; and Anna Louise Strong, "Chinese Strategy in the Taiwan Strait," *New Times* (Moscow), no. 46 (November 1958), pp. 8–11.

127. Evidently, opposition to this method of dealing with the Quemoy garrison was anticipated or was occurring, for as Peng said in his October 13 order to the front: "Some Communists may not understand this [order] for the time being. How comes such an idea? We don't understand! We don't understand! Comrades! You will understand after a while." *Peking Review,* October 14, 1958 (supp.), p. 1.

128. Talbott, ed. and trans., *Khrushchev Remembers,* p. 263.

129. Speech before the Supreme State Conference, September 8, 1958, in *Mao Zedong sixiang wansui,* p. 237.

130. *Documents of the Chinese Communist Party Central Committee,* 1: 123–48.

131. JPRS, *Miscellany of Mao Tse-tung Thought,* p. 138.

132. Mao, "Organize the Militia in a Big Way," *Renmin ribao,* October 30, 1958, in *Chinese Law and Government* 4 (Fall/Winter 1971/72): 261.

133. JPRS, *Miscellany of Mao Tse-tung Thought,* p. 136.

134. Radio Beijing, November 15, 1958.

135. Eisenhower reported in his memoirs (*Waging Peace,* pp. 300–301) that by September 11, 1958, the Joint Chiefs of Staff were of the opinion that the offshore islands should be abandoned or maintained only as outposts. Secretary of Defense Neil McElroy shared that view in the belief Chiang wanted to promote a Sino-U.S. war that would lead to a GMD invasion of the mainland. Eisenhower and Dulles, as was previously noted, also considered the offshore-islands deployments excessive and of little usefulness. As a result of a visit by Dulles to Taiwan in October, Chiang Kai-shek agreed in a joint statement that the "use of force" should not be the "principal means" of "restor[ing]" freedom on the mainland (*New York Times,* October 24, 1958, p. 3). Eisenhower was able to obtain a small reduction in the Quemoy garrison, "but not to the extent I thought desirable" (Eisenhower, *Waging Peace,* p. 304). Chiang remained unleashed and, in return for his promises to Dulles, received increased U.S. military aid and a reaffirmation of the defense treaty.

Chapter 4

1. Fang Zhong, "All-Round Improvement in China's Economy," *Peking Review,* August 23, 1963, p. 8.

2. "A Special Correspondent Report," *Far Eastern Economic Review,* September 27, 1962, p. 588.

3. Yong Longgui, "The Socialist Economy Moves Ahead," *China Reconstructs* 12 (December 1962), in *Selections from Mainland China Magazines* (hereafter cited as *SCMM),* no. 345 (December 27, 1962), p. 13.

4. According to Wu's calculation, the estimation was made on the basis of 285 kilograms of unprocessed grain per adult and a population of 650 million by the end of 1961. Wu Yuan-li, "Farm Crisis in Red China," *Current History* 43 (September 1962): 164.

5. *People's Daily* editorial, "Building an Independent, Comprehensive, and Modern National Economic System," *Peking Review,* December 6, 1962, p. 10.

6. Fang Zhong, "All-Round Improvement," p. 8.

7. Robert Michael Field, "Civilian Industrial Production in the People's Republic of China, 1949-74," in *China: A Reassessment of the Economy,* a compendium of papers submitted to Joint Economic Committee, Congress of the United States, 94th cong., 1st sess., 1975, p. 151.

8. Liao Luyan, "The Whole Party and the Whole People Go in for Agriculture in a Big Way," *Peking Review,* September 14, 1960, p. 33.

9. Barry M. Richman, *Industrial Society in Communist China* (New York: Vintage Books, 1972), pp. 612-13.

10. Gilbert Etienne, "Difficulties of Chinese Economy," *Far Eastern Economic Review,* December 28, 1961, p. 597.

11. *The Bulletin of Activities of the PLA,* p. 284.

12. Ibid., p. 744.

13. Ibid., pp. 296-99.

14. Ibid., p. 284.

15. Ibid., p. 287.

16. Charles P. Ridley, ed., *Rural People's Communes in Lienchiang* (Stanford: Hoover Institution, 1969), pp. 98—99.

17. *The Bulletin of Activities of the PLA,* pp. 190-91.

18. Liao Luyan, "The Whole Party and the Whole People Go in for Agriculture," pp. 35-36.

19. "Communiqué of the Ninth Plenary Session of the Eighth Central Committee of the Communist Party of China," *Peking Review,* January 27, 1961, pp. 5-7.

20. Ibid.

21. "Press Communiqué on the National People's Congress," ibid., April 20, 1962, pp. 3-7.

22. "Mao's Talk at an Enlarged Central Work Conference," January 30, 1962, in Schram, ed., *Chairman Mao Talks to the People,* p. 178; *People's Daily editorial,* "Building an Independent, Comprehensive, and Modern National Economic System," p. 10.

23. Stanley Karnow, *Mao and China: From Revolution to Revolution* (New York: Viking Press, 1972), p. 128.

24. Alexander Eckstein, *China's Economic Revolution* (Cambridge: At the University Press, 1977), p. 250.

25. Liao Luyan, "The Whole Party and the Whole People Go in for Agriculture," p. 33.

26. *The Bulletin of Activities of the PLA,* p. 746.

27. Ibid., p. 747.

28. The 1962 New Year's Day editorial of *People's Daily,* in *Peking Review,* January 5, 1962, pp. 6-9.

29. Zhang Yikuan, "A Few Problems on Incentive Bonus Work in Commercial Enterprises," *Dakong bao,* June 1, 1962, in *SCMP,* no. 2768 (June 28, 1962), pp. 4-7.

30. Yang Ling, "Seriously Increase Leadership over Production Teams," *Shishi shouci,* no. 7 (April 1962), in *SCMM,* no. 315 (May 28, 1962), pp. 15-17.

31. Xue Wen, "Collective Production versus Private Family Production," *Shishi shouci,* nos. 3-4 (February 17, 1962), ibid., no. 318 (June 18, 1962), pp. 35-37.

32. Zhu Jilin, "Industrialization—the Mass Way," *Peking Review,* December 2, 1958, pp. 6-7.

33. Franz Schurmann, *Ideology and Organization in Communist China,* 2d ed. (Berkeley: University of California Press, 1968), pp. 400, 492.

34. Richard Baum and Frederick C. Teiwes, *Ssu-ch'ing: The Socialist Education Movement of 1962-66* (Berkeley: University of California Press, 1968), pp. 11-13.

35. Parris H. Chang, "Research Notes on the Changing Loci of Decision in the Chinese Communist Party," *China Quarterly,* no. 44 (October–December 1970), p. 172.

36. Zhang Yikuan, "A Few Problems on Incentive Bonus Work," pp. 4–7.

37. Concerning the basic principles of the constitution of the Anshan Iron and Steel Company, see Charles Bettelheim, *Cultural Revolution and Industrial Organization in China* (New York: Monthly Review Press, 1974), pp. 18, 70–71.

38. J. D. Simmonds, *China: The Evolution of a Revolution, 1959–66* (Canberra: Australian National University, 1968), p. 18.

39. Solomon, *Mao's Revolution,* pp. 418–19.

40. Zhou Enlai's "Report on the Work of the Government," Third National People's Congress, First Session, December 21–22, 1964, in *Peking Review,* January 1, 1965, pp. 12–13.

41. Thornton, *China, the Struggle for Power,* p. 251.

42. "Long Live the Invincible Thought of Mao Tse-tung," *Jiefang ribao,* in *CB,* July 8, 1969, p. 19; "Background of Antirevolutionary Incident of Chen Guan Lou," in Ting Wang, ed., *Zhonggong wenhua dageming zeliao huibian* [Collection of Documents on the Chinese Communist Great Cultural Revolution] (Hong Kong: Contemporary China Research Institute, 1968), pp. 561–62.

43. "From the Defeat of P'eng Teh-huai to the Bankruptcy of China's Khrushchev," *Red Flag,* no. 13 (1967), in *The Case of P'eng Teh-huai,* p. 137.

44. Merle Goldman, "The Unique Blooming and Contending of 1961–1962," *China Quarterly,* no. 37 (January–March 1969), pp. 79–80.

45. "From the Defeat of P'eng Teh-huai to the Bankruptcy of China's Khrushchev," p. 138.

46. Ibid.

47. "The Third Confession of Liu Shao-ch'i," *Chinese Law and Government* 1 (Spring 1968): 78–79.

48. "Thoroughly Expose Liu Shao-ch'i's Counterrevolutionary Revisionist Crimes in Political and Legal Work," ibid., p. 78; "The Confession of Wu Leng-fei," *Hongse xin hua* [New Red China] 43 (May 1968), ibid. 2 (Winter 1969/70): 78.

49. Goldman, "The Unique Blooming and Contending of 1961–1962," pp. 76–83; Karnow, *Mao and China,* p. 133.

50. One example is the comment made by Parris Chang that during most of 1961 and 1962 "Mao was himself in the second line in the Politbureau Standing Committee" and "Liu was in charge of the Party's daily administration." See Chang, "Research Notes on the Changing Loci of Decision," p. 177.

51. "Mao's Talk," January 30, 1962, p. 168.

52. "Mao's Talk at the Lushan Conference," July 23, 1959, in Schram, ed., *Chairman Mao Talks to the People,* p. 139.

53. "Mao's Talk," January 30, 1962, pp. 171–72.

54. Ibid., p. 173.

55. Ibid., pp. 175–76.

56. Simmonds, *China,* pp. 33–34.

57. "Mao's Talk," January 30, 1962, pp. 176–77.

58. "Liu Shao-ch'i's Self-criticism Made at the Work Conference of the CCP Central Committee," October 23, 1966, in *Issues and Studies* 6 (June 1970): 94–95.

59. "Mao's Speech at the Tenth Plenum of the Eighth Central Committee," September 24, 1962, in Schram, ed., *Chairman Mao Talks to the People,* p. 196.

60. Ibid., p. 192.

61. Ibid., p. 194.

62. "Communiqué of the Tenth Plenary Session of the Eighth Central Committee of the Communist Party of the China," *Peking Review,* September 28, 1962, p. 6.

63. Ibid., p. 7.
64. Schram, ed., *Chairman Mao Talks to the People*, pp. 194–95.
65. Gittings, *The Role of the Chinese Army*, chap. 2.
66. Joffe, *Party and Army*, pp. 114–37.
67. As for Lin Biao's support for Mao's policies during the debate, see Hsieh, *Communist China's Strategy in the Nuclear Era*, pp. 176–80.
68. *Peking Review*, October 18, 1960, pp. 7–8.
69. Ellis Joffe, "The Chinese Army under Lin Piao: Prelude to Political Intervention," in John H. Lindbeck, ed., *China: Management of a Revolutionary Society* (Seattle: University Press of Washington, 1971), p. 359.
70. "Four-Good Company Movement Gains Further Momentum," *People's Daily*, August 2, 1962, in *SCMP*, no. 2801 (August 17, 1962), p. 17.
71. Joffe, *Party and Army*, p. 139.
72. Ibid., p. 141.
73. Tang Pingzhu, "On the Basic Level Construction of the Armed Forces," *People's Daily*, May 15, 1962, in *SCMP*, no. 2753 (June 6, 1962), pp. 4–5.
74. *The Bulletin of Activities of the PLA*, pp. 186–87.
75. Gittings, *The Role of the Chinese Army*, p. 182.
76. On July 29, 1962, the New China News Agency recorded the PLA's contribution to agricultural production and to construction tasks as two million work days during the first seven months of 1962; see *SCMP*, no. 2792 (August 3, 1962), p. 3.
77. Ellis Joffe, "The Conflict between Old and New in the Chinese Army," in Roderick MacFarquhar, ed., *China under Mao: Politics Takes Command* (Cambridge, Mass.: MIT Press, 1966); Gittings, *The Role of the Chinese Army*, pp. 195–96.
78. S. C. Chen and Charles P. Ridley, eds., *Rural People's Communes in Lien-Chiang: Documents concerning Communes in Lien-Chiang County, Fukien Province, 1962–63* (Stanford: Hoover Institution, 1969), pp. 96–98.
79. "Develop the Glorious Tradition of the PLA," in *SCMP*, no. 2794 (August 8, 1962), pp. 3–4.
80. See Chapter 3.
81. Gittings, *The Role of the Chinese Army*, p. 309.
82. *The Bulletin of Activities of the PLA*, p. 749.
83. Ibid., p. 190.
84. Ibid.
85. Ibid., p. 671.
86. "Liu Shao-chi's Self-criticism," p. 94.
87. *SCMP*, no. 2797 (August 13, 1962), pp. 3–5.
88. *Nanfang ribao*, July 28, 1962, ibid., no. 2800 (August 16, 1962), pp. 6–7.
89. Joffe, *Party and Army*, p. 158.
90. "Mao's Talk," January 30, 1962, pp. 178–79.
91. *The Bulletin of Activities of the PLA*, p. 482.
92. Ibid.
93. Ibid., pp. 727–35.
94. Ibid., p. 192.
95. Ibid.
96. Xiao Hua, "The Chinese Revolution and the Armed Struggle," *Hongqi*, August 1, 1962, in *SCMM*, no. 328 (August 27, 1962), p. 9.
97. Alice Langley Hsieh, "China's Secret Military Papers: Military Doctrine and Strategy," *China Quarterly*, no. 18 (April–June 1964), pp. 94–95.
98. *The Bulletin of Activities of the PLA*, p. 480.

99. *SCMP*, no. 2801 (August 17, 1962), p. 14.

100. Neville Maxwell, *India's China War* (London: Jonathan Cape, 1970), p. 75.

101. Ibid., pp. 76–77.

102. Ibid., pp. 93–95.

103. Text of agreement in *Notes, Memoranda, and Letters Exchanged and Agreements Signed between the Governments of India and China: White Paper* (hereafter cited as *White Paper*), vols. 1–8 (New Delhi: Ministry of External Affairs, Government of India, 1959–63), 1: 98–101.

104. H. Arthur Steiner, "Chinese Policy in the Sino-Indian Border Dispute," *Current Scene,* November 7, 1961, pp. 1–3.

105. Chinese note, December 26, 1959, in *White Paper,* 3: 66–68.

106. In 1956, India published a political map that delimited Indian-claimed portions of the N.E.F.A., Uttar Pradesh, as well as Eastern Ladakh. In July 1958, China published a map in *China Pictorial* that showed a different version of the boundaries compared to the Indian map. See *White Paper,* 1: 46; *China Pictorial* 95 (July 1958): 20–21.

107. In October 1958, the Indian government for the first time formally protested that the Aksai Chin highway had been constructed on the eastern part of India's Ladakh region. See G. F. Hudson, ed., *St. Anthony's Papers,* no. 14 (Carbondale, Ill.: Southern Illinois University Press, 1963), pp. 9–10.

108. Nehru's letter to Zhou, December 11, 1958, in *White Paper,* 1: 48–50.

109. Zhou's letter to Nehru, January 23, 1959, ibid., pp. 52–54.

110. George N. Patterson, "China and Tibet: Background to the Revolt," *China Quarterly,* no. 1 (January–March 1960), pp. 97–99.

111. Zhou's letter to Nehru, December 17, 1959, in *Documents on the Sino-Indian Boundary Question* (Beijing: Foreign Languages Press, 1960), p. 22.

112. *White Paper,* 1: 60–62.

113. *New York Times,* April 19, 1959.

114. Maxwell, *India's China War* (1970), pp. 103–5, 263

115. Xinhua News Agency communiqué, March 28, 1959, in *Peking Review,* March 31, 1959, p. 7.

116. Editorial Department of *People's Daily,* "The Revolution in Tibet and Nehru's Philosophy," May 6, 1959, ibid., May 12, 1959, pp. 9–10.

117. Zhou's letter to Nehru, September 8, 1959, in *Documents on the Sino-Indian Boundary Question,* p. 9.

118. Maxwell, *India's China War* (1970), pp. 109–11.

119. A *People's Daily* article on May 6, 1959, strongly condemned the Indian intervention in Tibetan affairs, saying that it reflected the nature of India's large bourgeoisie and consequently certain influences of the imperialist policy of intervention. See "The Revolution in Tibet and Nehru's Philosophy," pp. 14–16.

120. *White Paper,* 1: 75–76.

121. *Documents on the Sino-Indian Boundary Question,* pp. 65–66.

122. Ibid., p. 27.

123. The border settlement with Burma (on terms that were generally considered rather generous to the Burmese side) was probably in some part motivated by the hope that the Burmese government would no longer let U.S. CIA aircraft fly over its territory en route to Tibet and northern India.

124. Maxwell, *India's China War* (1970), p. 160.

125. Ibid., p. 164–65.

126. Zhou's letter to Nehru, December 17, 1959, in *Documents on the Sino-Indian Boundary Question,* p. 20.

127. Maxwell, *India's China War* (1970), pp. 166–69.

128. Ibid., pp. 161–62.

129. Ibid., pp. 175, 235; P.V.R. Rao, *Defense without Rift* (Bombay: Popular Prakashan, 1970), p. 309.

130. Brij M. Kaul, *The Untold Story* (Bombay: Allied Publishers, 1967), p. 281.

131. Maxwell, *India's China War* (1970), pp. 199–205.

132. K. Subrahmanyam, "Nehru and India-China Conflict," in B. R. Nanda, ed., *Indian Foreign Policy: The Nehru Years* (Honolulu: University Press of Hawaii, 1976), p. 117.

133. Kaul, *The Untold Story,* p. 281.

134. Margaret Fisher, Leo E. Rose, and Robert C. Huttenback, *Himalayan Battleground: Sino-Indian Rivalry in Ladakh* (London: Pall Mall Press, 1963), p. 131.

135. Ibid.

136. *New York Times,* August 15, 1962; Fisher, Rose, and Huttenback, *Himalayan Battleground,* p. 131.

137. Maxwell, *India's China War* (1970), pp. 221–23.

138. Twelve cases had been recorded from June 1961 to March 1962 (*White Paper,* 6: 1-2, 48), and 109 cases from April 1962 to October 1962 (ibid., pp. 38–39, 40, 46, 54–55, 59, 67, 78–79, 85; and ibid., 7: 11, 13, 76).

139. By mid-1962, the Chinese protests against Indian intrusions into Chinese-claimed territory almost entirely concerned the intrusions into both the western and middle sectors.

140. Seventy-two sorties were recorded during the last half of 1961; see *White Paper,* 6: 106–8, 111–13.

141. Ibid., 7: 151.

142. Ibid.

143. Maxwell, *India's China War* (1970), p. 230.

144. *Hindustan Times* "Observer," June 8, 1962, in *Peking Review,* July 27, 1962, pp. 13–14.

145. Kaul, *The Untold Story,* p. 339.

146. *White Paper,* 6: 3.

147. Zhou Chunli, "Sino-Indian Border Situation Worsens," *Peking Review,* July 20, 1962, p. 16.

148. Ibid., July 13, 1962, p. 11.

149. Maxwell, *India's China War* (1970), p. 237.

150. Allen S. Whiting, *The Chinese Calculus of Deterrence: India and Indochina* (Ann Arbor: University of Michigan Press, 1975), p. 79; Maxwell, *India's China War* (1970), pp. 237–38.

151. Maxwell, *India's China War* (1970), pp. 238–39.

152. Ibid.

153. Whiting, *The Chinese Calculus of Deterrence,* p. 84.

154. Zhang Ji, "The Sino-Indian Boundary Question," *Peking Review,* August 17, 1962, p. 6.

155. "The Afterthoughts of Premier Chou," interview with Neville Maxwell, *Times* (London), December 19, 1971.

156. Ibid.

157. *White Paper,* 7: 3–4.

158. Maxwell, *India's China War* (1970), p. 245.

159. *White Paper,* 7: 36–37.

160. Zhang Ji, "The Sino-Indian Boundary Question," p. 6.

161. A *People's Daily* editorial, September 7, 1962, in *Peking Review,* September 14, 1962, pp. 10–11.

162. *White Paper,* 7: 73.

163. Ibid., p. 78.

164. Ibid., pp. 97–98.

165. Ibid., p. 102.

166. *SCMP,* no. 2840 (October 17, 1962), p. 6.

167. Klaus H. Pringsheim, "China, India, and Their Himalayan Border, 1961–63," *Asian Survey* 3 (October 1963): 488.

168. *Peking Review,* October 12, 1962, p. 8.

169. Ibid., October 19, 1962, pp. 6–7.

170. George N. Patterson, "The Situation in Tibet," *China Quarterly,* no. 6 (April–June 1961), pp. 84–85; idem, "Recent Chinese Policies in Tibet and towards the Himalayan Border States," ibid. 12 (October–December 1962): 191–93.

171. Retired Air Force Colonel L. Fletcher Prouty, who served in 1959 as coordinator between the CIA and the U.S. Air Force, recalled in the *Denver Post* on February 6, 1972, that "the CIA operation that enabled the Dalai Lama to escape to India . . . was one of the agency's most masterful performances." See Whiting, *The Chinese Calculus of Deterrence,* pp. 18, 255.

172. Ibid., pp. 15–19; Victor Marchetti and John D. Marks, *The CIA and the Cult of Intelligence* (New York: Knopf, 1974), pp. 138, 146.

173. Marchetti and Marks, *The CIA and the Cult of Intelligence,* p. 116.

174. *People's Daily* "Observer," "No Interference in Tibet Allowed," April 22, 1962, in *Peking Review,* April 27, 1962, p.8.

175. Ibid., p. 9.

176. Patterson was informed by Indian military leaders in early 1962 that in India, such a decision was a definite possibility in the event of any serious military engagement of India with Communist China. See Patterson, "Recent Chinese Policies in Tibet," pp. 192–93.

177. Edgar Snow, *The Long Revolution* (New York: Random House, 1971), pp. 195–96; Zhang Chingwu, "Democratic Reform in Tibet," *Peking Review,* June 8, 1962, p. 6.

178. *People's Daily* editorial, "The Current Laotian Situation," in *Peking Review,* January 12, 1962, pp. 6–7; Hong Lan, "SEATO—Instrument of U.S. Aggression," ibid., March 2, 1962, pp. 7–8; Kong Ming, "U.S.-Thai Military Collaboration," ibid., April 13, 1962, pp. 8–9.

179. *People's Daily* editorial, May 19, 1962, ibid., May 25, 1962, p. 11.

180. Ibid., May 6, 1962, p. 13.

181. *Far Eastern Economic Review,* August 23, 1962, p. 334; Frank Robertson, "Refugees and Troop Moves—A Report from Hong Kong," *China Quarterly,* no. 11 (July–September 1962), p. 111.

182. Robertson, "Refugees and Troop Moves," p. 113; Whiting, *The Chinese Calculus of Deterrence,* pp. 30–31.

183. Stanley Karnow, "Sinkiang: Soviet Rustlers in China's Wild West," *The Reporter,* June 18, 1964, pp. 38–39.

184. Ibid., p. 39.

185. Ibid.

186. Ibid., p. 37.

187. Ann Sheehy, "Soviet Views on Sinkiang," *Mizan* (London) 11 (September–October 1969): 275.

188. Karnow, "Sinkiang," p. 39.

189. Editorial departments of *People's Daily* and *Red Flag,* "The Origin and Development of the Differences between the Leadership of the CPSU and Ourselves," *Peking Review,* September 13, 1962, p. 18.

190. "Ch'en Yi's Interview with Japanese Journalists," May 29, 1962, cited in Whiting, *The Chinese Calculus of Deterrence,* p. 64.

191. Roger Hilsman, *To Move a Nation* (Garden City, N.Y.: Doubleday, 1967), p. 310.

192. Whiting, *The Chinese Calculus of Deterrence,* p. 69.

193. Hinton, *Communist China in World Politics,* p. 271.

194. Ibid.

195. Robertson, "Refugees and Troop Moves," pp. 114–15.

196. *SCMP,* no. 2811 (September 4, 1962), pp. 6–8.

197. *Peking Review,* June 29, 1962, pp. 5–7.

198. Young, *Negotiating with the Chinese Communists,* pp. 250–51.

199. Whiting, *The Chinese Calculus of Deterrence,* p. 63.

200. *Peking Review,* July 13, 1962, p. 11.

201. Ibid., July 27, 1962, pp. 13–14.

202. John Kenneth Galbraith, *Ambassador's Journal* (Boston: Houghton Mifflin, 1969), p. 381.

203. *New York Times,* June 10, 1962.

204. "U.S. Aid and India's Anti-Chinese Campaign," *Peking Review,* October 26, 1962, p. 15.

205. According to the article, by the end of July 1962, U.S. aid to India was continuing to increase from the level of aid given in the second half of 1959, when India had launched a vigorous anti-China campaign. The amount as of July 1962 was $3.9 billion, an annual average of $1.3 billion, compared to $1.9 billion (or an average of $0.6 billion a year) from the second half of 1956 to the end of the first half of 1959, when the Indian government gradually deviated from its nonalignment policy. See "More on Nehru's Philosophy in the Light of the Sino-Indian Boundary Question," in *The Sino-Indian Boundary Question,* enl. ed., 2 vols. (Beijing: Foreign Languages Press, 1962–65), 1: 168.

206. *People's Daily* "Observer," "The Pretense of Non-Alignment Falls Away," *Peking Review,* November 16, 1962, p. 6.

207. John Gittings, *Survey of the Sino-Soviet Dispute: A Commentary and Extracts from the Recent Polemics, 1963–67* (London: Oxford University Press, 1968), pp. 89–109, 116–19.

208. Donald S. Zagoria, *The Sino-Soviet Conflict: 1956–61* (Princeton: Princeton University Press, 1962), pp. 319–39, 343–69.

209. Gittings, *Survey of the Sino-Soviet Dispute,* pp. 129–43.

210. Editorial Department of *People's Daily,* "The Truth about How the Leaders of the CPSU Have Allied Themselves with India against China," *Peking Review,* November 8, 1963, p. 19.

211. Gittings, *Survey of the Sino-Soviet Dispute,* pp. 112–13.

212. Ibid., p. 115; Maxwell, *India's China War* (1970), pp. 278–79.

213. Arthur Stein, *India and the Soviet Union: The Nehru Era* (Chicago: University of Chicago Press, 1969), p. 117.

214. *Hindu,* September 21, 1959; see ibid.

215. Stein, *India and the Soviet Union,* pp. 120–21.

216. "The Truth about . . . the Leaders of the CPSU," p. 19

217. Ibid.

218. Edward Crankshaw, *The New Cold War: Moscow v. Peking* (Baltimore: Penguin, 1963), pp. 108, 127.

219. Stein, *India and the Soviet Union,* pp. 125, 178–79.

220. Ibid., p. 177.

221. Ibid., p. 126; Whiting, *The Chinese Calculus of Deterrence,* p. 73; Maxwell, *India's China War* (1970), pp. 285–86.

222. Ian C. C. Graham, "The Indo-Soviet MIG Deal and Its International Repercussions," *Asian Survey* 4 (May 1964): 823–24.

223. Ibid., p. 828.

224. Pringsheim, "China, India, and Their Himalayan Border," p. 485.

225. "The Truth about . . . the Leaders of the CPSU," p. 20.

226. Colina McDougal, "The Sino-Soviet Dialogue," *Far Eastern Economic Review,* December 13, 1962, p. 561.

227. Alexander Dallin et al., eds., *Diversity in International Communism: A Documentary Record, 1961–63* (New York: Columbia University Press, 1963), p. 655.

228. Ibid.

229. *People's Daily* editorial, "The Infamy of Modern Revisionism," September 17, 1962, in *Peking Review,* September 21, 1962, pp. 12–15; Ren Guping, "The Tito Group," ibid., October 12, 1962, pp. 11–16.

230. Schram, ed., *Chairman Mao Talks to the People,* pp. 192–93.

231. *The Sino-Indian Boundary Question* (enl. ed.), 1: 127.

232. Ibid., 2: 4.

233. "The Truth about . . . the Leaders of the CPSU," p. 22.

234. Kaul, *The Untold Story,* pp. 434–35; Girilal Jain, "The Border Dispute in Perspective," *China Report* 6 (November–December 1970): 60.

235. Hilsman, *To Move a Nation,* pp. 177–78, 180.

236. Whiting, *The Chinese Calculus of Deterrence,* pp. 151–52. Hilsman has discussed the procedure of deception used in Washington before Kennedy announced the decision to quarantine Cuba; see *To Move a Nation,* pp. 198–99, 207.

237. *The Sino-Indian Boundary Question* (enl. ed.), 2: 4–5.

238. Premier Zhou's "Report on the Work of the Government," pp. 12–13; *Jiefang ribao* editorial, "Long Live the Invincible Thought of Mao," *CB,* July 8, 1969, pp. 20–21.

239. "Down with Lo Jui-ch'ing, Usurper of the Army Power," a pamphlet published by the Liaison Center of Repudiating Liu, Deng, and Tao, China Science and Technology University's Dongfanghong Commune, Red Guard Congress, July 1967, reprinted in *SCMM,* no. 641 (January 20, 1969), pp. 2–3.

240. A pamphlet distributed by the Printing System Committee of the Guangzhou Area Worker's Revolutionary Committee, March 1968, reprinted in *CB,* March 17, 1969, p. 4.

241. The argument is based on the charges made against Liu-Deng-Luo revisionists in the Cultural Revolution document *Agricultural Machinery and Technique: Special Issue on Revolutionary Mass Criticism,* September 1968, reprinted in *Union Research Service,* no. 53 (October 22–25, 1968), pp. 88–97.

242. "Liu Shao-chi's Self-criticism," p. 94.

243. Schram, ed., *Chairman Mao Talks to the People,* pp. 180–82.

244. *Peking Review,* April 20, 1962, pp. 3–4.

245. Ibid., January 5, 1962, pp. 8–9.

246. Editorial departments of *People's Daily, Red Flag,* and the *Liberation Army Daily,* "Commemorate the 50th Anniversary of the Communist Party of China," ibid., July 2, 1971, p. 15.

247. For instance, as Chen Yi noted in his interview with Japanese journalists on May 29, "We are faced with two tests: to overcome the internal economic difficulties and to cope with the external aggression of imperialism." See Whiting, *The Chinese Calculus of Deterrence,* p. 64.

248. *Peking Review,* April 20, 1962, pp. 3–7.

249. For the Chinese and Indian governments' exchange of notes and the statement made by the spokesman for the Chinese Foreign Ministry, see ibid., pp. 10–20.

250. *White Paper,* 6: 37–39.

251. Whiting, *The Chinese Calculus of Deterrence,* p. 60.

252. A Chinese note, May 19, 1962, in *White Paper,* 6: 46.

253. *White Paper,* 7: 32–33.

254. Zhou recalled that Menon and Chen Yi had basically agreed to issue a joint communiqué. Menon had said that there wasn't enough time to work out such a communiqué in Geneva, but that after he returned to Delhi and reported to his government, such a communiqué could be issued by the two governments. After Menon returned to Delhi, however, the Indian government suggested nothing about negotiations. Zhou commented that the collapse of the talks was due not to Menon himself but to external pressure from the Indian Parliament. See "The Afterthoughts of Premier Chou," *Times* (London), December 19, 1971.

255. *White Paper,* 7: 73.

256. The troop movement to the front in Tibet appeared moderate, probably because the concept of regional defense in the Chinese armed forces meant that the defense of Tibet was based on its permanent garrison. The PLA's strength in Tibet was recorded as 140,000–150,000 by fall, slightly over the 125,000 recorded in early summer. See Griffith, *The Chinese People's Liberation Army,* p. 282.

257. Major Sital Ram Johri, *Chinese Invasion of Ladakh* (Lucknow: Himalaya Publications, 1969), p. 84.

258. Whiting, *The Chinese Calculus of Deterrence,* p. 98.

259. Chu-ko Liang (Pinyin: Zhuge Liang) (181–234), China's prime minister during the minor Han dynasty, was renowned for "his great prudence and foresight" as a military strategist throughout his life. Lü Tuan (Pinyin: Lu Duan) a minister of the Song dynasty in the tenth century, was known as "a fool in small matters, but not in big ones." See Schram, ed., *Chairman Mao Talks to the People,* pp. 195, 323.

260. *White Paper,* 7: 80–81.

261. Ibid., pp. 84–85.

262. *Peking Review,* September 28, 1962, p. 6.

263. Ibid., October 5, 1962, pp. 6–7.

264. Whiting, *The Chinese Calculus of Deterrence,* pp. 103–4.

265. J. P. Dalvi, *Himalayan Blunder* (Bombay: Thacker and Co., 1969), p. 376.

266. Kaul, *The Untold Story,* p. 430.

267. Whiting, *The Chinese Calculus of Deterrence,* p. 121.

268. For a description of the mass rallies and for excerpts from high-level Chinese leaders' speeches, see *Peking Review,* November 2, 1962, pp. 3–4; and ibid., November 9, 1962, pp. 4–5.

269. *White Paper,* 8: 2–4.

270. Ibid., pp. 4–7.

271. On India's anti-China mobilization, see Zhou Baoru, "New Delhi Prepares Further Attacks on China," *Peking Review,* November 9, 1962, pp. 20–22; and the Chinese note of November 6, 1962, in *White Paper,* 8: 62–64.

272. Maxwell, *India's China War* (1970), p. 388.

273. Ibid., pp. 395–96.

274. General Kaul reminds us that India's November 14 attack was the first since the October fighting, and on November 16 Indian newspapers hailed the action under the headline "Jawans Swing into Attack." See Maxwell, *India's China War* (1970), pp. 393–94.

275. Galbraith described the panic in New Delhi as follows: "Yesterday [November 20] was the day of ultimate panic in Delhi, the first time I have ever witnessed the disintegration of public morale—and for the first time I began to wonder what the powers of resistance might be. The rumors flew around the town, the most widely believed being that a detachment of 500 paratroopers was about to drop in New Delhi with, in addition to taking over the town, the even more engaging task of reinstalling Krishna Menon. Rumors of the advance of the Chinese

reached massive proportions, and at one stage they were said to be virtually on the outskirts of Tezpur" (*Ambassador's Journal,* p. 487).

276. *Peking Review,* November 30, 1962, pp. 5–7.

277. "Ch'en Yi's Interview with Japanese Journalists," in Whiting, *The Chinese Calculus of Deterrence,* p. 63.

278. *The Sino-Indian Boundary Question* (enl. ed.), 1: 6–36.

279. For instance, the Chinese government's November 21, 1962, announcement of a cease-fire and withdrawal expressed such a hope for negotiations.

280. The October 27, 1962, article by the Editorial Department of *People's Daily* asserted that "as to how India should solve its economic and political problems, that is entirely the Indian people's own affair, and China has never interfered," and that "the Chinese people sincerely hope [there will soon be a] prosperous, democratic and strong India on the continent of Asia" ("More on Nehru's Philosophy in the Light of the Sino-Indian Boundary Question," in *The Sino-Indian Boundary Question* [enl. ed.], 1: 132–33).

281. Zhou's letter of November 4, 1962, in *Peking Review,* November 9, 1962, p. 14.

282. Statement of the P.R.C., November 21, 1962, in *The Sino-Indian Boundary Question* (enl. ed.), 1: 44–45.

283. Kaul, *The Untold Story,* pp. 395, 401.

284. Maxwell, *India's China War* (1970), p. 409.

285. According to Maxwell's citation of former Permanent Undersecretary at the British Foreign Office Lord Caccia's remarks in 1966 on China's unilateral withdrawal, it was "the first time in recorded history that a great power has not exploited military success by demanding something more" (*India's China War* [1970], p. 419).

286. *Peking Review,* October 26, 1962, p. 8.

287. The statement was published prior to October 25, the date that the PLA occupied Tawang, sixty miles south of Chedong. This is not considered evidence that any military commander saw a sudden collapse of Indian armies at Chedong after an initial offensive on October 20, exploited a military victory, and chased defeated Indian armies across the McMahon line. Nor does it suggest that the Defense Ministry merely justified or confirmed PLA activities beyond the line after the PLA crossed it.

288. As has been discussed, in a meeting with Nehru in April 1960, Zhou tried to concede China's claims to the N.E.F.A. in exchange for Aksai Chin. We have noted that since the spring of 1962 numerous government notes had focused China's protests on India's newly created posts, intrusions, and military provocations in Xinjiang and western Tibet.

289. An approximate accounting of casualties among Indian troops in the N.E.F.A. and Ladakh during the war of October and November 1962 is as follows:

	Killed	Wounded	Missing	Total
N.E.F.A.	1,150	500	1,600	3,250
Ladakh	230	50	60	340

Cited in Kaul's *The Untold Story,* p. 433.

290. Fisher, Rose, and Huttenback, *Himalyan Battleground,* p. 135.

291. "The Truth about . . . the Leaders of the CPSU," p. 22.

292. *Peking Review,* November 9, 1962, p. 21.

293. Ibid., November 16, 1962, pp. 6–7.

294. As was made clear in Zhou Baoru's article of November 9, China was aware of U.S. support to India before the November offensive: "Two days later [October 31], Lincoln White, U.S. State Department spokesman, announced that the U.S. would immediately begin airlifting light infantry weapons, ammunition, transport and communications equipment to India. According to U.S. Brigadier-General Robert D. Foreman, who accompanied the arms

arriving at Calcutta, U.S. aircraft bringing arms landed in India every three hours, each aircraft carrying about 30,000 pounds of military equipment" (*Peking Review,* November 9, 1962, pp. 21–22.)

295. Ibid., November 30, 1962, p. 31.

296. Mao Sun, "A Great Initiative for a Peaceful Settlement," ibid., pp. 22–25.

297. Later the Chinese described how Moscow betrayed Peking: "During the Caribbean crisis, they spoke a few seemingly fair words out of consideration of expediency. But when the crisis was over, they went back on their words. They have sided with the Indian reactionaries all the time. The stand taken by the leaders of the CPSU on the Sino-Indian boundary question is a complete betrayal of proletarian internationalism" ("The Truth about . . . the Leaders of the CPSU," p. 20).

298. Wu Yuchang, "The October Socialist Revolution," *Peking Review,* November 9, 1962, pp. 5–7; *People's Daily* editorial November 7, 1962, ibid., pp. 8–10; *Red Flag* editorial, November 16, 1962, ibid., November 30, 1962, pp. 16–19.

299. "The Moscow Declaration and the Moscow Statement," ibid., November 30, 1962, pp. 26–30.

300. The first article to vigorously condemn Nehru's nonalignment policy appeared on October 27 under the title "More on Nehru's Philosophy in the Light of the Sino-Indian Boundary Question"; see *The Sino-Indian Boundary Question* (enl. ed.), 1: 93–134, esp. pp. 115–21. See also *People's Daily* "Observer," "The Pretense of Non-Alignment Falls Away," pp. 5–7; "Premier Chou's Letter to the Leaders of Asian and African Countries . . .," November 15, 1962, in *The Sino-Indian Boundary Question* (enl. ed.), 1: 33–35; *People's Daily* editorial, "An Unshakable Principle," December 10, 1962, in *Peking Review,* December 14, 1962, pp. 5–7.

301. Solomon, *Mao's Revolution and the Chinese Political Culture,* pp. 429, 444; Griffith, *The Sino-Soviet Rift,* p. 7; Nanda, ed., *Indian Foreign Policy,* p. 19.

302. Schram, ed., *Chairman Mao Talks to the People,* pp. 194–95.

303. Willem F. Van Eekelen, *Indian Foreign Policy and the Border Dispute with China,* 2d ed. rev. (The Hague: Martinus Nijhoff, 1967).

304. Speech of Luo Ruiqing, in *SCMP,* no. 2801 (August 17, 1962), p. 14; Chen Yi's speech, in *Peking Review,* November 9, 1962, p. 21.

305. Fang Zhong, "All-Round Improvement in Chinese Economy," p. 12; Zhou Enlai "Report on the Work of the Government," pp. 12–13.

306. Subrahmanyam, "Nehru and the India-China Conflict of 1962," pp. 117–19.

307. Kaul, *The Untold Story,* pp. 386–87.

308. Whiting, *The Chinese Calculus of Deterrence,* pp. 166–69.

Chapter 5

1. See Doris Rich, "Who Will Carry On? The Search for Red Heirs," *Current Scene,* February 1, 1965.

2. See "Cultivating and Training Millions of Successors to the Proletarian Revolution," *Renmin ribao,* August 3, 1964, p. 1. The importance of the campaign was indicated by the presence of Mao, Liu Shaoqi, Zhou Enlai, and other central leaders at the Ninth Congress of the Communist Youth League, held in Beijing June 11–29, 1964.

A related campaign involved serious discussion of ways to restructure the educational system so as to reduce the imbalance between vocational training and job openings. Proposals were widely circulated to modify academic curricula and revise the criteria for the admission and promotion of students. At year's end, the decision was made to reintroduce the system of half-work, half-study that the schools had established during the Great Leap Forward. The purpose of these reforms was both to make the curricula more relevant to the nation's manpower needs and to make educational opportunities available to a broader segment of China's youth.

3. The five requirements were: (1) "they must be genuine Marxist-Leninists"; (2) "they must be revolutionaries who wholeheartedly serve the majority of the people of China and the whole world"; (3) "they must be proletarian statesmen capable of uniting and working together with the overwhelming majority"; (4) "they must be models in applying the Party's democratic centralism, must master the method of leadership based on the principle of 'from the masses, to the masses,' and must cultivate a democratic style and be good at listening to the masses"; and (5) "they must be modest and prudent and guard against arrogance and impetuosity; they must be imbued with the spirit of self-criticism and have the courage to correct mistakes and shortcomings in their work" (Mao, "On Krushchov's Phoney Communism and Its Historical Lessons for the World," *Peking Review,* July 17, 1964, pp. 26–27).

4. See Donald J. Munro, "The Yang Hsien-chen Affair," *China Quarterly,* no. 22 (April–June 1965), pp. 75–82.

5. See "A Great Revolution on the Cultural Front," *Hongqi,* no. 12 (1964). For summaries of the 1964 intellectual rectification campaign, see Adam Oliver, "Rectification of Mainland China Intellectuals, 1964–65," *Asian Survey* 5 (October 1965): 475–90; and Jack Gray and Patrick Cavendish, *Chinese Communism in Crisis: Maoism and the Cultural Revolution* (New York: Praeger, 1968), chap. 4.

6. Chen and Ridley, eds., *The Rural People's Communes in Lien-Chiang.*

7. See Baum and Teiwes, *Ssu-Ch'ing;* and idem, "Liu Shao-ch'i and the Cadre Question," *Asian Survey* 8 (April 1968): 323–45.

8. An Ziwen, "Cultivating and Training Revolutionary Successors Is a Strategic Task of the Party," *Hongqi,* nos. 17–18 (1964), in *SCMM,* no. 438 (October 12, 1964), pp. 1–12.

9. See John Gittings, "The 'Learn from the Army' Campaign," *China Quarterly,* no. 18 (April–June 1964), pp. 153–59; and Ralph L. Powell, "Commissars in the Economy: 'Learn from the PLA' Movement in China," *Asian Survey* 5 (March 1965): 125–38.

10. New Year's Day statement to the army, Radio Beijing domestic broadcast, December 31, 1964; italics added.

11. Morton H. Halperin and John Wilson Lewis, "New Tensions in Army-Party Relations in China, 1965–1966," *China Quarterly,* no. 26 (April–June 1966), pp. 58–67.

12. See "Down with Lo Jui-ch'ing, Usurper of the Army Power," a document prepared in July 1967 by the Liaison Center for Repudiating Liu, Deng, and Tao of the Red Guard Congress of the Chinese Science and Technology University's Dongfanghong Commune. A translation appears in *SCMM,* no. 641 (January 20, 1969), pp. 1–12. (The charges in this text are virtually identical to those in a document purported to be the report of the Central Committee Work Group formed in December 1965 to investigate Lo: "Report on the Question of the Errors Committed by Lo Jui-ch'ing," April 20, 1966, in *Issues and Studies* [Taibei] 5 [August 1969]: 87–101.) For more on the military tournaments, see "Big Military Competition Is Big Exposure of Lo Jui-ch'ing's Plot to Usurp Army Leadership and Oppose the Party," *Renmin ribao,* August 28, 1967, in *SCMP,* no. 4022 (September 15, 1967), pp. 1–6.

13. Luo Ruiqing, "The Road to the Growth of Young Soldiers," *Zhongguo qingnian* [China's Youth], no. 6 (1964), in Wuhao zhanshi ["Five-Good" Soldiers] (Shanghai: Renmin Chubanshe, 1965). According to Luo: "It is indeed important that young soldiers earnestly study theory and grasp certain theoretical knowledge. But even more important is tempering in revolutionary struggle. Chairman Mao said [in "Strategic Problems of China's Revolutionary

War"]: 'Reading books is study, applying [what is read] is study, and moreover is even more important study.' Knowledge is incomplete, is partial when one has book knowledge and no practical tempering. . . . Youthful officers who have not been through tempering in war and basic-level tempering must uniformly go down to the ranks and serve as ordinary soldiers, live a strict soldier's life for a time and let that serve as a supplementary course. A youth who has not been through wind and rain and has not seen the world cannot become a strong revolutionary soldier."

14. See, for example, "The Strongest Pillar of the Proletarian Dictatorship," *Peking Review,* August 4, 1967, pp. 40–42; "Hold High the Great Red Banner of Mao Tse-tung's Thought, Thoroughly Criticize and Repudiate the Bourgeois Military Line," *Jiefangjun bao* [Liberation Army Daily] editorial, July 31, 1967, translated in *Peking Review,* August 4, 1967, pp. 42–45; and "Unswervingly Take the Road of Putting Politics to the Fore," *Jiefangjun bao* editorial in *SCMP,* no. 4014 (September 5, 1967), pp. 20–26.

15. "Down with Lo Jui-ch'ing," p. 9.

16. "Selected Edition of Liu Shao-chi's Counter-revolutionary Revisionist Crimes," Nankai University, August 18 Red Rebel Regiment, Liaison Station (under the banner, "Pledging to Fight a Bloody Battle with Liu-Teng-T'ao to the End"), April 1967, in *SCMM,* nos. 651–53, (April 22, 28, and May 5, 1969).

17. There are many other quotations in Red Guard documents that purport to document Luo's adherence to the "bourgeois military line." Most of them, however, are undated.

18. James N. Townsend, "Communist China: The New Protracted War," *Asian Survey* 5 (January 1965): 1–11.

19. See, for example, Mei Zhijin, "The U.S. Vainly Struggles on in Southeast Asia," *Shijie zhishi* [World Knowledge], March 10, 1964, pp. 7–10.

20. *Renmin ribao* editorial, July 1, 1964, p. 3.

21. Ibid., July 8, 1964, p. 1.

22. The undated interview was given in Shanghai to Dr. Hugo Portisch, whose newspaper, *Der Kurier* (Vienna), published it on August 1. Although Zhou was not identified, the context—the speaker's statement that he had recently visited Pakistan, which Zhou had done the previous February—indicates it was he. Zhou said that China would directly intervene "only if, perhaps, the United States would send up their 'special warfare' [forces] toward the north, if they attacked North Vietnam." On China's response, Zhou said: "A very wide and a very broad front can be set up there [in Southeast Asia]. Such a war would not remain isolated in a narrow space. It would also involve Vietnam, Laos, and Cambodia, perhaps also Thailand." Zhou said with respect to the scope of fighting: "If they [the Americans] want a small war, well, then a small war it will be. If they want a big war, then it will be a big war. It all depends on the Americans. We do not want any war whatsoever. But if it is forced upon us, they will find us ready."

23. *Renmin ribao* editorial, August 6, 1964, p. 1: "Whenever U.S. imperialism intrudes into the territory, territorial waters and airspace of the DRV, the Chinese people, without hesitation, will resolutely support the just war of the Vietnamese people resisting the American aggression. The Chinese Government has repeatedly seriously warned the U.S. Government that if it dares to launch an attack against the DRV, the Chinese people will definitely not sit idly by without helping."

24. See Richard M. Bueschel, *Communist Chinese Air Power* (New York: Praeger, 1968), p. 83.

25. Allen S. Whiting, "How We Almost Went to War with China," *Look,* April 29, 1969, p. 76.

26. A Chinese broadcast of August 13 (reported in the *New York Times,* August 14, 1964, p. 3) specifically linked the maneuvers to pledges by the P.R.C. leadership to support Hanoi against U.S. aggression.

27. Edgar Snow, "Interview with Mao," *The New Republic,* February 27, 1965, pp. 17–23.

28. William E. Griffith, "Sino-Soviet Relations, 1964–1965," *China Quarterly,* no. 25 (January–March 1966), pp. 60–63.

29. Peng Zhen, *Speech at the Aliarcham Academy of Social Sciences in Indonesia (May 25, 1965)* (Beijing: Foreign Languages Press, 1965), p. 21. Peng's posts included membership on the Chinese Communist party (CCP) Central Committee Politburo and its Secretariat.

30. Griffith, "Sino-Soviet Relations," pp. 64–65.

31. For an argument that certain Chinese leaders took this position, see Uri Ra'anan, "Peking's Foreign Policy 'Debate,' 1965–1966," in Tang Tsou, ed., *China in Crisis,* vol. 2, *China's Policies in Asia and America's Alternatives* (Chicago: University of Chicago Press, 1968), pp. 23–72.

32. *Renmin ribao,* February 11, 1965, p. 2.

33. Ibid., February 14, 1965, p. 1.

34. In a speech at a North Korean embassy reception, ibid., February 9, 1965, p. 1.

35. Contrary to the interpretation of Uri Ra'anan that Luo was here "hinting at intervention" by the Chinese "as in Korea." See Ra'anan, "Peking's Foreign Policy 'Debate,'" p. 36.

36. Jay Tao, "Mao's World Outlook: Vietnam and the Revolution in China," *Asian Survey* 8 (May 1968): 422.

37. See the congratulatory message sent by Mao, Liu Shaoqi, and others to Soviet party and government leaders on February 13, in NCNA, *Daily Bulletin,* February 14, 1965, pp. 7–8. Liu Ningyi, in his previously cited speech of February 10, had also called upon the socialist countries to "unite" on the Vietnam question; but the context makes clear that he did not believe unity then existed (contrary to Ra'anan, "Peking's Foreign Policy 'Debate,'" p. 35) or was just around the corner.

38. In a letter of July 14, 1965, from the CCP Central Committee to the Soviet Communist party (CPSU), a genuine copy of which (with only minor deletions) was published in an article by Edward Crankshaw in *The Observer* (London), November 14, 1965, p. 5. See also "Refutation of the New Leaders of the C.P.S.U. on 'United Action,'" (hereafter cited as "Refutation") by the Editorial departments of *Renmin ribao* and *Hongqi,* November 11, 1965, in *Peking Review,* November 12, 1965, pp. 15–16.

39. According to a secret letter sent by the CPSU in early 1966 to Communist party offices in the Soviet Union and to other "fraternal" parties, Kosygin, while in Beijing, had proposed that polemics be discontinued, trade be expanded, and technical cooperation begin anew. The Chinese leadership is said to have rejected all these overtures. An excerpted version was published in *Die Welt* (Hamburg), March 21, 1966.

40. Guo Moruo's speech of February 13 is in NCNA, *Daily Bulletin,* February 14, 1965, pp. 17–21. For Chen Yi's speech of February 15, see ibid., February 16, 1965, pp. 5–6. Both speeches were made during celebrations to mark the fifteenth anniversary of the Sino-Soviet Treaty of Friendship and Mutal Defense.

41. See CCP Central Committee letter of July 14, 1965 (cited in note 38); and "Refutation," p. 16.

42. Chinese military aid then consisted of some additional subsonic MIGs, infantry weapons, and ammunition; economic aid included trucks, construction materials, pharmaceuticals, and rice.

43. *New York Times,* January 17, 1965, p. 1. The AAA units were probably detailed to protect PLA logistical personnel as well as North Vietnamese military targets.

44. See ibid., August 12, 1966, p. 4; and Whiting, "How We Almost Went to War with China," p. 77.

45. Work on the rail and road links was necessary after June, when they became targets of U.S. air strikes. The first Chinese units arrived in the early fall of 1965, the last in the spring of 1966 (Whiting, "How We Almost Went to War with China," p. 77). Their arrival freed North Vietnamese soldiers to perform similar tasks on the transportation lines between North and South Vietnam.

46. Bueschel, *Communist Chinese Air Power,* p. 83, mentions Mengze in Yunnan as one of the bases used by the North Vietnamese beginning in late 1965.

47. A *Renmin ribao* editorial (March 25, 1965, p. 2), for instance, responded to the NLF's five-point statement of March 22 by not only promising "all necessary material assistance" but also announcing China's willingness "at once to send our own personnel to fight together with the Vietnamese people . . . when the Vietnamese people need them."

48. "A Comment on the March Moscow Meeting," by the Editorial departments of *Renmin ribao* and *Hongqi,* March 23, 1965, in *Peking Review,* March 26, 1965, pp. 7–13. As the article explains, the Chinese had tried to persuade the new Soviet leaders to abandon plans for holding such an "illegal schismatic meeting." The Soviets' persistence "only goes to prove that they are still bent on deepening the differences, wrecking unity and doing fresh damage to the international communist movement. . . . Quite obviously, the new leaders of the C.P.S.U. have gone a step further in destroying the basis for the unity of the Communist Parties. In these circumstances we would like to ask: When they exclaim [in the conference communiqué], 'what unites the Communist Parties greatly outweighs that which at the present time disunites them,' what is this if not an effort to conceal their revisionist and schismatic essence?"

49. Ibid., p. 10: "At a time when the Democratic Republic of Viet Nam is being wantonly bombed by the U.S. gangsters, all the countries of the socialist camp and the revolutionary people throughout the world should, as a matter of course, unite and wage a tit-for-tat struggle against the U.S. aggressors."

50. According to a Chinese account ("Malinovsky Is a Liar," a statement by the Chinese Foreign Ministry, ibid., May 6, 1966, pp. 25–26), the transit arrangements were agreed upon in February.

51. The Central Committee of the CPSU did not publicly ratify the defense agreement reached when Kosygin was in Hanoi until March 26. It then probably took another few months before the Soviets shipped the first surface-to-air missiles (SAMs) and related equipment to North Vietnam, since not until late July did the first SAM attack U.S. jets. There are several possible explanations for these delays. One is that Soviet leaders were anxious not to close the door on D.R.V.-U.S. negotiations, which might have resulted from the proposed talks on Cambodia's neutrality in the spring of 1965. Other possible reasons are that the Soviets were uncertain about China's reliability in transporting the goods; they needed to be sure about how the United States would react to new aid deliveries (perhaps recalling the blockade of Cuba); and they needed time to draw up a "menu" of goods that the North Vietnamese could best use.

52. *New York Times,* April 8, 1965, p. 1.

53. The trilateral conference proposal is mentioned, though without a date, in "Refutation," p. 17. The other Soviet proposals are referred to in the Chinese reply of July 14, 1965 (cited in note 38), and in an interview with Liao Chengzhi (Liao Ch'eng-chih) (deputy director of the Staff Office for Foreign Affairs) given over Tokyo television on July 15, 1965.

54. The text of Beijing's April letter is unavailable, but the CCP's July 14 letter restates its main points.

55. On the Soviets' aid, see "Commentator," "Drive the U.S. Aggressors Out of Vietnam," *Hongqi,* no. 4 (1965): "Their deeds do not tally with their words. Posing as benefactors, they utter a lot of ballyhoo about helping the Vietnamese people. They have given some aid but it is merely for the purpose of making capital out of it in order to bargain with the United States, undermine the anti-U.S. revolutionary struggle of the people of Vietnam and

the rest of the world, and to serve U.S. imperialism. In a word, the modern revisionists are feigning support but, in reality, betraying the Vietnamese people's patriotic anti-U.S. struggle."

56. The *Renmin ribao* statement of March 25, promising Chinese personnel "when the Vietnamese people need them," was qualified on April 20. A resolution of the Sixth Session of the Standing Committee of the Third National People's Congress made the promise conditional also on "the needs of the common struggle" against the Americans (*Renmin ribao,* April 21, 1965, p. 1). Chen Yi, interviewed by a French correspondent on May 29, made the policy of self-reliance explicit when he said: "Yes, I think the Vietnamese people are perfectly capable, by relying on their own forces, to drive the American aggressors out of their country." See *Peking Review,* June 4, 1965, p. 15.

57. In "Drive the U.S. Aggressors Out of Vietnam," *Hongqi's* "Commentator" had stated that the American strategy was to use bombing in two ways: first, as "blackmail" to induce North Vietnam to the conference table; second, as a "smoke screen" to conceal escalation.

58. "Commemorate the Victory over German Fascism! Carry the Struggle against U.S. Imperialism through to the End!," *Hongqi,* no. 5 (1965), in *Peking Review,* May 14, 1965, pp. 7–15.

59. "The Historical Experience of the War against Fascism," *Renmin ribao,* May 9, 1965, ibid., pp. 15–22.

60. A different interpretation of Luo's comments about Munich has been offered by Maury Lisann in "Moscow and the Chinese Power Struggle," *Problems of Communism* 18 (November–December 1969): 32–41. Lisann argues that Luo's reference to the failure of Chamberlain and Daladier to align with the Soviet Union against Nazi Germany constituted an indirect admonition to Mao and Lin Biao to accept the Soviet proposals of April. But Lisann seems to be reading into Luo's statement much more than was intended. Luo was apparently in complete accord with Mao's view that the Soviet Union, in working for Vietnam negotiations, was risking "another Munich" in the same way that Chamberlain and Daladier did.

61. Although the editorial stated that "it is much more difficult for the United States to unleash a world war," it left open the possibility than one might occur. It spoke of "U.S. imperialist plans for aggression and war" and of the United States "following in Hitler's footsteps" by daring "to impose a world war on the people."

62. The argument that Luo did urge "unity" with Moscow is made by Ra'anan, "Peking's Foreign Policy 'Debate,'" pp. 43–44. He cites, as have others, Luo's assertion that "the United States' monopoly of the atom bomb was broken many years ago." The presumption is that Luo was referring to the Soviets' nuclear capability, and was really saying that a reduction in Sino-Soviet tensions would assure China's protection. But Lin Biao, in his September article on people's war (see n. 86 below), used precisely Luo's words; and a more accurate translation of them would be that the U.S. monopoly "has *long since* been broken," which could refer to *China's* bomb.

63. On this point, Alice Langley Hsieh has written: "Lo may have been advocating a series of 'quick fixes' (much as certain of his predecessors had in the mid-50s) in China's defense posture to deter, if not counter, any inclination on the part of the United States to extend the bombing to the mainland" (*Communist China's Military Policies, Doctrine, and Strategy* [Santa Monica, Calif.: Rand Corporation, P-3960, October 1968], pp. 29–30). This concern about surprise attack was hardly new in Chinese military thinking; several senior military leaders had referred to it and to the need for active air defense in the early 1960s. See Hsieh, "China's Secret Military Papers," pp. 82–84, 92.

64. During 1965, most estimates agree, China's jet-fighter capability was mainly in old-model MIG-15s and MIG-17s—according to one source about 1,000 of the former and 400 of

the latter (Laurence L. Ewing and Robert C. Sellers, eds., *The Reference Handbook of the Armed Forces of the World* [Washington, D.C.: Sellers and Associates, 1966]). A small number of MIG-19s—about 70, according to *The Reference Handbook*—also were available. China's production of MIG-21s did not get under way until 1965, and then only in limited numbers, whereas the North Vietnamese were receiving advanced-models MIG-21s in 1965. See Bueschel, *Communist Chinese Air Power,* pp. 89–91.

65. In February, it will be recalled, Kosygin had offered to resume economic and technical assistance, not military aid. According to the *Die Welt* excerpt of the secret CPSU letter (see note 39), in April and July the Soviet leaders also proposed cooperation on industrial and nuclear research, which the Chinese also turned down.

66. As Luo said: "The strategy of active defense does not stop with driving the aggressor out of the country, but requires strategic pursuit to destroy the enemy at his starting point, to destroy him in his nest. As Stalin put it, we must not allow a wounded beast to crawl back to recuperate; we must follow on its heels in hot pursuit and finish it off in its own lair. . . . We seriously warn the U.S. imperialists that they must not expect us to refain from counterattacking once they have attacked us. Nothing comes so cheap."

Ishwer Ojha has interpreted this passage as a recommendation that China undertake immediate action, under the guise of "strategic pursuit," against American forces in Vietnam. See Ishwer C. Ojha, "China's Cautious American Policy," *Current History* 53 (September 1967): 135–40, 175–76. This interpretation strains Luo's analogy between the Vietnam conflict and World War II. It is more likely that Luo was threatening that China would counterattack across its borders if American forces invaded China, just as Stalin had pursued Hitler's armies back into Germany. Luo may also have been arguing that since American forces had attacked North Vietnam, the D.R.V. had the right to send forces into the South to stage counterattacks against American installations. If so, this was not a novel position; Chinese spokesmen had granted Hanoi this "right" in February.

67. See Liu Yunzheng, "The Role of People's Militia," *Peking Review,* February 5, 1965, pp. 17–20. In "sudden war" situations, the author noted, there is the possibility that the rear areas might be attacked first, in air raids and by "air-dropped enemy forces." The militia would play a vital role in such a situation; it would "effectively maintain social order, steadfastly carry on production, safeguard communications, consolidate the rear and co-ordinate operations with and support the fighting at the front."

68. Luo said that "victory in war" required "close co-operation among the different armed services, of which the ground forces, and particularly the infantry, are primary."

One charge leveled against Luo after his purge was that he had "obstructed and opposed" Mao's guidelines for building up the local forces and militia, the implication being that Luo did not consider them of much value and preferred to rely on the professional standing army. See "Basic Differences between the Bourgeois and Proletarian Military Lines," by a Red Guard group in the PLA General Staff headquarters, ibid., November 24, 1967, pp. 13–14; and "Down with Lo Jui-ch'ing," p. 3. Whether this charge, like so many others, referred to 1965 is unclear. During the early 1960s, Luo seemed to be on both sides of the fence with regard to the militia: he defended maintaining a large militia even in peacetime, but he also insisted that its primary function be production and that it engage in military training only during leisure hours. See Luo's article in *Hongqi,* no. 10 (1960), as broadcast by NCNA (Beijing), May 15, 1960; and Gittings, *The Role of the Chinese Army,* p. 218.

69. Thus Luo mentioned that in World War II the Soviets correctly implemented active defense against the Nazi invaders by forming a defense line that took advantage of both geographic ("high mountains") and man-made barriers ("fortified cities"). Irregular troops operated in the rear to disrupt the enemy's supply lines. Eventually, the Nazis were routed at Stalingrad. Luo's preferred defense line, we may surmise, was not necessarily at the border but was close to it.

70. "Basic Differences between the Bourgeois and Proletarian Military Lines," p. 15. The "passive" strategy referred to in the civil war period was promoted by Zhou Enlai and Liu Bocheng (Liu Po-ch'eng) during the Guomindang's fourth encirclement campaign (June 1932–March 1933). A plan to "halt the enemy beyond the gate," it prevailed over Mao's strategy of "luring deep" (today called "active defense"). See Jerome Ch'en, *Mao and the Chinese Revolution* (New York: Oxford University Press, 1967), p. 177.

71. Luo's statement—"We will not attack unless are are attacked; if we are attacked, we will certainly counter-attack"—is not given due weight in the account of Donald S. Zagoria, *Vietnam Triangle: Moscow, Peking, Hanoi* (New York: Pegasus, 1967). Zagoria contends, with Ra'anan, that Luo was a "hawk" on Vietnam who favored accommodating the Soviets in order to improve China's defense and interventionist options in Vietnam.

72. The purported Central Committee work group's "Report on the Question of the Errors Committed by Lo Jui-ch'ing" (p. 98), accuses Luo of having requested the Standing Committee's approval of "a massive increase in troop strength" and a merger of "the various military regions" in 1965.

73. During the first months of 1965, China reported having shot down six U.S. jets and U-2 reconnaissance planes that had allegedly violated Chinese air space. When, as in mid-April, these incidents were commented on by Lin Biao, they were termed provocations, not signs of impending American attack. Lin's order for alertness was given in a NCNA (Beijing) domestic broadcast of April 18, 1965. Significantly, the one U.S. plane reported by the Chinese (NCNA, April 9) to have been downed in a dogfight with Chinese aircraft—the first such engagement reported since the Korean War—was said to have been destroyed by the missile of another American plane. Beijing refused to claim credit for the "kill." See *New York Times*, April 10, 1965, pp. 1, 3.

74. As broadcast by NCNA's international service (Beijing), June 1, 1965.

75. *Renmin ribao* editorial, July 13, 1965, in *Peking Review*, July 16, 1965, pp. 6–7.

76. The transmittal of Mao's views through *Jiefangjun bao*, the organ of the General Political Department, became more frequent later in 1965. That paper may have been chosen because of the reliability of its editorial staff as much as because it was the appropriate vehicle for communicating the party's view's to the PLA command. Since 1958, the deputy editor (and probably de facto chief) of *Jiefangjun bao* had been Tang Pingzhu (T'ang P'ing-chu), a lieutenant general with civil war service and experience mainly on the political side of the PLA system. A measure of his reliability is that after the Cultural Revolution began, Tang was named the "responsible person" of *Renmin ribao* (August 1966) and then (in October 1966) its acting managing editor, replacing Wu Lengxi (Wu Leng-hsi), who was purged for allegedly serving the Liu Shaoqi line. In January 1967 Tang also became a member of the All-PLA Cultural Revolutionary Group; although he was criticized by Red Guards the same month, he apparently survived the ordeal with his positions intact. See Union Research Institute, *Who's Who in Communist China* (Hong Kong: Union Research Institute, 1970), 2: 602; and *Zuguo yuekan* [Homeland Monthly], no. 36 (March 1967), p. 49 and no. 55 (October 1968), p. 8.

77. *Jiefangjun bao* editorial, June 10, 1965, excerpted in *Renmin ribao*, June 11, 1965, p. 2. The likelihood that Luo was a specific target of this editorial is enhanced by a thinly veiled reference to tournaments: "If [in training] one chases after championism and formalism, the fact that he scores brilliantly in shooting and throws a grenade for a distance of 45 meters does not mean that his consciousness has been raised." The abolition of ranks, awards, and insignia in the PLA by decision of the State Council in May 1965 was in keeping with the editorial's message on party authority.

78. Editorial departments of *Renmin ribao* and *Hongqi*, "Carry the Struggle against Khrushchev Revisionism through to the End," in *Peking Review*, June 18, 1965, pp. 5–10.

79. *Peking Review*, July 23, 1965, pp. 12–14.

80. Speech of July 28, ibid., August 6, 1965, pp. 23–26.

81. *Renmin ribao,* July 22, 1965, ibid., July 30, 1965, pp. 10–11.

82. *Renmin ribao,* August 3, 1965, ibid., August 6, 1965, pp. 17–19.

83. *Renmin ribao,* August 2, 1965, p. 1.

84. Huo Long, "Democratic Tradition of the Chinese People's Liberation Army," *Peking Review,* August 6, 1965, pp. 6–17; the article was originally published in *Hongqi, Renmin ribao,* and *Jiefangjun bao.*

85. Text in *Renmin ribao,* September 4, 1965, pp. 2–3.

86. In *Peking Review,* September 3, 1965, pp. 9–30; the original is in *Renmin ribao,* September 3, 1965, pp. 1–4.

87. A *Renmin ribao* editorial of September 2, 1965 (pp. 1–2), likewise said that China was sufficiently prepared: "If U.S. imperialism stubbornly wants to expand the war to the Chinese people, the Chinese people and the Chinese PLA will determinedly accompany it to the end. The Chinese people are mobilized, organized, armed." Similar statements about China's preparedness were made by *Renmin ribao*'s "Commentator" on September 21 and by Chen Yi in his memorable news conference on September 29 "welcoming" a showdown battle with all enemies (*Peking Review,* October 8, 1965, p. 14). Further interesting evidence of the leadership's attitude is the *Renmin ribao* editorial of September 21 on the strategic importance of the militia, appearing as it did in the same issue that reported the downing of a U.S. F-104 jet over Hainan and the capture of its pilot. The editorial stressed that "arming the masses" should proceed simultaneously with the ongoing modernization of the regular forces, since "strengthening the militia is an extremely important measure for dealing with U.S. imperialism's expansion of aggressive war."

88. Actually, Luo's September speech included the sharpest language he had used in characterizing the Soviet leaders and their policies.

89. This paragraph draws upon the essay by Richard Baum, "Revolution and Reaction in the Chinese Countryside: The Socialist Education Movement in Cultural Revolutionary Perspective," *China Quarterly,* no. 38 (April–June 1969), pp. 92–119.

90. Philip Bridgham, "Mao's 'Cultural Revolution': Origin and Development," ibid., no. 29 (January–March 1967), p. 15.

91. Ibid.

92. William Whitson has suggested to us that party dissidents with influence on *Renmin ribao* may have been motivated to support Luo Ruiqing's position on the external (U.S.) threat partly in order to divert Mao from continuing or broadening the Socialist Education Movement. Perhaps Mao's awareness of this strategy further intensified his dissatisfaction with the party leadership.

93. On Peng Zhen's reading of the Yao article, see Bridgham, "Mao's 'Cultural Revolution,'" p. 18.

94. Mao is quoted as having said in 1965 that "the crux of *Hai Jui Dismissed from Office* is the question of dismissal from office. The Emperor Chia Ching dismissed Hai Jui from office. In 1959 we dismissed P'eng Teh-huai from office. And P'eng Teh-huai is 'Hai Jui' too" ("From the Defeat of P'eng Teh-huai to the Bankruptcy of China's Khrushchev," *Hongqi,* no. 13 [1967], in *Peking Review,* August 18, 1967, p. 20).

95. The first official accusation linking Luo to Peng, Yang, and Lu came in Lin Biao's address on May 18, 1966, to an enlarged session of the CCP Central Committee Politburo, in which he said: "Chairman Mao, in recent months, has paid particular attention to the prevention of a counterrevolutionary coup d'état and adopted many measures. After the Lo Jui-ch'ing problem, he talked about it. Now the P'eng Chen problem has been exposed, and he again summoned several persons and talked about it, dispatched personnel and had them stationed in the radio broadcasting stations, the armed forces and the public security systems in order to prevent a counterrevolutionary coup d'état and the occupation of our crucial points." Lin went on to note that "coups d'état have today become a fad," with an average of

eleven in the last six years. The original text of Lin's speech is in *Zhonggong yanjiu* [Studies on Chinese Communism], May 10, 1970, pp. 124–31. The translation used here is from *Issues and Studies* (Taibei) 6 (February 1970): 81–92.

96. Luo's final public appearance (until his rehabilitation in 1979) was in the last week of November 1965. On December 8, 1965, a conference reportedly convened by Mao and the Central Committee opened in Shanghai to "expose and criticize" Luo's errors (see "Report on the Question of the Errors Committed by Lo Jui-ch'ing"). Investigation of Luo was then carried out by a work group appointed by the Central Committee. It held two sets of meetings between March 4 and April 8; but halfway through the proceedings, on March 18, Luo reportedly attempted suicide by jumping from the building. The Soviet news agency TASS reported on December 24, 1966, that Luo and Peng Dehuai had been formally arrested by Red Guard groups—twenty days after Peng Zhen was dragged out for public condemnation.

97. Yang was last mentioned in the Chinese press on October 24, 1965. He, the three other members of the "four-family village" (*sizhuangdian*), and Kang Sheng had been members of the Central Committee Cultural Revolution Group that Mao had established in 1964 (under Peng Zhen) to deal with reform of the Beijing opera. The report issued by this group—the so-called February (1966) Outline—was the basis for the removal of Peng Zhen, who was accused of trying to prevent a cultural revolution in the arts and in the party. Of the five members of the Cultural Revolution Group, only Kang Sheng survived; all five were secretaries or alternate secretaries in the Secretariat of the Central Committee. The fall of Yang and Luo was therefore in great part the first round of a Maoist assault on the party Secretariat. For further background, see *Zuguo yuekan*, no. 44 (November 1967), p. 17.

98. See the discussion in Bridgham, "Mao's 'Cultural Revolution,'" pp. 19–20. Briefly, Lin's five-point directive was: the "creative study and use of Chairman Mao's works"; persistence in the "four firsts"; the involvement of leading cadres in the ranks and in directing the "four-good" company movements; the promotion of superior commanders and soldiers to responsible positions; and hard drilling, mastery of technique, close-range fighting, and night-fighting tactics.

99. *Renmin ribao*, January 19, 1966, p. 1. The work conference was said to have been attended by Zhou Enlai, Zhu De, Deng Xiaoping, and Peng Zhen, with speeches delivered by Ye Jianying, Xiao Hua, and Yang Chengwu.

100. Only excerpts of the speech were published; see *ibid.*, January 25, 1966, pp. 1–2.

101. In 1966, for example, the Japanese Communist party (JCP) admitted the importance of the doctrinal questions in the Sino-Soviet dispute, but argued than the failure of China and the Soviet Union to agree on the practical question of aid to Hanoi was directly responsible for America's escalation of the war. See "In Order to Strengthen the International Action and United Front against U.S. Imperialism," *Akahata*, February 4, 1966. It is possible that in the spring of 1965, the JCP or other Communist parties already held these views and communicated them privately to Beijing.

102. Had Luo been in favor of united action with the Soviet Union, Russian accounts of the Cultural Revolution could be expected to treat Luo favorably. There are Soviet references to disagreements within the Chinese leadership over the question of united action. For example, three members of the Institute of Far Eastern Studies of the U.S.S.R. Academy of Sciences write: "Some of the CPC leaders saw that the independent existence of China was threatened by Mao Tse-tung's 'special' line, particularly by his refusal to rely on the socialist camp in face of U.S. imperialist intervention in Southeast Asia, and demanded a reassessment of China's discredited foreign policy. Differences arose in the CPC leadership between those who desired more active resistance to U.S. imperialism on the basis of unity with the socialist camp, and the Maoists, who counted on attaining their goals by balancing between the socialist camp and the USA, halting active support for the struggle of the Vietnamese people and demonstrating their anti-Sovietism" (B. Zanegin, A. Mironov, and Y. Mikhailov, *Developments*

in China [Moscow: Progress Publishers, 1968], p. 78). On the other hand, one of the few direct references to Luo that we could locate accuses him of an anti-Soviet position: "It is true that they [Luo, Liu Shaoqi, and Deng Xiaoping] came out against completely replacing Marxism with the 'ideas of Mao,' but it is also true that it was precisely they themselves who for a long time promoted the cult of Mao Tse-tung, and tried to 'combine' internationalism with nationalism and anti-Sovietism" (Fedor Burlatskii, *Maoizm—ugroza sotsializmu v Kitae* [Maoism—Threat to Socialism in China] [Moscow: Politizdat, 1968], p. 63).

103. The Chinese, understandably, never specified what form this "stronger action" might take. Nor are the conditions that would have triggered "stronger action" completely clear. They may well have included an American invasion of North Vietnam, the bombing of the Red River dikes, or other American actions that would threaten the stability of the Hanoi government. Recall, for example, Zhou's warning in 1964 that China might directly intervene "if, perhaps, the United States would send their 'special warfare' [forces] toward the north, if they attacked North Vietnam" (*Der Kurier,* August 1, 1964).

104. It is true that in his speech of September 2, Luo emphasized different things in his discussion of aid to North Vietnam and the Viet Cong than did Lin Biao. In "Long Live the Victory of People's War!" Lin emphasized both the self-reliant struggle of the Chinese Red Army during the anti-Japanese war and the role of self-reliance in modern wars of national liberation. Luo, while also referring to the self-reliance of the Red Army, went on to advocate "still more effective" (*genghaode*) support for the "Vietnamese people." This passage does contrast with the mood of Lin's article, and suggests that Luo may have sought to increase the level of Chinese aid to the North Vietnamese and the NLF. Luo did not, however, mention what kind of "support" he had in mind; the word *zhiyuan* could refer to anything from combat troops to propaganda. And of the three major themes in Luo's speech, his call for "more effective support" was the only one on which he did not elaborate.

105. It is also possible that Luo differed from Mao on a fourth point, the wisdom of strategic pursuit. The evidence is fairly complex. In his May article, Luo spoke out in favor of counterattacking across China's boundaries, but his motive may have been to deter American attack, not to suggest a set strategy. Zhou Enlai, in 1966, also warned of the possibility of strategic pursuit. In his four-point formulation of China's America policy, Zhou declared: "Once the war breaks out, it will have no boundaries. Some U.S. strategists want to bombard China by relying on their air and naval superiority and avoid a ground war. This is wishful thinking. Once the war gets started with air or sea action, it will not be for the United States alone to decide how the war will continue. If you can come from the sky, why can't we fight back on the ground?" (*Peking Review,* May 13, 1966, p. 5). Mao seems to have been totally opposed to strategic pursuit. In his interview with Edgar Snow in January 1965, he stated that Chinese troops would not go outside Chinese boundaries to fight. At the First Plenum of the Ninth Central Committee in April 1969, Mao again promised (in referring to the Sino-Soviet conflict) that "if the enemy should invade our country, we would refrain from invading his country. As a general rule, we do not fight outside of our own country" (U.S., Department of Commerce, Joint Publications Research Service [JPRS], no. 50,564 [*Translations on Communist China,* no. 104], May 21, 1970, p. 6).

106. Our argument here is slightly different from that of Franz Schurmann ("A Special Feature: What Is Happening in China?" *New York Review of Books,* October 20, 1966, pp. 18–25). Schurmann concluded that a basic difference between Luo and the Maoists was the former's desire for preattack preparations, as against the latter's reliance on postattack mobilization. Red Guard criticisms of Peng Dehuai for failing to make adequate preparations against American attack lead us to believe that Schurmann is in error. See "Settle Accounts with P'eng Teh-huai for His Crimes of Usurping Army Leadership and Opposing the Party," *Jinggangshan Guangdong wenyi zhan bao* (Guangzhou), September 5, 1967. We believe

that the *nature* of the preparations advocated by Luo is much more important than their *timing,* and that the Maoists did not in fact rely solely on postattack mobilization.

107. *New York Times,* May 6, 1965, p. 9.

108. According to these charges, Luo, as well as Peng Dehuai before him, sought to restrict and retard defense research; resisted guidelines formulated by Mao and other authorities; dismissed achievements that had been recorded; and wanted to take over the leadership of research institutions (in keeping with the "quick fix" approach) in order to bend research to meet the production needs of the regular forces. See "Down with Lo Jui-ch'ing, Usurper of the Army Power," pp. 6–7; and the NCNA's international service broadcast of August 27, 1967.

109. *Jiefangjun bao* editorial, June 10, 1965.

110. "Big Military Competition Is Big Exposure of Lo Jui-ch'ing's Plot"; italics added. We assume here that the accusation concerns Luo's activities in 1965.

111. Mao's move against Luo might not have occurred had not the Maoists then perceived a threat to Mao's authority in the party from "capitalist roaders." The insecurity of Mao's position may have been a significant factor in his determination to purge Luo. In more stable circumstances, Luo's contrariness might have been tolerated.

112. See the comments of Zhou Enlai in "Chairman Mao and the Chiefs of the Central Administration Comment on Public Safety, Prosecution, and Law—Paramount Instructions," *Chinese Law and Government* 2 (Winter 1969/70): 4–5.

113. Though Luo was purged, other military leaders who might have agreed with his position emerged from the Cultural Revolution with their political positions strengthened. Huang Yongsheng, the commander of the Canton Military Region (the location of many defense preparations both before and during the Cultural Revolution) became chief of staff and a member of the Politburo. (Yang Chengwu, air defense commander in 1965, was Huang's predecessor as Chief of Staff. Yang was purged in March 1968.) Wu Faxian (Wu Fa-hsien), commander of the air force, also became a member of the Politburo and a deputy chief of staff. In addition, the air force political commissar, and several deputy commanders and deputy commissars, were added to the Ninth Central Committee.

It is possible that these men survived the Cultural Revolution because they were not linked with Mao's opponents in the civilian party apparatus; because they supported (or at least did not oppose) Mao's use of the PLA during the GPCR; and because they were willing to sacrifice Luo Ruiqing at Mao's request.

Chapter 6

1. Lin Biao, "Report to the Ninth National Congress of the Communist Party of China," *Peking Review,* April 28, 1969, p. 19.

2. "Decision of the CCP Central Committee concerning the Great Proletarian Cultural Revolution," August 8, 1966, in *Documents of the Chinese Communist Party Central Committee,* 1: 207–17.

3. Lin Biao, "Report to the Ninth National Congress," p. 18.

4. Juliana P. Heaslet, "The Red Guards: Instruments of Destruction in the Cultural Revolution," *Asian Survey* 11 (December 1972): 1044–45; Philip Bridgham, "Mao's Cultural Revolution in 1967: The Struggle to Seize Power," *China Quarterly,* no. 34 (April–June 1968), pp. 7–10.

5. On July 19, Chen Caidao (Ch'en Ts'ai-tao), Wuhan Garrison commander, favored public order and the smooth development of the Cultural Revolution; supported the conservative faction of the rebels, which had kidnapped two members of the Cultural Revolutionary Group (CRG) of the Central Committee; and disobeyed the order from the

center to support the radical faction. By July 26, the Wuhan mutiny had been subdued by the Maoists after the center dispatched a main force division, some warships of the East Sea Fleet, and local air force units to Wuhan. See Thomas W. Robinson "The Wuhan Incident: Local Strife and Provincial Rebellion during the Cultural Revolution," *China Quarterly,* no. 47 (July–September 1971), pp. 417–34.

6. For instance, Wang Li, one of the radicals in the CRG, was said to claim: "Ninety percent of the leadership in the armed forces is conservative, and only one to two percent is revolutionary." Under the slogan "Attack by reason, defend by force," he urged selected rebels to arm. See "Purge of the 'Wang, Kuan, Chi, and Lin Anti-Party group,'" *Facts and Features,* May 1, 1968, p. 15.

7. Concerning public disorder during the "hot summer" of 1967, see K. S. Karol, *The Second Chinese Revolution* (New York: Hill and Wang, 1973), pp. 277–85.

8. For instance, Mao's and Lin's comments on civil disorder at the meeting of the Red Guard leaders in Beijing in July 1968; see "Dialogues with Responsible Persons of Capital Red Guards Congress," July 28, 1968, in JPRS, *Miscellany of Mao Tse-tung Thought,* 2: 473, 481, 487.

9. Charles Neuhauser, "The Impact of the Cultural Revolution on the Chinese Communist Party Machine," *Asian Survey* 8 (June 1968): 465–86.

10. Richard K. Diao, "The Impact of the Cultural Revolution on China's Economic Elite," *China Quarterly,* no. 42 (April–June 1970), pp. 65–87.

11. Gurtov, "The Foreign Ministry and Foreign Affairs," pp. 94–95.

12. Parris H. Chang, "China's Eclipse of the Moon," *Far Eastern Economic Review,* January 16, 1969, pp. 97–99; and "Nieh Jung-chen: Men to Watch 46," *China Topics,* YB no. 494 (August 13, 1968), pp. 1–7.

13. "Premier Chou's Important Speech of February 2, 1968," in *SCMP,* no. 4154 (April 8, 1968), p. 6.

14. "Dialogues with Responsible Persons," p. 475.

15. Richard Baum, "China: Year of the Mangoes," *Asian Survey* 9 (January 1969): 1–17, esp. 14–17.

16. Karnow, *Mao and China,* pp. 446–47.

17. *Peking Review,* September 13, 1968, pp. 3–5.

18. A joint editorial of *People's Daily* and the *Liberation Army Daily,* September 26, 1968, ibid., September 27, 1968, pp. 3–4; and communiqué of the Twelfth Plenum, ibid., November 1, 1968 (supp.), pp. i–viii.

19. Ibid., November 29, 1968, pp. 10–13.

20. See Chapter 5.

21. Mao's principles in scientific research, which stressed "going all out," "self-reliance," and "hard work" to catch up with the most advanced scientific levels, were set forth in 1958 when Mao decided to manufacture nuclear weapons without relying on Soviet aid. "Counterrevolutionary Revisionist Line in National Defense Research Repudiated," *Peking Review,* September 8, 1967, pp. 9–10; "Mao Tse-tung's Thought—Banner of Victory in Scaling the Heights of Science and Technology," ibid., November 3, 1967, pp. 13–15.

22. "Decision concerning the PLA's Resolute Support of the Revolutionary Masses of the Left," January 23, 1968, in Michael Y. Kau, ed., *The People's Liberation Army and China's Nation Building* (White Plains, N.Y.: International Arts and Sciences Press, 1973), pp. 317–19.

23. *China News Analysis,* June 14, 1968, pp. 12–14.

24. Ralph L. Powell, "Soldiers in the Chinese Economy," *Asian Survey* 11 (August 1971): 753–55.

25. Ralph L. Powell and Chong-kun Yoon, "Public Security and the PLA," ibid. 12 (December 1972): 1082–100.

26. NCNA (Beijing), report in English, February 11, 1969, in *SCMP,* no. 4361 (February 20, 1969), p. 15.

27. One piece of evidence is a Radio Harbin broadcast of October 6, 1967: "The handful of leaders in the Provincial Party Committee taking the capitalist road said . . . that the Provincial Military District was not a part of the national defense army, and its principal leadership was the Provincial Party Committee" (cited in John Gittings, "Army-Party Relations in the Light of the Cultural Revolution," in John Wilson Lewis, ed., *Party Leadership and Revolutionary Power in China* [Cambridge: At the University Press, 1970], p. 390). A directive of the MAC on April 6, 1967, warned that the "decision on whether an organization is Leftist, Rightist, or Centrist can't be based upon whether it has broken into military organs." See *China Topics,* YB, no. 463 (February 1968), p. iv; and the *Liberation Army Daily* editorial, "Earnestly Implement the Principle of Supporting the Left, But Not Any Particular Faction," January 28, 1968, in *Peking Review,* February 2, 1968, pp. 8–9.

28. Harvey Nelsen, "The Military Forces in the Cultural Revolution," *China Quarterly,* no. 51 (July–September 1972), p. 454.

29. New members included Wu Faxian, chief commander of the air force; Qiu Huizuo (Ch'iu Hui-tso), director of the General Rear Service Department; and Zhang Xiuquan (Chang Hsiu-chu'an), head of the Navy Political Department. See Thornton, *China, the Struggle for Power,* p. 312.

30. "Some Directives concerning the Dispatching of the 'Central Support-the-Left Units' in All Military Regions and Provincial Military Districts by the CCPCC, the State Council, MAC, and CRG, June 10, 1968," in Kau, ed., *The People's Liberation Army,* pp. 322–28.

31. Nelsen, "The Military Forces in the Cultural Revolution," pp. 454–55, 472–74; Thornton, *China, the Struggle for Power,* p. 384.

32. Nelsen, "The Military Forces in the Cultural Revolution," pp. 457–59.

33. Chien Yu-shen, *China's Fading Revolution: Army Dissent and Military Division, 1967–68* (Hong Kong: Centre of Contemporary Chinese Studies, 1969), p. 14.

34. Ibid., pp. 17–25.

35. Jurgen Domes, "The Role of the Military in the Formation of Revolutionary Committees, 1967–68," *China Quarterly,* no. 44 (October–December 1970), pp. 132–42.

36. Zhou's speech at a meeting of army cadres, local leaders, and Red Guards in Beijing, September 26, 1967, in *SCMM,* no. 611 (January 2, 1968), pp. 8–11; "Chou's Talk at a Reception for Revolutionary Masses of XX Industrial Systems," *Cultural Revolution Storm* (Guangzhou), February 1968, in *SCMP,* no. 4148 (March 28, 1968), pp. 3–9.

37. Chien, *China's Fading Revolution,* p. 326.

38. Ibid., p. 322.

39. *Union Research Service,* October 29, 1968, p. 110.

40. Ting Wang, "The Emergent Military Class," in William W. Whitson, ed., *The Military and Political Power in China in the 1970s* (New York: Praeger, 1972), p. 130.

41. *China Topics,* YB, no. 463 (February 1968), p. xi.

42. Concerning Lin Biao's personal role in dealing with the conflict between the radical wing and army commanders, see Ellis Joffe, "The Chinese Army after the Cultural Revolution: The Effects of Intervention," *China Quarterly,* no. 55 (July–September 1973), pp. 461–64; and Thomas W. Robinson, "Lin Piao: A Chinese Military Politician," in Whitson, ed., *The Military and Political Power in China,* pp. 82–85.

43. Lin Biao's speech, August 9, 1967, in *China Topics,* YB, no. 463 (February 1968), pp. xiii–xv.

44. "Great Supreme Commander Inspects Kiangsi Province," *Politics and Law Red Flag* (Guangzhou), October 17, 1967, in *SCMP,* no. 4070 (November 30, 1967), p. 6.

45. Lin Biao's speech at a meeting of army cadres, March 25, 1968, in *SCMP,* May 8, 1968, pp. 1–4.

46. Lin Biao, "On the Question of Giving Prominence to Politics," November 1967, in Michael Y. Kau, ed., *The Lin Piao Affair* (White Plains, N.Y.: International Arts and Sciences Press, 1975), pp. 455–59.

47. Lin Biao, "Important Directives to the Army," April 6, 1968, in Kau, ed., *The Lin Piao Affair,* pp. 501–8.

48. Chien, *China's Fading Revolution,* pp. 200–202.

49. Lin Biao's directives of April 6, 1968, in Kau, ed., *The Lin Piao Affair,* p. 508.

50. U.S., Congress, Joint Economic Committee, *China: A Reassessment of the Economy,* 94th Cong., 1st sess., July 10, 1975, p. 23.

51. Concerning the impact of the reduced industrial output in 1967–68 on China's GNP, see "China's Economy in 1968," *Current Scene,* May 3, 1969, pp. 1–3; and *China Topics,* YB, no. 485 (May 28, 1968), pp. 1–5.

52. International Institute of Strategic Studies (IISS) London, *The Military Balance, 1968–69,* p. 23; U.S., Arms Control and Disarmament Agency, *World Military Expenditure and Arms Trade, 1963–73* (Washington, D.C.: Government Printing Office, 1975), p. 85.

53. The restriction of China's national budget ceilings has stemmed in part from the decentralized authority over political, economic, and military resources, which has made it difficult for the central authorities to tax regional surpluses excessively or to transfer the resources of wealthier regions to poorest ones. See William W. Whitson, "Domestic Constraints on Alternative Chinese Military Politics and Strategies in the 1970s," *Annals of the American Academy of Political and Social Science,* July 1972, p. 46.

54. Manfredo Macioti, "Scientists Go Barefoot," *Survival,* July 1971, pp. 232–38.

55. *The Military Balance, 1967–68,* pp. 9–12; *The Military Balance, 1968–69,* pp. 9–12.

56. International Institute of Strategic Studies (IISS), London, *Strategic Survey, 1968,* pp. 41–42.

57. Steve Washenko, "Agriculture in China: Priorities and Prospects," *Current Scene,* October 7, 1971, p. 2.

58. *Union Research Service,* July 5, 1969, p. 103.

59. Ibid., pp. 104–6.

60. Washenko, "Agriculture in China," p. 4.

61. *Peking Review,* August 4, 1967, pp. 14–35.

62. The two statements on the detonation of the hydrogen bombs hailed Mao's correct decision in 1958 to be self-reliant in making atomic and hydrogen bombs and proclaimed the victory of Mao's military line over the revisionist line. See "Press Communiqué of China's First Hydrogen Bomb Test," June 17, 1967, ibid., June 23, 1967, pp. 6–7; "Press Communiqué of China's Second Hydrogen Bomb Test," December 28, 1968, ibid., January 3, 1969, pp. 5–6.

63. "Press Communiqué of China's First Hydrogen Bomb Test," p. 6.

64. NCNA (Beijing), English translation, January 31, 1968, in *SCMP,* no. 4111 (February 5, 1968), pp. 52–53.

65. Jonathan D. Pollack, "Chinese Attitudes towards Nuclear Weapons, 1964–1969," *China Quarterly,* no. 50 (April–June 1972), p. 249.

66. Nelsen, "The Military Forces in the Cultural Revolution," p. 446.

67. Gurtov, "The Foreign Ministry and Foreign Affairs," pp. 83–85; Van Ness, *Revolution and Chinese Foreign Policy,* pp. 213–26, 236–87; Daniel Tretiak, *The Chinese Cultural Revolution and Foreign Policy: The Process of Conflict and Current Policy,* Advanced Studies Group Monograph no. 2 (Waltham, Mass.: Westinghouse Electric Corp., 1970), pp. 1–31.

68. Edward E. Rice, *Mao's Way* (Berkeley: University of California Press, 1972), pp. 360–62.

69. *Peking Review,* February 3, 1967, pp. 23–24.

70. Statement of the Chinese government, ibid., February 10, 1967, pp. 6–7.

71. Concerning the mass demonstrations, see ibid., pp. 9–10; on the Beijing rally, see ibid., February 17, 1967, pp. 12–14, 19.

72. NCNA (Beijing), English-language broadcast, February 10, 1967, in *Foreign Broadcast Information Service* (hereafter cited as *FBIS*), February 13, 1967, p. BBB9.

73. Thomas W. Robinson, "Chou En-lai and the Cultural Revolution," in Robinson, ed., *The Cultural Revolution in China,* p. 267.

74. *Peking Review,* February 10, 1967, pp. 7–8.

75. For the monitored text of Zhou's speech, see *FBIS,* February 13, 1967, pp. BBB5–6.

76. Editor's note, ibid.

77. Fu Zhongbi, "Liquidation of Armed Struggle Means Shameful Betrayal of the Proletarian Revolutionary Cause," *People's Daily,* July 7, 1967, in *Peking Review,* July 21, 1967, pp. 26–28.

78. *Peking Review,* August 18, 1967, p. 37.

79. Clubb, *China and Russia,* p. 487.

80. Ibid.

81. *People's Daily* "Commentator," "We Have Friends All Over the World," August 14, 1967, in *Peking Review,* August 25, 1967, pp. 18–19; *People's Daily* "Commentator," "It Is a Good Thing for Us That the Enemy Attacks China," August 17, 1967, ibid., pp. 19–20.

82. Gurtov, "The Foreign Ministry and Foreign Affairs," p. 90; Rice, *Mao's Way,* p. 378.

83. *Red Flag* editorial, in *Peking Review,* September 22, 1967, pp. 5–6.

84. Gurtov, "The Foreign Ministry and Foreign Affairs," pp. 92–93; Van Ness, *Revolution and Chinese Foreign Policy,* p. 243.

85. For instance, one Red Guard document revealed this view. See *Dongfanghong Dianxun* [East Is Red Telegraph], no. 3 (July 1968), in *SCMP,* no. 4231 (August 2, 1968), pp. 20–23.

86. Premier Zhou's important speech, February 2, 1968, ibid., no. 4154 (April 8, 1968), pp. 5–6.

87. Young, *Negotiating with the Chinese Communists,* pp. 294–98.

88. NCNA (Beijing), May 28, 1968, in *SCMP,* no. 4191 (June 5, 1968), p. 18.

89. Oleg B. Borisov, and B. T. Koloskov, *Soviet-Chinese Relations, 1945–70* (Bloomington: Indiana University Press, 1975), p. 342.

90. For instance, Lin's speech at the Beijing rally commemorating the fiftieth anniversary of the October Revolution, in *Peking Review,* November 10, 1967, pp. 5–8.

91. Rice, *Mao's Way,* pp. 372–73.

92. Whiting, *The Chinese Calculus of Deterrence,* pp. 228, 241–42.

93. Thomas Gottlieb, *Chinese Foreign Policy Factionalism and the Origins of the Strategic Triangle* (Santa Monica, Calif: Rand Corporation, November 1977), pp. 72–73.

94. Dennis J. Doolin, *Territorial Claims in the Sino-Soviet Conflict: Documents and Analysis* (Stanford: Hoover Institution, 1965), pp. 15–19.

95. Excerpts from "A Comment on the Statement of the Communist Party of the U.S.A.," *People's Daily* editorial, March 8, 1963, ibid., pp. 29–31.

96. Excerpts from "Letter of CCPCC to CPSUCC," February 29, 1964, in Gittings, *Survey of the Sino-Soviet Dispute,* pp. 163–64.

97. Excerpts from "Soviet Government Statement," September 20, 1963, in Doolin, *Territorial Claims in the Sino-Soviet Conflict,* pp. 32–33.

98. Hinton, *Communist China in World Politics,* p. 325.

99. Thomas W. Robinson, "The Sino-Soviet Border Dispute: Background, Development, and the March 1969 Clashes," *American Political Science Review* 66 (1972): 1179–81; Hinton, *Communist China in World Politics,* pp. 326–27; Gittings, *Survey of the Sino-Soviet Dispute,* pp. 158–59.

100. The discussion below was reconstructed in light of the Chinese documents published after the March 1969 clashes. See the note of the Ministry of Foreign Affairs of the P.R.C. to

the Soviet Embassy in China, March 3, 1969, in *Peking Review*, March 7, 1969, p. 12; statement of the Information Department of the Chinese Foreign Ministry, March 11, 1969, ibid., March 14, 1969, pp. 14–15; statement of the Chinese government, May 24, 1969, ibid., May 30, 1969, pp. 3–9; document of the Ministry of Foreign Affairs of the P.R.C., October 8, 1969, ibid., October 10, 1969, pp. 8–15; Robinson, "The Sino-Soviet Border Dispute," pp. 1179–83; Neville Maxwell, "A Note on the Amur/Ussuri Sector of the Sino-Soviet Boundaries," *Modern China* 1 (January 1975): 116–26.

101. Document of the Ministry of Foreign Affairs of the P.R.C., October 8, 1969, p. 14.

102. Mao's statement to the Japanese Socialist delegation, in Doolin, *Territorial Claims in the Sino-Soviet Conflict*, pp. 42–44.

103. Radio Free Europe, *China: Sino-Soviet Relations* (June 3, 1966), pp. 2–5.

104. *Pravda* editorial, "In Connection with Mao Tse-tung's Talk with a Group of Japanese Socialists," September 2, 1964, in Doolin, *Territorial Claims in the Sino-Soviet Conflict*, pp. 47–56.

105. J. Malcolm Mackintosh, "The Soviet Generals' View of China in the 1960s," in Garthoff, ed., *Sino-Soviet Military Relations* (New York: Praeger, 1966), pp. 183–92, esp. pp. 190–91; I.I.S.S., *Strategic Survey, 1966*, pp. 16–19.

106. Soviet troops had not been garrisoned in Mongolia since 1957. As a result of the signing of a new Soviet-Mongolian defense accord in January 1966, according to Western press dispatches in early 1967, Soviet troops reentered Mongolia. See Salisbury, *War between Russia and China*, pp. 152–53; and Thomas W. Wolfe, *Soviet Power and Europe, 1945–1970* (Baltimore: Johns Hopkins Press, 1970), p. 467.

107. Concerning Soviet build-up and redeployment of troops along the Sino-Soviet and Sino-Mongolian borders, see Harrison E. Salisbury, "Soviet-Chinese Hostility Found along Their Frontier," *New York Times*, August 17, 1966, pp. 1, 4; Robinson, "The Sino-Soviet Border Dispute," p. 1186.

108. "Communiqué of Plenary Session of the Central Committee of the Communist Party of the Soviet Union," December 13, 1966, in *Current Digest of the Soviet Press* (hereafter cited as *CDSP*), January 4, 1967, pp. 3–4.

109. *New York Times*, January 11, 1967, p. 3.

110. Ibid., January 21, 1967, p. 2.

111. Gottlieb, *Chinese Foreign Policy Factionalism*, pp. 51, 80–81.

112. Chief editor of the Vienna *Kurier* Hugo Portisch, who visited Siberia in mid-1967, interviewed Soviet military officials on the far eastern border and provided such information. See *Atlas* 14 (September 1967): 15–19.

113. *New York Times*, December 11, 1966, p. 3.

114. *CB*, October 21, 1969, p. 50.

115. Directive of the Military Affairs Committee, January 28, 1967; see Chien, *China's Fading Revolution*, p. 246.

116. On March 26, 1967, Chen Yi was quoted as having made such a comment in a speech before representatives of bourgeois democratic parties. See Borisov and Koloskov, *Soviet-Chinese Relations*, p. 313.

117. Gottlieb, *Chinese Foreign Policy Factionalism*, p. 51; Wolfe, *Soviet Power and Europe*, p. 467.

118. Cited in Gottlieb, *Chinese Foreign Policy Factionalism*, p. 68.

119. *China Topics*, YB, no. 523 (May 1, 1969), p. 11.

120. Gottlieb, *Chinese Foreign Policy Factionalism*, pp. 71–72.

121. Statement of the Chinese government, May 24, 1969, in *Peking Review*, May 30, 1969, p. 6.

122. A tabloid published by *Red Flag Bulletin* (Guangdong), May 26, 1968; see *SCMP*, no. 4202 (June 20, 1968), pp. 25–29.

123. Note of the Ministry of Foreign Affairs to the Soviet Embassy in China, March 3, 1969, p. 12.

124. *China Topics,* YB, no. 523 (May 1, 1969), p. 9.

125. "Report from Sinkiang," a tabloid edited by the revolutionary workers of the 8th Peasant Corps of the Xinjiang Red 2nd Headquarters, January 24, 1968, in *Union Research Service,* March 5, 1968, pp. 234–40.

126. *China Topics,* YB, no. 516 (February 20, 1969), p. 8; YB, no. 539 (November 18, 1969), p. 20.

127. Ibid., YB, no. 523 (May 1, 1969), p. 10.

128. Tai Sung An, *The Sino-Soviet Territorial Dispute* (Philadelphia: Western Press, 1972), p. 85.

129. *China News Analysis,* April 11, 1969, p. 6.

130. *Washington Post,* January 6, 1967, p. 9.

131. One of the regulations of January 13, 1967, frequently referred to as *gongan liutiao* ("six rules of public security"), strictly stipulated that any person who maintained "illicit relations with foreign countries" and engaged in sabotage and subversive activities would be severely punished. See *SCMP,* no. 4235 (August 9, 1968), pp. 1–2. The order of September 5, 1967, stipulated that "in the complex, acute class struggle, all revolutionary mass organizations must strictly guard against any attempt to weaken or lower the PLA's fighting strength and prestige." See *China Topics,* YB, no. 463 (February 1968), p. xii.

132. *Peking Review,* March 22, 1968, pp. 15–16.

133. Ibid., March 7, 1969, p. 6.

134. Concerning Sino-Soviet relations in 1966–67, see Clubb, *China and Russia,* pp. 480–90; Borisov and Koloskov, *Soviet-Chinese Relations,* pp. 294–345.

135. According to Moscow's version, Moscow asked Beijing to convene the fourteenth session of the Soviet-Chinese Navigation Commission at the end of July 1967, but Beijing allegedly ignored the Soviet proposal. In the meantime, Moscow appeared to raise a strong protest to the P.R.C. that China's unilaterally declared regulations in April 1966 to govern foreign ships on frontier rivers violated the 1958 Treaty of Commerce and Navigation between the two countries, which guaranteed the ships of both the right to move freely along contiguous waterways and into connecting streams in the Amur and Ussuri rivers. It seems likely that at that time the Beijing leadership did not feel it was necessary to discuss unresolved problems of improving conditions for navigation along the two rivers. The reason was that such a discussion would affect the Chinese regulations that required Soviet ships and personnel on the two rivers to report and turn over weapons, ammunition, and radar equipment to the Chinese Harbor Supervision Office; it was a time when the Chinese suspected the Soviets of espionage and sabotage activities on China's border. See Salisbury, "Soviet-Chinese Hostility," p. 4; Robinson, "The Sino-Soviet Border Dispute," pp. 1181–82; Borisov and Koloskov, *Soviet-Chinese Relations,* pp. 341–42.

136. Alfred D. Low, *The Sino-Soviet Dispute: An Analysis of the Polemics* (London: Associated University Presses, 1976), pp. 237–40.

137. Concerning bureaucratic politics in Soviet leadership on the issue of Czechoslovakia and the P.R.C., see Jiri Valenta, "Soviet Decision Making and the Czechoslovak Crisis of 1968," *Studies in Comparative Communism* 8 (Spring–Summer 1975): 147–73, esp. 152–54; Harold C. Hinton, *Three and a Half Powers: The New Balance in Asia* (Bloomington: Indiana University Press, 1975), pp. 103–4; Lisann, "Moscow and the Chinese Power Struggle," p. 39.

138. *Pravda,* February 29, 1968, p. 4.

139. Excerpts and comments on the six articles appeared in *China Topics,* YB, no. 497 (August 23, 1968), pp. 1–15.

140. *International Affairs* (Moscow), February 1968, pp. 14–22.

141. *China Topics,* YB, no. 497 (August 23, 1968), pp. 6–9.

142. *Pravda,* April 11, 1968, in *International Affairs* (Moscow), May 1968, pp. 3–4.

143. *FBIS,* June 28, 1968, pp. A15–16.

144. *Peking Review,* February 23, 1968, p. 30; see also *People's Daily* "Commentator," "A Foul Performance in Budapest," March 18, 1968, ibid., March 22, 1968, pp. 9–10.

145. "Soviet Revisionist Clique Can't Escape the Punishment of History," ibid., March 8, 1968, pp. 22–25; *People's Daily* "Commentator," "A Clumsy Anti-China Performance," April 29, 1968, ibid., May 17, 1968, p. 29.

146. Ibid., August 9, 1968, pp. 12–14.

147. *Pravda* and *Izvestia,* August 21, 1968, in *CDSP,* September 11, 1968, p. 3.

148. "Defense of Socialism Is the Highest International Duty," *Pravda,* August 22, 1968, ibid., pp. 5–14; TASS communiqué of August 22, 1968, ibid., p. 3.

149. Beijing's first comment on Czechoslovakian modern revisionism was made when the *Peking Review* published an article by the Editorial Department of the Albanian paper *Zeri Popullit;* see "Soviet Revisionism and Czechoslovakia," *Peking Review,* August 16, 1968, pp. 16–19.

150. NCNA report, *Peking Review,* August 23, 1968 (supp.), pp. vi-viii; *People's Daily* "Commentator," "Total Bankruptcy of Soviet Modern Revisionism," August 23, 1968, ibid., pp. iv–vi; *People's Daily* "Commentator," "Deal Made at Bayonet Point," August 30, 1968, ibid., September 6, 1968, pp. 8–9.

151. Ibid., August 23, 1968 (supp.), pp. iii–iv.

152. Concerning the Brezhnev doctrine, see S. Kovalev, "Sovereignty and the Internationalist Obligations of Socialist Countries," *Pravda,* September 26, 1968, in *CDSP,* October 16, 1968, pp. 10–12.

153. Yin Jingyao, "A New Historical Stage in the Peiping-Moscow Struggle," *Issues and Studies* (Taibei) 5 (June 1969): 5–7.

154. *Peking Review,* September 20, 1968, p. 41; italics added.

155. "Premier Chou En-lai's Speech at Peking Banquet," *CB,* June 16, 1969, p. 44.

156. Excerpt from a speech by Wang Enmao, October 18, 1968, in *Peking Review,* October 18, 1968, pp. 29–30; Radio Wulumuzhi, January 11, 1969, in *China Topics,* YB, no. 516 (February 20, 1969), p. 9.

157. *China News Analysis,* April 18, 1969, pp. 6–7.

158. *People's Daily* "Observer," "Vile Soviet Revisionist Declaration to Persist in Treacherous Policy," June 26, 1967, in *Peking Review,* June 30, 1967, pp. 16–17; *People's Daily* "Observer," "Big Betrayal at Hollybush," July 3, 1967, ibid. July 7, 1967, pp. 23–25; *People's Daily* "Commentator," "Insidious U.S.-Soviet Collaboration Policy," July 23, 1967, ibid., July 28, 1967, pp. 12–13.

159. For instance, the Beijing leadership pointed out that before and after the Glassboro talks, the leaders of Burma, Indonesia, and Mongolia were rewarded by Washington and Moscow with cash and weapons in return for their anti-China campaigns. See *People's Daily* "Commentator," "U.S. Imperialism and Soviet Revisionism Are Backstage Managers of Anti-China Force," August 11, 1967, ibid., August 25, 1967, pp. 17–18.

160. *People's Daily* "Commentator," "Nuclear Hoax Cannot Save U.S. Imperialism and Soviet Revisionism," ibid., September 8, 1967, p. 34; *People's Daily* "Commentator," "A Nuclear Fraud Jointly Hatched by the United States and the Soviet Union," June 13, 1968, ibid., June 21, 1968, pp. 17–18.

161. An article in the *Peking Review* on March 8, 1968, revealed that during the Glassboro conspiracy, Moscow and Washington reached "tacit agreement" on the question of "how to use their nuclear weapons to contain China," that at the end of 1967, Washington was determined to start building an ABM system aimed at China and that the Soviets were also preparing an ABM system against China. See "Soviet Revisionist Clique Cannot Escape the Punishment of History," p. 25.

162. "Dirty Deal on Deal," *Peking Review,* July 5, 1968, p. 33.

163. This Chinese apprehension was revealed for the first time in January 1967 when Ye Jianying, vice-chairman of the National Defense Council, spoke out at a mass rally in Beijing, and it was frequently reiterated in the Chinese press. See Ye's speech in *FBIS,* January 16, 1967, pp. BBB5–9. Concerning other Chinese comments, see "Soviet Revisionist Clique Cannot Escape the Punishment of History," pp. 24–25; and "Dirty Deal on Deal," p. 33.

164. David I. Hitchcock, "Joint Development of Siberia: Decision Making in Japanese-Soviet Relations," *Asian Survey* 11 (March 1971): 279–300.

165. *People's Daily* "Commentator," "Total Collaboration between Soviet Revisionist Clique and Japanese Reactionaries," August 10, 1967, in *Peking Review,* August 18, 1967, pp. 34–35.

166. An, *The Sino-Soviet Territorial Dispute,* pp. 87–89.

167. "Total Collaboration," p. 35; Chen Yi's speech at Korean National Day reception, September 9, 1968, in *CB,* June 16, 1969, p. 42.

168. "Total Collaboration," p. 35; NCNA (Beijing), report in English, December 20, 1968, in *SCMP,* no 4326 (December 27, 1968), pp. 18–19.

169. *SCMP,* no. 4322 (December 19, 1968), pp. 21–22.

170. Note of the Chinese Foreign Ministry to the Indian embassy in Beijing, September 10, 1967, in *FBIS,* September 10, 1967, p. BBB9.

171. "Indian Armed Provocations against China Cannot Be Denied," *Peking Review,* September 22, 1967, p. 31.

172. NCNA correspondent, "Indian Defense Minister Singh Slanders CPR," September 14, 1967, in *FBIS,* September 15, 1967, p. BBB2.

173. *People's Daily* "Commentator," "The Soviet Revisionist Clique Is the Vicious Enemy of the Asian People," February 17, 1967, in *Peking Review,* February 23, 1967, pp. 28–29; "Soviet Revisionists Intensify Collaboration with Asian, African, and Latin American Reactionaries," ibid. May 17, 1968, pp. 24–26.

174. Article by *People's Daily* "Commentator" in *FBIS,* September 14, 1967, pp. BBB1–2.

175. NCNA (Beijing), September 8, 1967, ibid., September 10, 1967, pp. BBB9–10.

176. Chen Daifu, "Resolutely Smash the Military Provocations by the Indian Reactionaries," ibid., September 14, 1967, pp. BBB3–4.

177. *FBIS,* September 14, 1967, p. BBB2.

178. *Liberation Army Daily* "Commentator," "The Indian Aggressors Must Rein in at the Brink of the Cliff," ibid., September 15, 1967, pp. BBB4–5.

179. "Indian Armed Provocations against China Cannot Be Denied," pp. 13–14.

180. New York Times Staff, *The Pentagon Papers,* pp. 510–41, esp. pp. 526–40.

181. Statements of the Chinese Foreign Ministry, January 12 and March 29, 1968, in *SCMP,* January 16, 1968, pp. 26–27; and ibid., April 2, 1968, p. 29.

182. *People's Daily* "Commentator," "Johnson's Brinkmanship Is Doomed to Failure," August 22, 1967, in *Peking Review,* September 1, 1967, pp. 29–30; statement of the Chinese Foreign Ministry, August 30, 1967, ibid., September 8, 1967, pp. 18–19; Premier Zhou Enlai's message to President Nguyen Huu Tho, Presidium of the Central Committee of the South Vietnam National Front for Liberation, February 2, 1968, ibid., February 9, 1968, p. 7.

183. "PLA's New Contributions in Serving the People," ibid., September 1, 1967, pp. 6–7; *Liberation Army Daily* editorial, "Grasp Revolution, Stimulate Preparedness against War, and Definitely Wipe Out the Intruding Enemy," September 9, 1967, in *FBIS,* September 11, 1967, pp. BBB7–8.

184. Statement of the Chinese Foreign Ministry, August 30, 1967, *Peking Review,* September 8, 1967, p. 19.

185. Concerning Johnson's decision and its impact on China's security, see Clark M. Clifford, "A Vietnam Reappraisal," *Foreign Affairs* 47 (July 1969): 601–22, esp. 614–16.

186. NCNA correspondent, "U.S. Imperialist Chieftain Johnson Tries New Fraud—'Partially Stopping Bombing' to Induce 'Peace Talks,'" April 5, 1968, in *Peking Review,* April 12, 1968, pp. 14–15; *People's Daily* "Commentator," "Murderous Intent Revealed before the Scheme Is Fully Unfolded," April 15, 1968, ibid., April 19, 1968, pp. 12–13.

187. "U.S. Imperialist Chieftain Johnson Tries New Fraud," pp. 14–15.

188. Clifford, "A Vietnam Reappraisal," pp. 615–16; Mozingo, *China's Foreign Policy,* pp. 41–43.

189. NCNA (Beijing), October 19, 1968, in *FBIS,* October 21, 1968, p. A1.

190. For instance, see Zhou Enlai's speech at the National Day reception given by the Vietnamese ambassador, September 2, 1968, in *Peking Review,* September 6, 1968, pp. 6–7.

191. Italics added. The article even revealed China's fear of joint U.S.-Soviet preparation of military provocations: "In rigging up the anti-China ring of encirclement, the first aim of U.S. imperialism and Soviet revisionism is of course to set up a strategic encirclement and prepare to launch military provocations against China." See *FBIS,* September 23, 1968, pp. A1–2.

192. Chiang Yi-shan, "Military Affairs in Communist China," *Communist China, 1968* (Hong Kong: Union Research Institute, 1968), pp. 243–44.

193. Wu Chin-yin, "Peiping's Efforts to Strengthen Defense Work in Desert Areas," *Chinese Communist Affairs* 6 (February 1969): 17–20.

194. *Peking Review,* September 13, 1968, pp. 6–7.

195. Ibid., October 4, 1968, pp. 14–15.

196. Concerning inconclusive arguments about the difference in emphasis in the Beijing leadership on pace and methods of internal consolidation during the second half of 1968, see Thornton, *China, the Struggle for Power,* pp. 321–28; Rice, *Mao's Way,* pp. 459–77; Karol, *The Second Chinese Revolution,* pp. 376–78; Philip Bridgham, "Mao's Cultural Revolution: The Struggle to Consolidate Power," *China Quarterly,* no. 41 (January–March 1970), pp. 1–25; Ralph L. Powell, "The Power of the Chinese Military," *Current History* 59 (September 1970): 129–33, 175–78.

197. *Peking Review,* September 13, 1968, p. 8.

198. Ibid., October 4, 1968, pp. 13–14.

199. The Twelfth Plenum communiqué reminded the audience that in 1967–68 the trend to reverse the correct verdict had occurred twice, and urged that for the work of party building, the nation should pay attention to Mao's instructions on "getting rid of the stale and taking in the fresh," that it should expel the bad elements that sneaked into the party. Ibid., November 1, 1968 (supp.), pp. vi–vii.

200. *FBIS,* September 23, 1968, pp. C3–4.

201. In talking to "responsible persons of Capital Red Guards Congress" on July 28, 1968, Mao explicitly revealed, in front of Lin, his dissatisfaction with the PLA's political work. Assigning the leading role in the revolution to the working class, he claimed: "Members of the Military Control Commissions are nothing but soldiers. . . . We should say that we must learn from the masses. . . . Didn't we say that the working class is the leading class?" (JPRS, *Miscellany of Mao Tse-tung Thought,* 2: 478–79).

202. Nanchang, Jiangxi provincial broadcasting station, report of July 31, 1969, cited in Robinson, "The Sino-Soviet Border Dispute," p. 1192.

203. *New China Daily* (Nanjing), December 16, 1968, cited in Ralph L. Powell, "The Party, the Government, and the Gun," *Asian Survey* 10 (January 1970): 452.

204. Bridgham, "Mao's Cultural Revolution in 1967: The Struggle to Seize Power," pp. 12–13.

205. For instance, NCNA (Guangzhou), "PLA Meets to Build Frontier Defense Politically," September 2, 1968, in *SCMP,* no. 4254 (September 10, 1968), p. 15.

206. NCNA (Beijing), "PLA Men Guarding Coasts and Frontiers Propagate Mao Tse-tung's Thought," February 21, 1969, ibid., no. 4364 (February 26, 1968), p. 14.

207. Ibid., p. 15.

208. "Grasp Military Training According to Chairman Mao's Line of Army Building," *Red Flag*, no. 5 (1972), in *Chinese Law and Government* 5 (Fall–Winter 1972/73): 125–32.

209. Neville Maxwell provided the information after interviewing the Chinese patrol commander of Zhenbao Island at the time of the March clashes, but indicated that such an order was issued by the patrol commander. See "Report from China: The Chinese Account of the 1969 Fighting at Chen Pao," *China Quarterly*, no. 56 (October–December 1973): 730–39. However, it seems unlikely that the patrol commander alone would be authorized to issue an order highly relevant to Chinese border security; he would be expected to receive the order from a higher defense authority like the Defense Ministry.

210. "Mao's Talk at the First Plenum of the Ninth Central Committee, April 28, 1969," in Schram, ed., *Chairman Mao Talks to the People*, pp. 285–86.

211. Maxwell, "Report from China," pp. 733–34.

212. Lo Siting, "On the Struggle between Patriotism and National Betrayal," *Red Flag*, no. 11 (1974), in *FBIS*, November 20, 1974, pp. E1–10, esp. pp. E3–5.

213. John Gittings, "Peking Walls Have Fears Too," *Far Eastern Economic Review*, January 30, 1969, pp. 175–76; and Gottlieb, *Chinese Foreign Policy Factionalism*, p. 94.

214. Gottlieb, *Chinese Foreign Policy Factionalism*, p. 19; Mozingo, *China's Foreign Policy*, pp. 45–46; Allen S. Whiting, "The Sino-American Detente: Genesis and Prospects," in Ian Wilson, ed., *China and the World Community* (Sidney, Australia: Angus and Robertson, 1973), pp. 70–76.

215. *Peking Review*, November 29, 1968, pp. 30–31.

216. Ibid., pp. 3–9, esp. p. 8.

217. Gottlieb, *Chinese Foreign Policy Factionalism*, pp. 105–7.

218. Foster Rhea Dulles, *American Policy toward Communist China, 1949–1969* (New York: Thomas Y. Crowell, 1972), pp. 239–40; Mozingo, *China's Foreign Policy*, pp. 44–45; Whiting, "The Sino-American Detente," pp. 78–79.

219. Statement of the Chinese Foreign Ministry's Information Department, February 6, 1969, in *CB*, August 15, 1969, p. 31.

220. *China Topics*, YB, no. 523 (May 1, 1969), p. 10.

221. Maxwell, "Report from China," pp. 732–33.

222. Gottlieb, *Chinese Foreign Policy Factionalism*, p. 109.

223. For instance, an article by a *People's Daily* and *Red Flag* commentator, "Confession in an Impasse," January 28, 1969, in *CB*, March 2, 1969, pp. 1–4.

224. Statement of the Chinese Foreign Ministry's Information Department, February 19, 1969, in *CB*, August 15, 1969, p. 31.

225. Chien, *China's Fading Revolution*, p. 108; Harold C. Hinton, *The Bear at the Gate: Chinese Policy Making under Soviet Pressure* (Stanford: Hoover Institution, 1971), p. 34.

226. Maxwell, "Report from China," p. 734.

227. John Gittings, "The Giants Clash," *Far Eastern Economic Review*, March 13, 1969, pp. 447–48.

228. Chinese note to the Soviet Embassy (Beijing), March 3, 1969, in *Peking Review*, March 7, 1969, p. 12; and joint editorial of *People's Daily* and the *Liberation Army Daily*, March 4, 1969, ibid., pp. 6–7.

229. Maxwell, "Report from China," p. 731.

230. Lin Biao, "Report to the Ninth National Congress," pp. 28–29.

231. Wang Zhaocai, "Tear Off the Wrappings from the Soviet Revisionists' 'Definition of Aggression,'" *Red Flag*, no. 5 (1969), in *Peking Review*, May 30, 1969, pp. 13–15; a joint editorial of *People's Daily, Red Flag*, and the *Liberation Army Daily*, June 9, 1969, ibid., June 13, 1969, pp. 6–8.

232. The Soviets charged that who fired first on March 2 was entirely reconstructed by numerous writers in terms of Soviet documents; only Maxwell provided a Chinese version of

the March 2 fighting. The Soviets alleged that on March 2 the Chinese shot first, but they would not deny that on March 15 they did strike the first blow in retaliation for the Chinese-initiated incident of March 2. See IISS "The Sino-Soviet Dispute," *Strategic Survey, 1969,* pp. 66–72; Robinson, "The Sino-Soviet Border Dispute," pp. 1187–89; Karnow, *Mao and China,* pp. 495–97; Harold C. Hinton, "Conflict on the Ussuri: A Clash of Nationalisms," *Problems of Communism* 20 (January–April 1971): 47–48; and Tsao Chih-ching, "Peiping-Soviet Border Clashes," *Issues and Studies* (Taibei) 8 (May 1969): 1–3.

233. See Robinson, "The Sino-Soviet Border Dispute," pp. 1187–89; Karnow, *Mao and China,* pp. 495–97; and Maxwell, "Report from China," p. 735.

234. Concerning Chinese mass rallies, see *Peking Review,* March 7, 1969, pp. 8–11.

235. Tillman Durdin's report in the *New York Times,* March 16, 1969, pp. 1, 11; William Beecher, "Border Restraint Noted," ibid., April 12, 1969, p. 11.

236. Lin Biao's report to the Ninth National Congress, p. 28; Xinhua News Agency's "Note on Release of the Soviet Government's March 29 Statement," May 24, 1969, in *Peking Review,* May 30, 1969, p. 9.

237. Hinton, *The Bear at the Gate,* p. 54; An, *The Sino-Soviet Territorial Dispute,* p. 101.

238. For instance, a Chinese government statement of May 24, 1969, declared: "The Soviet Government will have completely miscalculated if it should take the Chinese Government's stand for a peaceful settlement of the boundary question as a sign that China is weak and can be bullied, thinking that the Chinese people can be cowed by its policy of nuclear blackmail and that it can realize its territorial claims against China by means of war" (*Peking Review,* May 30, 1969, p. 9).

239. Robinson, "The Sino-Soviet Border Dispute," pp. 1192–93.

240. For Chinese criticism of the restoration of capitalism in the Soviet system, see Hong Xuan, "Soviet Revisionists' 'New System' Is a New Means to Exploit the Working People," *Peking Review,* March 22, 1968, pp. 34–35; Gong Huiwen, "Trade Unions under Soviet Revisionism," ibid., May 3, 1968, pp. 28–29; "Soviet Institutes of Higher Learning Turned into Tools for All-round Capitalist Restoration," ibid., August 2, 1968, pp. 27–28; Xinhua News Agency's commentary, "Soviet Workers in Abyss of Suffering," ibid., October 18, 1968, pp. 22–24; "Soviet Revisionist Komsomol—Tool for Restoring Capitalism," ibid., December 20, 1968, pp. 27–28.

241. Daniel Tretiak, "Changes in Chinese Attention to Southeast Asia, 1967–1969: Their Relevance for the Future of the Area," *Current Scene,* November 1, 1969, pp. 1–17, esp. pp. 10–13; Linda D. Dillon, Bruce Bruton, and Walter C. Soderlund, "Who Was the Principal Enemy?: Shifts in Official Chinese Perceptions of the Two Superpowers, 1968–1969," *Asian Survey* 17 (May 1977): 456–73.

242. Hinton, "Conflict on the Ussuri," p. 47; Tsao Chih-ching, "Peiping-Soviet Border Clashes," p. 2.

243. Roger Glenn Brown, "Chinese Politics and American Policy: A New Look at the Triangle," *Foreign Policy,* no. 23 (Summer 1976), pp. 3–23. For support of this view, see Gottlieb, *Chinese Foreign Policy Factionalism,* pp. 115–18.

244. Harvey Nelsen, "The Sino-Soviet Border Clashes of March 1969: A Comment," *Contemporary China* 1 (December 1976): 12.

245. Joffe, "The Chinese Army after the Cultural Revolution," pp. 451–54.

246. "Mao's Talk at Enlarged Meeting of the Political Bureau," March 20, 1966, in JPRS, *Miscellany of Mao Tse-tung Thought,* 2: 375.

247. Schram, ed., *Chairman Mao Talks to the People,* p. 285.

248. "The August 28, 1969, Directive," which was circulated within the Chinese Communist party, indicated that the border units were not to be allowed to travel to exchange revolutionary experience. See *Chinese Law and Government* 3 (Winter 1970/ 71): 274–77.

249. Schram, ed., *Chairman Mao Talks to the People,* p. 285.

Chapter 7

1. With a view to the future, it should be added that at times of internal vulnerability, external pressures that threaten China's border security, whether with invasion, subversion, or the occupation of a buffer area, have not deterred China, but rather have provoked drastic Chinese responses. In the 1979 invasion of Vietnam, which we treat briefly later in this chapter, such a provocation was a major factor in China's claim that "punishment" of Vietnam was necessary.

2. Most writers on bureaucratic politics neglect the relationship between bureaucratic interests and ideology. They consider bureaucratic politics an independent motive force in policy making, whereas we assume that in China, bureaucratic competition takes place within a philosophical framework that is bounded by the three "impulses" and the dialectical method of analysis. (We would also maintain that ideological consensus bounds policy debates and bureaucratically motivated stances therein in all other governments, the United States included.) See, for example, the introduction to Morton H. Halperin and Arnold Kanter, eds., *Readings in American Foreign Policy: A Bureaucratic Perspective* (Boston: Little, Brown, 1973).

3. Mao, "Speech at the First Plenum of the Ninth Central Committee," in JPRS, no. 50,564 (*Translations on Communist China,* no. 104), May 21, 1970, p. 6.

4. As Mao wrote in "On Contradiction" (*Selected Readings,* p. 120), internal factors always account for change more than external factors do. But neither this nor any other aspect of the concept of contradictions has been incorporated into most Western studies of Chinese foreign policy, which today commonly interpret it in terms of balance of power and national security.

5. On the differences between the two, see the exceptional study by Kenneth Lieberthal, "The Politics of Modernization in the PRC," *Problems of Communism* 27 (May–June 1978): 1–17.

6. The most cogent argument in support of this view is by Charles Bettelheim, "The Great Leap Backward," in Bettelheim and Neil Burton, *China since Mao* (New York: Monthly Review Press, 1977).

7. *Three Worlds,* p. 4, quotes Mao as having outlined the theory to an unnamed Third World leader, saying: "In my view, the United States and the Soviet Union form the first world. Japan, Europe and Canada, the middle section, belong to the second world. We are the third world."

8. Many writers have commented on China's strategic reasons in the 1950s and 1960s for supporting Third World revolutions, especially in nearby countries, and for confronting the United States over Taiwan. Peaceful coexistence, in the Chinese view, was hardly possible when the United States was intervening in other countries' affairs. Very little has been written, however, about the domestic political context in which Chinese criticisms of peaceful coexistence took place. If Mao and his supporters had endorsed détente with the United States, they would have risked eroding the class struggle and dictatorship of the proletariat within China, paving the way for revisionism of the kind Khrushchev was accused of practicing. In Mao's view, resisting imperialism and securing the Chinese and other revolutions required strengthening socialism at home just as much as they required supporting anti-imperialist revolutions abroad.

9. A very clear statement of these priorities is Foreign Minister Huang Hua's foreign-policy report of July 30, 1977, in *Issues and Studies* (Taibei) 13 (November 1977): 89–90.

10. See Kent Morrison, "Domestic Politics and Industrialization in China: The Foreign Trade Factor," *Asian Survey* 18 (July 1978): 687–705.

11. Interview by U.S. television commentators, January 31, 1979, in *Beijing Review,* February 16, 1979, p. 17.

12. See Wang Jiaxiang, "In Refutation of Modern Revisionism's Reactionary Theory of the State," *Peking Review,* June 24, 1958, pp. 6–11; and Editorial departments of *Renmin ribao* and *Hongqi,* "Is Yugoslavia a Socialist Country?," ibid., September 27, 1963, pp. 14–27.

13. See E. L. Wheelwright and Bruce McFarlane, *The Chinese Road to Socialism: Economics of the Cultural Revolution* (New York: Monthly Review Press, 1970), pp. 69–70, 87–88.

14. See Wang Jiaxiang, "In Refutation of Modern Revisionism's Reactionary Theory of the State."

15. See, for instance, *Peking Review,* September 1, 1978, pp. 13–15, for Hua's speech in Belgrade and an article on Yugoslavia's "Achievements in Socialist Construction."

16. An excellent survey has been written by Daniel Tretiak and Gabor Teleki, "The Uneasy Triangle: The Sino-Yugoslav Rapprochement and Its Implications for Sino-Albanian Relations," *Current Scene* 15 (October 1977): 1–18.

17. Xue Muqiao, "A Study in the Planned Management of the Socialist Economy," *Beijing Review,* October 26, 1979, pp. 14–20. See also his follow-up article on profitability in enterprises, "On Reforming the Economic Management System (II)," ibid., March 24, 1980, pp. 21–25.

18. See Huang Hua's "Report on the World Situation," *Issues and Studies* (Taibei) 14 (January 1978): 96.

19. Ibid., p. 97. Here, the foreign minister asks the audience, "Should we unite with an individual like Tito? What do you think?" He is greeted with silence, which, he says, "suggests that you have not caught the essence of the problem." In a similar vein, Vice-Premier Deng, speaking before the CCP Central Committee ten days before Hua, noted: "Some people at home and abroad denounce us for breaking our promise by opposing revisionism on the one hand and practicing revisionism on the other hand" ("Teng Hsiao-ping's Talk at the Third Plenary Session of the Tenth CCPCC," ibid. 14 [July 1978], p. 106).

20. Deng Xiaoping's speech, ibid., pp. 100–101.

21. Prior to the invasion of Kampuchea, *Renmin ribao* had stated: "There is a limit to the Chinese people's forbearance and restraint." It repeated the longstanding Maoist dictum that China "will not attack unless it is attacked; but if it is attacked, it will certainly counterattack" (NCNA [Beijing] broadcast, December 24, 1978, in *FBIS*/P.R.C., December 26, 1978, p. A13). In February 1979 there were warnings to Vietnam from, among others, the Chinese Foreign Ministry and Vice-Premier Li Xiannian (ibid., February 16, 1979, pp. A2–3, and February 12, 1979, pp. A7–8). Of these, the clearest were Deng Xiaoping's statements in the United States, where he said that China would have to "teach Vietnam a lesson," and in Japan, where he said that "China is considering taking an appropriate counteraction in Vietnam even if such an action involved some risk. Vietnam must be punished" (*San Francisco Chronicle,* February 18, 1979, pp. 1, 27). The invasion followed within days.

22. *Renmin ribao* editorial, December 25, 1978, as broadcast by New China News Agency and translated in *FBIS*/P.R.C., December 26, 1978, p. A16.

23. See *Los Angeles Times,* March 7, 1979, p. 19, for these quotations.

24. The debate resulted in decisions to cut back the pace and scope of industrial targets and to increase investments in agriculture. See *Beijing Review,* February 16, 1979, pp. 6–7; April 6, 1979, p. 3; and April 20, 1979, p. 3. A number of Mao's supporters were reportedly purged during this "readjustment" process; see *Los Angeles Times,* April 25, 1979, p. 1.

25. When Deng Xiaoping visited Washington, he said that where there was a united will, Soviet expansionism could be defeated. Referring to the overthrow of the shah of Iran, Deng said that while China could do nothing to prevent it, there were countries that could (and should) if they were strong-minded enough. See interview with U.S. television commentators in *Beijing Review,* February 16, 1979, p. 19. By invading Vietnam, China was showing what a useful ally it could be.

26. Although U.S. leaders reportedly objected to Chinese plans to "punish" Vietnam, the U.S. position during the invasion supported China. In particular, Washington took the same position as Beijing that the appropriate way to resolve the crisis was for China to withdraw from Vietnam and for Vietnam to withdraw from Kampuchea. Direct criticisms of Chinese actions were held to a minimum; and later high-level visits by U.S. officials (Secretary of Commerce Michael Blumenthal, Vice-President Walter Mondale, and National Security Council director Zbigniew Brzezinski) reflected the U.S. desire to go forward with economic exchanges and consultation on "parallel" global strategy.

27. *Renmin ribao* editorial, February 18, 1979.

28. *Peking Review,* July 17, 1964, pp. 7–27.

Glossary of Pinyin Names

In January 1979 the government of the People's Republic of China officially adopted the Pinyin system of romanization. Accordingly, the list below consists of the Pinyin spelling of most of the personal and place names mentioned in the text, followed by a modified Wade-Giles spelling, which to many will be the more familiar of the two. Among the names that we have not converted to the Pinyin system are Chiang Kai-shek, Tibet, Manchuria, Inner and Outer Mongolia, and the Pescadores. Also absent are names that have changed only in form (hyphenation, diacritical marks, etc.), not in spelling.

Anhui (Anhwei)
An Zhiyuan (An Chih-yuan)
An Ziwen (An Tzu-wen)
Beijing (Peking)
Bo Yibo (Po I-po)
Chen Caidao (Ch'en Ts'ai-tao)
Chengdu (Ch'eng-tu)
Chen Xilian
Chongqing (Chungking)
Dachen (Tachen)
Dalian (Darien)
Deng Tuo (Teng T'o)
Deng Xiaoping (Teng Hsiao-p'ing)
Deng Yongya (Teng Yung-ya)
Deng Zehui (Teng Tzu-hui)
Dong Biwu (Tung Pi-wu)
Donghua (Tunghua)
Fan Hong (Fan Hung)
Fujian (Fukien)
Fuzhou (Foochow)
Gaer (Gartok)
Gansu (Kansu)
Gao Gang (Kao Kang)
Guangdong (Kwangtung)
Guangxi (Kwangsi)
Guangzhou (Kwangchow, or Canton)

Guizhou (Kweichow)
Guo Moruo (Kuo Mo-jo)
Hangzhou (Hangchow)
Heilongjiang (Heilungkiang)
Henan (Honan)
Hetian (Hotien)
Hobei (Hebei)
Hongqiling (Hung Ch'iling)
Hua Guofeng (Hua Kuo-feng)
Huang Xinding (Huang Hsin-ting)
Huang Yongsheng (Huang Yung-sheng)
Hubei (Hupeh)
Huibin (Harbin)
Huo Long (Ho Lung)
Jiang Qing (Chiang Ch'ing)
Jiangsu (Kiangsu)
Jiangxi (Kiangsi)
Jilin (Kirin)
Kangda (K'ang-ta)
Lanzhou (Lanchow)
Lianjiang (Lien-chiang)
Liao Chengzhi (Liao Ch'eng-chih)
Liao Heshu (Liao Ho-shu)
Liao Luyan (Liao Lu-yen)
Lin Biao (Lin Piao)
Liu Bocheng (Liu Po-ch'eng)

Liu Shaoqi (Liu Shao-ch'i)
Li Xiannian (Li Hsien-nien)
Longze (Longju)
Lu Dingyi (Lu Ting-yi)
Lu Duan (Lü Tuan)
Luo Ruiqing (Lo Jui-ch'ing)
Mao Zedong (Mao Tse-tung)
Nanjing (Nanking)
Nie Rongzhen (Nieh Jung-chen)
Nie Yanrong (Nieh Yen-jung)
Ni Jieliang (Ni Chieh-liang)
Ningxia (Ningsia)
Peng Dehuai (P'eng Teh-huai)
Peng Zhen (P'eng Chen)
Qiao Guanhua (Ch'iao Kuan-hua)
Qingdao (Tsingtao)
Qinghai (Chinghai)
Qiu Huizuo (Ch'iu Hui-tso)
Shandong (Shantung)
Shanxi (Shansi)
Shenxi (Shensi)
Sichuan (Szechwan)
Taibei (Taipei)
Tang Pingzhu (T'ang P'ing-chu)
Tianjin (Tientsin)
Wang Bingnan (Wang Ping-nan)

Wu Faxian (Wu Fa-hsien)
Wu Lengxi (Wu Leng-hsi)
Wulumuzhi (Urumchi)
Wure (Wu-je)
Wu Xiuquan (Wu Hsiu-ch'uan)
Xiao Hua (Hsiao Hua)
Xinhua she (Hsinhua she)
Xinjiang (Sinkiang)
Xisha (Paracel)
Yanan (Yenan)
Yangze (Yangtse)
Yan Hongyan (Yen Hung-yen)
Yang Xianzhen (Yang Hsien-chen)
Yanjing (Yenching)
Yao Dengshan (Yao Teng-shan)
Ye Jianying (Yeh Chien-ying)
Yining (Kuldja)
Yu Zhaoli (Yü Chao-li)
Zhang Guohua (Chang Kuo-hua)
Zhang Wentian (Chang Wen-t'ien)
Zhang Xiuquan (Chang Hsiu-chu'an)
Zhejiang (Chekiang)
Zhenbao (Chen Pao)
Zhou Enlai (Chou En-lai)
Zhu De (Chu Teh)
Zhuge Liang (Chu-ko Liang)

Bibliography

General Sources

Books and Monographs on Domestic and Foreign Policy

Barnett, A. Doak. *China and the Major Powers in East Asia.* Washington, D.C.: Brookings Institution, 1978.
———ed. *Communist Strategies in Asia.* New York: Praeger, 1963.
Bettelheim, Charles, and Burton, Neil. *China Since Mao.* New York: Monthly Review Press, 1977.
Clubb, Oliver Edmund. *China and Russia: The Great Game.* New York: Columbia University Press, 1971.
Dutt, Vidya P. *China and the World.* New York: Praeger, 1966.
Farrell, R. Barry, ed. *Approaches to Comparative and International Politics.* Evanston: Northwestern University Press, 1966.
Gittings, John. *The Role of the Chinese Army.* London: Oxford University Press, 1967.
———. *The World and China, 1922-1972.* New York: Harper and Row, 1974.
Gurtov, Melvin. *China and Southeast Asia—The Politics of Survival: A Study of Foreign Policy Interaction.* Baltimore: Johns Hopkins University Press, 1975.
Halperin, Morton H., and Kanter, Arnold, eds. *Readings in American Foreign Policy: A Bureaucratic Perspective.* Boston: Little, Brown, 1973.
Hinton, Harold C. *China in World Politics.* Boston: Houghton Mifflin, 1966.
Karnow, Stanley. *Mao and China.* New York: Viking Press, 1972.
Kennan, George F. *The Cloud of Danger: Current Realities of American Foreign Policy.* Boston: Little, Brown, 1977.
Mozingo, David P. *China's Foreign Policy and the Cultural Revolution.* Cornell University, International Relations of East Asia Monograph, March 1970.
———. *Chinese Policy Toward Indonesia, 1949–1967.* Ithaca, N.Y.: Cornell University Press, 1975.
New York Times Staff. *The Pentagon Papers.* New York: Bantam Books, 1971.
Ojha, Ishwer C. *Chinese Foreign Policy in an Age of Transition: The Diplomacy of Cultural Despair.* Boston: Beacon Press, 1969.
Rice, Edward E. *Mao's Way.* Berkeley: University of California Press, 1972.

Robinson, Thomas W., ed. *The Cultural Revolution in China.* Berkeley: University of California Press, 1971.

Rosenau, James N., ed. *Linkage Politics: Essays on the Convergence of National and International Systems.* New York: Free Press, 1969.

Schurmann, Franz. *Ideology and Organization in Communist China.* 2d ed. Berkeley: University of California Press, 1968; 2d ed., enl., 1971.

Simmonds, James D. *China: Evolution of a Revolution 1959–1966.* Canberra: Australian National University, 1968.

———. *China's World: The Foreign Policy of a Developing State.* New York: Columbia University Press, 1970.

Snow, Edgar. *The Long Revolution.* New York: Random House, 1971.

Solomon, Richard C. *Mao's Revolution and the Chinese Political Culture.* Berkeley: University of California Press, 1971.

Teng, Ssu-yu, and Fairbank, John K. *China's Response to the West: A Documentary Survey, 1839-1923.* New York: Atheneum, 1969.

Thornton, Richard C. *China, the Struggle for Power, 1917–1972.* Bloomington: Indiana University Press, 1973.

Van Ness, Peter. *Revolution and Chinese Foreign Policy: Peking's Support for Wars of National Liberation.* Berkeley: University of California Press, 1970.

Wang, Gungwu. *China and the World since 1949: The Impact of Independence, Modernity, and Revolution.* New York: St. Martin's Press, 1977.

Wheelwright, E. L., and McFarlane, Bruce. *The Chinese Road to Socialism: Economics of the Cultural Revolution.* New York: Monthly Review Press, 1970.

Whiting, Allen S. *Chinese Domestic Politics and Foreign Policy in the 1970s.* Ann Arbor: Center for Chinese Studies, University of Michigan, 1979.

Whitson, William W., ed. *The Military and Political Power in China in the 1970s.* New York: Praeger, 1972.

Articles

Deng Xiaoping. "Talk at the Third Plenary Session of the Tenth CCPCC" (July 20, 1977). *Issues and Studies* (Taibei) 14 (July 1978): 103–8.

Huang Hua. "Report on the World Situation" (July 30, 1977). *Issues and Studies* (Taibei) 13 (November 1977): 78–84; 14 (January 1978): 94–116.

Lieberthal, Kenneth. "The Politics of Modernization in the PRC." *Problems of Communism* 27 (May–June 1978): 1–17.

Los Angeles Times, March 7 and April 25, 1979.

Morrison, Kent. "Domestic Politics and Industrialization in China: The Foreign Trade Factor," *Asian Survey* 18 (July 1978): 687–705.

San Francisco Chronicle, February 18, 1979.

Tretiak, Daniel, and Teleki, Gabor. "The Uneasy Triangle: Sino-Yugoslav Rapprochement and Its Implications for Sino-Albanian Relations." *Current Scene* 15 (October 1977): 1–18.

Zimmerman, William. "Issue Area and Foreign-Policy Process: A Research Note in Search of a General Theory." *American Political Science Review* 67 (1973): 1204–12.

Documents and Periodicals

In Chinese

Center for Research on China Problems, ed. *Lin Biao quanji* [Collected Writings of Lin Biao]. Hong Kong: Zelian Chubanshe, 1970.

Ding Wang, ed. *Zhonggong wenhua dageming zeliao huibian* [Collection of Documents on the Chinese Communist Great Cultural Revolution]. Hong Kong: Contemporary China Research Institute, 1968.

Mao Zedong sixiang wansui [Long Live the Thought of Mao Zedong]. Beijing, 1969.

Mao Zedong xuanji [Selected Works of Mao Zedong]. Vols. 1–4. Beijing: People's Publishing House, 1967.

Renmin ribao [People's Daily] (Beijing), 1950–79.

Shijie zhishi [World Knowledge]. Beijing: Shijie zhishi Chubanshe, 1949–58.

Zhonghua renmin gongheguo duiwai guanxi wenjian ji [Documents of the Foreign Relations of the P.R.C.]. Vol. 5 (1958). Beijing: Shijie zhishi Chubanshe, 1959.

In English

Bowie, Robert R., and Fairbank, John K., eds. *Communist China, 1955–59: Policy Documents with Analysis.* Cambridge, Mass.: Harvard University Press, 1962.

The Case of P'eng Teh-huai. Hong Kong: Union Research Institute, 1968.

Chen, S.C., and Ridley, Charles P., ed. *Rural People's Communes in Lien-Chiang: Documents concerning Communes in Lien-Chiang Country, Fukien Province, 1962–63.* Stanford: Hoover Institution, 1969.

Cheng, J. Chester, ed. *The Politics of the Chinese Red Army: The Bulletin of Activities of the PLA.* Stanford: Hoover Institution, 1966.

Chinese Communist Party Documents of the Great Proletarian Cultural Revolution, 1965–1967. Hong Kong: Union Research Institute, 1968.

Documents of the Chinese Communist Party Central Committee, September 1956–April 1969. Hong Kong: Union Research Institute, 1971.

Foreign Broadcast Information Service (Washington, D.C.), 1962–79.

New York Times, 1950–80.

Peking Review, 1958–80.

Renmin ribao, Editorial Department. *Chairman Mao's Theory of the Differentiation of the Three Worlds Is a Major Contribution to Marxism-Leninism.* Beijing: Foreign Languages Press, 1977.

Schram, Stuart R., ed. *Chairman Mao Talks to the People: Talks and Letters, 1956–1971.* New York: Pantheon Books, 1974.

———. *The Political Thought of Mao Tse-tung.* Rev. ed. New York: Praeger, 1969.

———. *Quotations from Chairman Mao Tse-tung.* New York: Bantam Books, 1967.

Selected Military Writings of Mao Tse-tung. Beijing: Foreign Languages Press, 1968.

Selected Readings from the Works of Mao Tse-tung. Beijing: Foreign Languages

Press, 1971.

Selected Works of Mao Tse-tung. Vols. 1–4. Beijing: Foreign Languages Press, 1961–77.

U.S., Consulate General, Hong Kong. *Current Background,* 1950–69.

———. *Selections from China Mainland Magazines,* 1962–69.

———. *Survey of China Mainland Press,* 1950–69.

U.S., Department of Commerce, Joint Publications Research Service. *Miscellany of Mao Tse-tung Thought (1949–1968).* Washington, D.C.: Government Printing Office, 1974.

———. No. 50,564 (*Translations on Communist China,* no. 104), May 21, 1970.

The Korean War

Books

Baldwin, Frank, ed. *Without Parallel: The American-Korean Relationship since 1945.* New York: Pantheon Books, 1974.

Beloff, Max. *Soviet Policy in the Far East, 1944–51.* London: Oxford University Press, 1953.

Chow, Ching-wen. *Ten Years of Storm.* New York: Holt, Rinehart, and Winston, 1960.

Dallin, Alexander. *The Soviet Union and the United Nations.* New York: Praeger, 1961.

Floyd, David. *Mao against Khrushchev.* New York: Praeger, 1964.

Friedman, Edward, and Selden, Mark, eds. *American's Asia: Dissenting Essays on Asian-American Relations.* New York: Vintage Books, 1971.

Garthoff, Raymond L., ed. *Sino-Soviet Military Relations.* New York: Praeger, 1966.

Gati, Charles, ed. *Caging the Bear: Containment and the Cold War.* Indianapolis: Bobbs-Merrill, 1974.

George, Alexander L. *The Chinese Communist Army in Action: The Korean War and Its Aftermath.* New York: Columbia University Press, 1967.

Griffith, Samuel B. *The Chinese People's Liberation Army.* New York: McGraw-Hill, 1967.

Han Suyin. *Wind in the Tower: Mao Tse-tung and the Chinese Revolution, 1949–75.* Boston: Little, Brown, 1976.

Hsiung, James C. *Ideology and Practice: The Evolution of Chinese Communism.* New York: Praeger, 1970.

Kennan, George F. *Memoirs, 1925–50.* Boston: Little, Brown, 1967.

MacFarquhar, Roderick, ed. *Sino-American Relations, 1949–71.* New York: Praeger, 1972.

Melby, John. *Mandate of Heaven: Record of a Civil War, China, 1945–49.* Toronto: University of Toronto Press, 1968.

Mosely, Philip E. *The Kremlin and World Politics.* New York: Vintage Books, 1960.

Panikkar, Kavalarm M. *In Two Chinas: Memoirs of a Diplomat.* London: George Allen and Unwin, 1955.

Salisbury, Harrison E. *War between Russia and China.* New York: W. W. Norton, 1969.

Service, John. *The Amerasia Papers.* Berkeley: Center for Chinese Studies, University of California, 1971.

Simmons, Robert R. *The Strained Alliance: Peking, P'yongyang, Moscow, and the Politics of the Korean Civil War.* New York: Free Press, 1975.

Stoessinger, John G. *Nations in Darkness: China, Russia, and America.* New York: Random House, 1971.

Talbott, Strobe, ed. and trans. *Khrushchev Remembers: The Last Testament.* Boston: Little, Brown, 1970.

Topping, Seymour. *Journey between Two Chinas.* New York: Harper and Row, 1972.

Tsou, Tang. *America's Failure in China, 1941-50.* Chicago: University of Chicago Press, 1963.

U.S., Department of the Army. *Korea: 1950.* Washington, D.C.: Government Printing Office, 1952.

Whiting, Allen S. *China Crosses the Yalu: The Decision to Enter the Korean War.* Stanford: Stanford University Press, 1960.

Whitney, Courtney. *MacArthur: His Rendezvous with History.* New York: Knopf, 1966.

Source Materials in Translation

Chinese Press Survey (Shanghai), 1949-50.

Huang Hua. "Report on the World Situation" (July 30, 1977). *Issues and Studies* (Taibei) 14 (January 1978): 94-116.

New China News Agency Daily News Release (Beijing: The China Information Bureau, Press Administration), 1950.

People's China (Beijing), 1950-51.

Review of Hong Kong Chinese Press, 1950-51.

Newspapers and Periodicals

Blum, Robert M. "Secret Cable from Peking." *San Francisco Chronicle,* September 27, 1978, p. F-1.

Far Eastern Economic Review, October 2, 1969.

Lieberthal, Kenneth. "Mao versus Liu? Policy towards Industry and Commerce, 1946-49." *China Quarterly,* no. 47 (July-September 1971), pp. 494-520.

San Francisco Examiner and Chronicle, August 13, 1978.

Vogel, Ezra. "Land Reform in Kwangtung, 1951-53: Central Control and Localism." *China Quarterly,* no. 38 (April-June 1969), pp. 27-62.

The Taiwan Strait Crisis

Books and Mongraphs

Ch'en Jerome, ed. *Mao Papers: Anthology and Bibliography.* London: Oxford University Press, 1970.

Eisenhower, Dwight D. *Waging Peace, 1956–1961.* Garden City, N.Y.: Double-day, 1965.

Halperin, Morton H., ed. *Sino-Soviet Relations and Arms Control.* Cambridge, Mass.: MIT Press, 1967.

Hsieh, Alice Langley. *Communist China's Strategy in the Nuclear War.* Englewood Cliffs, N.J.: Prentice-Hall, 1962.

Patterson, George N. *Tibet in Revolt.* London: Faber and Faber, 1960.

Tsou, Tang. *The Embroilment over Quemoy: Mao, Chiang, and Dulles.* Logan: Institute of International Studies, University of Utah, 1959.

Young, Kenneth T., Jr. *Negotiating with the Chinese Communists: The United States Experience, 1953–67.* New York: McGraw-Hill, 1968.

Articles

Barnett, Robert W. "China and Taiwan: The Economic Issues." *Foreign Affairs* 50, no. 3 (April 1972): 444–58.

Clubb, Oliver Edmund. "Formosa and the Offshore Islands in American Policy, 1950–55." *Political Science Quarterly* 74, no. 4 (December 1959): 517–31.

Kallgren, Joyce. "Nationalist China's Armed Forces." *China Quarterly,* no. 15 (July–September 1963), pp. 35–44.

MacFarquhar, Roderick. "Communist China's Intra-party Dispute." *Pacific Affairs* 31, no. 4 (December 1958): 323–35.

Oksenberg, Michel. "Policy-making under Mao Tse-tung, 1949–1968." *Comparative Politics* 3, no. 3 (April 1971): 323–60.

Sigal, Leon V. "The 'Rational Policy' Model and the Formosa Straits Crisis." *International Studies Quarterly* 14, no. 2 (June 1970): 121–56.

Strong, Anna Louise. "Chinese Strategy in the Taiwan Strait." *New Times* (Moscow), no. 46 (November 1958), pp. 8–11.

Thomas, John R. "Soviet Behavior in the Quemoy Crisis of 1958." *Orbis* 6, no. 1 (Spring 1962): 38–64.

Tsou, Tang. "Mao's Limited War in the Taiwan Strait." *Orbis* 3, no. 3 (Fall 1959): 332–50.

———. "The Quemoy Imbroglio: Chiang Kai-shek and the United States." *Western Political Quarterly* 12, no. 4 (December 1959): 1075–91.

Whiting, Allen S. "Quemoy 1958: Mao's Miscalculations." *China Quarterly,* no. 62 (June 1975), pp. 263–70.

Documents and Newspapers

Chinese People's Institute of Foreign Affairs, ed. *Oppose U.S. Military Provocations in the Taiwan Strait Area.* Beijing: Foreign Languages Press, 1958.

Documents of the Chinese Communist Party Central Committee, September 1958–April 1969. Vol. 1. Hong Kong: Union Research Institute, 1971.

Renmin ribao [People's Daily] October 30, 1958 (*Chinese Law and Government* 4 [Fall/Winter 1971/72]: 260–69).

Shijie zhishi [World Knowledge], July 5 and August 5, 1958.

U.S., Department of Commerce, Joint Publications Research Service. Nos. 49,826 and 50,792 (*Translations on Communist China,* nos. 90 and 109), February 12 and June 23, 1970.

U.S., Department of State. *Department of State Bulletin*, vol. 37, no. 935 (May 27, 1957), pp. 854–55; vol. 37, no. 942 (July 15, 1957), pp. 91–95; vol. 39, no. 1002 (September 8, 1958), pp. 385–90.

Zhongyang ribao [Central Daily News] (Taibei), 1957–58.

The Sino-Indian Border War

Books and Monographs

Bettelheim, Charles. *Cultural Revolution and Industrial Organization in China.* New York: Monthly Review Press, 1974.

Crankshaw, Edward. *The New Cold War: Moscow v. Peking.* Baltimore: Penguin, 1963.

Dallin, Alexander, et al., eds. *Diversity in International Communism: A Documentary Record, 1961–63.* New York: Columbia University Press, 1963.

Dalvi, J. P. *Himalayan Blunder.* Bombay: Thacker and Co., 1969.

Eekelen, Willem F. Van. *Indian Foreign Policy and the Border Dispute with China.* 2d rev. ed. The Hague: Martinus Nijhoff, 1967.

Fisher, Margaret; Rose, Leo E.; and Huttenback, Robert C. *Himalayan Battleground: Sino-Indian Rivalry in Ladakh.* New York: Praeger, 1963.

Galbraith, John Kenneth. *Ambassador's Journal.* Boston: Houghton Mifflin, 1969.

Griffith, William E. *The Sino-Soviet Rift.* Cambridge, Mass.: MIT Press, 1964.

Hilsman, Roger. *To Move a Nation.* Garden City, N.Y.: Doubleday, 1967.

Joffe, Ellis. *Party and Army: Professionalism and Political Control in the Chinese Officer Corps, 1949–1964.* Cambridge, Mass.: Harvard University Press, 1965.

Johri, Sita Ram. *Chinese Invasion of Ladakh.* Lucknow: Himalaya Publications, 1969.

Kaul, Brij M. *The Untold Story.* Bombay: Allied Publishers, 1967.

MacFarquhar, Roderick, ed. *China under Mao: Politics Takes Command.* Cambridge, Mass.: MIT Press, 1966.

Marchetti, Victor, and Marks, John D. *The CIA and the Cult of Intelligence.* New York: Knopf, 1974.

Maxwell, Neville. *India's China War.* London: Jonathan Cape, 1970; Garden City, N.Y.: Doubleday, Anchor, 1972.

Nanda, B. R., ed. *Indian Foreign Policy: The Nehru Years.* Honolulu: University Press of Hawaii, 1976.

Richman, Barry M. *Industrial Society in Communist China.* New York: Vintage Books, 1972.

Stein, Arthur. *India and the Soviet Union: The Nehru Era.* Chicago: University of Chicago Press, 1969.

Whiting, Allen S. *The Chinese Calculus of Deterrence: India and Indochina.* Ann Arbor: University of Michigan Press, 1975.

Zagoria, Donald S. *The Sino-Soviet Conflict: 1956–61.* Princeton: Princeton University Press, 1962.

Articles

Chang, Parris H. "Research Notes on the Changing Loci of Decision in the Chinese Communist Party." *China Quarterly,* no. 44 (October–December 1970), pp. 169–94.

Goldman, Merle. "The Unique Blooming and Contending of 1961–1962." *China Quarterly,* no. 37 (January–March 1969), pp. 57–84.

Graham, Ian C. C. "The Indo-Soviet MIG Deal and Its International Repercussions." *Asian Survey* 4 (May 1964): 823–32.

Hsieh, Alice Langley. "China's Secret Military Papers: Military Doctrine and Strategy." *China Quarterly,* no. 18 (April–June 1964), pp. 79–99.

Jain, Girilal. "The Border Dispute in Perspective." *China Report* 6 (November–December 1970): 56–63.

Karnow, Stanley. "Sinkiang: Soviet Rustlers in China's Wild West." *The Reporter,* June 18, 1964, pp. 37–39.

Maxwell, Neville. "The Afterthoughts of Premier Chou." *Times* (London), December 19, 1971.

Patterson, George N. "China and Tibet: Background to the Revolt." *China Quarterly,* no. 1 (January–March 1960), pp. 87–102.

————"Recent Chinese Policies in Tibet and towards the Himalayan Border States." *China Quarterly,* no. 12 (October–December 1962), pp. 191–202.

————"The Situation in Tibet." *China Quarterly,* no. 6 (April–June 1961), pp. 81–86.

Powell, Ralph L. "Politico-Military Relationships in Communist China." Mimeographed. U.S. Department of State Policy Research Study, October 1963.

Pringsheim, Klaus H. "China, India, and Their Himalayan Border, 1961–63." *Asian Survey* 3 (October 1963): 474–95.

Robertson, Frank. "Refugees and Troop Moves—A Report from Hong Kong." *China Quarterly,* no. 11 (July–September 1962), pp. 111–15.

Sheehy, Ann. "Soviet Views on Sinkiang," *Mizan* (London) 11 (September–October 1969): 271–83.

Steiner, H. Arthur. "Chinese Policy in the Sino-Indian Border Dispute." *Current Scene,* November 7, 1961, pp. 1–9.

Wu, Yuan-li. "Farm Crisis in Red China." *Current History* 43 (September 1962): 162–67.

Documents

"The Confession of Wu Leng-hsi." *Hongse xin hua* [New Red China], 43 (May 1968), in *Chinese Law and Government* 2 (Winter 1969/70): 63–86.

"Criticism of Liu Shao-ch'i's *On How to Be a Good Communist." Chinese Law and Government* 1 (Spring 1968): 61–67.

Documents of the Sino-Indian Boundary Question. Beijing: Foreign Languages Press, 1960.

Notes, Memoranda, and Letters Exchanged and Agreements Signed between the Governments of India and China: White Paper. Vols. 1–8. New Delhi: Ministry of External Affairs, Government of India, 1959–63.

The Sino-Indian Boundary Question. Enl. ed. 2 vols. Beijing: Foreign Languages Press, 1962–65.
"The Third Confession of Liu Shao-ch'i." *Chinese Law and Government* 1 (Spring 1968): 75–80.
U.S., Congress, Joint Economic Committee. *China: A Reassessment of the Economy,* 94th Cong., 1st sess., July 10, 1975.

The Vietnam War

Books and Monographs

Baum, Richard, and Teiwes, Frederick C. *Ssu-Ch'ing: The Socialist Education Movement of 1962–66.* Berkeley: University of California Press, 1968.
Bueschel, Richard M. *Communist Chinese Air Power.* New York: Praeger, 1968..
Burlatskii, Fedor. *Maoizm—ugroza sotsializmu v Kitae* [Maoism—Threat to Socialism in China]. Moscow: Politizdat, 1968.
Ch'en, Jerome. *Mao and the Chinese Revolution.* New York: Oxford University Press, 1967.
Gray, Jack, and Cavendish, Patrick. *Chinese Communism in Crisis: Maoism and the Cultural Revolution.* New York: Praeger, 1968.
Hsieh, Alice Langley. *Communist China's Evolving Military Strategy and Doctrine.* Arlington, Va.: Institute for Defense Analyses, International and Social Studies Division, 1970.
————*Communist China's Military Policies, Doctrine, and Strategy.* Santa Monica, Calif.: Rand Corporation, P-3960, October 1968.
Sellers, Robert C., ed. *The Reference Handbook of the Armed Forces of the World.* Washington, D.C.: Sellers and Associates, 1966.
Tsou, Tang, ed. *China in Crisis,* vol. 2, *China's Policies in Asia and America's Alternatives.* Chicago: University of Chicago Press, 1968.
Who's Who in Communist China. Vols. 1–2. Hong Kong: Union Research Institute, 1970.
Zagoria, Donald S. *Vietnam Triangle: Moscow, Peking, Hanoi.* New York: Pegasus, 1967.
Zanegin, B.; Mironov, A.; and Mikhailov, Y. *Developments in China.* Moscow: Progress Publishers, 1968.

Articles

Baum, Richard. "Revolution and Reaction in the Countryside: The Socialist Education Movement in Cultural Revolutionary Perspective." *China Quarterly,* no. 38 (April–June 1969), pp. 92–119.
Baum, Richard, and Teiwes, Frederick C. "Liu Shao-ch'i and the Cadre Question." *Asian Survey* 8 (April 1968): 323–45.
Gittings, John. "The 'Learn from the Army' Campaign." *China Quarterly,* no. 18 (April–June 1964), pp. 153–59.
Griffith, William E. "Sino-Soviet Relations, 1964–1965." *China Quarterly,* no. 25 (January–March 1966), pp. 3–143.

Halperin, Morton H., and Lewis, John Wilson. "New Tensions in Army-Party Relations in China, 1965–1966." *China Quarterly,* no. 26 (April–June 1966), pp. 58–67.

Munro, Donald J. "The Yang Hsien-chen Affair." *China Quarterly,* no. 22 April–June 1965), pp. 75–82.

Ojha, Ishwer C. "China's Cautious American Policy." *Current History* 53 (September 1967): 135–41, 175–76.

Oliver, Adam. "Rectification of Mainland China Intellectuals, 1964–65." *Asian Survey* 5 (October 1965): 475–90.

Portisch, Hugo. "Interview with Chou En-lai." *Der Kurier* (Vienna), August 1, 1964.

Powell, Ralph L. "Commissars in the Economy: 'Learn from the PLA' Movement in China." *Asian Survey* 5 (March 1965): 125–38.

Rich, Doris. "Who Will Carry On? The Search for Red Heirs." *Current Scene,* February 1, 1965.

Schurmann, Franz. "A Special Feature: What Is Happening in China?" *New York Review of Books,* October 20, 1966, pp. 18–25.

Snow, Edgar. "Interview with Mao." *The New Republic,* February 27, 1965, pp. 17–23.

Tao, Jay. "Mao's World Outlook: Vietnam and the Revolution in China." *Asian Survey* 8 (May 1968): 416–32.

Townsend, James N. "Communist China: The New Protracted War." *Asian Survey* 5 (January 1965): 1–11.

Whiting, Allen S. "How We Almost Went to War with China." *Look,* April 29, 1969, pp. 76–79.

Yahuda, Michael. "Kremlinology and the Chinese Strategic Debate, 1965–66." *China Quarterly,* no. 49 (January–March 1972), pp. 32–75.

Documents and Newspapers

"Chairman Mao and the Chiefs of the Central Administration Comment on Public Safety, Prosecution, and Law—Paramount Instructions." *Chinese Law and Government* 2 (Winter 1969/70): 4–5.

Hongqi [Red Flag], 1965.

Issues and Studies (Taibei), 5 (August 1969): 87–101; 6 (February 1970): 81–92.

Jiefangjun bao [Liberation Army Daily], 1965.

Jinggangshan Guangdong wenyi zhan bao [Jinggangshan Canton Literary Combat Daily] (Guangzhou), September 5, 1967.

New China Agency. *Daily Bulletin,* 1965.

Peng Zhen. *Speech at the Aliarcham Academy of Social Sciences in Indonesia (May 25, 1965).* Beijing: Foreign Languages Press, 1965.

Shijie zhishi [World Knowledge], March 10, 1964, pp. 7–10.

U.S., Department of Commerce, Joint Publications Research Service. No. 50,564 (*Translations on Communist China,* no. 104), May 21, 1970.

Wuhao zhanshi ["Five-Good" Soldiers]. Shanghai: Renmin Chubanshe, 1965.

Zuguo yuekan [Homeland Monthly], no. 36 (March 1967); no. 44 (November 1967); no. 55 (October 1968).

The Sino-Soviet Border Clashes

Books and Monographs

An, Tai Sung. *The Sino-Soviet Territorial Dispute.* Philadelphia: Westminster Press, 1973.
Borisov, Oleg B., and Koloskov, B. T. *Soviet-Chinese Relations, 1945–70.* Bloomington: Indiana University Press, 1975.
Chien, Yu-shen. *China's Fading Revolution: Army Dissent and Military Divisions, 1967–68.* Hong Kong: Centre of Contemporary Chinese Studies, 1969.
Dulles, Foster Rhea. *American Policy toward Communist China, 1949–1969.* New York: Thomas Y. Crowell, 1972.
Gittings, John. *Survey of the Sino-Soviet Dispute: A Commentary and Extracts from the Recent Polemics, 1963–67.* London: Oxford University Press, 1968.
Gottlieb, Thomas. *Chinese Foreign Policy Factionalism and the Origins of the Strategic Triangle.* Santa Monica, Calif.: Rand Corporation, November 1977.
Hinton, Harold C. *The Bear at the Gate: Chinese Policy Making under Soviet Pressure.* Stanford: Hoover Institution, 1971.
———. *Three and a Half Powers: The New Balance in Asia.* Bloomington: Indiana University Press, 1975.
Johnson, Chalmers, ed. *Ideology and Politics in Contemporary China.* Seattle: University Press of Washington, 1973.
Karol, K. S. *The Second Chinese Revolution.* New York: Hill and Wang, 1973.
Low, Alfred D. *The Sino-Soviet Dispute: An Analysis of the Polemics.* London: Associated University Presses, 1976.
Tretiak, Daniel. *The Chinese Cultural Revolution and Foreign Policy: The Process of Conflict and Current Policy.* Advanced Studies Group Monograph no. 2. Waltham, Mass.: Westinghouse Electric Corp., 1970.
Wolfe, Thomas W. *Soviet Power and Europe, 1945–1970.* Baltimore: Johns Hopkins Press, 1970.
Young, Kenneth T., Jr. *Negotiating with the Chinese Communists: The United States Experience, 1953–1967.* New York: McGraw-Hill, 1968.

Articles

Baum, Richard. "China: Year of the Mangoes." *Asian Survey* 9 (January 1969): 1–17.
Bridgham, Philip. "Mao's Cultural Revolution in 1967: The Struggle to Seize Power." *China Quarterly,* no. 34 (April–June 1968), pp. 6–37.
———. "Mao's Cultural Revolution: The Struggle to Consolidate Power." *China Quarterly,* no. 41 (January–March 1970), pp. 1–25.
Brown, Roger Glenn. "Chinese Politics and American Policy: A New Look at the Triangle." *Foreign Policy,* no. 23 (Summer 1976), pp. 3–23.
Clifford, Clark M. "A Vietnam Reappraisal." *Foreign Affairs* 47 (July 1969): 601–22.
Dillon, Linda D.; Bruton, Bruce; and Soderlund, Walter C. "Who Was the Principal Enemy?: Shifts in Official Chinese Perceptions of the Two Superpowers, 1968–1969." *Asian Survey* 17 (May 1977): 456–73.

Domes, Jurgen. "The Role of the Military in the Formation of Revolutionary Committees, 1967–68." *China Quarterly,* no. 44 (October–December 1970), pp. 112–45.

Gurtov, Melvin. "The Foreign Ministry and Foreign Affairs during the Cultural Revolution." *China Quarterly,* no. 40 (October–December 1969), pp. 65–102.

Heaslet, Juliana P. "The Red Guards: Instruments of Destruction in the Cultural Revolution." *Asian Survey* 11 (December 1972): 1032–47.

Hinton, Harold C. "Conflict on the Ussuri: A Clash of Nationalisms." *Problems of Communism* 20 (January–April 1971): 45–61.

Joffe, Ellis. "The Chinese Army after the Cultural Revolution: The Effects of Intervention." *China Quarterly,* no. 55 (July–September 1973), pp. 450–77.

Lisann, Maury. "Moscow and the Chinese Power Struggle." *Problems of Communism* 18 (November–December 1969): 32–41.

Macioti, Manfredo. "Scientists Go Barefoot." *Survival,* July 1971, pp. 232–38.

Maxwell, Neville. "The Chinese Account of the 1969 Fighting at Chenpao." *China Quarterly,* no. 56 (October–December 1973), pp. 730–39.

Nelsen, Harvey. "The Military Forces in the Cultural Revolution." *China Quarterly,* no. 51 (July–September 1972), pp. 444–74.

Pollack, Jonathan D. "Chinese Attitudes towards Nuclear Weapons, 1964-1969." *China Quarterly,* no. 50 (April–June 1972), pp. 244–71.

Portisch, Hugo. "Red Russia–Red China: The Bristling Border." *Atlas* 14 (September 1967): 15–19.

Powell, Ralph L. "The Party, the Government, and the Gun." *Asian Survey* 10 (June 1970): 441–71.

Robinson, Thomas W. "The Sino-Soviet Border Dispute: Background, Development, and the March 1969 Clashes." *American Political Science Review* 66 (December 1972): 1175–1202.

————"The Wuhan Incident: Local Strife and Provincial Rebellion during the Cultural Revolution." *China Quarterly,* no. 47 (July–September 1971), pp. 413–38.

Tretiak, Daniel. "Changes in Chinese Attention to Southeast Asia, 1967–69: Their Relevance for the Future of the Area." *Current Scene,* November 1, 1969, pp. 1–17.

Valenta, Jiri. "Soviet Decisionmaking and the Czechoslovak Crisis of 1968." *Studies in Comparative Communism* 8 (Spring–Summer 1975): 147–73.

Wu, Chin-yin. "Peiping's Efforts to Strengthen Defense Works in the Desert Areas." *Chinese Communist Affairs* 6 (February 1969): 17–20.

Yin, Ching-yao. "A New Historical Stage in the Peiping-Moscow Struggle." *Issues and Studies* (Taibei) 5 (June 1969): 1–13.

Documents and Periodicals

China Topics: Documentation of Specific Current Topics Taken Mainly from the Press and Radio of the Chinese People's Republic, 1967–69.

Current Digest of the Soviet Press, 1968–69. Published weekly by the Joint Committee on Slavic Studies.

Doolin, Dennis J. *Territorial Claims in the Sino-Soviet Conflict: Documents and Analysis.* Stanford: Hoover Institution, 1965.

Far Eastern Economic Review, 1967–68.

International Institute for Strategic Studies (London). *The Military Balance,* 1967–69.

————. *Strategic Survey,* 1967–69.

Kau, Michael Y., ed. *The Lin Piao Affair: Power Politics and Military Coup.* White Plains, N.Y.: International Arts and Sciences Press, 1975.

————.*The People's Liberation Army and China's Nation-building.* White Plains, N.Y.: International Arts and Sciences Press, 1973.

New York Times, 1966–68.

U.S., Arms Control and Disarmament Agency. *World Military Expenditure and Arms Trade, 1963–73.* Washington, D.C.: Government Printing Office, 1975.

Index

327

This book was composed in Quadritek Times Roman text and
Benguiat display type by Brushwood Graphics from a design by
Alan Carter. It was printed on 50-lb. Publishers Eggshell
Cream and bound by Universal Lithographers, Inc.